SONOMA COUNTY

DRUGGISTS

Frank A. Sternad and John C. Burton

Aperitifs Publishing Company
Santa Rosa, California

Published by Aperitifs Publishing Company
Santa Rosa, California

Copyright © 2021 by John C. Burton. All rights reserved.

ISBN: 978-1-7324530-3-6
Library of Congress Control Number: 2021910274

Printed in the United States of America

No part of this book may be reproduced, stored in a retrieval system, or transmitted in any form or by any means, electronic, mechanical, photocopying, recording, scanning or otherwise, without written permission from the authors and the publisher.

Every effort has been made to provide accurate information regarding the subject material. Like all books attempting to describe collectibles, this one is not complete. It is hoped that publication will stimulate interest and result in the discovery of more artifacts and history related to Sonoma County druggists and drug stores.

John C. Burton
johncburton@msn.com
707-523-1611

Frank A. Sternad
fsternad@sonic.net

ACKNOWLEDGEMENTS

I can't say enough about Merle Avila and Dan Brown for providing knowledge and encouragement while undertaking this endeavor. Also my thanks to both for allowing access to their bottles and other collectibles for photography, and to Merle for his proofreading time.

Appreciation is extended to Helmut & DeAnna Jordt, Lou & Leisa Lambert, Eric McGuire, Rick Siri, Richard Siri, James Arietta, Mike Burgess and John Louder for contributing photographs of their druggists bottles and related items.

It should also be mentioned that the *Sonoma County Library, Newspapers.com, Ancestry.com* and *California Digital Newspaper Collection* websites have been indispensable for obtaining digital images and historical information.

Finally, special recognition goes to co-author Frank Sternad who stepped in during the final stages to edit the original draft, upgrade images, and contribute additional illustrations and research.

I think you will agree that the cooperative effort has resulted in a valuable reference for collectors.

JCB

CONTENTS

Druggist Bottles and Medicine Glasses	*vi*
Contributors	*xii*
Sonoma County Prescription Forms	*xiv*

THE DRUGGISTS—

CLOVERDALE

Boggs, Dr. J. O.	5-6
Carico, Dr. John W.	8-10
Cloverdale Drug Store	5, 19
Cloverdale Pharmacy	11-12, 17-18
Dineen, Daniel L. Rexall Store	11-14
Gawthrop, Lester	17-18
Grant, Dr. C. F.	3
Grant and Riechers	3-4
Holladay, Elias	6-7
Hudson, T. F.	19
Magill Pharmacy, James Magill	15-16
Markell, Dr. R. S.	1-4
Mason, Dr. D. E.	7
May, Charles	14
Model Pharmacy	8-10
Oldham Drug Company (Wm.)	15, 184
Peoples Drug Store	6-7
Riechers, Dr. Fred	3-4
Shipley, William C.	10, 14, 18
Smith, Dr. Q. C.	1

FORESTVILLE

Jewett Drug Store	20

GEYSERVILLE

Burnett, Roy O.	30-31
Callwell, Bert	31
Carico, John H.	28-29
Geyserville Pharmacy	21-32
Grubstick, Alex	32
Hawkins, James W.	28-30
Lock, Ernest L.	24-26
Merrithew, Edwin	21
Rexall Store	22, 28, 33
Sellgren, Fred	27, 308
Sohler Bros. – Frank & Will	21-23
Wanted – A Drug Store	21
Wetzler, Dale B.	26-28

GLEN ELLEN

Benson, Arthur	32, 108
Dowdell, Richard E.	32

GRATON

Graton Pharmacy, Rexall Store	33
Upp, Arthur F.	33

GUERNEVILLE

Belden & Upp (BC & AF)	34
Guerneville Drug Store	34
Ruddock, Edward J.	34, 313

HEALDSBURG

Bamford, Dr. W. Drug Store	36
Baxter, Hall William	94
Brown, George R. (see Brown-Wolfe)	
Brown, Henry K. (see Wright & Brown)	
Brown-Wolfe Drug Store	35, 64, 86-88
Brownlee, Walter S.	61-62
Burr, Frank	58, 95-98
Canan, W.S.	36, 38 - 40
Canan & Fike	38-39
Canan & Hutton	40
Carpenter's Pharmacy (C.M.)	84-86
Carroll, William F.	86
Carver, Rollo (see Nichols & Carver)	
Clark's Drug Store	45
Clough' Pharmacy (Oliver T.)	67, 69
Corrick, Frank J. (see Corrick & Meese)	
Corrick & Meese	101
Cuneo, Joseph T.	35, 104-106
Evans & Kruse (C.D. & August)	79
Evans, Clarence D.	75, 79-83
Ewing, James E.	92, 94-95, 194
Ewing & Burr (James & Frank)	95
Fenno, James	42, 48
Fike, Nathan (see Canan & Fike)	
Fox, Henry	90-94

Gregory & Co.	68	**MONTE RIO**	
Haigh, W. Rainey	58-60, 62, 99-100	Tomasco, Ralph A.	106
Haigh & Carver (W.R. & Rollo)	50, 59	Torr's Drug Store	107
Haigh & Peck (W.R. & John)	50, 60		
Hayes, M. H.	36	**PENNGROVE**	
Hobson, Jerome C.	50, 54-56, 64, 66	Penngrove Drug Store	108
Hobson & Kruse (J.C. & F.A.)	56		
Huntington, H. L.	84-85	**PETALUMA**	
Hutton, Charles R.	36, 40	Antlers Drug Store	125
Jones & Hobson (O. L. & J. C.)	50-51, 54-56, 73	Black's Drug Store	133-134
Jones, Oliver L.	50-51, 55	Blackburn Drug Co.	139
Knickerbocker, Miss L. M.	103	Chicken Pharmacy	109
Knight, Peter J. (see Knight & Schmitz)		Clark Drug Co.	137-138
Knight & Schmitz (P.J. & L.A.)	50, 63	Dean & Young (L. & C.H.)	157
Kruse, August W.T.	79	Dilberger & Lynn (F.C. & C.W.)	154-156
Kruse, Fred A.	50, 55, 57, 75	Edelmann. George L.	140, 141
Laymance, F.M.	45-46	Geary Pharmacy (Warren F.)	169
Luedke, Julius Jr.	50, 65, 81	Haydon, Stephen C.	110, 141
Macy, William	36	Herold Drug Co.	168
Max, W. A.	36	Hitchcock's Drug Store (F.N.)	135
Medico Drug Co.	105-106	James Drug Store (Louis)	123-124
Meese, Arthur	35, 101	Lessel, Adolph	130
Miller & Hobson (Lou & J.C.)	50, 66	Lovegrove, Charles P. & Co.	126, 127
Miller & Whitney (G.T. & W.B.)	50-55, 73	Lynn, C. Walter	154-156
Miller, George T.	50, 51	Maggetti, Clarence B.	125
Miller, Lou	50, 55, 66	Maynard & Co. (FT & H.Hoyer)	143
Nichols & Carver (H.S. & R.)	50, 58-61, 98	Maynard Pharmacy, The	154-157
Nichols, Horace S.	50, 58-59, 65, 94,98	Maynard, Frank T.	142-151
Palace Pharmacy/Drug Store	50-69	Maynard, Harry H.	152-153
Peck, John W.	50, 59-60	McGuire, Thomas (Sr & Jr)	158-164
Peoples Drug Store	90-91, 95	Morris Drug Co. (H. Morris)	171
Piper & Laymance (J.J. & F.M.)	45-46	O'Neill Drug Co. (Fred A.)	172
Piper, J. J.	45-47	Petaluma Drug Company	124-125
Rathke, Wm. E.	64, 69-72	Petaluma Drug Store	126-129
Red Front Drug Store	58, 90, 92, 94-95	Pheonix Drug Store	142
Rexall Store	99-101	Poehlmann, Otto Henry	125
Richardson, Edgar	97	Red Front Drug Store	140
Riley & Fox (T.J. & Henry)	90-91	Robbins & Vaslit	128, 129
Riley, Thomas J.	89-91, 248	Ruffin, D. T.	132
Schmitz, Leo A.	50, 63-65	Scanlon, A. B.	171
Tomasco Drug Co.	105	Towne, Smith D.	111-121, 306
Whitney & Kruse (W.B. & F.A.)	50-51, 57, 73	Towne, Walter	122-123, 139, 306
Whitney, William B.	51, 64, 73-78	Treuholtz, E. M.	131
Winham, W. P. L.	49	Tuttle & Squires	137, 188
Wolfe, F. M.	86	Vaslit & Robbins	128, 129
Wright & Brown (H.K. & A.)	41, 42, 75, 78	Wagener, S. H. & Co.	141-142
Wright, Albert	43, 44	Webb's Drug Store	136

Weck & Wood Drug Co.	170
Yellow Front Drug Store	135-137
Young Drug Co.	165-166
Young-Herold Drug Co.	167

SANTA ROSA

Alban, Dr. W.G.	174
Bacci, John	175-176, 186
Baldwin's Drug Co. (W.E.)	177-178
Belden & Upp	179-180, 188
Bennett, Lizzie McG.	181
Bogle, Dr. J. A.	182
Bryant, W. E.	183
Butler, Clarence Ray	184-185, 188, 203
Butler, Geo. C. & Geo. R.	208
Butler-Winans Drug Co.	184
City Pharmacy	279, 281
Claypool, Capt. J.W.	188, 210-216
Claypool, Mrs. Mollie	188, 250
Davis, Harry S.	189
Dean, James B.	190
Dignan, Michael H.	191-192
Dozier & Hall (L. & W.R.)	193
Economy Drug Store	277
Empire Drug Co.	203-205
Ewing, James E.	95, 194-5, 227, 237
Exchange Drug Store	281
Exclusive Prescription Pharmacy	178, 280
Farmer, Eugene C.	196-200, 224
Fischer, C. G.	194-195
Franchetti, Angelo J.	185, 269, 274, 302
Frazee, Charles D.	201-202
Gambini, Al	203
Garloff, Carl	206-208
Goldberg, Louis	209, 231
Hahman, Paul T.	210-217
Hall Brothers, Theron & Lowell	218-219
Hall, Walter R.	193
Hendley, John	220-221
Hill & Eberhard	191, 222
Hill & Wheeler	222
Hooper & Farmer (J.N. & E.C.)	224
Hooper's Drug Store (J.N.)	223
Hudson, T. F.	19, 183, 225
Humphries, R. J.	281-282
Johnson, Guy E., Drug Store	226, 236
Juell's Drug Store (Nels)	177, 227-228
Keller, C. F.	190, 229
Kellogg, H. D.	230, 248
Lauchere, Herman	206, 209, 231
Lunn, James H.	223, 232, 242, 257
Luttrell & Rutherford	235
Luttrell, George M.	209, 233-234
McGaughey, Lizzie	181, 289, 300
McLain, A. F.	236
Medico Drug Co.	185-187
Model Drug Store	189, 237, 257
Morrison & Hill	240
Morrison, Oscar	238-239
Muller, Martin	189, 237
Newman, F. Harry	173, 241
Norton & Tuttle (H.D. & O.R.)	178
Peoples Drug Store	194-5, 227, 237, 247
Pioneer Drug Store	201, 232
Plaza Drug Store	183, 268
Pye, Major Richard J.	232, 242
Reed, Wm. C.	245-246, 282
Reedy, Ray B.	194-195, 237, 247
Rexall Drug Store	197, 204-207
Richardson, Jos. H.	243-244
Riley, T. J. & Co.	89, 230, 248
RPS (monogram) Drug Store	254
Rutherford, Wm. E.	219, 235, 249, 251
Santa Rosa Drug Store	221, 243, 234
Service Drug Store	206-208, 231
Smith, Dr. Robert Press	253-254
Snodgrass, W. B.	255
Sontag Drug Store	256
Spencer, Thomas	252
St. Rose Drug Store	257-266
Standard Drug Co.	178
Stewart, Even McK.	264-266, 276
Stewart, Wm. McKenzie	257-263
Stewart Manufacturing Co.	257
Temple, Rufus A.	252-253, 267
Titus, I. S. & Company	268, 281
Tomasco Drug Company	186, 269-276
Toschi, Eugene J.	277-278
Traill, George E.	279
Tuttle, Oliver Roy	178, 213, 280
Van Valkenburg, C.C.	255, 279
Warboys, J. W.	218, 229, 283-286
Winans, Ray J.	184-186, 188
Zimmerman, John M.	238, 268, 287

SEBASTOPOL

Analy Drug Store	308-311
Bennett, Lizzie McG.	289-290, 300
Collins, William "Bill"	312, 319
Finley, N. C.	288
Forsyth, Jesse	310
Franchetti, Angelo J.	302
Hill, Irwin J. "Pete"	302-303
Hite, Burtis and Fred	293, 300-301
Momboisse, Raymond	301, 305
Morse, Mrs. F.E.	311
Parr, Wm. W.	289-292
Pease, George	312-319
Rexall Store	299
Sebastopol Drug Store	292
Sellgren, Fred	308
Tomasco Drug Co.	302-305
Towne's Drug Store	306-307
Towne, Walter and Lester	306-307
Weeks, Curtis M.	308-309
Worth, Thomas R.	293-299
Worth's Drug Store	293-301, 305

SONOMA

Eastland, Orin	323
Lambert, Louis F.	324-325
Simmons, Lloyd S.	321-322
Wegner, Edward	320

DRUGGIST BOTTLES and MEDICINE GLASSES
Frank A. Sternad, Pharm.D.

Embossed druggist bottles, also called *drugstore, pharmacy* and *prescription* bottles, are popular with today's collectors because they are relatively easy to connect to a particular person, place and time. They were commonly used for dispensing physician's prescriptions, but just as often for repackaging liquids from bulk stock to be sold over-the-counter. One popular style, the so-called Philadelphia Oval, was made with a flared, sharp edged mouth, the so-called "Prescription Lip" that enabled liquid medication to be dispensed by the drop as well as spoonful. Such a precise finish on a mouth-blown bottle was accomplished by special tools in the hands of skilled glassworkers. During the early to mid-1870's, when railroad networks enabled eastern glassworks to make high quality bottles widely available, the majority of American drugstores became reliant on uniformly blown "prescription ware," ranging in capacity from a tiny 1/2 fluid ounce to a massive quart. Fortunately for today's collector, a significant percentage of these merchants took advantage of an irresistible option offered for prescription bottles—low cost custom embossing.

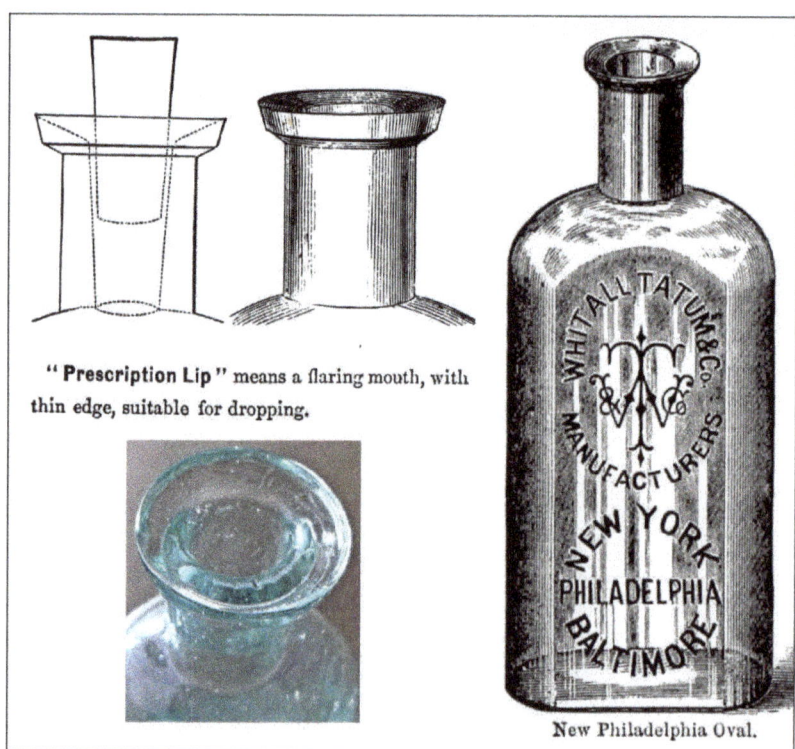

"**Prescription Lip**" means a flaring mouth, with thin edge, suitable for dropping.

New Philadelphia Oval.

Illustrations from Druggists Glassware, Whitall, Tatum & Co., 1880

Beginning in 1868, the leader in providing embossed prescription bottles to the nation's drugstores was Whitall, Tatum & Co. of Philadelphia and New York, with glassworks in Cumberland County, New Jersey. The firm's 1876 catalog devoted four pages of text and illustrations describing their sets of lettered plates, "prepared for the insertion of names without the expense of making a new mould." Inspired by James J. Christie's 1867 patent, custom-engraved movable plates were inserted into apertures in bottle molds, yielding embossed bottles at prices only slightly higher than un-embossed ware. The charge for each lettered plate ranged from $4 to $7 (reduced to $1.50 to $6 in 1880), depending on physical size plus the amount of lettering and devices engraved on the plate. Most dramatically, the custom plates did away with the greater expense of cutting letters into deep, angular interiors of large mold pieces. Instead, small flat plates of cast iron, easily engraved by mechanical routing equipment, resulted in uniform lettering and detailed design work at substantial savings. The venting of trapped air via tiny channels drilled into each letter allowed for greater glass-to-mold contact and ensured strong embossing.

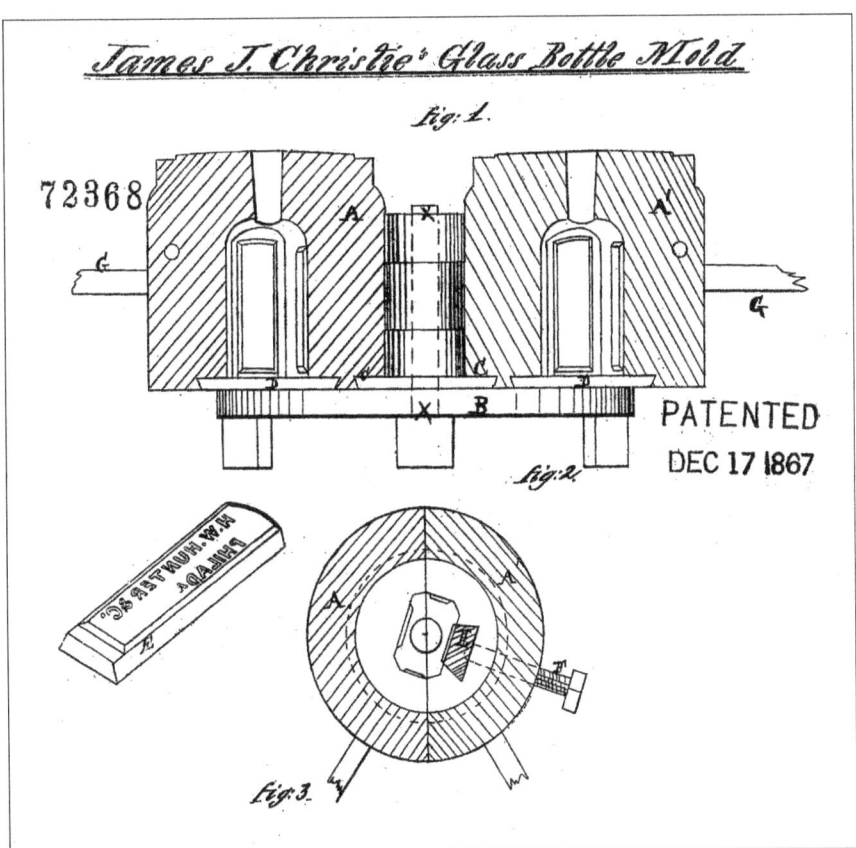

Drawing for U.S. Patent No. 72368, registered December 17, 1867 by James J. Christie.

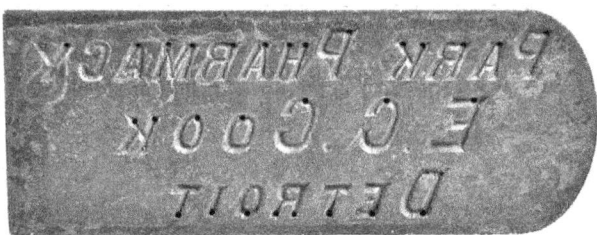

Cast iron lettered plate similar to one pictured in Christie's patent drawing. Lettering is engraved in reverse for positive embossing in the glass.

A typical embossed druggist bottle displays the pharmacist's or store name, title (*druggist, pharmacist, apothecary, chemist*), town and state. But other information could be included such as street address, building, professional degree, slogans, and decorative elements like monogrammed initials, mortar & pestle, and fancy borders. A separate plate was required for each bottle size (see pages 202 and 286 for graduated sets of embossed bottles).

Prescription bottles could be ordered in a dozen different shapes and just as many sizes. Styles commonly referred to as *French Square* and *Boston Round* were offered by glassworks as early as the 1860s. Later, improved designs were developed by American factories and registered with the U. S. Patent Office. Dates for such registrations are often found embossed on the base of bottles.

Design patents registered by Whitall, Tatum & Company (W.T. & Co.):
- January 22, 1878 (D10407, Millville Round)
- May 7, 1878 (D10675, Double Philadelphia Oval)
- January 18, 1881 (D12139, D12140, Keystone Oval)
- April 3, 1888 (D18221, Seal Square)
- January 5, 1892 (D21285, Manhattan Oval)
- December 11 1894 (D23874, Knickerbocker Oval)
- January 18, 1898 (D28182, Penn Oval)

JAN. 18, 1881

PAT. JAN. 5, 1892

PAT. DEC. 11, 1894

The company initials "W. T. & Co." were embossed on bases of bottles prior to the firm's incorporation as Whitall Tatum Co. in 1901. Molds then gradually changed to "W. T. CO."

Apothecary symbols for bottle volumes commonly embossed on bottles:

℥ss	one-half fluid ounce	℥iv	four fluid ounces
℥i	one fluid ounce	℥vi	six fluid ounces
℥ii	two fluid ounces	℥viii	eight fluid ounces
℥iii	three fluid ounces	℥xvi	sixteen fluid ounces

Glass colors offered by Whitall, Tatum & Co. in 1880 were green (actually a light blue-green or aquamarine), flint (clear, colorless), and blue (cobalt). Not yet available was the orange-brown color commonly called amber. The base price for a gross of 4-ounce French Squares in 1880 was: $7.25 (flint), $7.50 (green), and $8.50 (blue). To this was added cost of the lettered plate on the first order.

The popularity of embossed, cork-stoppered prescription ware began to diminish during the second decade of the 20th century as mass production of screw-cap bottles by automatic machinery gradually replaced short runs of custom handwork.

Sonoma County Druggist Bottles

As soon as commercial centers began to develop in Sonoma County in the mid-1850s, druggists appeared among the pioneer merchants in almost every town. One of the first was Stephen C. Haydon, a druggist in Petaluma as early as August 1855. In 1857 he moved into a storefront at the north end of the newly constructed, 3-story Phoenix Block. Defying the competition, Samuel H. Wagener opened his Phenix Drug Store at the south end of the same building in August 1857. Haydon sold to Smith D. Towne in August 1858; and when the new owner ordered personalized bottles in the mid-1870's, he had no qualms about having them embossed "1855" to assure his patrons they were dealing with the oldest drugstore in town (see bottle PET-D-04, page 114). Frank T. Maynard, who had worked in San Francisco since 1849, came up river to Petaluma in 1861, bought out Wagener, and continued until 1896 when his son took over the business. Maynard's clear round bottle, circa 1870 (PET-D-36, see below) is believed to be the first embossed bottle used by a Sonoma County druggist.

John Hendley was an early druggist in Santa Rosa, hanging up his sign in 1858 and lasting until 1860. Dr. William G. Alban came to town that year, followed by Joseph H. Richardson who ran a store on the plaza for nine years starting in October 1861. The earliest known Santa Rosa druggist bottles are those made for T.F. Hudson (SR-D14, page 225) and Charles D. Frazee (SR-D-07, page 202), both circa 1874-75.

In Healdsburg, Dr. W. Bamford advertised himself as druggist in 1858, followed by the short-lived partnership of Hayes & Max 1860-61. The earliest Healdsburg druggist bottle appears to be the ball neck panel embossed for the partnership of Albert Wright and Henry K. Brown about 1875 (HBG-D-31, page 41).

F.T. MAYNARD PETALUMA   circa 1870

MEDICINE GLASSES

Prior to the 19th century, small glass measuring devices were utilized almost exclusively by pharmacists and physicians. Markings indicated volumes in minums (drops), fluid drams, and fluid ounces. Gradual demand for accurate household dosing of medicines, however, led to production of "medicine glasses." These devices were graduated in more common measures: *teaspoon, dessert-spoon, tablespoon* and *wineglass*. One of the first commercial offerings was by the firm of J. and S. Maw in London. Their 1832 catalog listed mouth blown, "Wine glasses, graduated to tea and table spoonfuls, one shilling and sixpence each." In 1883, Whitall, Tatum & Company, a major American supplier of personalized prescription ware, offered press-molded, tumbler-shaped medicine glasses. The tumbler was popular because of low cost, sturdy construction, and most importantly, the availability of custom embossing.

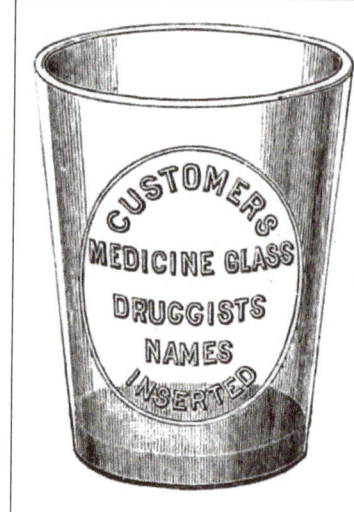

Whitall, Tatum & Co. catalog, 1883

As with bottles, a lettered plate could be inserted in the mold to personalize the ware. Cost was about 7 cents per glass for the tablespoonful size in gross lots, plus a modest $2 for the lettered plate. It was suggested that the inscription would be noticed by the customer each time it was filled for a dose; thus, the "Customers Medicine Glass" was recommended not only as a medical aid but as a promotional gimmick for the druggist. John M. Maris & Company's 1893 catalog stated, "This is a capital way of advertising—the price being so low the tumbler can be given away." The "tablespoon" size tumbler averaged 1.9 inches tall with a 1.5 inches diameter mouth.

Free blown and turn molded medicine glasses required all inscriptions to be done by wheel engraving. Each glass was calibrated by marking the levels of introduced volumes of water. With the advent of semi-automatic machinery, volumes became more consistent, and teaspoon graduations could be embossed in the glass. Nevertheless, as late as 1902, medicine glasses that were completely embossed, completely engraved, or a combination of the two were still available from Whitall Tatum Company.

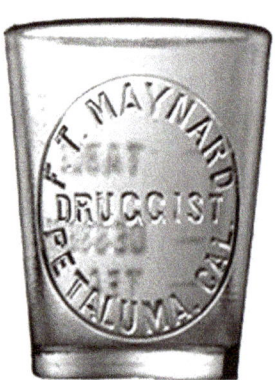  

Medicine glasses: embossed graduations center, wheel engraved at right, circa 1890

In 1905 Whitall Tatum Co. introduced a new style of medicine glass, particularly designed to permit accurate measurement of smaller doses. The conical vase-shape was claimed to be the only medicine glass with a ½ teaspoonful graduation. "To insure accuracy the graduating is done by hand, and the lines are engraved on the glass, not pressed... Druggists' names can be pressed on the underside of the foot so as to be read from above, through the glass." This style cost 12.5 cents each in two gross lots. The conical measure averaged 2.9 inches tall, 2.2 inches diameter mouth, and held up to two tablespoons.

In the venerable Apothecaries system of weights and measures, a *teaspoon* was taken as equivalent to a fluid dram (1/8 fluid ounce, or about 4 ml in the metric system). A *dessertspoon* contained two teaspoons, and a *tablespoon* held the volume of 4 teaspoons (1/2 fluid ounce). The capacity of a *wineglass* was 2 fluid ounces or 4 tablespoons. Although household flatware was the source of this terminology, no consistency of volume could be expected where art rather than science dictated construction. One survey revealed that teaspoons selected at random varied in capacity from 3 to 7 ml.

Whitall Tatum Co. Annual Price List, 1913

C.D. EVANS DRUGGIST
Conical medicine glass, Healdsburg, circa 1906
ex Frank Sternad collection

CONTRIBUTORS

MERLE AVILA: The man is tenacious. The amount of time and effort he has put into this book is invaluable--not just the Sebastopol chapter (I call his collection the "Sebastopol Smithsonian") but the entire edition. He allowed us to photograph items from his collection, and he helped with the basic organizing of the book. To Merle I am extremely grateful.

JAMES ARIETTA: Many thanks for his addition of paper labeled medicine bottles and photos. It's truly a pleasure to know a young collector who has an interest in our local history. I have to get to the flea markets and garage sales earlier now because of James.

DANIEL S. BROWN: Mr. Petaluma! Truthfully, he is the one that "jump-started" the book on Sonoma County druggists. I've been to his home twice, once with John Louder photographing bottles, the second time because his collection is overwhelming and I could not remember everything I saw. We appreciate his patience and especially the finger sandwiches provided by his wife Lisle.

DALE CHASE: Compared to the rest of us, Dale is a "newbie" bottle collector but an advanced toy collector. That said, he willingly participates in any and all Northwestern Bottle Collectors functions and is always willing to do what's asked of him.

HELMUT & DEANNA JORDT: Look around and you will see both Helmut and DeAnna at antique shows, estate and garage sales, flea markets, and antique bottle shows. Helmut is past president of the Northwestern Bottle Collectors, and along with DeAnna has amassed an amazing collection of antique bottles, breweriana advertising and pinball machines. You will find many images of their bottles and dose glasses in this book. Ever grateful. Thank you.

LOU & LEISA LAMBERT: Diggers! This is where many of the "new finds" come from. This couple penetrates the earth with great enthusiasm. Because of Lou and Leisa, and people like them, history can change with each new dig. They bring formerly unknown items to the surface, nudging historians to rewrite their stories.

JOHN LOUDER: John has proven himself invaluable for local history research and providing information for this publication. He has spent numerous hours at the Sonoma County Library and the Sonoma County Recorder's Office for our benefit. John started collecting at four or five while playing at the old house on Santa Rosa's Stewart Street. He would occasionally find a marble or a toy soldier, and just plain enjoyed finding something old that he dug out of the ground. His mother would tell him "that must have belonged to a little boy who lived here a long time ago." He questioned, "Who was that kid and what became of him?" Today, John's curiosity hasn't changed, "Who were the people and what became of them," but now he researches the answers.

ERIC McGUIRE: This man has an unbelievable knowledge of history, has authored numerous articles for collectors' journals, and can answer just about any question you might have regarding glass. Eric is Western Region Director of the Federation of Historical Bottle Collectors.

RICK SIRI: Rick and his wife Delores, have amassed a wonderful collection of California medicine and citrate bottles, small town California whiskey bottles, Cathedral and pepper sauce bottles. Rick is former President of the Northwestern Bottle Collectors and current vice president of the club.

RICHARD SIRI: If you don't know what it is, ask Richard. A consummate collector, he maintains numerous, diverse collections. He does seem partial to Nevada casino chips, 1957 Chevrolets, and oh yes, he has amassed one of the most complete collections of Western bitters bottles, the top 25 western whiskeys, and enviable collections of Hostetter's Stomach Bitters and USA Hospital Dept. bottles. Richard is a past president of the Federation of Historical Bottle Collectors (2008-10). In 2009 he introduced the concept of developing the FOHBC Virtual Museum, and now serves on the museum board of directors. In 2018 he was inducted into the FOHBC Hall of Fame. His wife Beverly, a collector herself, is a patient woman.

FRANK STERNAD: Frank is a retired pharmacist and has been active in collecting and writing about bottles since the 1970's. His special interests are western proprietary medicine and druggist bottles, plus a more recent obsession with merchandise sold in The Rexall Store (see his blog: capnrexall.blogspot.com). Another passion is vintage picture postcards, a few of which are reproduced on these pages.

SONOMA COUNTY LIBRARY: Before the COVID-19 pandemic, John Louder and I would often visit the downtown Annex Building which houses the Sonoma County History and Genealogy Library. The expert direction we received there from Katherine J. Rinehart, MA saved us many wasted hours. Katherine's colleagues, Simone Kremkau, MLIS and Joanna Kolosov, MLIS also provided much needed assistance.

—John C. Burton

℥ii *Worth's Drug Store,* KINGSBURY BLOCK, *Sebastopol, Cal.*
Merle Avila collection

SONOMA COUNTY PRESCRIPTION FORMS

Prescriptions pictured here were filled by Healdsburg druggists Henry Fox, Ewing & Burr and their successors during the period 1888-1900. Although druggist-personalized blanks were provided gratis to local physicians with the intent of influencing where they might be filled, the patient was free to make that decision. Occasionally the choice was a pharmacy in a different town, which explains why some Santa Rosa Rx forms appear in this group.

All prescriptions courtesy Richard Siri

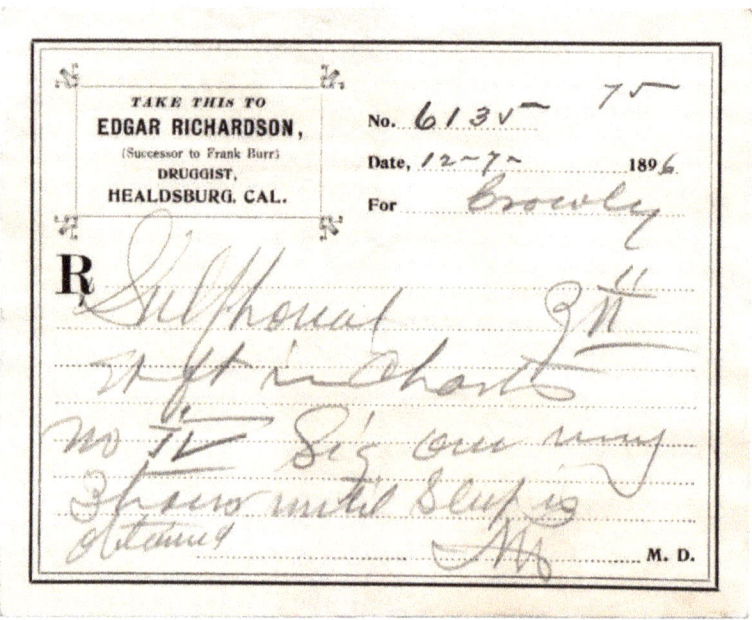

Prescription, written December 7, 1896 on Edgar Richardson's Rx blank for Sulphonal, a long-acting sleep medication. A dose of 30 grains was to be taken "every 3 hours until sleep is obtained." Richardson's Healdsburg proprietorship was short-lived, see page 97.

Prescription written by Dr. J.R. Swisher of Healdsburg on Ewing & Burr's form, filled August 28, 1892. The mixture of squills, morphine, ethyl nitrite, peppermint and tolu was likely used to treat cough and fever.

xiv

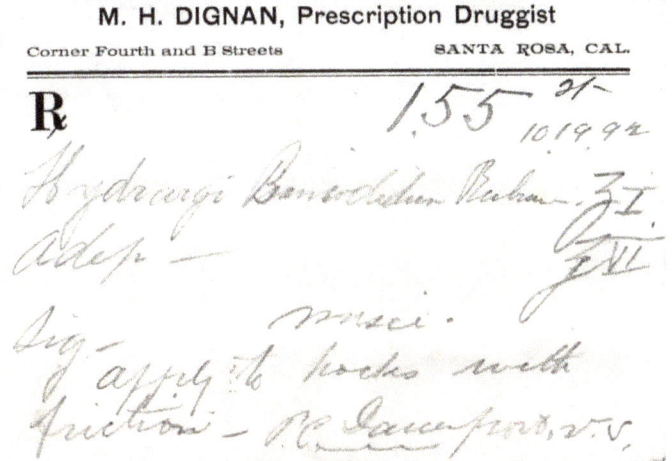

M.H. Dignan, Santa Rosa, October 19, 1892

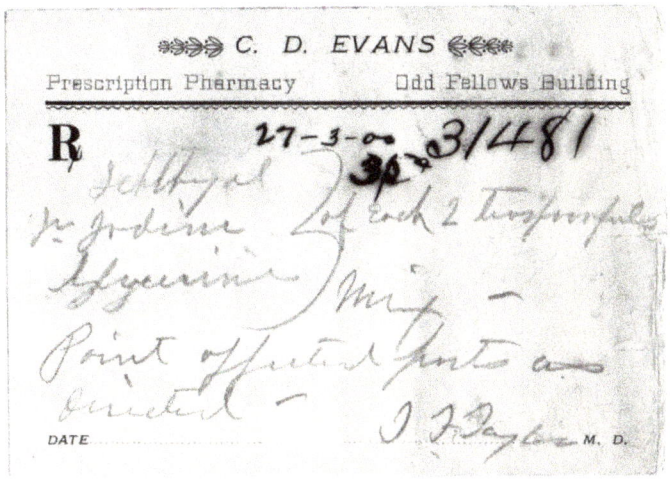

C.D. Evans, Healdsburg, March 27, 1900

Ewing & Burr, Healdsburg, Nov. 30, 1896

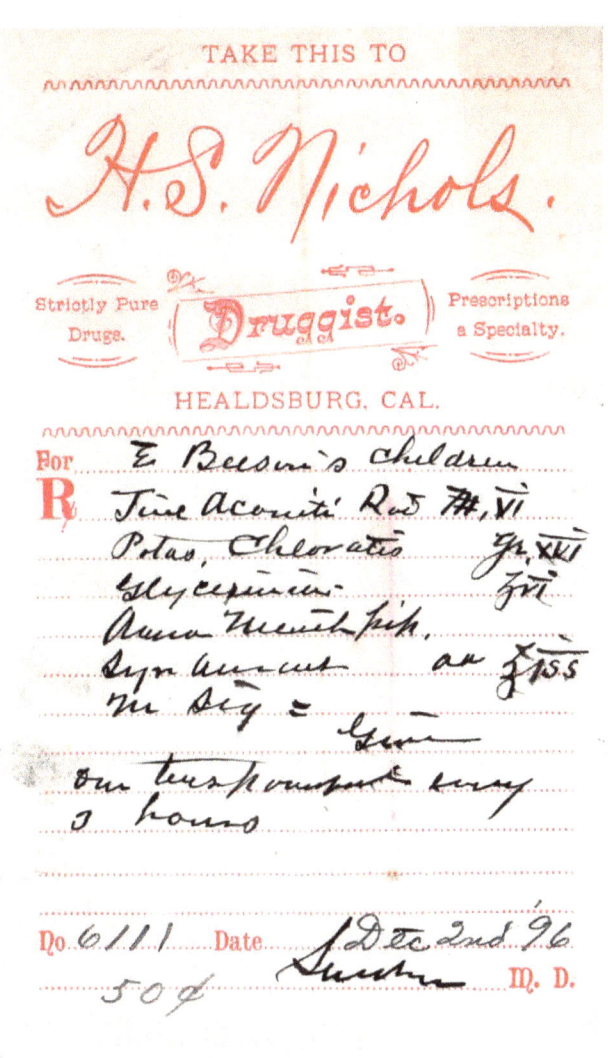

Nichols & Carver, Healdsburg, May 1, 1899

H.S. Nichols, Healdsburg, Dec. 2, 1896.
Rx is for "E. Beeson's children," containing aconite, potassium chlorate, glycerin, and peppermint; possibly for croup or chicken pox.

DRS. STONE & WEAVER,
South Side of Plaza.

HEALDSBURG, CAL.

Henry Fox, Druggist,
Healdsburg,
California.

Give ½ teaspoonful every 4 or 5 hours with a little nourishment

for John Ferguson's child
13210
8-14-88-60

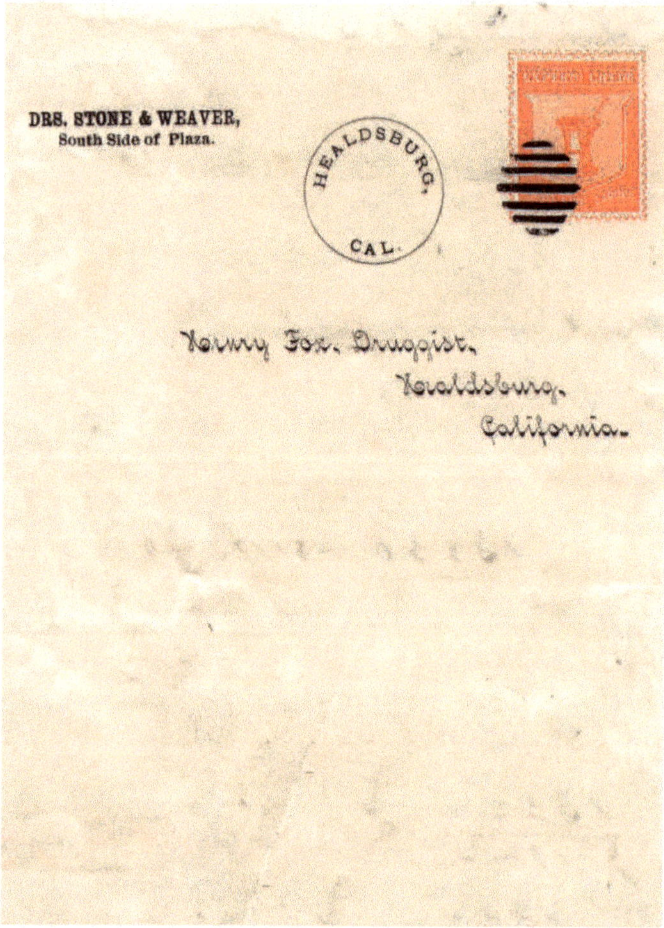

Henry Fox, Healdsburg, August 14, 1888

Reverse of this prescription is printed to simulate a stamped envelope, with physician as sender and druggist as addressee. The fantasy postage stamp reads, *Experto Crede* which is Latin for "Trust one Experienced," and *Nihil Sine Labore*, "Nothing without work." A fake handstamp cancel adds to the illusion.

FRANK BURR,
Druggist,
HEALDSBURG, CAL.

No. 24455

Date, Nov 5 1897

For Miss Hall

R

M.D.

Frank Burr, Healdsburg, November 5, 1897

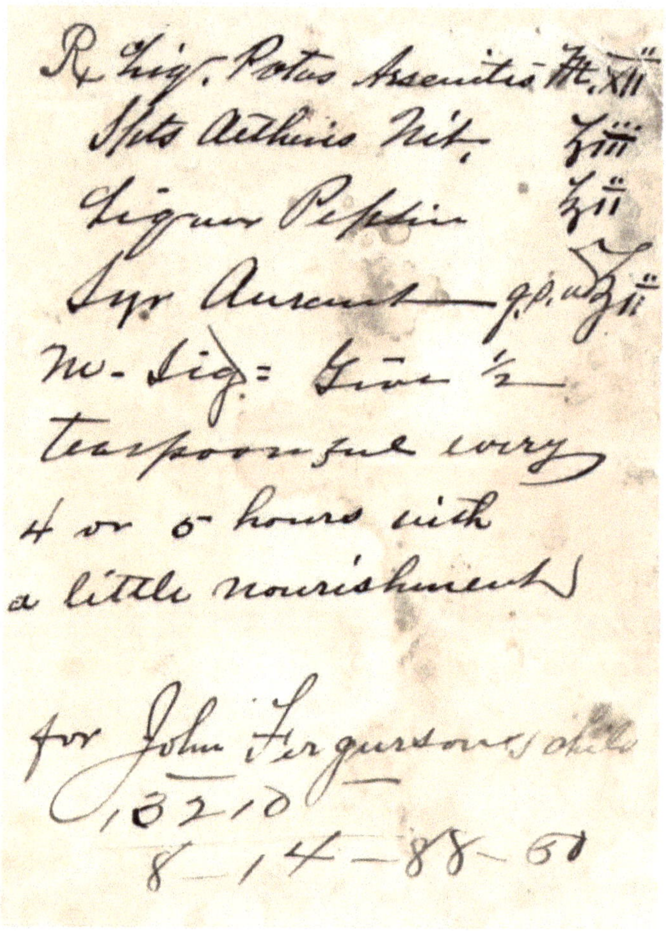

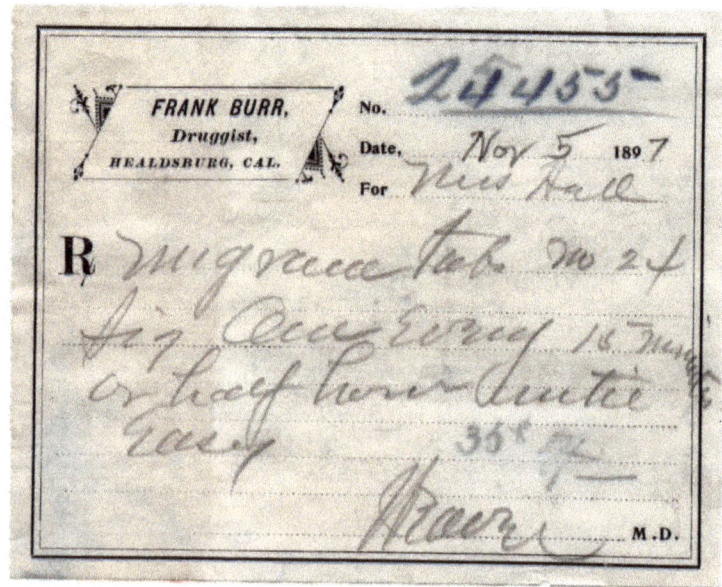

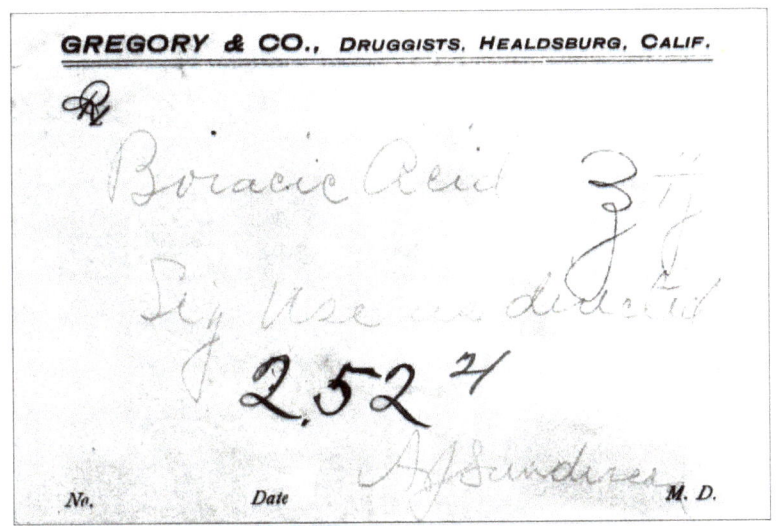
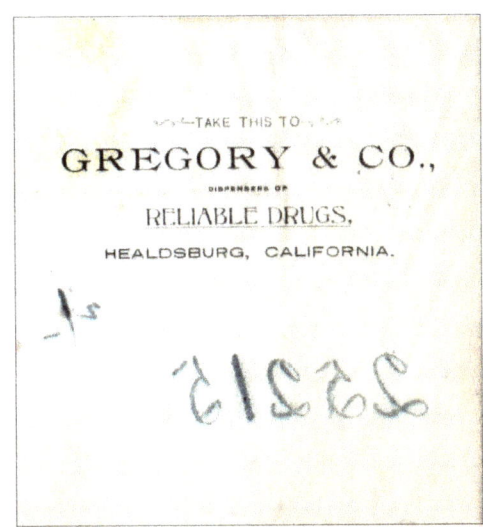

Gregory & Co., Healdsburg, December 22, 1892; back imprint from September 1897

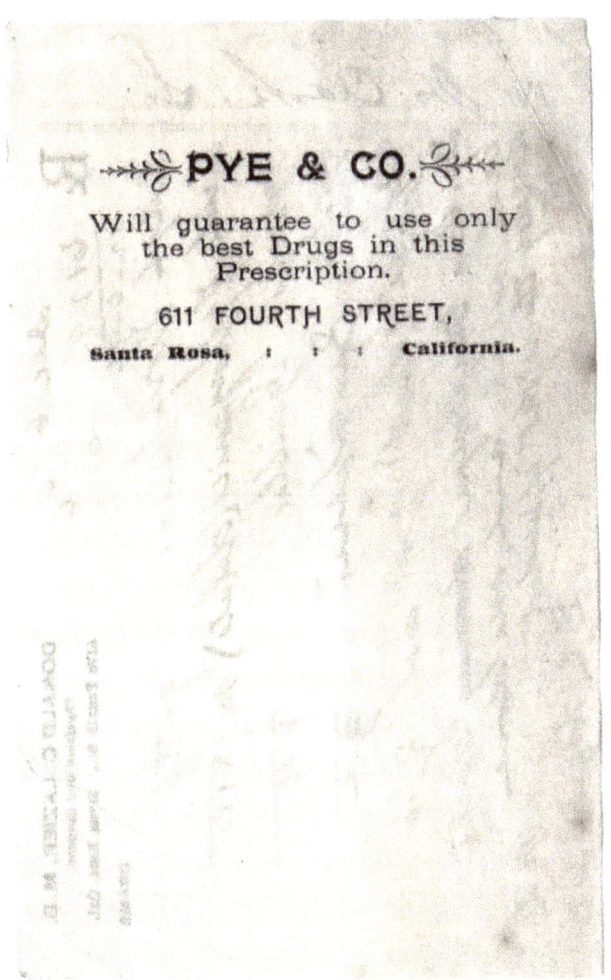

Pye & Co., Santa Rosa, back imprint
December 1892

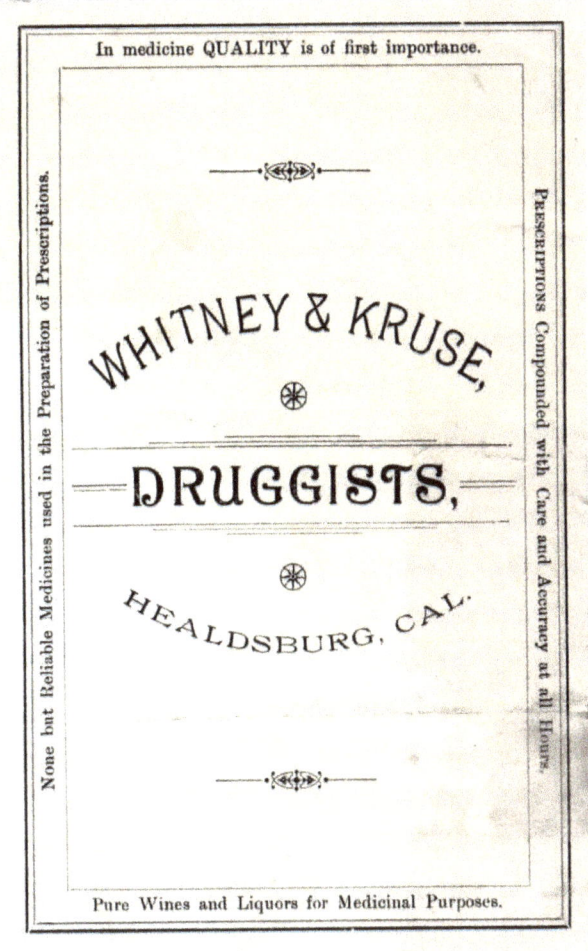

Whitney & Kruse, Healdsburg, back imprint
December 1894

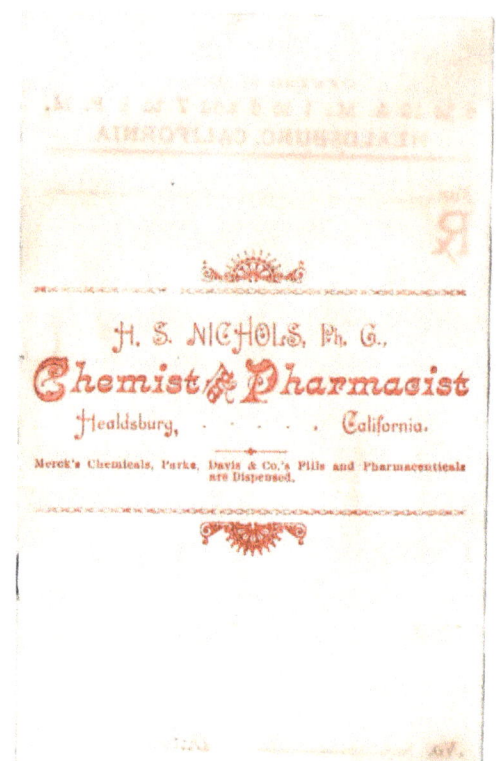
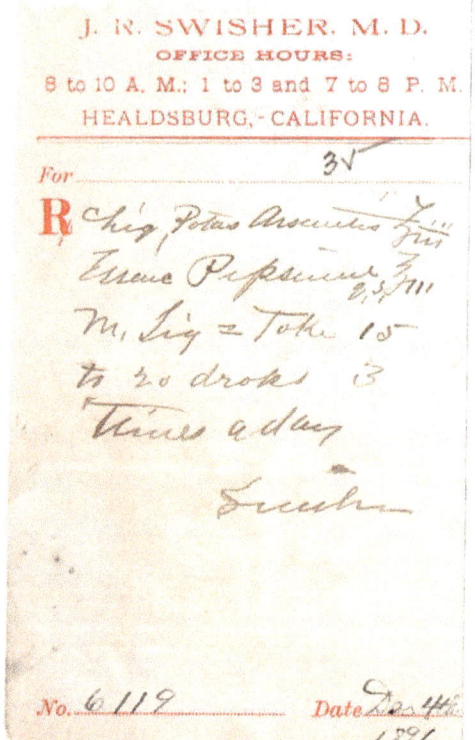

H.S. Nichols, Healdsburg, December 4, 1896

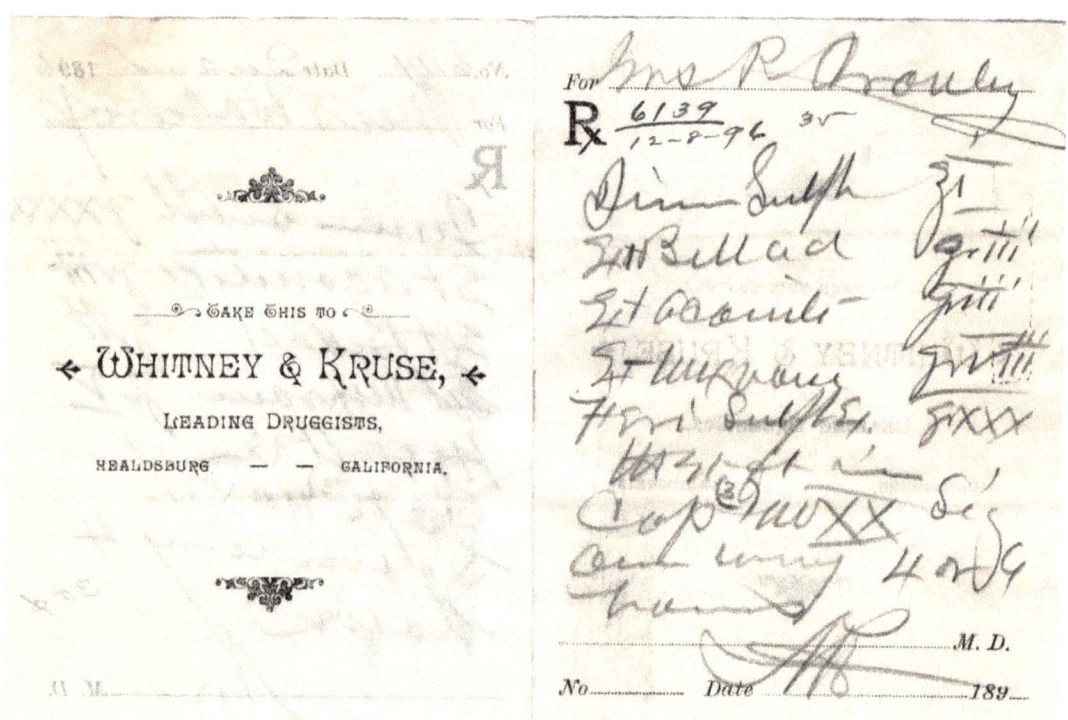

Whitney & Kruse, Healdsburg, December 8, 1896

Rx: Quinine, belladonna, aconite, nux vomica (strychnine), and iron sulfate--punched into 20 capsules with a dose of one every 4 to 6 hours. This is a classic "shotgun" formula containing several active ingredients, each possessing more than one therapeutic application. The female patient was possibly suffering from digestive and/or menstrual problems.

Model Drug Store, Martin Muller, Prop., Santa Rosa, April 4, 1899

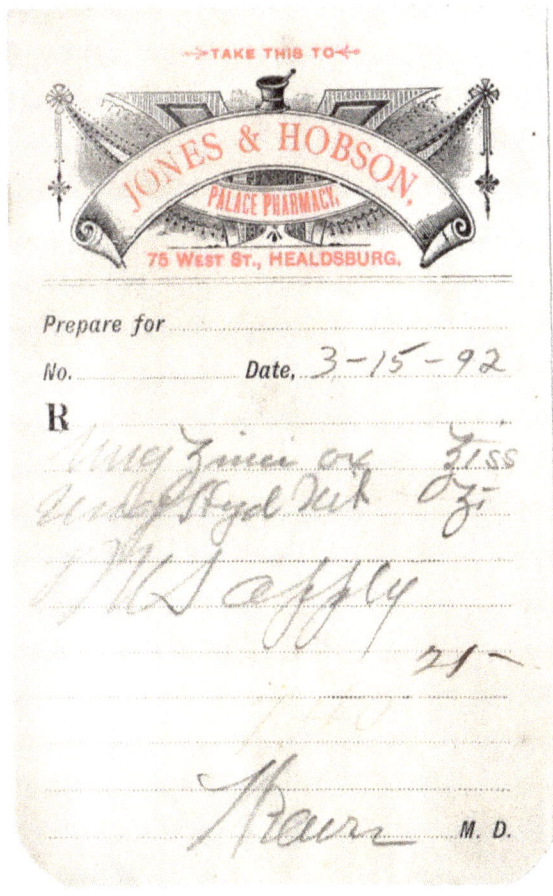

Jones & Hobson, Healdsburg, March 15, 1892

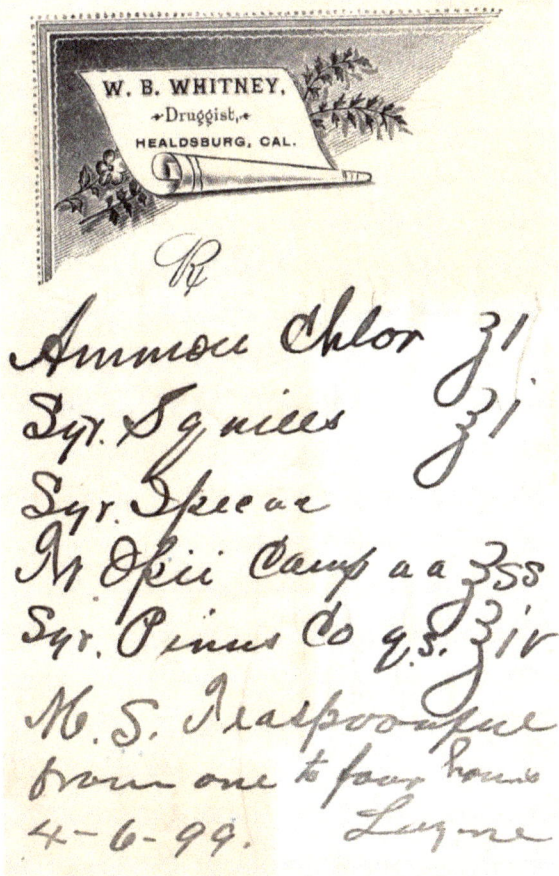

W.B. Whitney, Healdsburg, April 6, 1899

Nichols & Carver, Healdsburg, back imprint
April 1899

J.E. Ewing, Santa Rosa, May 5, 1899

Edgar Richardson, Healdsburg, October 20, 1897

CLOVERDALE

- **Dr. Q. C. Smith**
  - N. West Street
  - 1874– December 1879
  - Purchased T.F. Hudson's store (see page 19); sold to Dr. R. S. Markell

Dr. Q. C. Smith took his departure for San Francisco last Friday morning. It was his intention to start on Tuesday of this week for Bloomfield, Mo. We wish the Dr. continued success wherever he may pitch his camp.

Sonoma West Times
November 20, 1879

The undersigned would respectfully announce to the people of Cloverdale and vicinity that he has sold out his entire business to his successor, Dr. R. S. Markell, who will be found at our old stand, ready to render such services as the latest teachings of Medicine and Surgery of the present day would dictate.
To those who have for years trusted the lives of themselves and families to our care, we would recommend them to a like confidence in the skill of our esteemed successor.
    Q. C. Smith, M. D.
Dr. Q. C. Smith is at present located at Bellevue Hospital, New York.

Sonoma West Times
December 4, 1879

DR. Q. C. SMITH.

Keeps for sale at his Drug Store,

Drugs & Medicines.

(Officinal, Domestic & Pate

A general assortment; also a full line of

General Stationery Goods,

Note, Letter and Cap Papers, [plain and fancy]; Envelopes, all styles, Pens, Inks and Pencils, Academic and common School Books, Legal blanks, Blank Books. Childrens Copy Books, and a full supply of Toilet Articles, soaps, hair oils and Perfumery, tooth brushes &c.
☞ Give him a call and get something to please you. 7-1-78.

July 1, 1878
Cloverdale News

- **Dr. Richard S. Markell**
- West Street (Carrie Block)
- December 1879 – February 1903 (operated by his widow Christina J. Markell, 1903-1906)
- Purchased drugstore from Dr. Q. C. Smith; sold to Grant & Riechers

DRUGS and MEDICINES !!

Dr. R. S. Markell,

Having purchased the Drug Store formerly occupied by Dr. Q.C. Smith, north West Street, Cloverdale, Cal., will keep constantly on hand a Full assortment o

DRUGS

Medicines, Chemicals, Proprietary Medicines,

Fancy Toilet Goods,

Perfumery, Notions.

Candies, Etc., Etc.

Also a General variety of

STATIONERY

SCHOOL AND OTHER BOOKS.

A liberal patronage is respectfully solicited. dec 11 17 6

Cloverdale Reveille
May 14, 1881

RESOLUTIONS OF RESPECT

Whereas, it has pleased the Supreme Grand master of the Universe through the grim reaper death to remove from our midst Brother R. S. Markell; and

Whereas, by his death this lodge has lost an earnest brother, his family a faithful, loving head, and the community active, respected and valued citizen.

Cloverdale Reveille
February 14, 1903

- **Grant and Riechers** (Dr. C.F. Grant and Fred Riechers)
- January 1906 – October 1911 (purchased Markell drugstore; sold to D.L. Dineen, page 11)
- Carrie Block, west side of West Street between 1st and 2nd Streets

SALES OF REAL ESTATE
Dr. C. F. Grant Buys H. C. Carrie Property

Henry C. Carrie has sold his brick building on West Street to Dr. C. F. Grant. This is the building in which Mrs. R.S. Markell's drug store, millinery and dressmaking parlors, and Dr. Grant's medical office are located. The new owner will greatly improve the property. The floor is to be lowered and up-to-date plate glass front to be put on the building. The interior will be entirely remodeled and nothing left undone to make the building modern in every respect. Mr. Carrie reserves the residence property at the rear of the drug store.

Cloverdale Reveille
November 25, 1905

Messrs. Grant and Riechers Buy Markell Drug Store

Tuesday, Dr. C. F. Grant, and Fred Riechers, the latter an old-time friend of Dr. Grant, purchased the Markell Drug Store from Mrs. C. J. Markell. This sale had been anticipated for some time and as a result of the change of ownership. This pharmacy, conducted successfully by the late Dr. R. S. Markell for more than twenty years, will be entirely remodeled and equipped in an up-to-date manner.

Dr. Grant and Mr. Riechers recently purchased the brick building in which the store is located and will immediately make extensive improvements to the property. A modern plate glass front will be put in and the floor lowered to the grade of the sidewalk. This work will require about a months' time, during which time the drug store will have temporary quarters in the old Cloverdale hotel.

Mrs. Markell will move her millinery parlor and dressmaking establishment to the Baer building on upper West Street. I. S. Lewis, who had his real estate office in the Baer Building for several years has taken quarters in the rear of the post office building.

Cloverdale Reveille
January 6, 1906

CLO-D-01
PURITY ACCURACY (outer circle)
OUR SUCCESS (inner circle)
GRANT
AND RIECHERS
DRUGGISTS
CLOVERDALE, CAL.
Clear oval
Tooled top
5 1/8 inches tall
Dan Brown collection

DEATH CAME UNEXPECTEDLY TO FRED RIECHERS
Succumbs at Mary Jesse Hospital Tuesday
Elks Hold Services Thursday
Remains Cremated

Cloverdale friends of Frederick Riechers learned with deep regret of his death last Tuesday afternoon, which occurred at the Mary Jesse Hospital in Santa Rosa.

Very few knew that he was ill, as up to the Friday previous he was preforming his duties at Grant & Riechers Drug Store as usual. He had, however, been in poor health for some time, but as he never complained, only his most intimate friends were aware he was not feeling well.

Saturday morning, he decided he would go to the hospital, where it was thought that he would recuperate. Even up to the day of his death he was not confined to his bed, but he was able to be up and around his room. A complication of troubles that could not be combatted caused his death.

Fred Riechers had been a resident of Cloverdale for a little more than five years. He and Dr. C. F. Grant for many years had been warm personal friends at Wheatland and when Dr. Grant succeeded Dr. R. S. Markell in Cloverdale and later purchased the drug store from Mrs. Markell, an opening was afforded Mr. Riechers to engage in business here.

This business he took advantage of and entered a partnership with his old time-friend in the drug business. Their business relationship and friendship continued to the end. He is survived by a sister and three brothers.

Cloverdale Reveille
May 13, 1911

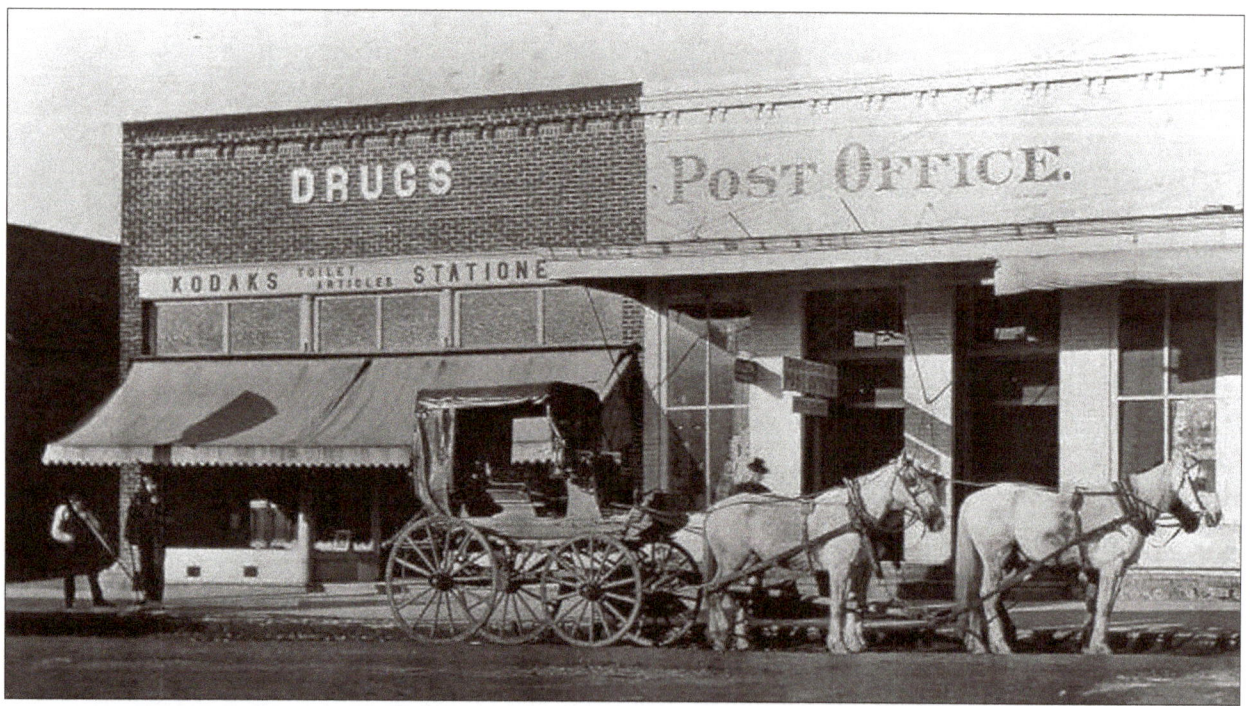

The 1875 Carrie Block on West Street, opposite intersection of Broad Street. Drugstore on the south side was successively occupied by Richard S. Markell, Grant and Riechers, Daniel L. Dineen, and Lester Gawthrop. Photo taken about 1912 when the store was known as Cloverdale Pharmacy, Daniel L. Dineen, proprietor (see page 11).

Courtesy, Sonoma County Library

- **Dr. Joseph O. Boggs**
  - Adjoining Menihan's Cloverdale Hotel
  - 1875 – October 1889 (Boggs died Oct 28, 1889, age 81)

Dr. J. O. Boggs' Cloverdale Drug Store has many fine items for the holiday's that have come in. Come see how cheap they are, they are selling like hot cakes!

Cloverdale Reveille
December 6, 1880

FRESH DRUGS AND MEDICINES!

—ALL THE POPULAR—
PROPRIETRY MEDICINES.
WITH
Perfumery,   Fancy Articles
Fine Toilet Soaps,
Tooth Brushes,
Hair Brushes,   Hand Mirrors
Etc., Etc.

FINE PAPETRIE AND STATIONERY

Autograph AND Photograph ALBUMS &c.,
Constantly on hand, and for sale CHEAP by

DR. J. O. BOGGS,

at the Drug Store adjoining Menihan's Cloverdale Hotel.

Sonoma West Times
September 10, 1881

J. O. BOGGS, M. D.
Physician and Surgeon, Cloverdale, Cal. Office in Cloverdale Drug Store,
West Street adjoining the Cloverdale Hotel.

Sonoma West Times
August 2, 1889

- **People's Drug Store**, Elias Holladay, prop.
- Successor to Dr. J. O. Boggs
- November 1889 – November 1890

A BUSINESS CHANGE
HOLLADAY & MAX PURCHASE DRUG STORE

Mr. E. Holladay and Mr. Albert Max have bought the tin ware stove store from Shaw & Williams which, in the future, will be conducted under the firm name of Holladay & Max. Mr. Holladay will move his drug store from the old stand formerly occupied by Dr. J. O. Boggs to the storeroom next to the stove store, and will open an archway between, which will enable him to conduct both branches of the business.

The new firm has our best wishes for their future success. Messrs. Shaw & Williams, the retiring firm, are young men, born and raised up in this community, and in whom we feel a deep interest, and who by their honesty and upright manners have won hosts of friends, who will join us in our regrets in losing them from our business circle. Success go with them.

Cloverdale Reveille
January 18, 1890

People's Drug Store.

PURE DRUGS, MEDICINE and CHEMICALS, SELECT TOILET ARTICLES,

ALSO

A Fine Line of Perfumery.

☞ Special attention given to compounding physicians and family prescriptions.

E. HOLLADAY, Prop'r.

Cloverdale Reveille
June 7, 1890

- **People's Drug Store**, Dr. D.E. Mason, prop.
- Successor to E. Holladay
- November 1890—April 1892 (moved to Oakland)

CO-PARTNERSHIP NOTICE

Notice is hereby given that Dr. D. E. Mason and A. Max have formed a co-partnership in the stove and hardware store and the business will be conducted under the firm name of A. Max & Co. The drug store will be conducted exclusively by Dr. Mason.

Cloverdale Reveille
November 12, 1890

A BUSINESS CHANGE

During the week just passed another business change has taken place. Mr. E. Holladay of the firm of Holladay & Max sold his drug store as well as his interest in the tin and stove store to Dr. D. E. Mason of this place. The business will hereafter be conducted under the firm name of A. Max & Co.

The drug store will be conducted exclusively by Dr. Mason. They have our best wishes for their future prosperity and success.

Mr. Holladay will remain some time to settle up in full his business affairs. He will then go in search of a new field in San Jose being probably his objective point.

The businessmen of Cloverdale will miss Mr. Holladay from their ranks, while the community will lose an estimable family who, during their residence in Cloverdale, has contributed much toward church entertainment by their musical talents which have always been greatly appreciated. The community receiving them may feel proud of their accession. Success attend them.

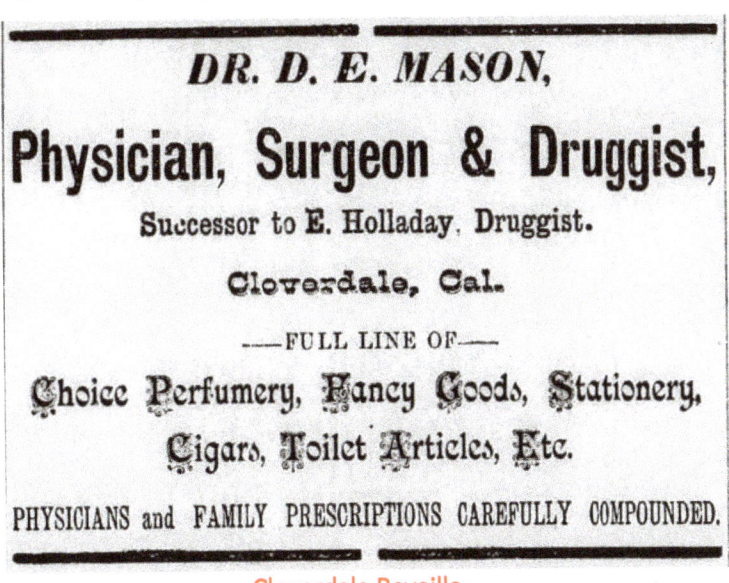

Cloverdale Reveille
November 15, 1890

- **Model Pharmacy**, Dr. John W. Carico, prop.
- NW corner of West and 2nd Sts. in Yordi-Hall Building after December 1905
- 1901 – March 22, 1909 ; sold to H.C. Trask & W.C. Shipley

> **Coulson's Balanced Ration**
> **• Egg Food •**
>
> **A Prepared Food for Laying Hens**
>
> To be fed as a mash once a day. Healthy hens and plenty of Eggs. Fifty tons a month used by poultry raisers in Sonoma county. For sale at the
>
> **Model Drug Store, Cloverdale**
>
> ☞ Send your address for free poultry paper and circulars to A. R. COULSON, MANUFACTURER, Petaluma, Cal.

Cloverdale Reveille
January 17, 1903

MACALONE TO BE EMPLOYED AT MODEL PHARMACY

M. Macalone, a graduate in pharmacy, arrived the first of the week from Sacramento and has accepted a position at the Model Pharmacy.

Cloverdale Reveille
September 12, 1903

GEGENBAUR TO BE EMPLOYED AT MODEL PHARMACY

F. A. Gegenbaur of San Francisco, a graduate in pharmacy and, until recently, manager of the Cooper College of Pharmacy, has accepted a position at the Model Pharmacy and entered upon his duties Thursday.

Cloverdale Reveille
November 7, 1903

Mr. YAGER TO REPLACE PETER MAYER AT MODEL PHARMACY

Mr. Yager, a graduate of pharmacy is the successor of Peter Mayer at the Model Pharmacy

Cloverdale Reveille
August 5, 1905

THE MODEL PHARMACY
NOW LOCATED IN HANDSOME NEW QUARTERS

Finest Equipped Drug Store in this part of The State invites you to visit its new home

Having outgrown its former quarters, the Model Pharmacy, always an attractive store, has been installed in the commodious corner room of the Yordi-Hall building, where everything in the way of equipment has been made as thoroughly up-to-date as the most pretentious pharmacies of the larger cities.

Here Dr. J. W. Carico, the owner of the Model Pharmacy, has spared neither money nor pains to give the people of Cloverdale a store that may be pointed to with pride by all progressive citizens. Entering the spacious doorway, one cannot but be favorably impressed with the rare good taste shown in the interior arrangement. Shelving, show cases, large prescription case, and other fittings are in cherry, producing an effect that is very pleasing to the eye.

Ordinarily, linoleum would be a neat and satisfying floor covering, but in the new Model Pharmacy the floor has been tiled the entire length of the room to a point where the prescription case stands, a distance of about forty feet. This tiling alone must have involved considerable expenditure of several hundred dollars; but when one takes into consideration that the Model Pharmacy has a heavy plate glass front, massive mirrors at the sides abutting the shelving, large double-deck showcase, and everything that goes to make strictly modern equipment, a tiled flooring is justified.

It will be noted also, that the ordinary counters are dispensed with, the eight large cases, four on each side, taking their place. It will be a source of gratification to Cloverdale people that all mill work for this new store is a product of a home institution, coming from the mill of Messrs. Stoner and Reisinger. On the south side, the shelving is enclosed with handsome sliding glass doors, ball bearing, where will be kept constantly in stock all the leading patent medicines etc.

The shelving on the opposite side is not enclosed, it being devoted exclusively to the pharmaceutical bottles bearing Latin labels – labels that are as Greek to most of us – but perfectly plain to Mr. Peter Mayer, the pharmacist in charge. Show cases are filled with toilet articles in abundance, the most fragrant perfumes, Kodaks and Kodak supplies, as well as many novelties suitable as gifts at this happiest time of year.

Jewel cases, toilet sets, and other articles calculated to gladden some dear one's heart, perhaps on Christmas day, are tastefully displayed in the show windows. While the Model Pharmacy has about three times the space in its former quarters, it does not follow that it will enter into other lines of mercantile trade. The stock will be greatly enlarged, but the general policy will be continued – that of keeping within the scope of all modern establishments of this nature – carrying ample stock in all branches of the drug trade. The public has a cordial invitation to visit the new Model Pharmacy and will find the stock complete in every detail.   —The Observer.

Cloverdale Reveille
December 23, 1905

SOLE AGENT FOR WITTER SPRINGS
The Model Pharmacy is sole agent for the Witter Springs Water.
Cloverdale Reveille
July 6, 1906

Cloverdale Reveille
May 23, 1908

THE MODEL PHARMACY

Now Owned by the Firm of Trask & Shipley.

Dr. J. W. Carico Retires From Drug Business and Will Devote Time to Professional Practice.

Monday morning the Model Pharmacy established by Dr. J. W. Carico eight years ago and successfully conducted by him during that period, opened with new proprietors. The new firm is Trask & Shipley and the name of the store has been changed to the Clover Leaf Pharmacy. It has been known in the business community for some time that Dr. W. C. Shipley and Dr. H. C. Trask, both well and favorably known physicians of Cloverdale, have been desirous of acquiring the Model Pharmacy; also that Dr. Carico has felt disposed to retire from the drug store business provided he acquires his price. The negotiations under way recently culminated satisfactorily to all concerned, hence the change. Dr. Carico has moved his office back to his quarters of a few years ago in the Carico building on upper West street, and is having the interior of the building remodeled to meet his requirements, and will continue the practice of the medical profession. Drs. Trask and Shipley have moved their offices from the Holloway building to the Clover Leaf Pharmacy and will continue the practice of the medical profession with well-equipped offices at that place. They will increase the already large stock carried and be in position to meet all demands of the trade.

Cloverdale Reveille
March 29, 1909

- **Cloverdale Pharmacy,** Daniel Louis Dineen, prop.
- Merged Wm. Shipley's Clover Leaf Pharmacy with Grant & Riechers store in Carrie Block
- Cloverdale Pharmacy: November 1911 – April 1912 (see page 4)
- Dineen's Pharmacy, *The Rexall Store*: April 1912 – March 1923 (see page 17)

CLOVERDALE PHARMACY

D L. DINEEN, Proprietor

Successor to GRANT & RIECHERS DRUG STORE
Holiday Stationery, Perfumes and Toilet Articles

A very complete line now in stock.

Kodaks and Camera Supplies
WEST ST., NEXT TO POSTOFFICE

Cloverdale Reveille
December 16, 1911

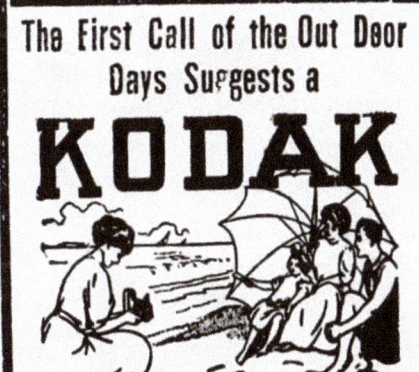

The First Call of the Out Door Days Suggests a **KODAK**

For then there is the pleasure of taking pictures added to the delights of the trips to the country and added to that the joy of having a picture story of your good time.

We have Kodaks that range in price from $1 up to as high as $25.

We Develop and Print Pictures.

DINEEN'S PHARMACY
West Street, One Door South of Postoffice, · CLOVERDALE

Cloverdale Reveille
April 6, 1912

CLO-D-2
> PURITY ACCURACY (outer circle)
> OUR SUCCESS (inner circle)
> CLOVERDALE PHARMACY
> D. L. DINEEN PROP.
> CLOVERDALE, CAL.
> Clear rectangular
> Tooled top
> 4 7/8 inches tall
> Base: W.T. CO P U.S.A. PAT. Dec 11, 1894
> Merle Avila collection
> 5 1/4 inches tall
> Base: W.T. CO P U.S.A. PAT. Dec 11, 1894
> Dan Brown bottle shown

CLO-D-03
> CLOVERDALE
> PHARMACY
> Clear rectangular
> Tooled top
> 3 1/2 to 5 1/8 inches tall
> Base: W.T. Co J USA PAT. Dec. 11, 1894
> Dan Brown collection

THE DINEEN ESTATE

The late Daniel W. Dineen [father of Daniel L. Dineen], city trustee and bank director, left an estate valued at over $150,000, including timber lands in Oregon valued at over $100,000.

The will of the deceased was filed for probate in the Superior Court by the executor named therein, Mrs. Elizabeth Dineen, widow of the deceased, through her attorney Ed Norton.

After making a bequest of $3,000 to a sister and bequeaths of 120 acres of land and $500 to other relatives, the deceased left all the residue of the realty and personality to his wife. In addition to the timber holding, Mr. Dineen owned a block of stock in the Bank of Cloverdale and other property.

> Healdsburg Enterprise
> August 9, 1913

Note: Daniel L. Dineen left Cloverdale in 1913 and his mother continued operating the drugstore with an employed pharmacist. By June 1917, Dineen was working for Wakelee's Pharmacies in San Francisco.

CLO-D-04

Paper label:
PERMANGANATE OF POTASH
POI (skull & crossbones) SON
94 to 99% Potass. Perman.
ANTIDOTE. (text)
Registered. No. C 868
DINEEN'S PHARMACY
CLOVERDALE
CAL.
Clear square
Tooled top
3 1/8 Inches tall
James Arietta collection

Cloverdale Reveille
January 23, 1915

Dr. William Shipley's Clover Leaf Pharmacy, circa 1910. Daniel L. Dineen moved Shipley's retail business four doors south into Grant & Riechers' drugstore in the Carrie Block, November 1911.
From a photo postcard

- **Charles L. May**
  - November 1915 – October 1916

HEART TROUBLE CAUSED DEATH

Charles Lawrence May, a well-known resident of Cloverdale for five years, passed away on Friday morning of last week at his home in the Carrie cottage on Commercial Street. The end came suddenly and death was due to dilation of the heart. Up to a few minutes of the time he was summoned, Mr. May was attending to business duties at his drug store as usual. At about 9 o'clock he complained of not feeling well and went home, with the intention of lying down awhile. Deceased was a native of Chicago, Illinois, aged 37 years. He had resided in Cloverdale for five years.

Cloverdale Reveille
May 27, 1916

MAY DRUG STORE SOLD

The latter part of last week, the stock of drugs in the May Drug Store was sold to F. R. Beaumont and shipped to San Francisco. Since the death of Mr. May about four months ago, Mrs. Margaret May continued the business, with C. E. Phelan as druggist.

Mrs. May and children have gone to San Francisco, where they will make their home with Mrs. May's father and brother. Mr. Phelan has gone to Sonoma, where he will have charge of one of the drug stores in that town.

Cloverdale Reveille
October 21, 1916

- **William Gunn Oldham Jr.** (lived 1897-1968)
- Oldham's Drug Store, 123 West St., *The Rexall Store*
- 1925 – May 1963 ; sold to Medico Drug Co.

Oldham Drug Company's Saturday Specials

35c. Vapo Rub, on sale	27c.
75c. Vapo Rub, on sale	63c.
40c. Fletcher's Castoria, on sale	29c.
$1.00 Horlick's Malted Milk, on sale	86c.
50c. Horlick's Malted Milk on sale	44c.
$1.00 Hind's Honey and Almond Cream, on sale	89c.
50c. Hind's Honey and Almond Cream, on sale	39c.
50c. Doriot Almond Lotion, on sale	33c.

Our Specials Will Save You Money

Prompt Delivery at all times — United Cigar Stores Agency

We give United Cigar Certificates not only in our Cigar Department, but with every purchase in our Store

Oldham Drug Company
Prescription Druggists
Cigars, Tobacco, Ice Cream and Stationery
We Solicit Mail Orders — West Street — Phone 1 — Cloverdale, Calif. — Developing & Printing

Cloverdale Reveille
November 20, 1925

Oldham's Drug Store – 123 West St.
1940's

JAMES MAGILL WITH OLDHAM DRUG STORE

James Magill, formerly of Hollywood, has accepted a position in the Oldham Drug Store. He leased the Sink residence in Cloverdale and has settled down with the intention of making this his home. He is quite well known here, having visited Cloverdale on a number of occasions. Mr. Magill is related to Miss Lottie Lambert and is the father of Mrs. R. R. Green, whose husband is a member of the firm of Heaney & Green, who conduct the Triangle Service Station.

Cloverdale Reveille
November 29, 1929

- **Magill Pharmacy** (James E. Magill)
- 1931 – October 1949 (destroyed by fire)
- West Street near 2nd St.

ARIZONA TEA
For Colds and Fever
at
MAGILL PHARMACY

Cloverdale Reveille
November 13, 1931

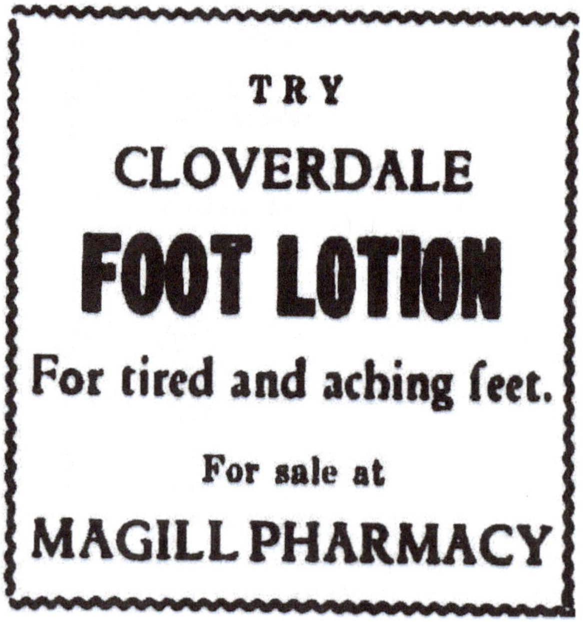

TRY
CLOVERDALE
FOOT LOTION
For tired and aching feet.
For sale at
MAGILL PHARMACY

Cloverdale Reveille
November 19, 1936

- **Cloverdale Pharmacy**, Lester Gawthrop, prop.
- Successor to Dineen's Pharmacy
- March 1923 – March 1931

Cloverdale Pharmacy

THE DEPENDABLE DRUGGISTS

LESTER GAWTHROP, Prop.

Cloverdale Reveille
January 14, 1929

Cloverdale Pharmacy, Carrie Block, circa 1925
Courtesy, Sonoma County Library

CERTIFICATE OF INDIVIDUAL DOING BUSINESS UNDER FICTITOUS NAME
Known By all men by these Presents;
That I, Lester Gawthrop, the undersigned, do hereby certify; that my name in full is Lester Gawthrop, and that my place of residence is Cloverdale, California; that I am transacting business in the state of California under the name and style of Cloverdale Pharmacy, and that I am the sole owner and proprietor of said business; that the place where the said business is carried on and conducted; and my principal place of business is West Street, Cloverdale, California.

Cloverdale Reveille
October 8, 1924

> We are giving a useful **Shopping Bag** With each purchase of **Nature's Remedy Tablets**
>
> The Ideal Laxative for Defective Elimination in Constipation, Biliousness, Sick Headache and Rheumatism.
>
> # CLOVERDALE PHARMACY
>
> LESTER GAWTHROP, prop.

Cloverdale Reveille
April 9, 1926

GAWTHROP STORE IS CLOSED INDEFINITELY
The Cloverdale Pharmacy operated by Lester Gawthrop, was closed Saturday and will not be reopened by him. Mr. Gawthrop has sold his home to C. P. Edmond. His family will occupy the cottage at the S. M. Reed Ranch until school closes and when they will probably leave Cloverdale. He expects to accept a position at Oakland which may keep him travelling throughout the state.

Cloverdale Reveille
March 6, 1931

- **T.F. Hudson**
- Cloverdale Drug Store, West Street,
- February 1872 – 1874 ; sold to Dr. Q. C. Smith
- See page 225

> **The Division of the County having proved a Failure,**
>
> I WOULD ANNOUNCE to my friends and the Public generally that I have purchased
>
> **The Cloverdale Drug Store,**
>
> On West street, Cloverdale, and will keep constantly on hand a complete and well assorted stock of fresh
>
> **DRUGS,**
>
> The best brands of
>
> LIQUORS,
>   CIGARS,
>   TOBACCO,
>   CONFECTIONARIES,
>   PAINTS, OILS, Etc., Etc.
>
> feb24 1m   T. F. HUDSON.

Sonoma Democrat
February 24, 1872

"The Division of the County having proved a Failure"

Note: In early 1872 Republican politicians in Petaluma attempted to split off the northern section of Sonoma County with a southern boundary near Santa Rosa. The new area was to be called Sotoyome County.

Note: T.F. Hudson was previously located in Ukiah (1870-72), stayed two years in Cloverdale, opened a drugstore in Santa Rosa, and moved to Tombstone, Arizona about 1880.

FORESTVILLE

- **Jewett's Drug Store**, John Egbert Jewett, prop.
- 1905 – 1922

John E. Jewett at left, circa 1905
David Henry collection

Elmer Anderson has resigned his position as clerk in Jewett's drug store.
Sonoma West Times
October 9, 1915

The smiling face of Willie Garland is seen on our streets once more.
He is now employed in Jewett' drug store.
Sonoma West Times
November 6, 1915

Mr. McLane who has been living in Jewett's old drug store has moved to the Scott place near Pocket Hill, and Jewett has moved his place of business from the Dinucci building back of his old store opposite I. O. O. F. Hall.
Sonoma West Times
December 9, 1916

Mrs. T. M. Norton, who has had charge of the Jewett drug store this summer, was obliged to go to Wheeler's Sanitarium at Healdsburg last week for treatment. Miss Wilma Clark has taken her place.
Sonoma West Times
July 27, 1917

GEYSERVILLE

- **Geyserville Pharmacy,** F.E. Sohler and W. A. Sohler, props.
- September 1907 – November 3, 1915, *The Rexall Store* (21035 Geyserville Ave.)
- Dr. Frank Ernest Sohler and his brother, William August Sohler; sold to Ernest L. Lock

WANTED – A DRUG STORE

Geyserville, with its immediate environment, represents a population of over 400. And although it is one of the most healthful sections known, yet people do get sick and need medicine.

We have a fine physician, but how can a carpenter work without tools? We are about nine miles from the nearest drug store, and if an emergency or extremity the patient might die before the necessary remedy could be procured. There is absolutely no risk in an investment of this kind here.

Who will be the first to erect a building – it need be neither large nor expensive – in which prescriptions may be compounded and where other necessary items in this line may be obtained? A bonanza for an experienced druggist with a little capital!

Geyserville Gazette
February 3, 1899

Drug Store Changes Hands.

Dr. F. E. Sohler and W. A. Sohler of Santa Rosa have purchased the practice and drug store of Dr. Edwin Merrithew of Geyserville. The latter will engage in the practice of his profession in Sacramento.

Healdsburg Tribune
September 12, 1907

Dr. Sohler has put about town some advertising benches calling attention to the Geyserville Drug Store. Should we have our usual band concerts, these will be highly appreciated for there has always been a lack of seats.

Healdsburg Enterprise
June 5, 1909

Mr. Will Sohler has graduated with honors at the College of Pharmacy and will soon return to take charge of the drug store.

Our druggist Mr. E. Mathews, is "gone again" and a new one, Mr. Mc Donald is "on again." There have been many changes in the one drug store within the last few months but we expect a steady hand at the helm when Mr. Will Sohler takes charge.

Healdsburg Tribune
May 4, 1910

Geyserville Pharmacy, circa 1909
Courtesy, Sonoma County Library

Geyserville Pharmacy, circa 1912
Courtesy, Sonoma County Library

FREE!

Come in and let us tell you how to get a $25 Phonograph ABSOLUTELY FREE

GEYSERVILLE PHARMACY

The Rexall Store

Phone 321 **SOHLER BROS.**

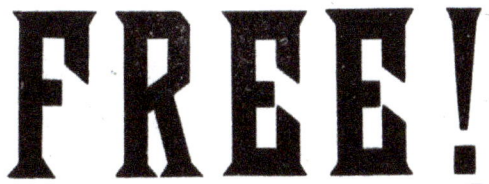

Geyserville Gazette
June 26, 1913

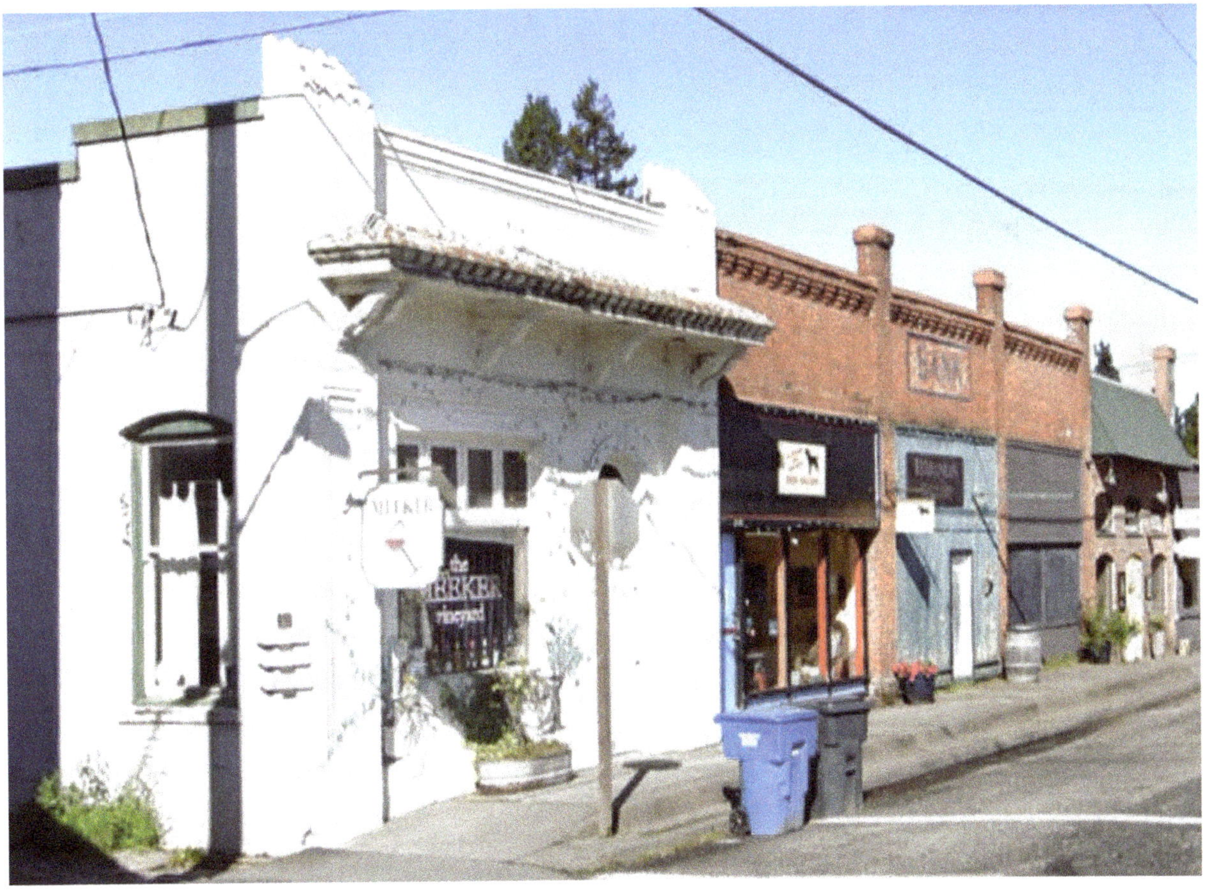

This white storefront at 21035 Geyserville Avenue occupies the site of Geyserville Pharmacy
Google photo, April 2019

- **Geyserville Pharmacy**, Ernest L. Lock, prop.
- Successor to Sohler Bros., *The Rexall Store*
- November 3, 1915 – October 1920

BUYS DRUG BUSINESS

On Wednesday, a deal was completed whereby the Geyserville Pharmacy was purchased by Mr. E. L. Lock from Sohler Bros. Mr. Lock has had considerable experience in the drug business, having spent some time with the Owl Drug Company in San Francisco, and recently has been employed in the drug business in Santa Rosa. Mr. Lock comes from a business family, his father being now in the grocery business in Petaluma.

Dr. Sohler will maintain offices as heretofore, and will be relieved in only the care of the business. Since his brother left for San Jose, he has been handicapped, and felt that it was best to dispose of the business. We are glad to welcome Mr. Lock to our city and hope he will like us all. He is a young man of sterling character and comes highly recommended.

Geyserville Gazette
November 5, 1915

NEW GEYSERVILLE DRUGGIST

Ernest L. Lock, formerly of Petaluma, has purchased the Geyserville pharmacy from Sohler Bros., and has taken possession of the business.

Healdsburg Enterprise
November 13, 1915

Patronize Your Own Drug Store

Where you can purchase the best goods at the most reasonable prices.

Come in and price our goods before you buy elsewhere.

Geyserville Pharmacy

E. L. LOCK

Geyserville Gazette
December 13, 1915

```
2nd PRIZE                    VALUE $12.00
              Donated by
         REXALL DRUG STORE
            E. L. Lock, Prop.

   I give a 12½-vote Coupon free with each 50c cash
   purchase.  Ask for Coupon.
```

GRAND PIANO CONTEST

Geyserville Gazette

February 25, 1916

DRUG STORE COMPLETED

The new drug store is now ready for business and the proprietor, Mr. E. L. Lock may well be proud of it. He has a completely new outfit of fixtures, show cases, etc., and the inside is finished in white. It is an institution the town may well be proud of.

Geyserville Gazette

February 23, 1917

```
             And Now
    WE CAN DELIVER TO
         YOUR DOOR

   Any Drug Store Article at
   Little or No Cost by Par-
   cel Post, promptly, safely

   Now when you need any drug store article it is a simple matter to
   phone, or mail your order, and it will be courteously and promptly at-
   tended to. The Parcel Post enables us to render this service to our
   out of town customers.


   GEYSERVILLE PHARMACY
```

```
   GEYSERVILLE                          CALIFORNIA
```

Geyserville Gazette

February 3, 1918

- **Geyserville Pharmacy**, Dale B. Wetzler, prop.
- Successor to E.L. Lock
- October 1920 – January 1929

LOCK SELLS DRUG STORE TO WETZLER

The drug store, for several years the property of Ernest Lock was sold last week to Dale Wetzler of Santa Rosa. We trust Mr. and Mrs. Wetzler may like their new home. The new druggist took charge today, Friday.

Healdsburg Enterprise
October 16, 1920

DRUGS══SPECIAL

Buy Your Goods at Your Home Pharmacy

GEYSERVILLE PHARMACY

Phone 32W   DALE B. WETZLER, Prop.

Healdsburg Enterprise
March 19, 1921

SPECIAL

WE ARE GIVING A FLY SWATTER FREE WITH EACH 25C PURCHASE.

GEYSERVILLE PHARMACY

Phone 32W   DALE B. WETZLER, Prop.

Let Us Supply Your Drug Wants

Healdsburg Enterprise
May 7, 1921

- **Geyserville Pharmacy,** Fred Sellgren, prop.
- Successor to Dale Wetzler
- January 1929 – November 1929

GEYSERVILLE DRUG STORE SOLD TO SAN FRANCISCAN

F. Sellgren of San Francisco will take possession of the Geyserville Pharmacy this week which he has purchased from Dale B. Wetzler. Wetzler is expecting to leave for Santa Rosa the latter part of the week with his family to make his home there.

Healdsburg Enterprise
January 10, 1929

GEYSERVILLE PHARMACY ENTERED BY THIEVES

Thieves broke into the Geyserville Pharmacy Wednesday night but nothing was taken. The entrance to the place was made through a window in the rear.

The cash register was opened but no money had been left in it. F. Sellgren, owner of the place, discovered that his place had been entered when he went to open up Thursday morning. A careful check-up of things revealed nothing missing. Sellgren recently purchased the place from Dale Wetzler who has moved to Santa Rosa. Constable Homer Cake was notified by Sellgren of the entrance of the store.

Healdsburg Enterprise
January 24, 1929

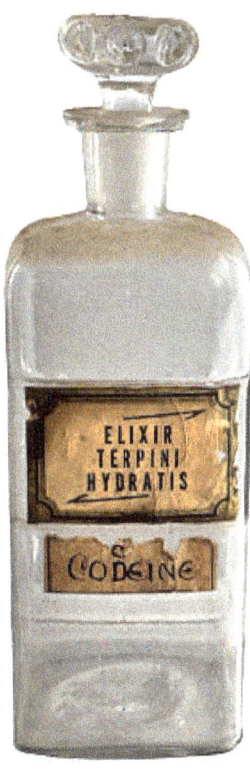

- **Geyserville Pharmacy**, John H. Carico, prop.
- November 1929 – April 1931
- Successor to F. Sellgren; son of Dr. John W. Carico of Cloverdale

CLOVERDALE MAN BUYS GEYSERVILLE DRUG BUSINESS

Sale of the Geyserville Rexall Drug Store by F. Sellgren to John H. Carico of Cloverdale was announced Thursday. Carico has been employed at the Oldham Drug Store in Cloverdale for the past two years and he will take over the new business the first of the month. Selgren purchased the drug store about eight months ago from Dale Wetzler. He has not made his future plans known.

Healdsburg Tribune
November 22, 1929

HAWKINS LEASES CARICO HOME

Mr. & Mrs. J. Hawkins have leased the home recently occupied by the John Carico family. Hawkins is the new proprietor of the Geyserville Pharmacy.

Healdsburg Tribune
May 2, 1931

CARICO ROBBED AT SANTA ROSA HAHMAN DRUG STORE

Santa Rosa has had another holdup robbery of a store. This time it was Hahman's drug store, where John Carico, on duty Wednesday night at 9:45, was robbed at gunpoint by a young bandit who took $10, half from the cash register and half from Carico's wallet, and disappeared out the front door without interference. Police were summoned but no trace of the young bandit, said to be about 19 years old, dressed in dark coat and light trousers.

Healdsburg Tribune, Enterprise and Scimitar
December 29, 1938

CARICO EXPECTED TO GO TO SAN FRANCISCO

John Carico, pharmacist in a Santa Rosa Drug Store, who was recently robbed in a holdup of the shop, has identified a photograph of George Warner, 19, being held in San Francisco with a companion as the pair responsible for a series of drug store robberies in the bay area. Carico is expected to go to San Francisco this week for a personal identification.

Healdsburg Tribune, Enterprise and Scimitar
January 16, 1939

- **Geyserville Pharmacy**, James W. Hawkins, prop.
- April 1931 – April 1934
- Successor to John Carico

GEYSERVILLE DRUG BUSINESS IS SOLD

John Carico, has disposed of the Geyserville Pharmacy and has moved his family to Healdsburg. Carico purchased the business about a year and a half ago. The purchaser, a San Francisco man, will take over the business the first of the month.

Healdsburg Tribune
April 24, 1931

J. W. Hawkins, San Francisco pharmacist, has purchased the John Carico interests in the Geyserville drug store and he and Mrs. Hawkins and their two daughters are now residents of Geyserville, the young ladies are of school age.

Mr. Hawkins is an expert pharmacist, a prescription specialist, and an experienced store manager. In addition to that, he is a live progressive citizen.

The Geyserville Pharmacy will now carry a new and complete stock of goods, offering weekly specials, and quoting metropolitan prices thereon. It will be a modern drug store in every sense of the term, and it will expand its trade into Geyserville's logical trade zone by advertising its specials, and serving its patrons promptly, politely and to their entire satisfaction.

Mr. Hawkins and family are a distinct acquisition to the business, professional, and social and club like of Geyserville.

Healdsburg Tribune
April 25, 1931

GEYSERVILLE DRUG STORE REOPENS

The Geyserville Pharmacy, which has been closed for a few days pending closing of the deal for its purchase, will reopen Tuesday morning under the management of J. W. Hawkins, an experienced pharmacist of San Francisco.
Hawkins, who takes over for John Carico, announces that a new and complete stock of goods is in route for the pharmacy, and that in future the store will be kept at high level of efficiency to give residents of Geyserville and vicinity all the service they might expect from a large city place. Prescriptions will be a specialty and Hawkins expect to have attractive weekly specials for the public.

Healdsburg Tribune
April 27, 1931

HAWKINS MOVES TO LOS ANGELES

J. W. Hawkins, who conducted the Geyserville Drug Store, has purchased a drug business in Los Angeles, and has moved his family there.

Healdsburg Tribune
May 9, 1934

- **Geyserville Pharmacy**, Roy O. Burnett, prop.
- April-May 1934
- Successor to James W. Hawkins

DRUG STORE SOLD

J. W. Hawkins has sold his drug store business here to Roy Burnett of Sacramento. Hawkins expects to enter business in a larger locality.

Healdsburg Tribune, Enterprise and Scimitar
April 12, 1934

DRUGGIST DIES SUDDENLY AT GEYSERVILLE

Roy Burnett, Geyserville Druggist, died suddenly Wednesday morning at the home of Mr. and Mrs. Parrott, with whom he made his home. Burnett had been ill for nearly a week, suffering from a heart ailment, but was thought to be improving.

Burnett came to Geyserville about three weeks ago, after purchasing the drug store from J. W. Hawkins. His wife, who had been summoned here from Sacramento by his illness, was with him when he died. Burnett was born in Humboldt County 55 years ago.

Healdsburg Tribune, Enterprise and Scimitar
May 10, 1934

- **Geyserville Pharmacy**, Robert E. "Bert" Callwell, prop.
- Successor to Roy. O. Burnett
- Sept. 19, 1934 – Sept. 1, 1942; Callwell opened Medico Drug Co. in Cloverdale, July 1951

BERT CALLWELL BUYS PHARMACY

Bert Callwell, widely known Santa Rosa Druggist, announced on Tuesday the purchase of the Geyserville Pharmacy from Mrs. R. O. Burnett, whose husband died suddenly several months ago. He will take over the business Wednesday, he announced. He plans to enlarge the stock and will carry a complete line of drugs and sundries.

Healdsburg Tribune - September 20, 1934

GEYSERVILLE
PHARMACY
BERT CALLWELL
Drugs, Notions
School Supplies
Next to Postoffice—Phone 32-W

Geyserville Press - April 19, 1940

Callwell Closing His Drug Store At Geyserville

Bert Callwell is closing his Geyserville Pharmacy September first and Tomasco Drug Co., which is purchasing the stock and prescription department, will transfer them to the Healdsburg store, Callwell announced today. It means Geyserville will be without a drug store.

Callwell, who has been in business in Geyserville for eight years, has not yet decided what he will do. He and Mrs. Callwell will go on a vacation after the first week in September and they will return to Geyserville on October first.

Healdsburg Tribune
August 27, 1942

"BERT" CALLWELL, GEYSERVILLE PHARMACY

When you wish a prescription filled, you feel better in the knowledge that the firm with whom you deal, is competent and conscientious. You want the purest ingredients to go into the compounding of the prescription, and in the exact quantity which your physician has indicated. Because the Geyserville Pharmacy, Geyserville, owned by Robert E. "Bert" Callwell, offers such a service, many Cloverdale and Geyserville people find their way in progressively increasing numbers to his pharmacy. Mr. Callwell is a stickler for using the very best obtainable ingredients, and he weighs them on a Torscon scale that is so finely adjusted that it will weigh down to even one-eighth of a grain in weight.

Robert E. Callwell—Bert, as he is known effectionately by many people—arrived in Geyserville in 1934. He had just been on a trip around the world, but none of the places he had seen appealed to him in the way Geyserville did, so he stayed and went into business.

Mr. Callwell was licensed as a pharmacist in 1925. Prior to locating in Geyserville, he worked in the drug business in San Francisco, Oakland, Porterville and Santa Rosa in California, and in Tonopah, Nevada. With regard to his experience in Santa Rosa, he was connected with Rutherford's Pharmacy, now Hall Bros., for 12 years.

Geyserville Press
October 24, 1941

- **Geyserville Pharmacy,** Alex Grubstick, prop.
- March 1950 – March 1952

IN GEYSERVILLE
Town's First Drug Store Now Operating

By MRS. ROBERT D. NEILL
Staff Correspondent
Phone 71-R

GEYSERVILLE, March 11 — Geyserville's first drug store was opened to the public Wednesday. It is owned by Alex Grubstick, who came to Geyserville from Vallejo.

The name of the store is "Geyserville Pharmacy." The owner has been a licensed pharmacist in California for 21 years.

Mr. Grubstick chose Geyserville for his location because the town has no other drug store and is small enough so that he will not have to work long hours.

Mr. Grubstick is married to the former Anita Casarotti of Sebastopol. They have two daughters, one five years and the other one year old.

The family likes the locale, the climate, schools and the "small-town neighborliness' of Geyserville.

The pharmacist attended the University of Chicago. Six years ago he managed the Sontag Drug Co. in Santa Rosa. He stayed in Napa two years before moving to Vallejo.

"The policy of the new drug store," Mr. Grubstick said, "will be to give good service whenever needed, day or night. Please do not hesitate to call us when the need arises. Our home phone is 114."

Press Democrat
March 12, 1950

GLEN ELLEN

- **Arthur Benson**
- **Richard E. Dowdall,** 1905-1911
- **L.F. Francis,** 1915

GRATON

- **Graton Pharmacy**, Arthur F. Upp, prop.
- 1924 – 1929

MAY START DRUG STORE IN GRATON SOON

Arthur Upp, resident of Graton Section, has purchased property in that place and is reported to be contemplating the opening of a drug and confectionary store there. Mr. Upp was formerly in the drug business in Santa Rosa, being a member of the firm of Belden & Upp, with a store in the Occidental building.

Sonoma West Times
May 2, 1924

GRATON NEWS IN DETAIL

A. F. Upp, local druggist, is making extensive improvements at his store here. An addition has been added to the west side of the building and half of the partition taken out of the main store. The new part will contain a new and larger prescription department and a large store room and ice cream parlor fitted with tables and chairs and a writing desk. Mr. Upp anticipates an unusually busy summer and will be well equipped to handle his trade much easier.

Sonoma West Times
April 19, 1929

GRA-D-01

Paper label:
Saffron
GRATON PHARMACY
A. F. UPP PROPRIETOR
THE REXALL STORE
GRATON   CALIFORNIA

Clear round abm
Richard Siri collection

GUERNEVILLE

- **Guerneville Drug Store** (Main Street, aka First St.– in IOOF Building)
- Dr. Edward J. Ruddock: 1906– 1910
- Benjamin C. Belden & Arthur F. Upp: August 1910 – November 30, 1915; Newton Lark became partner in 1912; Lark and Fred L. Warne purchased business in 1915.

LOCAL FIRM PURCHASES GUERNEVILLE DRUG STORE
Belden & Upp, the local Santa Rosa druggists, have purchased the Guerneville Drug Store, which has been conducted there by Dr. E. J. Ruddock. The new firm has taken charge of the purchase and Newton Lark, for many years with G. M. Luttrell here, will conduct the business.

Belden & Upp will make some important changes in their Guerneville store, and will carry a much larger and more complete stock than was formerly handled there. The importance of this deal can be realized when it is considered that Guerneville is the center of population for thousands of summer visitors each year.

Santa Rosa Republican
August 15, 1910

Guerneville Drug Store,
Main Street, circa 1910
Photo by W.A. Turner

Lark & Warne, 1916
Courtesy, Sonoma County Library

LARK & WARNE IS NAME OF NEW FIRM

Newton Lark, who as a member of the firm, has managed the Guerneville store of the Belden & Upp Drug Co., for the past five years, and Fred L. Warne, a brother of Mrs. H. J. Harrie of Bellevue, have purchased and taken over the store, as stated several days ago. Hereafter the firm will be Larke & Warne. Mr. Lark has made a large circle of friends since going to Guerneville, and the new firm are assured of a good business established by fair dealing and courteous treatment of the public in the past which will be continued by the new firm.

Press Democrat
December 10, 1915

HEALDSBURG

This 1936 photo shows the Brown-Wolfe Drug Store on the corner of West and Matheson Streets. To the north is the Wm. B. Whitney Building, Fox's Masonic Hall building, Joseph Cuneo's Pharmacy in the Swisher & Coffman Block, and Art Meese's Pharmacy under the Hotel Plaza.

From a photo postcard by Frank L. Patterson
ex Frank Sternad collection

- **Dr. W. Bamford**, physician, surgeon and druggist
- April-August 1858

> **Healdsburg Advertisements.**
>
> **NEW DRUG STORE.**
>
> HEALDSBURG, SONOMA CO., CAL.
>
> DR. BAMFORD would respectfully announce to the inhabitants of Russian River, that he has **Opened a New Drug Store in Healdsburg** where he intends to keep a supply of such Drugs and Medicines as are required.
>
> **DR. W. BAMFORD,**
>
> PHYSICIAN AND SURGEON.
>
> Office at Drug Store.
> Healdsburg, April 29, 1858.—3m.

> **NEW DRUG STORE.**
>
> HEALDSBURG, SONOMA CO., CAL.
>
> DR. BAMFORD would respectfully announce to the inhabitants of Russian River, that he has **Opened a New Drug Store in Healdsburg** where he intends to keep a supply of such Drugs and Medicines as are required.
>
> **DRS. BAMFORD & COUSTOLL,**
>
> PHYSICIANS AND SURGEONS.
>
> Office at Dr. Bamford's Drug Store.
> Healdsburg, April 29, 1858.—3m.

Sonoma Democrat
April 29, 1858

The friends of Dr. Coustoll, who went from this place to Paris a short time before the war, have been very anxious regarding his fate during the siege of that city, and now that the war is over several have written to him but no news has yet been received.

Russian River Flag
March 16, 1871

- **Hayes & Max** (M.H. Hayes & W.A. Max), druggists
- 1860-1861

This partnership opened a store in 1860 which was destroyed by fire the following year.

Portable apothecary cabinets, 19th century.

- **William Smythe Canan** (lived 1822-1891)
- First operated a drugstore in Healdsburg in 1862.
- Nathan Fike joined Canan in business on West Street 1865-66, succeeded by Charles R. Hutton as partner 1868-71. Canan and Hutton also started a money-exchange which they eventually incorporated in June 1874 as the Bank of Healdsburg.

- **Canan & Fike** (Wm. S. Canan & Nathan Fike)
- August 1865 – September 12, 1866

CANAN & FIKE,

Druggists & Apothecaries,

HEALDSBURG, CAL.

MOTT'S PILLS,
GRAFFENBERG'S PILLS,
MOFFATT'S PILLS,
CHEESEMAN'S FEMALE PILLS,
CLARK'S FEMALE PILLS,
Holloway's Pills and Ointment,
Kennerdy's Medical Discovery,
Marshall's Catarrh Snuff,
Baker's Pain Panacea,
Electric Oil,
HAMBURG TEA!
WELL'S PLASTER,
RUSSIAN SALVE,
McALLISTER'S OINTMENT,
JAPANESE SALVE,
PERUVIAN SIRUP,
COD LIVER OIL,
Brown's Bronchial Troches,
Faustick's Vermifuge,
Jaynes' Vermifuge,
Roman Eye Balsam,
Pettit's Eye Salve,
Graffenburg's Eye Lotion,
OXYGINATED BITTERS,
Hostetter's Bitters,
WISTAR'S WILD CHERRY,
Rarey's Condition Powders,
And all popular Patent Medicines.
SCHOOL & MISCELLANEOUS
BOOKS,
STATIONERY,
FANCY GOODS,
LAMPS, etc.

Russian River Flag
December 27, 1865

CANAN & FIKE,

Druggists & Apothecaries,

HEALDSBURG, CAL.

Have constantly for sale,

Compound Extract of Cloves,

A sure remedy for Toothache,

AYER'S CHERRY PECTORAL,

AYER'S SARSAPARILLA,

Ayers' Fever and Ague Cure,

AYERS' CATHARTIC PILLS,

JAYNES' ALTERNATIVE,

JAYNES' EXPECTORANT,

JAYNES' VERMIFUGE,

Jaynes' Hair Tonic,

Jaynes' Carminative Balsam,

Graffenberg's Consumption Cure,

Graffenberg's Grand Catholicon,

GRAFFENBERG'S SARSAPARILLA,

Osgood's Cholagogue,

Old Dr. Townsend's SARSAPARILLA,

S. P. Townsend's Sarsaparilla,
Bull's   do.
Tarrant's   do.
Bristol's   do.
Hall's   do.
Hall's Pulmonary Balsam,
Hall's Lung   do.

Russian River Flag
December 27, 1865

DISSOLUTION OF CO-PARTNERSHIP

The co-partnership heretofore existing between W. S. Canan and N. Fike is this day dissolved by mutual consent. All accounts of the late firm of Canan & Fike will be settled by W. S. Canan. Healdsburg, Sept. 12th, 1866. W.S. Canan will continue the business of druggist at the old stand on his own account.

Sonoma Democrat
September 15, 1866

- **Canan & Hutton** (Wm. S. Canan & Charles Hutton)
- April 1868 – April 1871

CANAN & HUTTON,

DRUGGISTS AND APOTHECARIES,

HEALDSBURG, CALIFORNIA.

HAVE CONSTANTLY ON hand a large and well selected stock of

Drugs,

Chemicals,

Paints,

Oils,

Dye Stuffs,

Glass,

Glassware,

Putty.

SURGICAL INSTRUMENTS,

Trusses, Shoulder Braces,

BOOKS AND STATIONERY,

SNUFF, TOBACCO AND CIGARS.

Physicians prescriptions carefully prepared.

AGENTS FOR

PHŒNIX AND ETNA,

Fire Insurance Companies.

ap-9-tf.

Russian River Flag
April 18, 1868

VINDICATION OF W. S. CANAN.

This gentleman, it will be remembered, was arrested in this city about the 1st of August by B. Wood, deputy sheriff of Sonoma county, Cal., and taken to Santa Rosa. The charges against Mr. Canan, as furnished the press reporters by Mr. Wood, was that he had embezzled $17,000 or over from the Mt. Jackson Quicksilver Mining Company, and $12,000 or $15,000 from the Healdsburg Bank—Mr. C. having been secretary of the former and president of the latter. In giving publicity to these charges at the time of the arrest we expressed the opinion that Mr. C. would prove his innocence, as he in no wise looked nor acted like a criminal, and it now gives us pleasure to publish that all reproach has been removed from his name. On his arrival in Santa Rosa a number of friends were on hand to go on his bail bond. A meeting of the mining company was had, and this is their report, as published in the leading column of the Healdsburg *Flag*:

HEALDSBURG, Aug. 20.

We, the undersigned directors of the Mt. Jackson Quicksilver Mining Co. find on making a second examination of *all* the books, papers and accounts of the company (a large part of the cash account having been kept upon the bank books of the old firm of Canan, Hutton & Smith, a fact unknown to the directors at the first examination) that there has not been any embezzlement or misappropriation of money, stock credit or property of the company; but, on the contrary, the account of receipts and disbursements exhibits a balance of $139.49 due W. S. Canan. D. H. ALDERSON,
ROBT. WEST,
J. H. VAUGHAN,
GEO. MULLIGAN,
Directors.

The charge against Mr. Canan (president) and Mr. Hutton (cashier), of having defrauded the bank of a large amount, on presentment to the grand jury, was unanimously dismissed on motion of the district attorney. The *Flag* adds: "We are confident the above statement, which entirely exonerates Mr. Canan from the grave charges that had been brought against him will be warmly welcomed by his many friends in this community."

We are informed by Mr. H. Denlinger, Mr. Canan's half brother, that it is probable he will return to Portland in the spring to make a home among us. Welcome to all such who have been "tried in the balance and not found wanting."

Oregonian
November 24, 1877

CANAN & HUTTON'S NEW DRUG STORE

Mr. H. D. Ley, painter and grainer, did a fine piece of work in Canan & Hutton's new drug store. Mr. Ley is a thorough workman and should be patronized. He is identified with the interests of Healdsburg, and for this alone, if not more, should have all the work in that line of business.

Russian River Flag
July 4, 1868

- **Wright & Brown** (Albert Wright & Henry K. Brown)
  - West Street, successors to Canan & Hutton; Masonic Bldg in 1877
  - June 1871 – July 1884

> WRIGHT & BROWN
> (Successors to Canan & Hutton)
> DRUGGIST & APOTHECARIES
> West Side of Plaza, Healdsburg
> CALL THE ATTENTION OF THE PUBLIC
> To their well stock of
> DRUGS, PATENT MEDICINES, PERFUMERY, TOILET ARTICLES,
> BOOKS, STATIONARY, PAINTS, OILS, VARNISHES, GLASS, ETC.
> Which they intend to render marketable, not only on account of
> Superiority and Freshness of Stock!
> BUT FROM THE LOWEST OF PRICES
> Having had long experience in the business, purchasers will find in their interest to deal with this firm. Their stock will always be composed of the
> BEST OF GOODS
> From first hands, which they will sell at the
> LOWEST PRICES
> All orders from a distance will be filled with dispatch, and satisfaction warranted.
> WRIGHT & BROWN
> Russian River Flag
> August 24, 1871

HBG-D-31
- W&B (monogram)
- WRIGHT & BROWN
- DRUGGISTS
- HEALDSBURG, CAL.
- Ball neck panel, 5.3" tall
- Clear, tooled top
- Ex Frank Sternad

HBG-D-32
- W&B (monogram)
- WRIGHT & BROWN
- DRUGGISTS
- HEALDSBURG, CAL.
- Clear oval, 6.8" tall
- Base: W.T. & CO.
- Tooled top
- Ex Frank Sternad

WRIGHT & BROWN
(Successors to Canan & Hutton,)

DRUGGISTS
—AND—
APOTHECARIES,
West Side of Plaza,
HEALDSBURG,

CALL THE ATTENTION OF THE Public to their well selected stock of

DRUGS,
PATENT MEDICINES,
PERFUMERY,
TOILET ARTICLES,
BOOKS,
STATIONERY,
PAINTS,
OILS,
VARNISHES,
GLASS, ETC., ETC.,

Which they intend to render marketable, not only on account of

Superiority and Freshness of Stock!
BUT FROM
LOWNESS OF PRICES!

Having had long experience in the business, purchasers will find it to their interest to deal with this firm. Their stock will always be composed of the

Best of Goods,
From first hands, which they will sell at the
LOWEST PRICES.

☞ All orders from a distance will be filled with dispatch, and satisfaction warranted.
3-21-tf   WRIGHT & BROWN.

Russian River Flag
July 13, 1871

REMOVAL!
REMOVAL!
REMOVAL!

WRIGHT & BROWN
WRIGHT & BROWN
WRIGHT & BROWN

DRUGGISTS and APOTHECARIES
DRUGGISTS and APOTHECARIES
DRUGGISTS and APOTHECARIES

HAVE REMOVED TO
HAVE REMOVED TO
HAVE REMOVED TO

Fenno's old Stand!
Fenno's old Stand!
Fenno's old Stand!

AND ARE PREPARED TO FURNISH

DRUGS,
PATENT MEDICINES,
PERFUMERY,
TOILET ARTICLES,
BOOKS AND STATIONERY,
PAINTS AND OILS,
VARNISHES,
GLASS, ETC., ETC.
—AT—
ASTONISHINGLY LOW PRICES!

HAVING HAD LONG EXPERIENCE IN the business, purchasers will find it to their interest to deal with this firm. Their stock will always be composed of the

BEST OF GOODS,
From first hands, which they will sell at the
Lowest Prices.
All orders from a distance will be filled with dispatch, and satisfaction warranted.
3-21-tf-5   WRIGHT & BROWN,

Russian River Flag
April 11, 1872

H. K. BROWN,   A. WRIGHT.
WRIGHT & BROWN,

HAVING REMOVED TO THE
NEW MASONIC BUILDING,
Still continue to keep one of
THE LARGEST
—AND—
BEST SELECTED STOCK
—OF—
DRUGS
—AND—
PROPRIETARY MEDICINES,

Ever brought into Sonoma county, and as it is a known fact that the wholesale rates of drugs have materially lowered during the past year, they have brought the prices of their large and

VARIED ASSORTMENT
To correspondingly
LOW FIGURES!

They carry a heavy stock of
Paints, Oils, Varnishes, Glass
—AND—
PAINTERS' MATERIALS
Throughout, and are selling at a slight advance on wholesale prices.

SCHOOL BOOKS & STATIONERY
Are made a specialty.
WRIGHT & BROWN
3-21-tf-5

Russian River Flag
May 17, 1877

When you go to the Post Office, examine Wright & Brown's stock of toilet soap and fancy goods; their show-cases are a credit to themselves and to the town.

Russian River Flag
April 27, 1876

- **Albert Wright**
  - 109 West Street
  - July 1884 – April 1886; sold to Miller & Whitney (see page 50)

HBG-D-01
AW (monogram)
A. WRIGHT
DRUGGIST
HEALDSBURG, CAL.
Tooled top
Clear oval
3.5 inches tall
Base: W T & CO. B
Merle Avila collection
5 1/4 inches tall
Base: W. T. & CO. C
Lou & Leisa Lambert bottle shown

The extensive drug and notion store of A. Wright. Esq., has been removed to commodious and convenient quarters in Koenig's Block, on the east side of West Street, between the Healdsburg Bank and John Daly's. The many friends and patrons of Mr. Wright will here find the same urbane and obliging attention that always characterized Mr. Wright and his clerks.
Russian River Flag
February 10, 1886

The many friends of Mr. A. Wright, will be pleased to learn that he is again in business. He has taken charge of the Seattle Pharmacy, in Seattle. His competency and his genial and friendly manners are bound to make his new venture a success. He has our best wishes.
Russian River Flag
July 28, 1886

Drugs, Perfumery, STATIONERY, Paints and Oils.

A. WRIGHT,

The Pioneer Druggist of Healdsburg,

Keeps these articles, and sells them at reasonable prices. He does a square and legitimate business, and deals fairly with every one.

☞ Prescriptions Carefully and Expeditiously Compounded. ☜

No mistakes are made in this establishment. This is the place where you can buy

Pure, Unadulterated Medicines,

of every kind, and depend on what you are getting.

Everything in the Fancy Goods and Toilet Line,

From a Tooth Brush to a Dressing Case.

Fine Perfumery a Specialty.

A. WRIGHT, The Druggist,

Having given satisfaction to his numerous friends and patrons in the past, takes this opportunity of thanking them for their favors and solicits a continuance of their patronage.

BOOKS!

School, Miscellaneous and blank books of every variety; and, in fact, a full line of everything usually carried in the stationery line, together with the largest assortment of patent medicines in any one store in the county.

Russian River Flag
January 20, 1886

DEATH OF ALBERT WRIGHT.

The following taken from the Examiner of Monday contains all the information as yet obtained in regard to the death of one of our former citizens Albert Wright:

SEATTLE (W. T.), July 14.—Dr. Albert Wright, about 50 years of age, committed suicide here to-night. He came here three years ago from Healdsburg, Cal., of which place he was at one time Postmaster. He started a drug store, which he sold three months ago, since which time he has seemed despondent. He has been in the habit of using morphine and to-night took a capsule containing ten grains, which resulted fatally.

He leaves two little girls, 14 and 9 years old, respectively. His wife died four years ago. He was well known in the country about Healdsburg as a political orator and writer.

Al. Wright, so well known in this section, was a native of Demoscotta, Maine, and at early age graduated with honors from Boldur College, and removed west, stopping for a few years in Nevada, coming to this city in 1870, where he entered into co-partnership with H. K. Brown under the firm name of Wright & Brown, doing a drug and stationery business. He served as Postmaster in this city for eight years under Grant's and Hayes' administrations.

In May, 1886, he removed from here to Seattle W. T., taking with him his two little girls, their mother having died in this place but a short time before.

Al. Wright was a popular and widely known man and held the esteem and honor of all with whom he was associated. Obliging and courteous in his business relations, a leader in political organizations, He was a Past Master of the F. and A. M. and at the time of his death was a member in good standing of the A. O. U. W. Lodge, No. 31, of this place, from which $2000 will be paid to his children.

Healdsburg Enterprise
July 18, 1888

- **Clark's Drug Store**, J. Clark, prop.
- September 1875 – May 1876
- Sold to Piper & Laymance

NEW BOTTLES
Clean and white, for Citrate Magnesia.
Ten cents given for return of bottles at Clarks Drug Store.
Russian River Flag - November 4, 1875

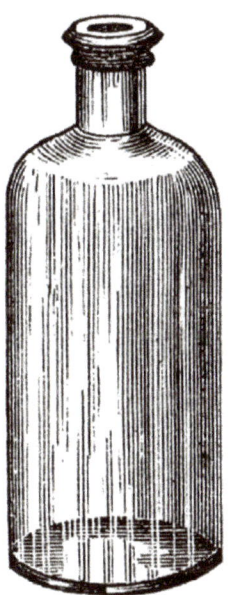

Whitall, Tatum & Co.
Druggists Glassware, 1876

Citrate of Magnesia.

FOR CHRISTMAS
Get a choice bottle of perfume or a nice hair brush. Good articles can be had at Clark's Drug Store
Russian River Flag
December 16, 1875

REMEMBER TOMORROW
Make some heart glad with a fine bottle of perfume, brush, cake of toilet soap, or some other useful article. Buy it at Dr. J. Clark's Drug Store.
Russian River Flag
December 23, 1875

CHEAP RENT
Cheap rent and light expenses are the main consideration for fair dealing. A cash business avoids making good customers pay for bad ones. This is the system now adopted at Clark's Drug Store, with reduced prices.
Russian River Flag
March 9, 1876

- **Piper, John J.** (lived 1830-1908)
  - April 24, 1873 – December 1878; NW corner of the plaza
  - Formed partnership with Francis M. Laymance to purchase Clarks Drug Store in September 1876. It was conducted until November 2, 1877.
  - Piper had been politically and fraternally active in Healdsburg since 1860. Previously he resided in Weaverville, Trinity County (1855-58) where he operated the Ridgeville Express.

NEW TO-DAY.

J. J. PIPER, M. D.,

PHYSICIAN, SURGEON AND OBSTETRIcian. Office—at his Drug Store, northwest corner of the plaza, Healdsburg.   [5-3

NEW DRUG STORE!

Dr. J. J. PIPER

Has opened a Drug Store

TWO DOORS SOUTH OF SOTOYOME HOUSE,

HEALDSBURG,

Where he will keep constantly on hand the Finest Quality of

Drugs and Medicines,

PAINTS AND OILS,

VARNISHES,

FANCY AND

TOILET ARTICLES,

DYE STUFFS, Etc.

Prescriptions Carefully Compounded.
5-3-tf-3

GRANGERS, FARMERS & CITIZENS
Remember that Dr. J. J. Piper's Drug Store is near the Farmer's and Mechanic's Bank and Granger's Store, and that it is supplied with a full stock of medicines, paints, oils, toilet articles, stationary, etc. Prices down.
Russian River Flag
February 28, 1876

Dr. J. J. Piper and F. Laymance have bought of Dr. J. Clark, the drug store adjoining Wells, Fargo and Co.'s office.
Russian River Flag
September 7, 1876

DISSOLUTION OF Co-PARTNERSHIP
Notice is hereby given that the partnership heretofore existing between Francis M. Laymance and John J. Piper is this day dissolved by mutual consent, the former retiring. All accounts may be settled with either party.
Russian River Flag
November 2, 1877

Russian River Flag
April 24, 1873

Dr. J. J. Piper, having purchased the interest of his late partner, hereafter conducts the business in his own name; the accounts of the late firm will be settled by either member. Prescriptions carefully compounded. Medicines, paints, oils, toilet articles, school books, and stationery always on hand.

Russian River Flag
November 15, 1877

GRAND
CLOSING OUT
SALE.

DR. PIPER'S DRUG STORE!

30 Days Only.

HOLIDAY PRESENTS

AT COST!

TOILET ARTICLES,

SOAPS, PERFUMES,

BOOKS, STATIONERY,

PAINTERS SUPPLIES,

DRUGS AND MEDICINES,

FIXTURES.

Splendid Opportunity to Fit Out a COUNTRY DRUG STORE!

HAVING DECIDED TO CLOSE-OUT MY business within the next 30 days, I will offer my entire stock of Drugs, Medicines, Perfumery, Toilet Articles, Books, Stationery, and in brief, everything kept in stock by me, at prices actually below cost. A fine opportunity is now offered to all who may need articles in my line, to supply themselves at a great saving. Many things suitable for holiday presents are comprised in the stock. I mean business, and you must come early to secure choice.

DR. J. J. PIPER.

Russian River Flag
November 21, 1878

DR. J. J. PIPER'S RIDGEVILLE EXPRESS!

connecting with

RHODES & Co.'s EXPRESS

to all parts of the Atlantic States and Europe, by every Steamer. Dr. Piper leaves Weaverville every TUESDAY and SATURDAY morning, for

BATES' RANCH,

CHELLIS' MILLS,

MINERSVILLE,

DIGGER CREEK,

MULE CREEK, and

RIDGEVILLE,

and will give particular attention to the carrying and delivery of LETTERS, PACKAGES, TREASURE, &c. DRAFTS purchased upon any Banking House in the State.

Collections made, and all business in the Express line carefully attended to.

 Gold Dust bought.   J. J. PIPER.

Weaver, July 18, 1857.

Trinity Journal
July 18, 1857

The remains of Dr. John J. Piper, who died in Spokane on June 20th, were brought to Healdsburg last week, and the funeral was held at T. G. Young's undertaking parlors Thursday, Rev. M. R. Wolfe officiating. Piper left Healdsburg about thirty years ago, after living here many years. Piper Street was named in his honor. He became a prominent citizen of Spokane, serving as superintendent of schools, as a supervisor, and in other positions of trust. He was aged 78 years.

Healdsburg Tribune
July 2, 1908

- **James E. Fenno**
  - December 1865 – September 1871

READ! READ!! READ!!!
GO TO
JAMES E. FENNO
HEALDSBURG, SONOMA COUNTY,
To buy your Drugs, Medicines, Watches, Clocks, Jewelry, Fancy Goods, Tobacco and Cigars,
SCHOOL BOOKS, GROCERIES AND PIPES.

DIRECT FROM THE EAST—PURE DRUGS, all the Patent Medicines, Pure Brandies and Wines.

Until further notice I will sell School at San Francisco prices.

Paints, Oils, Turpentine, Window Glass, Coal Oil, Machine Oil, Lard Oil, Castor Oil, Sweet Oil, Gold Pens, Stationary, Letter Paper, Envelopes, Inks, Pens of all Descriptions. The best assortment of Pipes, Cigars, Tobacco and Tobacco Boxes. Wall Paper, Window Shades, Curtain Fixtures, Candy, Nuts, Figs, Raisins, etc.

☞ Proscriptions carefully compounded and prepared at all times, day and night.

Watches, Clocks, Jewelry, and Accordeons, repaired, all at San Francisco prices.

All orders for Drugs, Medicines, Paints, Oils, Varnishes, School Books, Paper, Ink, Pens, Jewelry, or PRESCRIPTIONS, left with or sent to Wm. J. Harrison (Chas. E. Mitchell's store), Cloverdale, or T. C. Philbrick, Ukiah, will receive prompt attention.   JAMES E. FENNO.
45v1itf.

Sonoma Democrat
April 28, 1866

JAMES E. FENNO
—Has opened a—
JEWELRY & GUNSMITH SHOP,
East of Norton's Law Office,
HEALDSBURG,
Where He is Prepared to do
ALL KINDS OF REPAIRING PROMPTLY
And at Reasonable Prices.

WATCHES, CLOCKS, JEWELRY, ACcordeons, Sewing Machines, Guns and Pistols repaired, and Keys fitted and Locks repaired. Sewing Machine Needles, Oil, etc., kept on hand constantly.

Give Him a Call With Your Work.
4-3tf

Russian River Flag
December 28, 1871

GO TO FENNO'S
HEALDSBURG, SONOMA COUNTY
For Prescriptions, Drugs, Medicines, Wines, Brandies and everything in the drug line
at less than San Francisco prices since I import my own goods.

Sonoma Democrat
July 1870

SHERIFF'S SALE
We regret that we are called upon to chronicle the failure of James E. Fenno, druggist, who has been a resident of this place for some years. His stock of goods was levied upon last Saturday evening by Deputy Sheriff Reynolds, who will sell the same at public auction today.

Sonoma Democrat
September 30, 1871

- **Winham's Drug Store** (W.P.L. Winham)
  - Meyer's Building
  - October 1867 – December 1868

Russian River Flag
October 1867

Palace Pharmacy / Palace Drug Store

This long-lived enterprise was located in the Swisher & Coffman Block at 109 West St., across from the plaza at mid-block. Starting with the partnership of Miller & Whitney in the mid-1880's, the business was called *Palace Pharmacy*. In early 1901, under owners Haigh & Peck, the name was altered to *Palace Drug Store*. Following the 1906 earthquake, the street number became 309; and when Oliver Clough took charge in January 1909, he re-named the store *Clough's Pharmacy*. The *Palace* thus enjoyed a run of over twenty years. The two-story building itself, along with every other structure on the west side of the block, was demolished January-June 1981 to make way for the upscale hotels and shops we see today (see pages 35 and 77).

Palace Pharmacy

- May 1886 – January 1891   Miller & Whitney (George T. & Wm. B.)
- January 1891 – April 1892   Jones & Hobson (Oliver L. & Jerome C.)
- April 1892 – May 1894   Hobson & Kruse (Jerome C. & Fred A.)
- May 1894 – April 1898   Whitney & Kruse (Wm. B. & Fred A.)
- April 1898 – August 1900   Nichols & Carver (Horace S. & Rollo)
- August 1900 – February 1901 Haigh & Carver (W. Rainey & Rollo)

Palace Drug Store

- February 1901 – May 1901   Haigh & Peck (W. Rainey & John W.)
- June 1901 – July 1902   Knight & Schmitz (Peter J. & Leo A.)
- July 1902 – November 1903   Leo A. Schmitz
- November 1903 – April 1906   Julius Luedke Jr.
- April 1906 – January 1909   Miller & Hobson (Lou & Jerome C.)

Palace Pharmacy at left, 109 West St., Swisher & Coffman Block circa 1897.
Illustrated Atlas of Sonoma County, 1898

- **Miller & Whitney** (George T. Miller & William B. Whitney)
- Palace Pharmacy, 109 West Street
- Successors to Albert Wright
- May 1886 – January 1891

NEW FIRM OF MILLER & WHITNEY

On May 1st the new Drug Store of Miller & Whitney in Healdsburg, was opened to the public under Mr. Whitney's management. The latter gentleman thoroughly understands the business, and has a beautiful establishment in which to conduct it. The store is elegant in its appointments, and on the shelves and in the show-cases may be seen every article usually kept in a first-class drug store

Russian River Flag
August 11, 1886

Oliver L. Jones, who has lately been in the employ of Miller & Whitney, goes to San Francisco Saturday where he will attend Cooper Medical College.

Healdsburg Tribune, Enterprise and Scimitar
May 29, 1890

NOTICE TO DEBTORS

The books of the late firm of Miller & Whitney have been placed in my hands at J. W. Rose's office, and all persons indebted to those parties will please call and settle without further delay.

C. H. POND.

Healdsburg Tribune, Enterprise and Scimitar
May 14, 1891

Mr. W. B. Whitney, who lately succeeded the old firm of Whitney & Kruse, Druggists, will make several improvements to his well-known store. The front will be changed and larger show windows put in, as well as other alterations made to the interior of the store. A new awning will also be put on.

Mr. Whitney bears the distinction of having been the first graduate at the California College of Pharmacy from Sonoma County. He is the oldest druggist in Healdsburg, having entered Wrights Drug Store in this city as a boy in 1873.

In 1886, the firm of Miller and Whitney was formed, which was succeeded by Jones & Hobson. The firm of Whitney & Kruse was established in 1893, and for the past five years they have merited and received a very large share of the patronage of the people in this part of the county.
Mr. Whitney will hereafter conduct the business as a sole proprietor, and the reputation he has already established for courteous treatment, fair prices, and first-class drugs will no doubt endure him a continued liberal patronage.

Healdsburg Tribune, Enterprise and Scimitar
April 14, 1898

HBG-D-02
M&W (monogram)
MILLER & WHITNEY
PHARMACISTS
HEALDSBURG
CAL'A
Clear rectangular
Tooled top
6 inches tall
Base: W.T. & CO.
Dan Brown collection

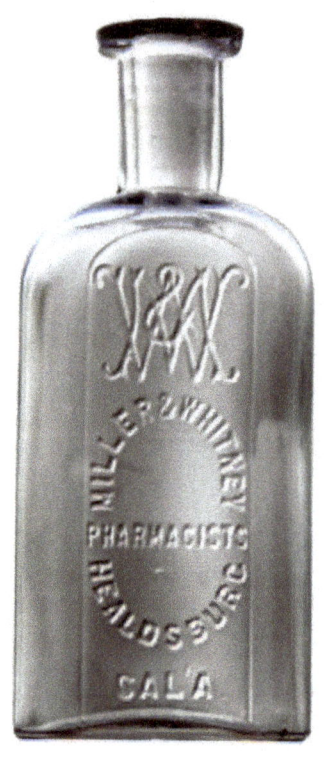

HBG-D-03
M&W (monogram)
MILLER & WHITNEY
PHARMACISTS
HEALDSBURG
CALA
Clear (sca) oval
Tooled top
7 Inches tall
Base: W.T. & CO. C
Lou & Leisa Lambert collection

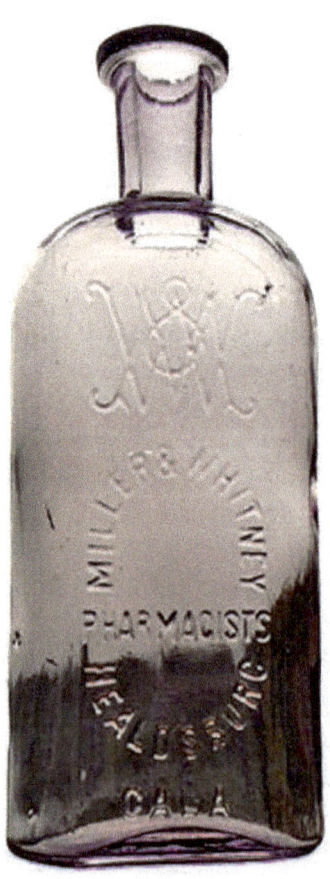

HBG-D-04
> MILLER & WHITNEY
> PHARMACISTS
> HEALDSBURG, CAL'A.
> Clear oval
> Tooled top
> 3 ½ inches tall
> Base: W T & CO   D
> Merle Avila collection

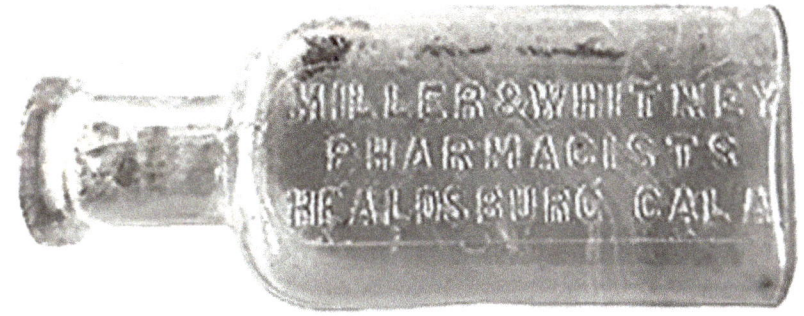

HBG-D-05
> COMPLIMENTS
> OF
> MILLER & WHITNEY
> HEALDSBURG
> Clear
> Medicine glass
> Helmut & DeAnna Jordt collection

- **Jones & Hobson** (Oliver L. Jones & Jerome C. Hobson)
- Palace Pharmacy
- January 1891 – April 1, 1892

Jones & Hobson have secured the service of a thoroughly competent druggist, a graduate of pharmacy who is also a registered State pharmacist. Miller & Whitney have always done the leading prescription business and the new firm intends to keep this department a leading feature. Prices still as low as ever.

Healdsburg Tribune
February 5, 1891

The mildew has already begun to attack grape vines in this section. The best preventive known is sulphur. To sulphur a large vineyard is a great expensive. This can be materially reduced by buying your sulphur at Jones and Hobson, proprietors of the Palace Drug Store. They buy in carload lots and can sell at the lowest prices.

Healdsburg Tribune
May 14, 1891

PROSPERITY

The prosperity of our town is shown by the condition and appearance of its stores. It is a pleasure for the Tribune to notice everything of merit and the firm of Jones & Hobson at the Palace Pharmacy certainly deserves great credit lor the successful management of this, Healdsburg's leading pharmacy.

Since the change of proprietors, the stock has been increased in value several thousand dollars. Every line and department have been restocked until now this model pharmacy has the most complete stock of any store in the Coast counties—there is scarcely a patent or proprietary medicine in the market, or known to the profession that is not for sale there.

The prescription department presided over by none but competent and experienced pharmacists, who have held positions in the largest and best drug store in the State, where they compounded literally thousands of prescriptions. Here a fresh and complete stock in every detail with all the necessary apparatus the public can depend on purity and perfectly compounded prescriptions.

Healdsburg Tribune, Enterprise and Scimitar
August 6, 1891

GO TO JONES & HOBSON'S
Palace Pharmacy and Christmas Bazaar
And be convinced of the superior quality and their
BARGAINS In HOLIDAY GOODS and CHRISTMAS GIFTS.
A complete stock of Patent Medicines, a fine line of Stationery, Pure Drugs. Prescriptions carefully compounded. Fine Imported Perfumery. Toilet Sets. Books in Prose and Poetry for almost a song.
Visit Jones and Hobson, Palace Pharmacy and you will have a
MERRY CHRISTMAS and a HAPPY NEW YEAR.

Healdsburg Tribune
December 17, 1891

THE PALACE PHARMACY

Formerly owned by Miller & Whitney, The Palace Pharmacy has enjoyed the well-earned reputation of doing a strictly honest prescription business, consequently commanding almost exclusively the entire trade of this vicinity in that line.

O. L. Jones, who during the past year has had charge of the prescription department, has always taken the most careful pains to sustain that reputation, although hampered and hindered by overwork (being the only druggist for many months in the establishment) has the well-earned confidence of the physicians and the public. O. L. Jones and J. C. Hobson, the present proprietors of the Palace Pharmacy, intend to improve their business in every department.

The books of the establishment which were formerly kept exclusively by Mr. Stephen Cavanagh, will be kept in an entirely different manner and according to business rules. The store will be enlarged to receive larger invoices of goods now ordered from standard makers in the East.

After much correspondence and at great expense the firm has secured the services of one of Oakland's best pharmacists, Mr. L. Miller. As a chemist and pharmacist, Mr. Miller is acknowledged by his professional capacity they have a right to know something of his qualifications. We know of no better way than to make public some of our correspondence with the largest drug house in Oakland in relation to him. The following being an exact copy:

Oakland, Feb. 2, 1891
Jones & Hobson, Druggists, Healdsburg,

Mr. L. Miller, head prescription clerk, is a thoroughly educated pharmacist; he is a graduate of the Ohio Slate Pharmaceutical Association and as a compounder of prescriptions he is among the foremost of this State. We are very sorry to lose him but he wants a change and we congratulate your firm in securing him to take charge of your prescription department.

Any time your firm desires to make any change communicate with us, as we would like to secure his services again. Our prescription business averages about 1,800 a month (in the winter 2,400); Mr. Miller had full charge of this department of our business. Mr. Miller deserves this recommendation from us as he has been in our employ seven years.

Hoping your success in your new enterprise, as you well deserve it, we are yours,
Osgood Bros.

Thanking the public for their generous patronage in the past and asking a continuance of the same, we are, Respectfully, Jones & Hobson.

Healdsburg Tribune, Enterprise and Scimitar
March 5, 1891

HBG-D-05A
JONES & HOBSON
PALACE PHARMACY
Clear oval, 4.5" tall
Clear rectangular, 5.5" tall
Tooled top
Base: W in diamond
ex Frank Sternad

- **Hobson & Kruse** (Jerome C. Hobson & Fred A. Kruse)
- Palace Pharmacy
- April 1, 1892 – May 1894

NOTICE.

THE FIRM OF JONES & HOBSON, DRUGgists, doing business under the firm name of Jones & Hobson, at the city of Healdsburg, County of Sonoma, State of California, is this day mutually dissolved. Mr. Hobson and Mr. Kruse having purchased the entire interest of Mr. Jones. All accounts due the firm of Jones & Hobson are payable to the firm of Hobson & Kruse and all liabilities and accounts due from or on account of said firm of Jones & Hobson have been assigned and will be paid by Hobson & Kruse.
O. L. JONES,
J. C. HOBSON,
F. A. KRUSE.

HEALDSBURG, April, 1, 1892.

Healdsburg Tribune, Enterprise and Scimitar
April 29, 1892

MORE VIRTUE IN
Dr. Robert's Golden Gate Medical Syrup
than in hundreds of cheap make-ups but extensively advertised stuff. To prove this fact all we ask you is to give it a try. We can give you references from hundreds of people who will testify to the above. Moreover, they say the G. G. M. S. must be taken more freely. No family ought to be without it. Small bottle 75 cents, large bottle $1.50.
Manufactured by
MRS. KATE ROBERTS
914 Fourth Street, Santa Rosa.
FOR SALE BY HOBSON & KRUSE, DRUGGISTS, HEALDSBURG, CAL.

Healdsburg Tribune, Enterprise and Scimitar
November 17, 1892

- **Whitney & Kruse** (William B. Whitney & Fred A. Kruse)
- Palace Pharmacy
- May 1894 – April 1898

HBG-D-05B
Whitney & Kruse
PHARMACISTS
75 WEST ST. HEALDSBURG
Clear rectangular
Tooled top
6.8 inches tall
Base: S.B.W.
ex Frank Sternad collection

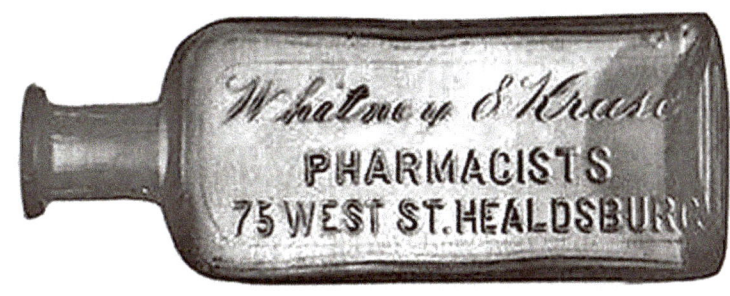

Healdsburg Tribune
March 3, 1898

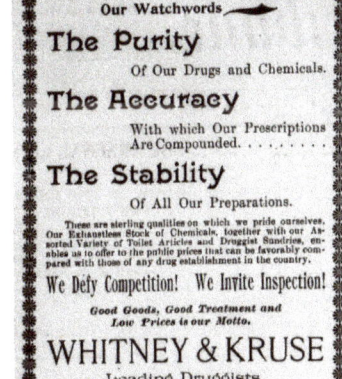

HBG-D-06
WHITNEY & KRUSE
PHARMACISTS
HEALDSBURG, CAL.
Clear rectangular
4 ½ inches tall
Helmut & DeAnna Jordt
5 ½ inches tall
John Burton collection

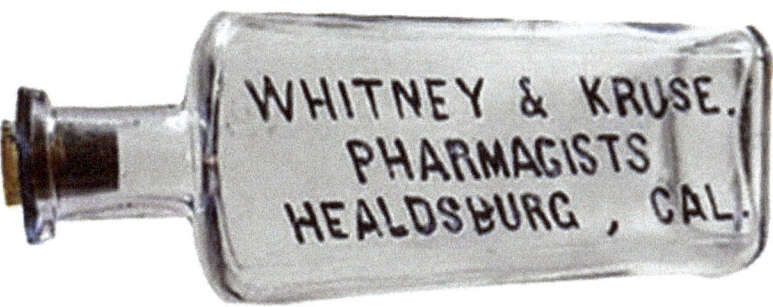

BG-D-12
WHITNEY'S
COUGH SYRUP
PUT UP BY
WHITNEY & KRUSE
HEALDSBURG, CAL.
Aqua rectangular panel
Tooled top
5 3/4 inches tall
Base: W.T. & Co.
ex Frank Sternad collection

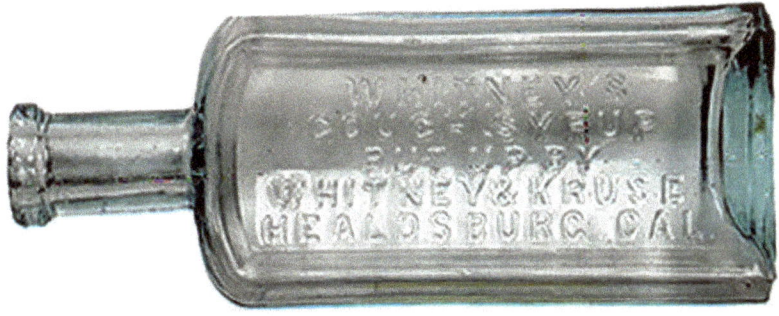

- **Nichols & Carver** (Horace S. Nichols & Rollo Carver)
- 105 West Street, Masonic Hall (former Frank Burr): September 1897 – April 1898
- Palace Pharmacy, Swisher & Coffman Block, 109 West St.: April 1898 – August 1900
- Horace Squires Nichols (1864-1930) also purchased the Red Front Drug Store at 111 West St. from H.W. Baxter in April 1890 (see page 94 and bottle below). After leaving Healdsburg in August 1900 to manage pharmacies in other cities, Nichols returned in January 1906.

Last Friday a 100-pound carboy of sulphuric acid exploded in the rear of Nichols' drug store and Rainey Haigh was badly burned on the legs

Sonoma Democrat
July 28, 1894

BURR'S DRUG STORE SOLD

H. S. Nichols and Rollo Carver have purchased Frank Burr's drugstore [105 West St.]. Both stores, Nichols' and Burr's, will be carried on as before, with Mr. Carver in charge of Burr's store. We wish the new firm of Nichols & Carver success.

Healdsburg Tribune
September 16, 1897

Nichols and Carver's [Palace] drug store is neat, well appropriated establishment, and contains everything that is usually found in drug stores of first class. Drugs, chemicals, toilet and fancy articles are on hand. Mr. H. S. Nichols, the senior member of the firm, is a graduate from the California College of Pharmacy of 1887, which is a sufficient guarantee of his fitness and ability to compound prescriptions. Mr. Nichols is a young man, but he has resided here for the past twenty-two years, has conducted his store for the last fourteen years in Healdsburg. Mr. Rollo Carver, is a native of Alexander Valley and of course is widely known. He has been associated with Mr. Nichols for about two years. Both gentlemen are popular young men.

Healdsburg Tribune, Enterprise and Scimitar
December 14, 1899

HBG-D-07
H. S. NICHOLS Ph.G.
DRUGGIST
HEALDSBURG, CAL.
Clear rectangular
4 1/2 inches tall
Dan Brown collection
5 1/8 inches tall
8 inches tall
Helmut & DeAnna Jordt collection

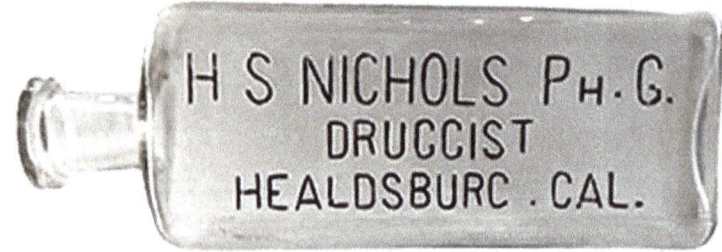

- **Haigh & Carver** (W. Rainey Haigh & Rollo Carver)
- Palace Pharmacy
- August 1900 – February 1901

W. RAINEY HAIGH RESIGNS FROM NICHOLS DRUG STORE

W. Rainey Haigh has resigned his position at Nichols store as prescription clerk and on Monday morning he went to San Francisco to perfect arrangements "on the road" for some Eastern houses. Rainey's territory will be extensive and include the thriftiest section of the state, so with his rustling gift there is no question of his success.

Healdsburg Tribune, Enterprise and Scimitar
August 6, 1895

W. RAINEY HAIGH PURCHASES HORACE NICHOLS SHARE OF DRUG STORE

W. Rainey Haigh has purchased the interest of Horace Nichols in the drug business of Nichols & Carver, and the new firm is Haigh & Carver. Mr. Haigh is an experienced druggist of many years practice, is a most popular young man, and the new firm will undoubtedly receive a large share of the patronage of the public.

Healdsburg Tribune, Enterprise and Scimitar
August 9, 1900

DEATH OF ROLLO CARVER

Consumption Carried off a Most Promising Young Man

Rollo G. Carver died Monday evening at the home of his guardian. Dr. J. R. Swisher, after an illness of several months. The deceased was born in Alexander Valley, May 4, 1876, and his life was spent in the Valley and Healdsburg.

He attended school here, but failing health compelled him to leave the high school. Later he began the study of medicine, but this, too, proved too great a stress, on his constitution and he was forced to abandon it. Some three years ago, he purchased an interest in the drug store with Horace Nichols, and recently disposed of it to John W. Peck, when it was seen that, his failing health would not permit him of the confinement.

The deceased was a young man of most upright character, and enjoyed the esteem and respect of the entire community. Both parents died a number of years ago, and but one family relative survives him, a sister, Miss Dora Carver, who arrived from Ogden last week. The funeral occurred on March 21, 1901.

Healdsburg Tribune, Enterprise and Scimitar
March 21, 1901

- **Haigh & Peck** (W. Rainey Haigh & John Wm. Peck)
- Palace Drug Store (Dr. James R. Swisher, owner of the building, was also an interim proprietor)
- February 1901 – May 16, 1901

NEW PARTNER
John W. Peck has purchased Rollo Carver's interest in the drugstore formerly owned by Nichols & Carver.

Healdsburg Tribune
February 7, 1901

At Truitt's Opera House on next Friday and Saturday evenings the queen of lion tamers Angie and her three large performing lions will appear, supported by the All-Star Orpheum Vaudeville Company, twelve in number, with the greatest program ever presented in Healdsburg.

The program comprises acrobatic performers, operatic singers, dancing, with a change of program nightly. The fearless Angie and her three mammoth lions are a whole show in themselves. It is something one cannot afford to miss. Angie, in a den with three ferocious lions, performs at the risk of her life many difficult acts. She sits on the large lion, Prince, puts her head in his terrible jaws, places his paws around her neck while she lies on his breast, dances a cake-walk with Trilby and fondles the three fierce brutes as if they were kittens.

Reserved seats now on sale at Haigh & Peck's drug store.

Healdsburg Tribune, Enterprise and Scimitar
February 14, 1901

Truitt's Opera House on Center Street, circa 1910
Courtesy, Vivian Hall

NEW DRUGGIST

The Petaluma *Argus* says: Mr. and Mrs. Walter Brownlee are to leave Petaluma and move to Healdsburg where Mr. Brownlee will take the management of the Palace Drug Store. If the business proves satisfactory after a few months trial, Mr. Brownlee will probably purchase an interest. Rollo Carver, who died last week in Healdsburg, was a partner in the store. Mr. & Mrs. Brownlee will leave Petaluma on April 1st

Healdsburg Tribune, Enterprise and Scimitar
March 28, 1901

Under New Management

Walter S. Brownlee has taken the management of the drug store recently owned by Nichols & Carver in Healdsburg. Mr. Brownlee has had twelve years' experience in the management of drug stores, and will conduct the store in a thoroughly first-class manner. The store has been christened "The Palace Drug Store," and will be known by that name hereafter. Attention is called to their new ad in this issue of the *Tribune*.

Healdsburg Tribune, Enterprise and Scimitar
April 11, 1901

---THE---
Palace Drug Store
(Formerly conducted by Nichols & Carver)
Is entirely under new management. You will find a complete stock of
PURE DRUGS
CHEMICALS
TOILET ARTICLES
STATIONERY
PHOTO GOODS
Prescriptions Carefully Compounded
PHONE, MAIN 66
WEST STREET,   OPPOSITE PLAZA

Healdsburg Tribune
April 11, 1901

The Palace drug store at Healdsburg. Swisher and Peck. proprietors, is under the management of Walter Brownlee. an experienced pharmacist. Some notable improvements are being made in the glass show windows and when completed will be one of the most attractive business places in town.

Petaluma Courier
May 1, 1901

W. S. Brownlee, formerly in the Palace drug store in this city, Is proprietor of the drug store in St. Helena.

Healdsburg Tribune
January 1902

AFTER THE 1906 EARTHQUAKE

Rainey Haigh is now located in Sacramento employed in a large drug store there.

Healdsburg Enterprise - June 9, 1906

J. E. Ewing, one of the organizers of the club, has trained his eye rather than his muscles, and although he is an enthusiast on all forms of club sport he excels in fencing, boxing and billiards. Another clever boxer is W. R. Haigh, who holds the bicycling championship of the county. He was born in the valley, and most of his glimpses of the outside world have been obtained from his wheel, on which he has toured through the extreme southern portion of the State. His nearest rival on the silent steed is H. S. Nichols, who frequently wheels to the bay and return in preference to paying fare on the railroad. Several century runs are to his credit.

W. R. HAIGH AND H. S. NICHOLS, TWO FAST RIDERS OF THE WHEEL. HAIGH IS THE ONE-MILE CHAMPION OF SONOMA COUNTY.
[From a photograph.]

San Francisco Examiner
January 6, 1894

W. Rainey Haigh, Horace S. Nichols and James E. Ewing — three young Healdsburg druggists who were active members of the Healdsburg Bicycle Club.

- **Knight & Schmitz** (Peter J. Knight & Leo A. Schmitz)
- Palace Drug Store
- June 10, 1901 – July 28, 1902

UNDER NEW MANAGEMENT

L. A. Schmitz of San Francisco has taken the management of the Palace Drug Store.

Healdsburg Tribune, Enterprise and Scimitar
May 16, 1901

Certificate of Copartnership.

WE, THE UNDERSIGNED, DO HEREBY certify that we are partners transacting business in the State of California, at the City of Healdsburg, in the County of Sonoma, under the firm name and style of PALACE DRUG STORE; that the full names of all the members of said partnership are Peter J. Knight and Leo A. Schmitz, and that the places of our respective residences are set opposite our respective names hereto subscribed.

In witness whereof we have hereto set our hands this 10th day of June, 1901.

PETER J. KNIGHT,
Residence, Healdsburg, California.
LEO A. SCHMITZ,
Residence, Healdsburg, California.

State of California, County of Sonoma—ss.

On this 10th day of June, in the year one thousand nine hundred and one, before me, J. T. Coffman, a Notary Public in and for the said county of Sonoma, residing therein, duly commissioned and qualified, personally appeared Peter J. Knight and Leo A. Schmitz, known to me to be the persons named in, whose names are subscribed to, and who executed the within instrument, and they and each of them duly acknowledged to me that they executed the same.

Witness my hand and the official seal this the day and year in this certificate first above written.

[Seal] J. T. COFFMAN,
Notary Public in and for the County of Sonoma, State of California. je13t

Your Doctor Fights

Disease with medicine. If the medicine is not right he can not conquer disease. If the druggist does his duty the medicine will be right, and your doctor will stand a fair chance of winning the victory.

You can help your doctor by having your prescriptions filled here.

Palace Drug Store

KNIGHT & SCHMITZ, Prop'rs.

Healdsburg Tribune
June 10, 1901

DISSOLUTION OF PARTNERSHIP

THE PARTNERSHIP HERETOFORE EXISTING between P. K. Knight and L. A. Schmitz, under the firm name and style of Knight & Schmitz and doing business as druggists and proprietors of the Palace drug store, in Healdsburg, California, has this day been dissolved by mutual consent, P. K. Knight retiring from that firm. L. A. Schmitz will continue business, and will pay all bills and collect all accounts outstanding.

Healdsburg, July 28, 1902

Healdsburg Tribune, Enterprise and Scimitar
September 4, 1902

- **Leo A. Schmitz**
- Palace Drug Store
- July 28, 1902 – November 30, 1903

Foley's Kidney Cure
makes kidneys and bladder right.
For sale by L. A. SCHMITZ

Physicians Prescibe It.

Many broad minded physicians prescribe Foley's Honey and Tar, as they have never found so safe and reliable a remedy for throat and lung troubles as this great remedy. Sold by L. A. Schmitz, druggist.

Healdsburg Tribune
November 20, 1902

L. A. Schmitz, former druggist in this city was here, last Saturday. He is now engaged in the real estate business in San Francisco at 16th and Valencia streets.

Healdsburg Tribune
September 1, 1906

L. A. Schmitz, former proprietor of the Palace Drug Store, was in Healdsburg on the Fourth. He is now employed at the Snake Drug Store in the Bay City.

Healdsburg Tribune, Enterprise and Scimitar
July 11, 1907

Former local Merchant Killed.

Leo A. Schmitz, twenty or more years ago a member of the firm of Knight & Schmitz, Healdsburg druggists, was killed by a hit and run auto driver near San Mateo last Sunday morning, and his murderer has not been apprehended.

Mr. Schmitz was engaged in the drug store business here in co-partnership with Mr. Knight in the present location of W. B. Whitney [307A West St.] Mr. Whitney's own store being then in the location of the Brown-Wolfe Drug Store [303 West St.].

Soon after the earthquake, Mr. Whitney retired from business to engage in farming and politics, and his store was managed by several different persons more or less successfully, until Mr. G.R. Brown took it over and has successfully conducted it for many years.

Mr. Whitney withstood the call of commerce for many years, only to return to mercantile life after Mr. Wm. Rathke died during the epidemic of influenza [d. February 6, 1920].

Sotoyome Scimitar
January 30, 1925

- **Julius James Luedke** (lived 1880-1944)
- Palace Drug Store
- November 30, 1903 – April 12, 1906 ; Luedke later became a store manager for Owl Drug.

PALACE DRUG STORE CHANGES HANDS

The Palace Drug Store is now under new management and Mr. Julius Luedke, who has been the efficient clerk for some time, is the new proprietor. The change was made Monday when Mr. L. A. Schmitz who has conducted the store for several years, sold out to Mr. Luedke.

Mr. Luedke is a Healdsburg boy, born and raised here, and is highly respected. He is an experienced druggist and in embarking in business for himself he has the best wishes from a wide circle of friends. Mr. Schmitz will continue in the store for some time until Mr. Luedke can secure a good assistant. Mr. Luedke will see that the Palace will lose none of its popularity but will endeavor to merit a wide patronage.

Healdsburg Enterprise
December 5, 1903

HBG-D-08

Palace Drug Store
J. Luedke Jr. Prop.
Healdsburg, Cal.
Clear oval
Tooled top
3 3/4 inches tall
Merle Avila collection
5 1/4 inches tall
Dan Brown's bottle shown

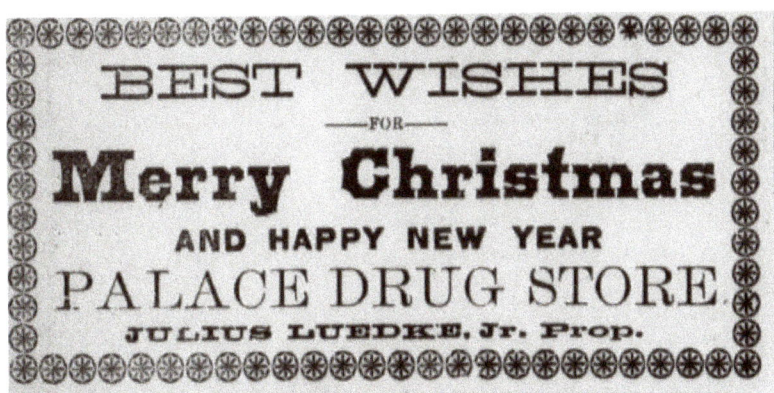

Healdsburg Enterprise
December 19, 1903

HORACE NICHOLS RETURNS TO HEALDSBURG

Horace Nichols has returned to Healdsburg and will take a position with the Palace Drug Store run by Julius Luedke. Mr. Nichols has been employed for some time in a drug store in Fort Bragg.

Healdsburg Tribune
February 1, 1906

- **Miller & Hobson** (Lou Miller & Jerome C. Hobson)
- Palace Drug Store
- April 12, 1906 – January 18, 1909

NEW DRUGGIST

Jerome Hobson and Lou Miller have purchased the Palace Drug Store, conducted for several years past by Julius Luedke. Mr. Miller was employed here in a drug store a number of years ago, but for some time has been manager for Osgood Bros., the well-known Oakland druggist.

Healdsburg Tribune, Enterprise and Scimitar
April 12, 1906

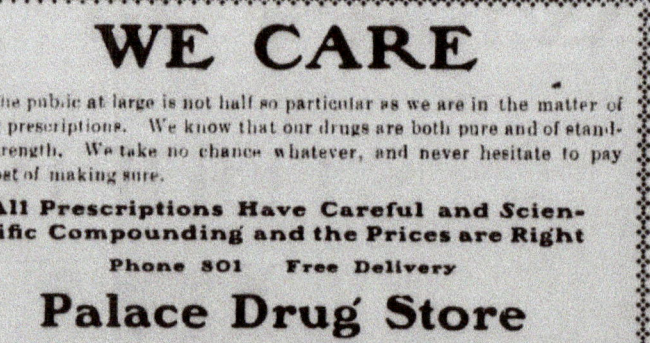

Healdsburg Tribune
January 3, 1907

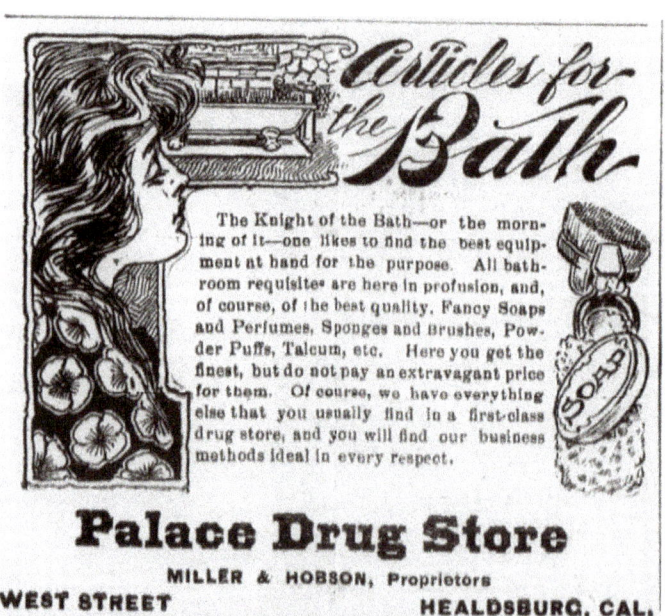

Healdsburg Tribune
May 30, 1908

A BOY BURGLAR

Deputy Sheriff Ben H. Barnes brought a youth named Hugh Rollins to this city from Healdsburg Saturday and lodged him in the county jail, charged with burglary. The lad has been in trouble before and is said to have burglarized the Palace Drug Store in Healdsburg. Rollins is a young dope fiend and in gaining access to the drug store broke out a glass in the rear and stole many articles. He was found with some of the property in his possession.

Santa Rosa Republican
September 14, 1908

- **Clough's Pharmacy**, Oliver T. Clough, prop.
- Purchased store from Miller & Hobson; sold to W.E. Rathke
- January 18, 1909 – September 1911
- Eliminated "Palace Drug Store" as store name

PALACE DRUG STORE HAS NEW PROPRIETOR

A business change took place last Monday when Mr. O. T. Clough, a druggist of many years' experience, purchased the Palace Drug Store, for the past several years conducted by Miller & Hobson. Mr. Clough is much impressed with our city and vicinity and being an enterprising young man will be a valuable addition to the business interests in our city.

He is a registered pharmacist of California and Washington and has held important positions in his line. For the past two years he has been the manager of the Martinez Pharmacy, Martinez, Cal., and prior to that was in charge of the Dispensary for the celebrated physician and surgeon, Dr. A. T. Leonard of San Francisco. Before coming to California, he held the position of head prescription clerk in the A. C. Smith Drug Co. of Salt Lake City, Utah.

Healdsburg Enterprise
January 23, 1909

HBG-D-09

CLOUGHS PHARMACY
THE PRESCRIPTION STORE
HEALDSBURG, CAL.
Clear oval
Tooled top
3 3/4 inches tall
5 5/8 inches tall
Base: W. T. CO. A U. S. A.
Merle Avila collection
5 1/4 inches tall
5 3/4 inches tall
6 ½ inches tall
Base: W.T. CO. USA
Dan Brown collection

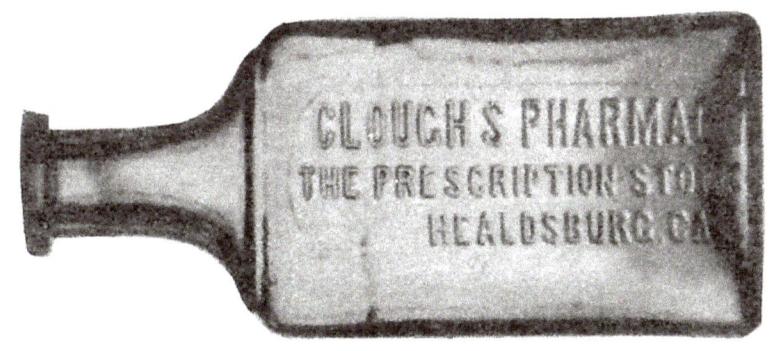

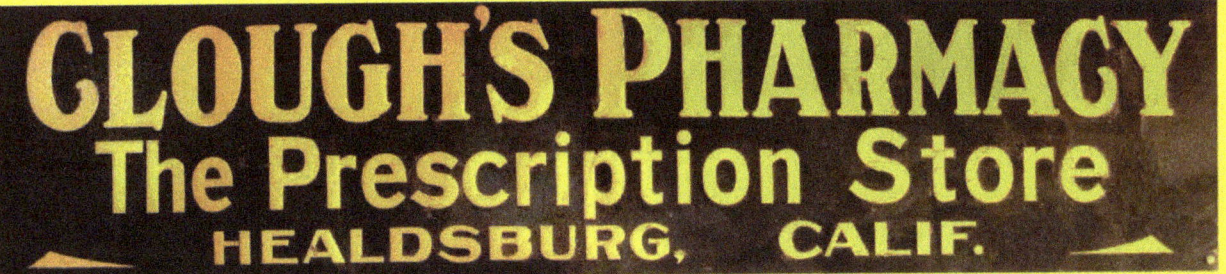

Embossed tin sign, circa 1910
ex Frank Sternad collection

- **Gregory & Co.** (James R. Gregory and Ernest B. Gregory)
- City Drug Store, Powell Street
- December 1891 – June 1898

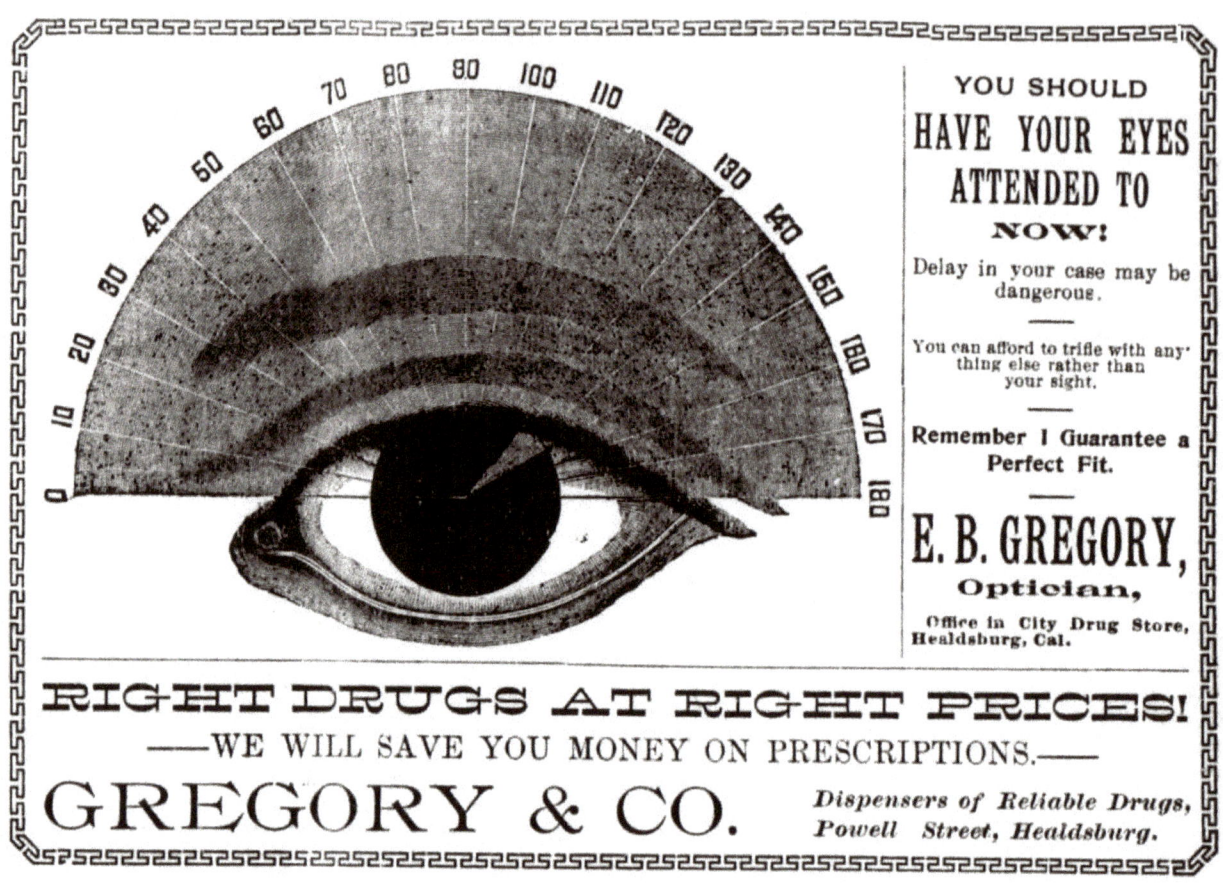

Healdsburg Tribune
April 30, 1896

Note: James Romeyn Gregory (1841-1906) attended College of Physicians and Surgeons in New York City in 1866, and was granted licensure as physician in California in January 1877. Prior to that he was a surgeon in the U.S. Army, and was a veteran of the Civil War and the Spanish-American War. His son, Ernest Bernhart Gregory (1864-1943) was also an MD. They came to Healdsburg from the Santa Cruz area. After closing the store in Healdsburg they moved to Santa Rosa, and then to Reno, Nevada about 1904.

- **Clough's Pharmacy**, Oliver T. Clough, prop.
- Purchased store from Miller & Hobson; sold to W.E. Rathke
- January 18, 1909 – September 1911
- Eliminated "Palace Drug Store" as store name

PALACE DRUG STORE HAS NEW PROPRIETOR

A business change took place last Monday when Mr. O. T. Clough, a druggist of many years' experience, purchased the Palace Drug Store, for the past several years conducted by Miller & Hobson. Mr. Clough is much impressed with our city and vicinity and being an enterprising young man will be a valuable addition to the business interests in our city.

He is a registered pharmacist of California and Washington and has held important positions in his line. For the past two years he has been the manager of the Martinez Pharmacy, Martinez, Cal., and prior to that was in charge of the Dispensary for the celebrated physician and surgeon, Dr. A. T. Leonard of San Francisco. Before coming to California, he held the position of head prescription clerk in the A. C. Smith Drug Co. of Salt Lake City, Utah.

Healdsburg Enterprise
January 23, 1909

HBG-D-09

CLOUGHS PHARMACY
THE PRESCRIPTION STORE
HEALDSBURG, CAL.
Clear oval
Tooled top
3 3/4 inches tall
5 5/8 inches tall
Base: W. T. CO. A U. S. A.
Merle Avila collection
5 1/4 inches tall
5 3/4 inches tall
6 ½ inches tall
Base: W.T. CO. USA
Dan Brown collection

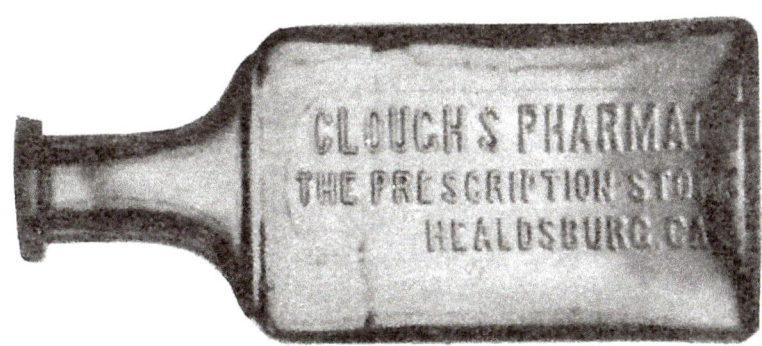

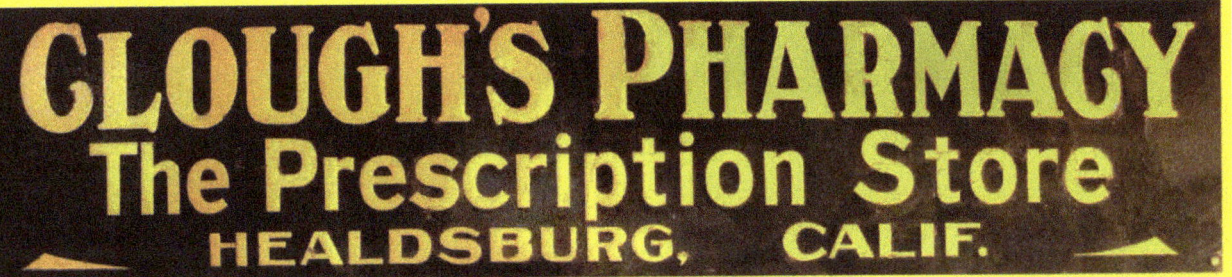

Embossed tin sign, circa 1910
ex Frank Sternad collection

- **Gregory & Co.** (James R. Gregory and Ernest B. Gregory)
- City Drug Store, Powell Street
- December 1891 – June 1898

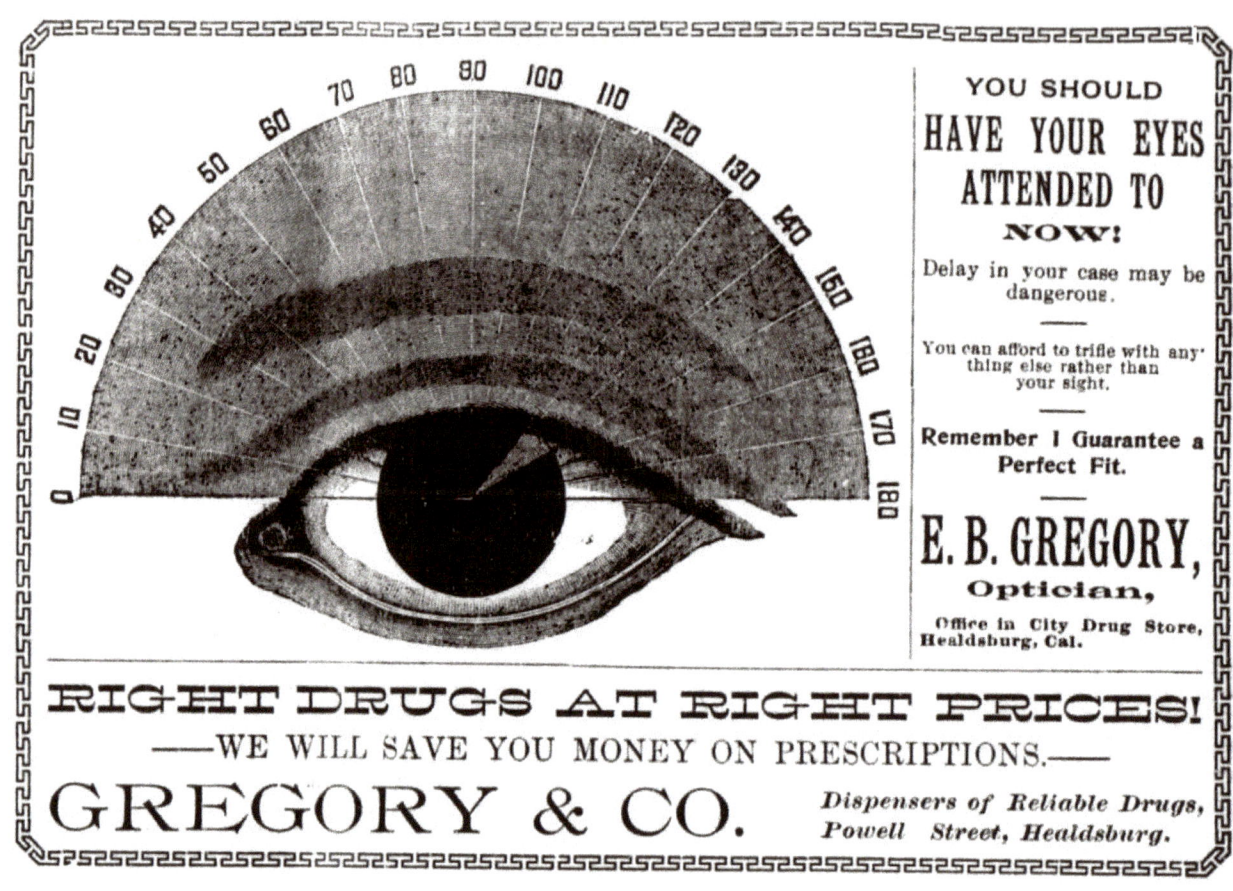

Healdsburg Tribune
April 30, 1896

Note: James Romeyn Gregory (1841-1906) attended College of Physicians and Surgeons in New York City in 1866, and was granted licensure as physician in California in January 1877. Prior to that he was a surgeon in the U.S. Army, and was a veteran of the Civil War and the Spanish-American War. His son, Ernest Bernhart Gregory (1864-1943) was also an MD. They came to Healdsburg from the Santa Cruz area. After closing the store in Healdsburg they moved to Santa Rosa, and then to Reno, Nevada about 1904.

- **Rathke's Pharmacy**, William Ernest Rathke, prop. (lived 1881-1920)
- Previously worked in Berkeley, Cal. 1906-1911
- Swisher & Coffman Block, 109 West Street, formerly Clough's Pharmacy
- September 25, 1911 – December 1920 ; sold to W.B. Whitney upon Rathke's untimely death

DRUG STORE HAS CHANGED HANDS

Mr. W. E. Rathke of Berkeley has purchased the drugstore of O. T. Clough, and is already in possession. Mr. Rathke is an experienced pharmacist with years of successful business training, and he is coming to Healdsburg believing he has established himself in one of the best locations in the state.

He has repeatedly tried to locate in this city and is pleased that he is finally settled in our midst, he is a pleasant gentleman and is a desirable acquisition to the business inters of our city. He is married and his family consists of his wife and three children.

Mr. Clough has been a resident of our city for the past two years, doing a successful business and only retires from business owning to poor health. He will continue to reside here for a time until he can decide to his future plans. Mr. Clough and wife have made many friends during their residence in our city and many regrets that they are to leave our midst, but all wish them success.

Healdsburg Tribune
September 30, 1911

See Your Doctor First

Stop trifling with your health by taking medicines that you don't know anything about.

When you are sick see your doctor at once, he's the man who prescribes medicines to suit your exact condition

We are the people who can fill the prescriptions that he writes with drugs of highest quality and purity.

Many a serious illness may be averted by seeing your doctor in time, and bringing the prescription to us — "See your doctor—then see us."

CLOUGH'S PHARMACY
W. E. RATHKE, Successor
The Prescription Store.   Phone 37

Healdsburg Tribune
September 27, 1911

W. E. RATHKE
The Prescription Store

WITH an experience in the Drug Business extending over a period of sixteen years and a reputation for reliable goods and square dealing, I can confidently solicit your patronage, either by mail or in person. The same courteous attention, whether your purchase be for a large or small amount.

Prescriptions Compounded by Registered Pharmacists Only

PURE DRUGS AND CHEMICALS

PHONE 37

WEST STREET   HEALDSBURG, CAL.

Healdsburg Tribune
July 3, 1913

Make It a Fountain Pen

A good Fountain Pen is one of the most useful of Christmas Gifts, and one which will bring the giver to mind every time a letter is written. For Father or Mother or for Young Man or Maiden a Founain Pen is always appropriate, and always brings lasting pleasure We have a good assortment of standard makes of Fountain Pens from which to select one tha will please.

FANCY STATIONERY
IVORY ARTICLES
THERMOS BOTTLES

And many oher useful and appropriate Christmas Gifts

Rathke's Drug Store
WEST STREET, FACING PLAZA

Healdsburg Enterprise
December 14, 1918

Rathke's Pharmacy (former Palace Drug Store) 109 West St., c.1915
Courtesy, Sonoma County Library

Death Came to W. E. Rathke Wednesday Night

What a sad thing is death. Wednesday night at about midnight it claimed another of our well known and well-beloved business men—William E. Rathke, proprietor of Rathke's Pharmacy succumbed to an attack of pneumonia, resulting from influenza. Always pleasant, always congenial, always cheerful, Mr. Rathke's death saddened the hearts of more warm friends than has the going away of any other man in this community for years. William Ernest Rathke was born in Pleasanton, California in October 1881, and was thirty-seven years of age when he passed away at his home on Tucker Street, surrounded by his beloved wife, mother, and family.

Sotoyome Scimitar
Feb 6, 1920

HBG-D-10

16 (fluid ounces)
Rathke's
PHARMACY
THE
PRESCRIPTION STORE
Clear oval
Tooled top
3 3/4 inches tall
Base: W. T. CO A USA
6 1/4 inches tall
Dan Brown collection

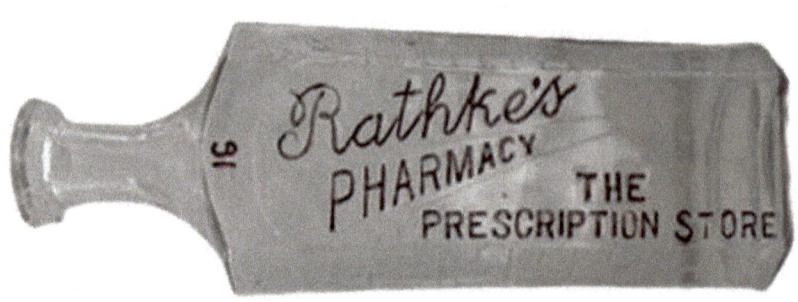

HBG-D-11

Rathke's
PHARMACY
THE
PRESCRIPTION STORE
Clear rectangular
Tooled top
5 ½ inches tall
Base: W.T. CO U.S.A.
John Burton collection

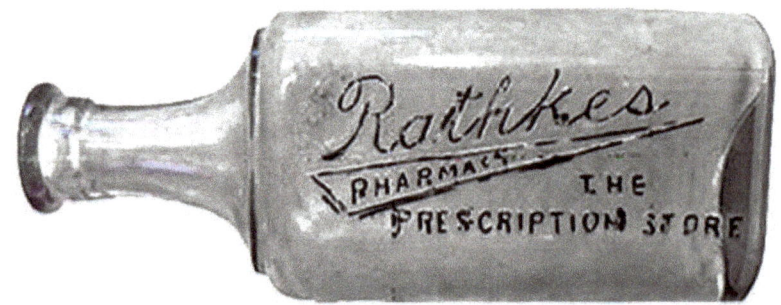

HBG-D-11

Rathke's
PHARMACY
THE
PRESCRIPTION STORE
Clear oval
6 1/4 inches tall
Base: half-moon
John Burton collection

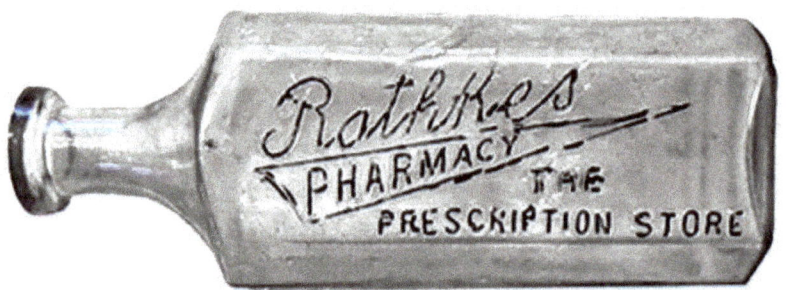

- **William B. Whitney** (lived 1852 -1931)
  - Whitney's Pharmacy, 103 West Street: 1897 – April 18, 1906
  - 309 West Street: Jan. 1921 – 1931 (aka 307A after 1928); sold to Jos. T. Cuneo, see p. 104

WHITNEY'S PHARMACY

Improvements in the Store to be made — Mr. Whitney's Record as a Druggist

Mr. W. B. Whitney, who lately succeeded the firm of Whitney & Kruse, druggists, will make several improvements in his well-known store. The front will be changed and larger show windows put in, as well as other alterations made in the interior of the store. A new awning will also be put on.

Mr. Whitney bears the distinction of having been the first graduate at the California College of Pharmacy from Sonoma County. He is the oldest druggist in Healdsburg, having entered the Wright & Brown drug store in this city as a boy in 1873.

In 1886 the firm of Miller and Whitney was formed, which was succeeded by J. C. Hobson & O. L. Jones. The firm of Whitney & Kruse was established in 1893, and for the past five years they have merited and received a very large share of the patronage of the people in this part of the county.

Mr. Whitney will hereafter conduct the business as a sole proprietor, and the reputation he has already established for courteous treatment, fair prices, and first-class drugs will no doubt endure him a continued liberal patronage.

Healdsburg Enterprise
June 1898

Whitney's Pharmacy circa 1900
Sonoma County Illustrated, James Milliken, 1901

EARTHQUAKE DAMAGE

Druggist W. B. Whitney is one of the heavy losers from the terrible disaster. His store building adjoining the Masonic Hall is a complete wreck. Some goods were saved, but only a trifle to what was destroyed. Mr. Whitney's damage was due to the falling walls of the adjacent Masonic Hall building crushing his roof onto his goods and wreaking general destruction.

Mr. Whitney says his loss is easily $10,000. Besides his business loss, his house was also damaged by being partially twisted from the foundation, and a falling chimney.

What is left of Mr. Whitney's drug stock is being placed in a bowling alley and adjoining room, and in a few days things will be arraigned and business carried on as before. Mr. Whitney is not discouraged and expects soon to be back in his old quarters, but in the meantime his old friends and patrons will find him doing business in the room adjoining Thornton's Harness Shop.

Healdsburg Enterprise
April 21, 1906

Collapsed wall of adjacent Masonic Hall destroyed W.B. Whitney's drugstore on April 18, 1906.
Courtesy, Healdsburg Museum

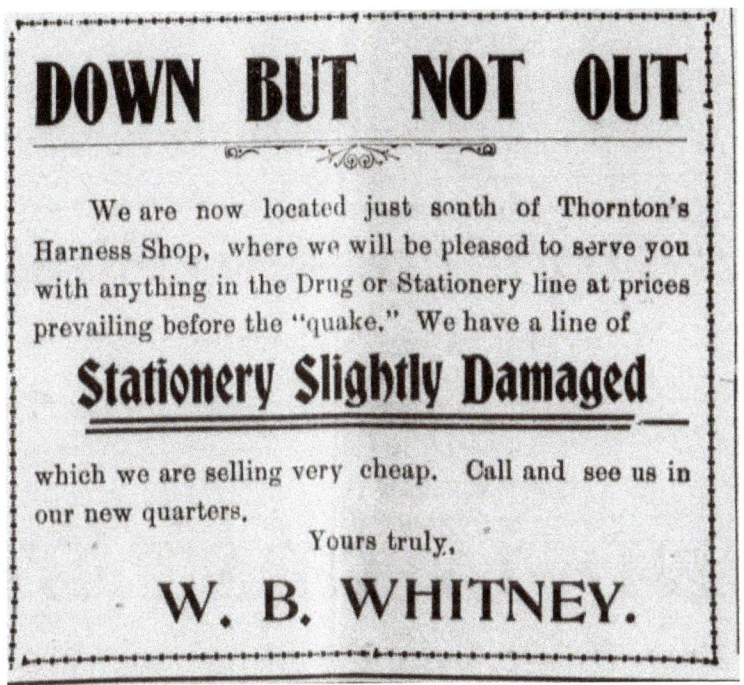

Healdsburg Enterprise
June 6, 1906

W. B. WHITNEY SELLS OUT DRUG STORE

Last week W. B. Whitney sold his entire stock of drugs and goodwill to C. D. Evans, one of our leading druggists, who will consolidate the same with his already large stock.

In 1873, Mr. Whitney while but a youth entered the drug service as an apprentice with Wright & Brown of this city and remained with them until 1882 when he departed to San Francisco and there completed a course in the California College of Pharmacy from which he graduated with honors. He was the first graduate of that institution from Sonoma County and undoubtedly ranks as the oldest druggist from point of service in the county. On his return from college he purchased the drug business of his former employers and since remained here as our leading druggist and one of our most influential and successful business men.

The community will greatly miss Mr. Whitney for he has been a leading factor in many enterprises tending toward welfare and advancement of our town. With his good business judgement and acumen, he has willingly given his aid in all projects that might lead to betterment of this section.

His business interest in Petaluma will require much of his time and attention and although his family will remain here, he will be obliged to spend most of his time away looking after his other business.

Before leaving he will put up a new building on the site of his former store on West Street, which was destroyed by the recent shakeup. The new building will be occupied by C. D. Evans who with the united stocks will have one of the largest and most modern drug stores north of the bay. Mr. Evans has been in business here for many years past and is widely known as a gentleman, courteous to all, careful and neat in his store and absolutely reliable in filling of all prescriptions. We predict for him unbounded success through the years to come.

Healdsburg Enterprise
June 23, 1906

HBG-D-13

℥iv
WBW (monogram)
WHITNEY'S
Pharmacy
HEALDSBURG, CAL.
Clear oval
3 3/4 inches tall
Dan Brown collection

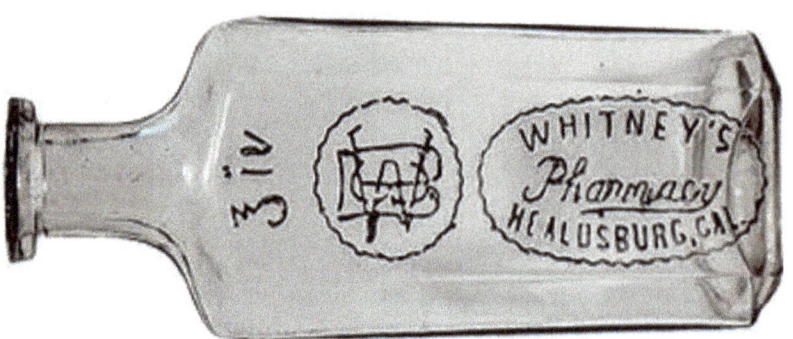

HBG-D-14

℥ii
WBW (monogram)
WHITNEY'S
Pharmacy
HEALDSBURG, CAL.
Clear oval
3 1/4 inches tall
Dan Brown collection

HBG-D-15

℥iii
WBW (monogram)
WHITNEY'S
Pharmacy
HEALDSBURG, CAL.
Clear oval
5 1/8 inches tall
Base: W T CO C U. S. A.
Merle Avila collection

HBG-D-16
> WBW (monogram)
> WHITNEY'S
> *Pharmacy*
> HEALDSBURG, CAL.
> Clear French square
> Tooled top
> 4 inches tall
> 5 ½ inches tall
> Base: PARIS
> Dan Brown collection

HBG-D-17
> WBW (monogram)
> WHITNEY'S
> *Pharmacy*
> HEALDSBURG, CAL
> Clear oval, tooled top
> 5 ½ inches tall
> Dan Brown collection
> 6 1/4 inches tall
> ex Frank Sternad coll.

Demolition of 300 block, Healdsburg Ave. — Whitney Building still standing, 2nd from left.
West Street was renamed Healdsburg Ave. in 1960.

Healdsburg Tribune
January 9, 1981

WHITNEY DIED SUNDAY

Billie Whitney is dead. So came the news to Healdsburg from the home he established here years and years ago, and though it was not unexpected, it brought a pause in the turbulence of life for those who knew him best. Billie Whitney has gone, and with him has gone some of the best things of life as he lived it, and for they who lived it with him.

Few men have lived a life charged with the very spirit of service as did Wm. B. Whitney. At home, in business; in the affairs of his town, of his county, of his state: in the minor events of a municipality. In the larger aspirations of a county: in the wider field of the state assembly, Mr. Whitney served, faithfully, intelligently and well, and throughout his life, taking it day by day his service brought him honors which he shed with a cheery wave of the hand, to take up other duties in the service of men, perhaps, more humble duties, perhaps more exalted ones —but always the faithful Billie Whitney in thought and deed and devotion.

Mr. Whitney was a native of Belfast, Maine, aged 77 years. He came to California with his parents in 1868 and grew up in Sonoma County, his father having settled on a ranch near Healdsburg. He was educated in the Healdsburg schools and entered Alexander Academy and later the College of Pharmacy of the University of California from which he graduated in 1884, being the first man from Sonoma County graduated from that institution. Returning to Healdsburg he clerked for a short time and in 1886 purchased the Wright & Brown drug store with which he has been connected ever since except for a time following the April 1906 disaster. He was elected to the Assembly in 1919 and served one term. Having retired from the drug store business in 1906 he purchased the present Whitney Pharmacy from the Wm. E. Rathke estate in January 1921.

Sotoyome Scimitar
May 21, 1931

William Benjamin Whitney
Taken about 1883 when he was attending California College of Pharmacy.
Photo by Andrew Price - Courtesy, Sonoma County Library

- **Evans & Kruse** (Clarence D. Evans & August Kruse)
- September 1899 – January 15, 1900
- IOOF Building, SE corner West and Matheson Streets

NEW DRUG STORE
Clarence Evans and August Kruse Will Open Pharmacy

Within a few weeks a new drug store will be opened in Healdsburg by Clarence Evens and August Kruse. It will be located in the Odd Fellows building. The young men are both well known in Healdsburg, Clarence Evans having been with W. B. Whitney for two years. He is a graduate in pharmacy, and previously worked in drug stores in San Francisco. He will give his personal attention to the prescription department, which will be a specialty of the new firm.

Store fittings for the new store are being made by Carpenter Goodrich, and no expense will be spared to make it one of the handsomest stores in the city. Both members of the new firm are very popular young men, and will no doubt build up a good business. The new store will be opened early next month.

Healdsburg Tribune - August 10, 1899

August Kruse came up from the ranch last Saturday. He will be here to stay next week looking after the fitting up of the Evans & Kruse Drug Store, which will open in the Odd Fellows building.

Healdsburg Tribune - August 31, 1899

Evans & Kruse last week added two Showcases to the drugstore for properly displaying the large assortment of toilet articles carried by them. The counters were made by Goodrich Bros., and are fine specimens of the cabinet-makers' art.

Healdsburg Tribune - November 2, 1899

"Evans for Drugs" pole sign at 303 West St. in new Whitney Bldg., c.1908
Lithographed postcard - Frank Sternad collection.

- **Evans' Drug Store**, Clarence Dewain Evans, prop. (lived 1876-1970)
- Odd Fellows Building, SE corner West and Matheson Streets until April 18, 1906
- 303 West St., Whitney Bldg. starting October 1906
- January 15, 1900 – March 1, 1910
- Sold to H.L. Huntington

What you need

When you buy your drugs is the purest and freshest— my stock is new and fresh

Bring me your Prescriptions

and get them filled with accuracy and at reasonable prices............

—o—

C. D. EVANS, Pharmacist

West Street, Healdsburg, Cal.

Healdsburg Tribune
January 18, 1900

Evans' Drug Store in the Whitney Building
May 9, 1909
Photo by Benjamin Wright
John Burton Collection

Clarence D. Evans has purchased the interest of August Kruse in the new drug store and will conduct the business in his own name. He will give special attention to compounding prescriptions, and his rates are very reasonable. Mr. Evans is well and favorably known in this section, and is receiving a good share of the public patronage.

Healdsburg Tribune
January 18, 1900

Evans-Haigh.

On Sunday last, at the home of the bride's parents, Mr. and Mrs. Robert Haigh, occurred the marriage of Miss Lena Haigh and Mr. Clarence D. Evans, two of Healdsburg's highly-respected young people. Rev. W. C. Driver performed the ceremony, and only the relatives and a few friends were present, as follows: Mr. and Mrs. Robert Haigh, Charles Haigh, Mrs. M. Haigh of Santa Rosa, Stella Haigh, Miss Lou Thompson, Miss Lynch and Rev. Driver and wife.

The bride is a native daughter of Healdsburg, and the groom has lived here for the past five years. Mr. Evans was until a few months ago clerk for W. B. Whitney, but is now proprietor of one of Healdsburg's leading drug stores and enjoys a liberal patronage. The TRIBUNE extends congratulations to the new couple, and wishes them happiness and prosperity.

Healdsburg Tribune
March 22, 1900

PLEASE CALL AND PAY
The almost complete destruction to our store leaves us in bad shape and we earnestly hope all those who are in our debt will call and give us what assistance they can.   —C. D. EVANS

Healdsburg Enterprise
April 21, 1906

C. D. EVANS
Julius Luedke, who had taken a position in San Francisco, before the earthquake, lost his place by that occurrence, and has accepted a position with C. D. Evans at his pharmacy.

Healdsburg Enterprise
May 26, 1906

IN NEW QUARTERS
Druggists C. D. Evans expects to occupy his new quarters next week, commencing to move Monday. His new store in the Whitney Building is fitted up in an elaborate manner and will be one of the handsomest furnished drug stores in the county.

Healdsburg Enterprise
October 6, 1906

EVANS' NEW DRUG STORE
One of the most prominent artistic buildings of Healdsburg that rose above the ruins made by the earthquake is the Whitney Building, a class A structure of concrete and steel. On the ground floor of the modern building is located Evans' drug store.

The interior is beautifully finished, the goods are being arranged on the shelves attractively, and when all is complete it will be one of the handsomest and most up-to-date drug stores in Northern California. All of the old stock went out with the earthquake, and everything is new and fresh.

Healdsburg Tribune
October 11, 1906

HBG-D-33
C. D. Evans
Druggist
Odd Fellows Bldg.
Healdsburg, Cal
Clear oval
Tooled top
5 3/4 inches tall
ex Frank Sternad coll.

HBG-D-18
C. D. EVANS
DRUGGIST
HEALDSBURG, CAL
Clear rectangular, tooled top
4 ½ inches tall
Base: W. T. CO.
Merle Avila collection

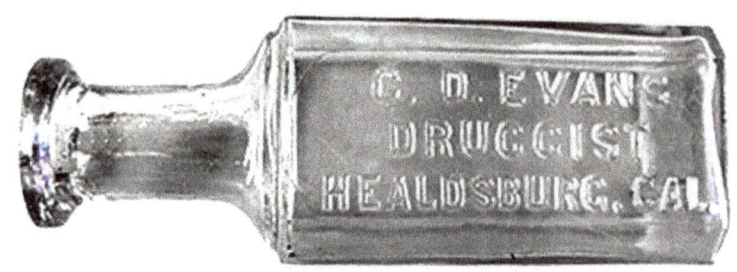

HBG-D-19
Evans
"THE PLACE TO BUY DRUGS"
HEALDSBURG, CAL.
Clear oval, tooled top
4 ½ inches tall
5 1/8 inches tall
5 ½ inches tall
ex Frank Sternad collection
shown

HBG-D-20
ʒvi
C. D. EVANS
DRUGGIST
HEALDSBURG, CAL.
Clear oval, tooled top
5 inches tall
Base: W. T. CO. F U.S.A.
John Burton collection

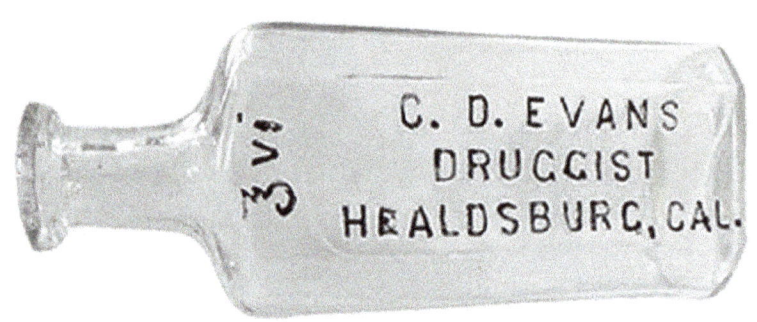

HBG-D-21
ʒiii
C. D. EVANS
DRUGGIST
HEALDSBURG, CAL.
Clear oval, tooled top
5 1/4 inches tall
Base: W. T. CO. A U.S.A.
John Burton collection

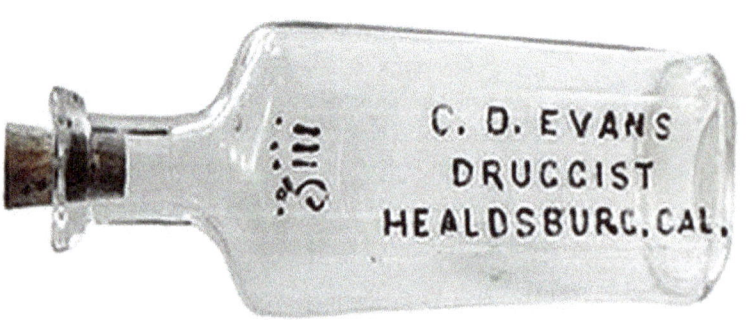

Evans-Haigh.

On Sunday last, at the home of the bride's parents, Mr. and Mrs. Robert Haigh, occurred the marriage of Miss Lena Haigh and Mr. Clarence D. Evans, two of Healdsburg's highly-respected young people. Rev. W. C. Driver performed the ceremony, and only the relatives and a few friends were present, as follows: Mr. and Mrs. Robert Haigh, Charles Haigh, Mrs. M. Haigh of Santa Rosa, Stella Haigh, Miss Lou Thompson, Miss Lynch and Rev. Driver and wife.

The bride is a native daughter of Healdsburg, and the groom has lived here for the past five years. Mr. Evans was until a few months ago clerk for W. B. Whitney, but is now proprietor of one of Healdsburg's leading drug stores and enjoys a liberal patronage. The TRIBUNE extends congratulations to the new couple, and wishes them happiness and prosperity.

PLEASE CALL AND PAY
The almost complete destruction to our store leaves us in bad shape and we earnestly hope all those who are in our debt will call and give us what assistance they can. —C. D. EVANS

Healdsburg Enterprise
April 21, 1906

C. D. EVANS
Julius Luedke, who had taken a position in San Francisco, before the earthquake, lost his place by that occurrence, and has accepted a position with C. D. Evans at his pharmacy.

Healdsburg Enterprise
May 26, 1906

Healdsburg Tribune
March 22, 1900

IN NEW QUARTERS
Druggists C. D. Evans expects to occupy his new quarters next week, commencing to move Monday. His new store in the Whitney Building is fitted up in an elaborate manner and will be one of the handsomest furnished drug stores in the county.

Healdsburg Enterprise
October 6, 1906

EVANS' NEW DRUG STORE
One of the most prominent artistic buildings of Healdsburg that rose above the ruins made by the earthquake is the Whitney Building, a class A structure of concrete and steel. On the ground floor of the modern building is located Evans' drug store.

The interior is beautifully finished, the goods are being arranged on the shelves attractively, and when all is complete it will be one of the handsomest and most up-to-date drug stores in Northern California. All of the old stock went out with the earthquake, and everything is new and fresh.

Healdsburg Tribune
October 11, 1906

HBG-D-33
C. D. Evans
Druggist
Odd Fellows Bldg.
Healdsburg, Cal
Clear oval
Tooled top
5 3/4 inches tall
ex Frank Sternad coll.

HBG-D-18
C. D. EVANS
DRUGGIST
HEALDSBURG, CAL
Clear rectangular, tooled top
4 ½ inches tall
Base: W. T. CO.
Merle Avila collection

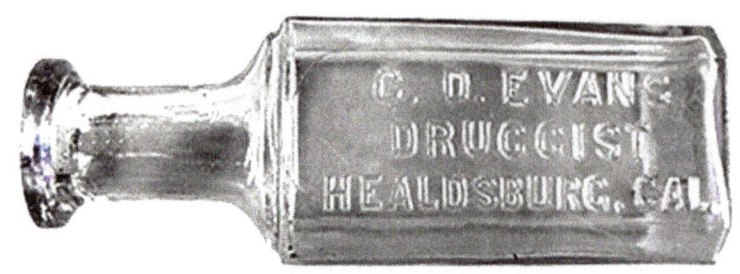

HBG-D-19
Evans
"THE PLACE TO BUY DRUGS"
HEALDSBURG, CAL.
Clear oval, tooled top
4 ½ inches tall
5 1/8 inches tall
5 ½ inches tall
ex Frank Sternad collection
shown

HBG-D-20
℥vi
C. D. EVANS
DRUGGIST
HEALDSBURG, CAL.
Clear oval, tooled top
5 inches tall
Base: W. T. CO. F U.S.A.
John Burton collection

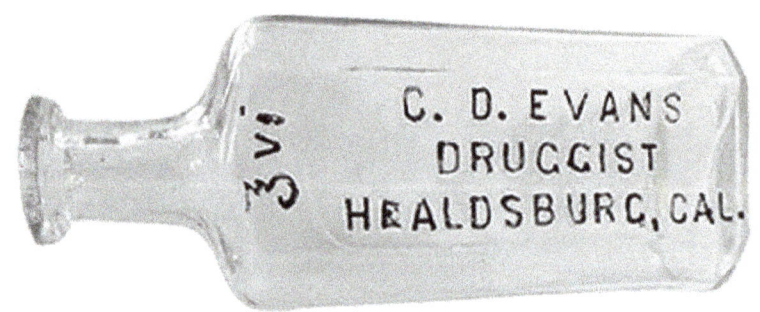

HBG-D-21
℥iii
C. D. EVANS
DRUGGIST
HEALDSBURG, CAL.
Clear oval, tooled top
5 1/4 inches tall
Base: W. T. CO. A U.S.A.
John Burton collection

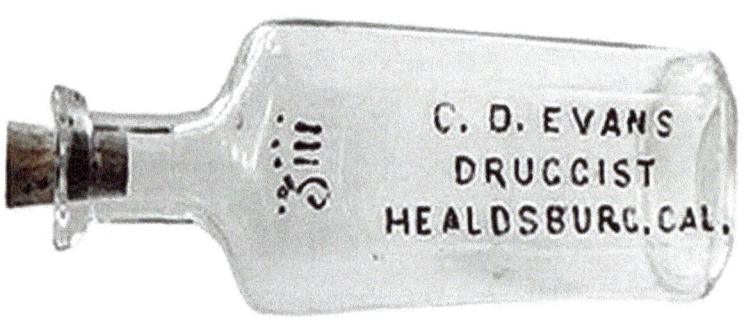

IMPORTANT BUSINESS CHANGE

A certain surprise was the announcement Thursday that Evans' Drug Store had changed hands. If the community were to suddenly find that the City Hall had disappeared it would have proven no greater surprise.

Evans' Drug Store is known throughout this entire part of Northern Sonoma County, and the wide publicity and the large patronage enjoyed by the store is due principally to the enterprise of Mr. Evans and the liberal use he made of printer's ink. It was generally commented on that Evans Drug Store was the best advertised place of business in this part of the county. Mr. H. L. Huntington is the purchaser, and is now in charge of the business.

Mr. Evans has been in the business in Healdsburg for close unto fourteen years. It is understood that Mr. Evans will give his entire time to the management of the Arabalene Company which manufactures the popular complexion powder of that name, of which he is the originator and to which he has given much of his attention.

Healdsburg Enterprise
April 2, 1910

For Your Complexion

Nothing is better than **Arabalene**, the liquid beautifier. It will keep your skin radiant, protect it from sunburn, tan and windburn; and is cooling and soothing in hot weather.

It **stays on smooth**, is positively invisible and imparts the natural glow of youth.

Its use will preserve a delicate skin and restore a discolored one. Cleans, bleaches and whitens the skin, besides making it soft and velvety. Get a 50 cent bottle of Arabalene at your druggist's today. Satisfaction guaranteed or the druggist will return your money.

Fresno Republican
June 30, 1914

The Arabalene Company has been incorporated at Santa Rosa to handle Arabalene and other drugs. The capital stock of the company is $50,000, of which $29,800 has been subscribed by the following incorporators: C. D. Evans, O. J. Lichfield, F. L. Bice, E. M. Norton, A. W. Garrett, J. McClish and George C. Alexander.

Pacific Pharmacist
May 1909

Promoting Arabalene

Druggist Evans spent Tuesday in San Francisco, looking after the interest of his Arabalene preparations. Mr. Evans stated that while in the city he made arrangements whereby Arabalene will be handled by such large corporations as the Emporium, Hales, etc., and that within two weeks it will be on sale at all prominent kindred establishments and large drug stores in the bay cities.

Healdsburg Tribune
December 10, 1909

Note: Clarence D. Evans (1876-1970) registered his "Arabalene Complexion Beautifier" as U.S. Trademark #50367 on March 13, 1906, claiming use of the brand since December 1903. The Arabalene Company was incorporated in 1909 at Santa Rosa with Evans as major stockholder, then located in San Francisco with Evans as secretary and manager in 1910. The firm moved into the new Hearst Building at Market & Third when it was completed in 1911. Arabalene was widely advertised on the Pacific Coast until 1926.

- **H. Lloyd Huntington**
  - Successor to Evans' Drug Store, 303 West St., *The Rexall Store*
  - March 31, 1910 – December 1, 1913

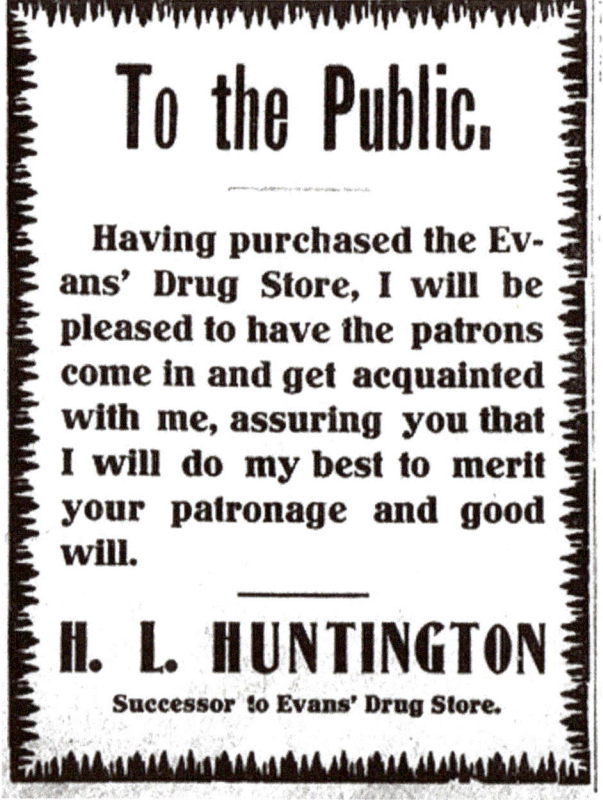

Healdsburg Tribune, Enterprise, and Scimitar
April 9, 1910

NEW SIGN FOR HUNTINGTON

H. L. Huntington, successor to C. D. Evans, is now sporting a fine new gold leaf sign on his windows which appears most resplendent in the summer sun.

Healdsburg Tribune, Enterprise, and Scimitar
August 10, 1910

DRUG STORE CHANGES OWNERS

H. L. HUNTINGTON has sold his store in Healdsburg to C. M. Carpenter, the transfer taking effect Monday, December 1st.

Mr. Carpenter has been a travelling man for the firm of Langley & Michaels for a number of years and has made regular trips to Healdsburg. He is a married man, and with Mrs. Carpenter will make his home in this city in about two weeks. Mr. Huntington has not made his plans public, but will remain in Healdsburg a few weeks.

Healdsburg Tribune, Enterprise, and Scimitar
December 4, 1913

- **Carpenter's Pharmacy**, Cecil M. Carpenter, prop.
  - Successor to H. L. Huntington, 303 West St., *The Rexall Store*
  - December 1, 1913 – December 9, 1915

Druggist C. M. Carpenter and wife have rented the Mascherini cottage on West Street and are now busy getting their household effects from Santa Rosa in place. Mr. Carpenter is the new proprietor of the Huntington Drug Store.

Mr. Carpenter has been coming to Healdsburg at regular intervals for the past eight years. He says he always did like the town and likes it better now that he has become identified with its business and social doings.

Healdsburg Enterprise
December 27, 1913

December 27, 1913
Healdsburg Enterprise

HEALDSBURG DRUGGIST HAS VALUABLE AGENCY

C. M. Carpenter has the Healdsburg agency for the simple mixture of buckthorn bark, glycerin, etc. known as *Adler-i-ka*, the remedy which became famous for curing appendicitis. This simple remedy has powerful action and drains such surprising amounts of old matter from the body that JUST ONE DOSE relieves sour stomach gas on the stomach and constipation almost IMMEDIATELY. The QUICK action of *Adler-i-ka* is astonishing.

Healdsburg Tribune, Enterprise, and Scimitar
November 25, 1915

- **Brown-Wolfe Drug Store** (George R. Brown & Francis M. Wolfe)
  - Successors to C. M. Carpenter
  - 303 West St., Whitney Bldg.: December 9, 1915 – September 1935
  - 301 West St., Seawell Bldg. cor. Matheson: Sept. 1935 – April 6, 1949 (see page 35)
  - Sold to William F. and Eleanor Carroll

DRUG STORE CHANGES HANDS

G. R. Brown and [his father-in-law] F.M. Wolfe of Watsonville have purchased the drug business from C. M. Carpenter. Both men have had a large experience in pharmacy and no doubt will merit the patronage of this community. The family of Mr. Brown arrived from Watsonville last week and has taken apartments at the Skinner house on East Street.

Healdsburg Tribune, Enterprise and Scimitar
December 9, 1915

Healdsburg Tribune, Enterprise, and Scimitar
December 16, 1915

HDG-D- 22
> Paper label:
> Net Contents *6* Fld. Ozs.
> CASTOR OIL
> (wolf's head)
> Brown-   PHONE
> Wolfe Drug Store   FOUR O
> HEALDSBURG, CAL.
> Clear rectangular
> 6 3/4 inches tall
> Merle Avila collection

HDG-D-23
> Paper label:
> (wolf's head)
> Brown-   PHONE
> Wolfe Drug Store   FOUR O
> HEALDSBURG, CAL.
> *(typewritten Rx label dated 11/4/50, prescribed by Dr. Dunlavy)*
> Amber round, metal screw cap abm
> 8 Inches tall
> James Arietta collection

GEORGE RAYMOND BROWN SUCCUMBS TO HEART ATTACK

Death took G. Raymond Brown, Healdsburg Druggist and owner of Brown-Wolfe Drug Store in this city, Wednesday, December 1.

Brown, a native of Piqua, Ohio, succumbed to a heart attack around noon Wednesday after spending the morning at the store.

He was 63 years old, had spent the last 36 years in Healdsburg living at 304 Powell Court and had operated a drug store on the corner of Matheson and West Streets for the past 33 years.

Healdsburg Tribune, Enterprise, and Scimitar
April 1, 1949

NOTICE OF INTENDED SALE

NOTICE IS HEREBY GIVEN: That MYRTLE E. BROWN, individually, and MYRTLE E. BROWN, Executrix of the estate of George Raymond Brown, deceased, doing business under the firm name and style of BROWN WOLFE DRUG STORE, at the City of Healdsburg, in Sonoma County, California, the address of said MYRTLE E. BROWN being 304 Powell Court, Healdsburg, California, does intend and propose, on the 6th day of April, 1949, to sell and convey unto WILLIAM F. CARROLL and ELEANOR CARROLL, his wife, whose address is 730 Darien Way, San Francisco, California, and the said last named persons propose to purchase on said 6th day of April, 1949, that certain drug business known as BROWN WOLFE DRUG STORE, together with the real property used in connection with said business located at 301 West Street, Healdsburg, California, and all the personal property connected with said business consisting of all the office and store equipment, stock on hand, liquor licenses and goodwill of said business; and that on the said 6th day of April, 1949 at the hour of eleven o'clock A.M., at the office of John A. Condit,

Healdsburg Tribune, Enterprise, and Scimitar
April 1, 1949

- **Riley The Druggist** (Thomas Jefferson Riley, lived 1842-1917))
  - Centennial Drug Store, Riley's Drug Store, City Drug Store
  - September 1876 – February 1878
  - March 1882 – August 1887 (West St. north of plaza, opp. Sotoyome House)
  - Opened another store with his son in Santa Rosa August 27, 1887, see page 248

Thomas Riley, who has been on our coast about a year and a half and finding Healdsburg agreeable to his tastes, has commenced business by opening a drug store in Wells' brick building, adjoining the Geyser Livery stables.

Russian River Flag
September 2, 1876

In a word, everything kept at a first-class drug store. Family recipes and physician's prescriptions accurately compounded. Call and convince yourself.

THOMAS RILEY
Russian River Flag
June 14, 1877

HBG-D-24

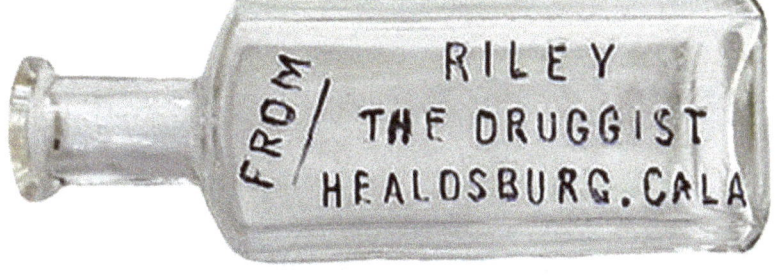

FROM
RILEY
THE DRUGGIST
HEALDSBURG, CALA.
Clear rectangle
Tooled top
3 3/8 inches tall
4 inches tall
4 3/8 inches tall
Base: W. T. & CO. H
Dan Brown collection
5 1/4 inches tall
Base: W. T. & CO. E
6 1/4 inches tall
Base: W. T. & CO. G
Merle Avila collection
7 5/8 inches tall
John Burton bottle shown

HBG-D-24A

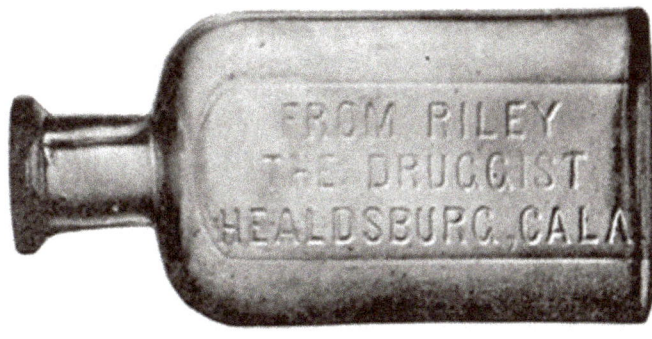

FROM RILEY
THE DRUGGIST
HEALDSBURG, CALA.
Clear oval
Tooled top
4.0, 4.5, 5.0 inches tall
ex Frank Sternad collection

- **Riley & Fox** (Thomas J. Riley & Henry Fox)
- Peoples Drug Store, IOOF Block: February 1878 – January 1879
- Red Front Drug Store, 111 West St.: January 1879 – January 11, 1882

NEW MEMBER OF THE FIRM

The new member of the firm of Riley & Fox is Mr. Henry Fox, late of Des Moines, Iowa and a gentleman experienced in business and bearing most excellent testimonials from prominent men of Des Moines, amongst whom is Ex-Governor Samuel Merrill. The new drug firm contemplates many improvements in their establishment, and from their wise appreciation of the local paper as an advertising medium and indirect benefactor, we prophecy their success in gaining popularity with the public.

Russian River Flag
February 28, 1878

For the Holidays
RILEY & FOX,

PICTURE BOOKS,
STORY BOOKS,
POETICAL BOOKS,
PHOTOGRAPH ALBUMS,
FLORAL ALBUMS,
AUTOGRAPH ALBUMS,
FANCY PAPERS (in boxes.)

People's Drug Store!

IN

Healdsburg.

We also sell the Celebrated

PACIFIC RUBBER PAINT

RILEY & FOX,

Southwest corner of the Plaza, I. O. O. F. Block.

Russian River Flag
December 26, 1878

Riley & Fox, having removed the People's Drug Store to the new quarters at Mulligan & Bros. old stand, take this opportunity to return thanks to their many patrons for past custom, and hope to merit a continuance of the same by pursuing the course of square dealing and one price to all that has heretofore characterized their business. Call and see them at their new quarters and be convinced that the People's Drug Store is what you want to buy in its line.

Healdsburg Enterprise
January 30, 1879

Riley & Fox have a fine article of pure Maryland Peach Brandy by the bottle or gallon.
Riley & Fox wish to call your attention to the celebrated Optimus Brandy, made by our townsman, Col. J. Scott.

Russian River Flag
January 5, 1882

DISSOLUTION OF Co-PARTNERSHIP

Notice is hereby given that the partnership existing between Henry Fox and T. J. Riley, in the city of Healdsburg, county of Sonoma, under the firm name of RILEY & FOX, druggists, stationers, etc., is this day dissolved by mutual consent. All accounts due the late firm will be collected by Mr. Fox, who will also settle all claims against the firm.   T.J. RILEY - HENRY FOX   January 11, 1882

Russian River Flag
January 12, 1882

HBG-D-25
    mortar & pestle
    RILEY & FOX (on garter)
    DRUGGISTS
    HEALDSBURG
    Clear square
    Tooled top
    4 1/8 inches tall
    Base: W T & CO   S
    Merle Avila collection

    6 inches tall
    Lou & Leisa Lambert

    8 ½ inches tall
    Base: W T & CO D
    Helmut & DeAnna Jordt collection

- **Henry Fox** (lived 1851-1916)
- Red Front Drug Store, 111 West St., north of Swisher & Coffman Block
- January 11, 1882 – January 29, 1890 ; sold to H.W. Baxter

TO THE PUBLIC

Having become the sole proprietor of the drug store lately conducted by Riley & Fox, I desire to thank all old customers and the public generally for past favors, soliciting a continuance of the same. I propose to keep myself supplied with the best drugs in the market, and will sell them at the lowest possible prices. In compounding prescriptions, I will be assisted by Dr. T. W. Brotherton whose recognized merit as a physician will insure public confidence. And finally, by close application to business and study of my patrons' interest, I will hope to merit a continuance of the confidence and patronage of the public.   HENRY FOX

Russian River Flag
January 11, 1882

WHITNEY EMPLOYED AT FOX'S RED FRONT DRUG STORE

If there is anybody that can handle drugs or holiday goods skillfully, it is Wm. B. Whitney at Fox's Red Front Drug Store.

Russian River Flag
December 13, 1883

RED FRONT DRUG STORE

The columns of the local newspaper are usually a reflex of the enterprise of business men. The columns of the Flag are always a reflex of the enterprise of Henry Fox, proprietor of the Red Front Drug Store. This week Mr. Fox is again to the front with a new announcement of new bargains in his store.

He directs attention to his mammoth stock of drugs, medicines, notions and fancy articles and he says, while wishing everybody a Happy New Year, he has some new bargains for those who wish to remember their friends with New Year's presents.

His new post office is on the way, and he wants to make room for it; and therefore, he will dispose of many articles very low. The Red Front Drug Store is worthy to be called one of the most enterprising business houses of Sonoma County, and we are glad to see Mr. Fox enjoying a large and growing trade.

Russian River Flag
December 29, 1886

James Ewing, a druggist from New York City, has accepted a position with Henry Fox of this city. He arrived on Tuesday last.

Healdsburg Enterprise
March 13, 1889

HBG—D-25A

    HENRY FOX
    DRUGGIST
    HEALDSBURG, CAL.
    Clear square, tooled top
    2 ½ inches tall
    ex Frank Sternad

Healdsburg Tribune
May 1, 1889

Note: Henry Fox was the Healdsburg agent for *Abietene* products made by D.F. Fryer, and also for preparations made by the *Abietine* Medical Co. (note slight spelling difference). Both lines were based on distilling Jeffrey and Gray pine pitch, and both firms were located in Oroville, California.

HBG–D-26
- HENRY FOX
- DRUGGIST
- HEALDSBURG, CAL.
- Clear oval
- Tooled top
- 3 ½ inches tall
- Merle Avila collection
- 3 ½ inches tall
- Base W. T. & CO A
- Helmut & DeAnna Jordt's bottle shown

HBG-D-26A
- HENRY FOX
- DRUGGIST
- HEALDSBURG, CAL.
- Clear oval
- Tooled top
- 4 3/4 inches tall
- Base W.T. & CO. A
- John Burton collection

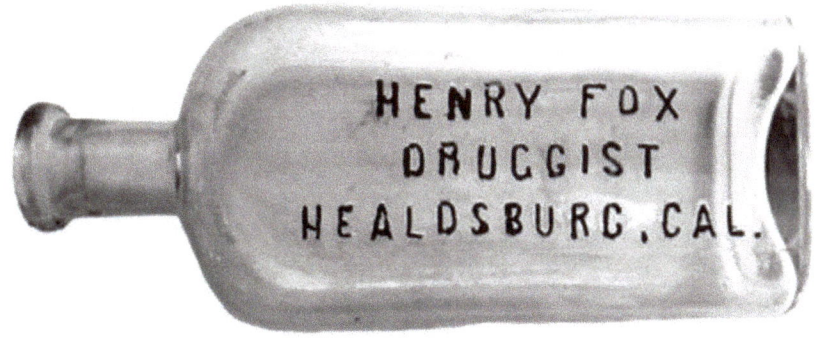

- **Baxter & Co.** (Hall William Baxter, lived 1850-1901)
- Red Front Drug Store, 111 West St.
- Successor to Henry Fox; sold to Horace S. Nichols
- January 29, 1890 – April 1890

A CARD

Having sold my drug store to Mr. H.W. Baxter of San Francisco, I wish to sincerely thank the people of Healdsburg and vicinity for their confidence and liberal patronage in the past and trust that they will extend the same to my successor, as he will be found in every way worthy of the same.

J. Ewing has been engaged as prescription clerk for H.W. Baxter and will continue to be found at his accustomed place in the post office building.

I wish to add that I consider myself permanently located and will always be one of you. I am positive that we have one of the finest little towns in this or any other State and I always expect to make it my home. Again thanking you sincerely for your many past favors, I remain very respectfully yours, Henry Fox.

Healdsburg Enterprise
February 5, 1890

J. Ewing will continue his vocation as pill maker under the new management at the Red Front store. Mr. Ewing is an excellent pharmacist and his retention by Mr. Baxter is a just tribute to his character and qualifications.

Healdsburg Tribune
February 8, 1890

RED FRONT DRUG STORE

If you cannot find what you want at the other stores, the Red Front Drug Store has it, "sure pop." The largest stock of Drugs, Stationery, Cigars and Tobacco, Fancy Goods and Cutlery, at the Red Front Drug Store, Baxter & Co., successors to Henry Fox.

Healdsburg Tribune, Enterprise and Scimitar
March 1, 1890

Fox's Asthma Cure will give you immediate relief. A wonderful medicine only 25 cents at Baxter & Co., successors to Henry Fox.

Healdsburg Tribune, Enterprise and Scimitar
March 1, 1890

> Horace Nichols, an old resident of Healdsburg, but late from San Francisco, has purchased the Red Front drug store of H. W. Baxter & Co. Notwithstanding the loss of an enterprising and respected merchant, Mr. Baxter, the people of Healdsburg are honored in exchange with the residence of Mr. Nichols, a proficient young man of equal enterprise and ambition of his predecessor. May he have success in his venture.

Healdsburg Tribune
April 12, 1890

- **Ewing & Burr** (James E. Ewing & Frank Burr)
- Ewing previously worked for Red Front Drug proprietors H.W. Baxter and H.S. Nichols (see page 58). He later invested in a store in Santa Rosa (see page 194)
- Masonic Hall, 105 West St.
- July 1892 – October 28, 1895

Last Saturday the new drug store of Ewing & Burr was opened for business and all-day long people thronged the place admiring the elegant fixtures and the fine display of goods. The proprietors are well pleased with the prospects of their venture and feel assured that they will receive a good share of Healdsburg's patronage.

Healdsburg Tribune, Enterprise and Scimitar
September 29, 1892

HBG–D-27

EWING & BURR
PHARMACISTS
HEALDSBURG, CAL.
Clear rectangular
Tooled top
4 7/8 inches tall
Base: W. T. & CO. D USA
Helmut & DeAnna Jordt collection

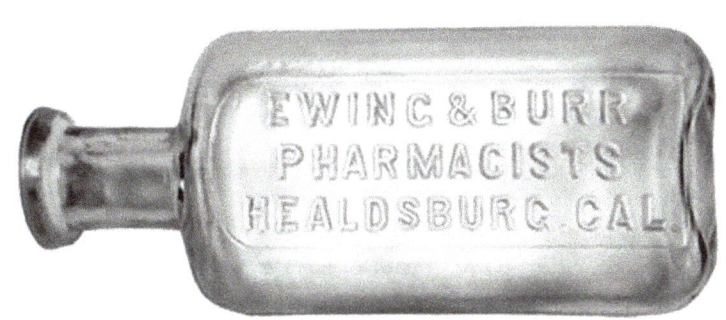

HOLIDAY GOODS,

Comprising a Full Line of

Dressing and Manicure Cases,

Bibles, Books, Photograph Albums, Etc.

EWING & BURR,

West Street, Healdsburg, Cal.

Healdsburg Tribune
December 15, 1892

DISSOLUTION NOTICE.

NOTICE IS HEREBY GIVEN THAT THE CO-partnership heretofore existing between the undersigned is by mutual consent this day dissolved. Frank Burr will continue in the business at the old stand and all accounts due the late firm are payable to him and he has assumed all indebtedness of the late firm.

[SIGNED]   FRANK BURR,
            JAMES E. EWING.

Dated at Healdsburg, County of Sonoma, State of California, this 28th day of October, A. D. 1895.

Healdsburg Tribune
November 29, 1895

- **Frank Burr**
  - Successor to Ewing & Burr, 105 West St.
  - October 28, 1895 – November 12, 1896; sold to Edgar Richardson

HBG–D-28

FRANK BURR
DRUGGIST
HEALDSBURG CAL.
Clear rectangular
Tooled top
4 3/8 inches tall
 Base: *** USA

4 ½ inches tall
Base: *** U S A PAT. JAN. 5, 1892
Helmut & DeAnna Jordt collection

HBG-D-29

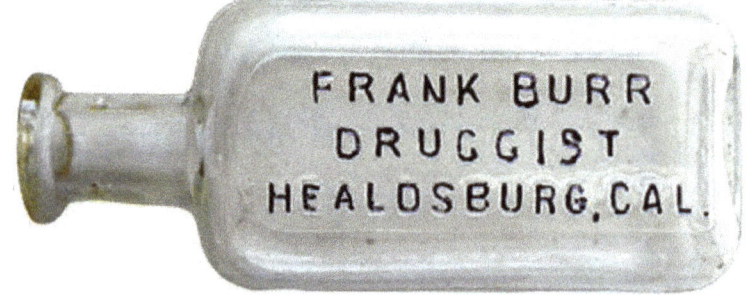

FRANK BURR
DRUGGIST
HEALDSBURG, CAL.
Clear rectangular
Tooled top
4 ½ inches tall
Base: *** 1 USA
John Burton collection

Frank Burr drugstore at left, circa 1896.
J. Hardy photo, courtesy Bruce Johnson

- **Richardson's Pharmacy** (Edgar Richardson)
- November 12, 1896 – May 1897
- Successor to Frank Burr, 105 West St.
- Because of Richardson's ill health, Frank Burr resumed control of store in late April 1897

TO WHOM IT MAY CONCERN

This is to inform the public generally that I have this day sold my drug business and good will to EDGAR RICHARDSON. Thanking you for past favors and soliciting a continuance of same for my successor,

I am Respectfully, Frank Burr   Healdsburg, Cal., Nov. 12, 1896.

Referring to the above I wish to solicit a share of the patronage of the public, and assure all who favor me with their trade that by just and liberal treatment, good goods and right prices. Respectfully, Edgar Richardson

Healdsburg Tribune, Enterprise and Scimitar
December 3, 1896

Wanted- A good house of five or six rooms, modern conveniences, centrally located. Apply at once to E. Richardson, successor to F. Burr, West Street.

Healdsburg Tribune, Enterprise and Scimitar
January 4, 1897

Country orders solicited and given the promptest attention by Richardson the pharmacist.

Healdsburg Tribune, Enterprise and Scimitar
January 4, 1897

On account of the illness of Mr. Richardson, Mr. Frank Burr has been occupying his old place in the drug store this week.

Healdsburg Tribune, Enterprise and Scimitar
April 29, 1897

OUR THANKSGIVING BIRD

Mr. Edgar Richardson, late proprietor of Richardson's Pharmacy, Healdsburg, but now engaged in the drug business in East Oakland, contributes an interesting article to the *Popular Science News* on the "Origin of the name Turkey." Mr. Richardson's contribution shows close study in its preparation, and is exceedingly logical and convincing.

The popular idea that the fowl derived its title in some way from the land of the ferocious Turk is shown to be a fallacy. He shows that in all probability the name comes from the Hebrew word tukki, for peacock, and as the turkey resembles a peacock in many ways, Mr. Richardson's idea is undoubtedly correct.

Healdsburg Tribune, Enterprise and Scimitar
November 4, 1897

- **Frank Burr**
  - May 1897 – September 1897
  - 105 West St.; sold store to Nichols & Carver (see page 58)

Frank Burr has again assumed control of the drug business formerly under his management. He solicits a fair share of the patronage of the people of Healdsburg and vicinity and will treat them with courtesy, good drugs and fair prices.

Healdsburg Tribune, Enterprise and Scimitar
May 27, 1897

BURR'S DRUG STORE SOLD

H. S. Nichols and Rollo Carver have purchased Frank Burr's drugstore. Both stores, Nichols' and Burr's, will be carried on as heretofore, with Mr. Carver in charge of Burr's store. We wish the new firm success.

Healdsburg Tribune - September 16, 1897

WILL LOCATE IN WINTERS

Mr. Frank Burr will leave Healdsburg this week and locate in Winters, Yolo County, where he will engage in the drug business. Mr. Burr has been a resident of Healdsburg for a number of years and he will carry with him the well-wishes of numberless friends. Mrs. Burr will join her husband at the expiration of her term as teacher of the Kellogg school, Knight's Valley.

Healdsburg Tribune, Enterprise and Scimitar
March 3, 1898

Mrs. Isabel Burr arrived from Winters Monday for a short visit with Miss Mina C. Emery. Before returning to Winters Mrs. Burr will visit friends in San Francisco. Mr. Frank Burr has lately purchased an interest in the Winters Hotel, and is prospering. He also retains an interest in the drug store, which he purchased after leaving Healdsburg.

Healdsburg Tribune, Enterprise and Scimitar
May 27, 1898

Coroner Frank L. Blackburn was called to Geyserville to hold an inquest over the remains of the late Mrs. Hellen Marion Malthum, who died from the effects of a dose of a drug supplied her at Miller's drug store. The sale was made by a young man named Frank Burr. He was interviewed and stated that all he knew about the matter was that he had sold a packet of salts.

The deceased was about sixty years of age. The coroner's jury is of the opinion that the seller of the salts was not sufficiently careful and the mistake cost Mrs. Malthum her life. Mr. Burr stated that he had nothing to do with the filling of prescriptions. Dr. Miller admits that the drug was not "Rochelle salts" but was another drug of poisonous nature. It seems there were two bottles on a shelf labelled "Salts," blown in the glass, but one bottle also bore a label on which was written the name of the real contents.

Mr. Burr, when he supplied the supposed salts for Mrs. Malthum, did not notice the second label on the bottle. She was sick at the time she took the fatal dose and suffered from heart weakness. District Attorney Pond is investigating the affair. Dr. Miller is a well-known practitioner and has been located at Geyserville for some time. Mr. Burr is not a novice in the drug business and is well thought of. Naturally Dr. Miller and Mr. Burr deeply regret the mistake. Dr. Miller was not in the store when the drug was sold.

Sotoyome Sun – September 9, 1903

- **Haigh's Drug Store** (Wm. Rainey Haigh)
- *The Rexall Store*, Hotel Plaza building
- February 1914 – 1919
- Haigh died Dec. 24, 1918 from influenza; Ken Hudson continued store for a few months

TO START WORK MONDAY

Rainey Haigh is here looking after matters incident to opening a new drug store in the Plaza Hotel. Work on the new front and placing the inside fixtures will be started Monday. He says he will have very attractive quarters with an entire new stock of drugs.

Healdsburg Enterprise
January 31, 1914

Haigh's Drug Store
Is the only Rexall Store in Healdsburg

READ THE FOLLOWING GUARANTEE WE GIVE THE PURCHASER OF THESE GOODS

THE ONLY AUTHORIZED AGENT FOR REXALL REMEDIES AND OTHER UNITED DRUG COMPANY PRODUCTS IN HEALDSBURG IS HAIGH'S DRUG STORE, AND ON ANY OF THESE GOODS PURCHASED FROM THIS STORE AND FOUND UNSATISFACTORY YOUR MONEY WILL BE PROMPTLY REFUNDED.

(Signed)   UNITED DRUG CO.

Healdsburg Tribune
May 23, 1914

HBG-D-30

PRESCRIPTION SPECIALISTS
HAIGH'S DRUG STORE   H (in circle)
HEALDSBURG, CALIF.
Clear oval, fluted neck
Tooled top
4 3/4 inches tall
Base: MARVEL
5 3/4 inches tall
Base: MARVEL
Merle Avila collection
6 ½ inches tall
10 to 11 inches tall
Base: ABM scar
John Burton bottle shown

W.R. Haigh (dark suit), Hotel Plaza building, circa 1915
Courtesy, Healdsburg Historical Society

Do Your Christmas Shopping Early
W. R. Haigh Rexall Drug Store
HOTEL PLAZA BUILDING

Our Motto: The Best in Drug Store Service
The Best in Drug Store Merchandise

Have your prescription filled by Haigh
Over 25 years' Experience

Christmas Suggestions

Parisian Ivory, Silverware, Toilet Articles,
Perfumes, Cameras, Stationery, Books
Christmas Cards, Novelties, Toys,
Dolls, and Haas' Candies

Our New Store

Offers an unusual opportunity to do your
Christmas shopping easily, convenient and economically

Healdsburg Tribune
December 6, 1917

- **Corrick & Meese** (Frank J. Corrick & Arthur Meese)
- Hotel Plaza Annex, 315 West Street, *The Rexall Store*
- March 1921 – December 1926 (Meese Pharmacy was successor)

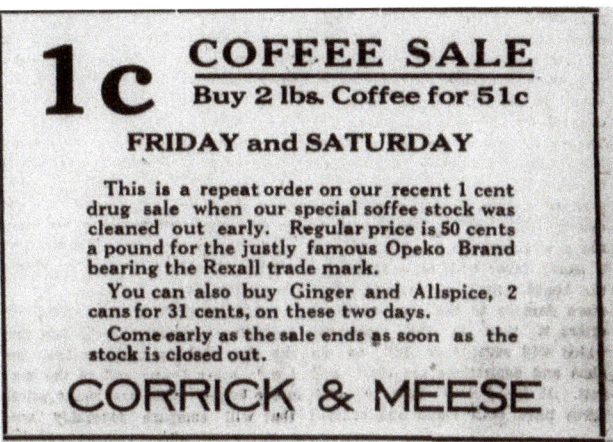

Healdsburg Tribune
December 1, 1921

LOCAL DRUGGISTS BUY BUILDING

The business building on West Street known as the Hotel Plaza Annex, has been sold by the Fox estate to Corrick & Meese, local druggists, who plan extensive alterations to the ground floor, and expect to occupy it with their drug store sometime in the early spring. The purchase was made necessary by the greatly expanding business of Corrick & Meese, who in the few years they have been in business here have built up a wonderful trade.

Healdsburg Tribune
December 25, 1924

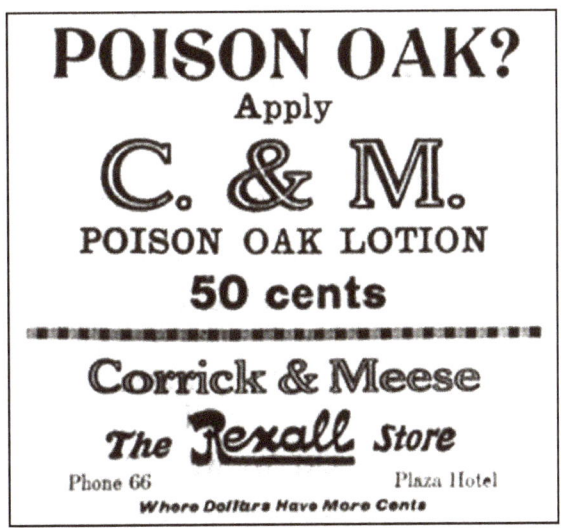

Sotoyome Scimitar
May 5, 1922

Broemmel's Pharmacy, San Francisco

A typical California pharmacy circa 1900 (pre-self-service)

The many glass-labeled pharmacy bottles seen on shelves at left contained chemicals and botanicals used for compounding doctors' prescriptions and other formulas. When required, they were transported to the pharmacy department in the rear, but were displayed on the sales floor to remind customers that professional pharmacy services were available.

- **Lena M. Knickerbocker**, registered pharmacist
  - September 1, 1915 – September 1917
  - Muller Building, corner West and North Streets

A DRUG STORE TO BE ADDED SOON

Healdsburg is to have an additional business enterprise about the first of September. Miss L. M. Knickerbocker has leased the Muller building on the corner of West and North streets, used for many years as a saloon, for the purpose of opening a drug store.

The building is being remodeled in part to fit it for the new business. A show window is being built on the West street front, and the interior is being arranged for its purpose.

Miss Knickerbocker comes from San Francisco, where she was in the drug business for many years.

She is a graduate druggist, and for a long time was in charge of the prescription department at the St. Francis hospital. She expects to have the store ready to open about the first of September.

Healdsburg Tribune, Enterprise and Scimitar
August 19, 1915

NEW DRUG STORE

The new drug store established by Lena M. Knickerbocker in the Muller building at the corner of West and North Streets was opened for business September 1st. The ladies in charge have equipped the place in an attractive manner. They hope to merit a share of the patronage of the public, and will spare no effort to please their patrons.

Healdsburg Tribune
September 9, 1915

Drug Store NEWS

Ladies who wish advice about their purchases may receive the same from a competent woman pharmacist at our store.

Remedies for coughs, colds and that troublesome sore throat that is now so prevalent.

OUR MOTTO
Quality, Accuracy, Quantity

LENA M. KNICKERBOCKER
Registered Pharmacist
Corner West and North Streets
HEALDSBURG, CAL.

September 25, 1915
Healdsburg Enterprise

MOVING DRUG STORE EQUIPMENT

The stock and equipment of the drug store formerly conducted by Miss Knickerbocker, at the corner of West and North streets, was taken to San Francisco Sunday night, by big auto truck from the city. The stock and fixtures were bought by Mrs. J. F. Fox of San Francisco. Miss Knickerbocker has returned to San Francisco to follow her vocation as a druggist.

Healdsburg Tribune, Enterprise and Scimitar
September 25, 1917

KNICKERBOCKER DRUG STOCK HAS BEEN SOLD

The drug stock belonging to Mrs. Knickerbocker and which has been situated in the Muller building at the corner of West and North streets was sold during the latter part of last week to San Francisco parties, and has been boxed up and shipped. Mrs. Knickerbocker left here about six weeks ago, and since that time the store has been closed.

Healdsburg Tribune
October 27, 1917

- **Cuneo's Pharmacy** (Joseph Theodore Cuneo, prop.)
- 307A West Street (this storefront was numbered 309 prior to 1928)
- Purchased the Whitney Pharmacy
- March 1932 – January 26, 1942

JOSEPH T. CUNEO BUYS WHITNEY PHARMACY HERE

Joseph T. Cuneo of Santa Rosa has purchased the Whitney Pharmacy at 307A West Street, Healdsburg. He is a graduate pharmacist and for the past three years, prior to coming to this city, was employed by the St. Rose Drug Store in Santa Rosa.

Sotoyome Scimitar
March 3, 1932

Sotoyome Scimitar
September 29, 1932

JOSEPH CUNEO SUCCUMBS IN UKIAH

Funeral arrangements are pending at the Fred Young and Company, Healdsburg, for Joseph Cuneo, who died suddenly on Wednesday morning, June 24 at his home in Ukiah. Mr. Cuneo, a well-known pharmacist and drug-store owner here for over twenty-years, was 48 years of age at his death.
For approximately ten years he had been owner-manager of the Cuneo Pharmacy here, and for 11 years prior to his assignment in Ukiah a year ago he was partner-manager of the Tomasco Pharmacy, which later became the Medico Drug Co. At the time of his death he was a partner-manager of the Medico Drug Co. in Ukiah and a partner in the Medico Drug Chain which maintains stores in Healdsburg, Vallejo, Santa Rosa as well as Ukiah.
A native of San Francisco, he was a graduate of Santa Rosa High School, Santa Rosa Junior College and the University of California. He was a member of the Ukiah Rotary Club. He is survived by his wife, Mrs. Gertrude B. Cuneo, Ukiah, his son, Timothy Joseph Cuneo, Ukiah, his parents, Mr. and Mrs. Frank Cuneo, Trenton, California, and a brother, Richmond Cuneo of Santa Rosa.

Healdsburg Tribune
June 25, 1953

- **Tomasco Drug Company** (Ralph A. Tomasco, et.al.)
- 333 West Street
- January 26, 1942 – 1950 (renamed Medico Drug Co., Joseph Cuneo, mgr.)

Tomasco Drug Co., 333 West St., May 1949

Starting Monday, January 26, Graham B. Mann and Joseph T. Cuneo, associated in Cuneo's Pharmacy, will be located at Tomasco Drug Co., 333 West Street, next to Plaza Theatre.
January 22, 1942
Healdsburg Tribune

Joseph Cuneo, partner in the Tomasco Drug store organization in Sonoma County, and operator of the local Tomasco Drug store, is recovering at his home this week from a leg operation. He will return to work at the store in about another week, it was learned.
Healdsburg Tribune, Enterprise and Scimitar
March 3, 1950

Medico Drug Co. Opens Fountain

It was announced today by Joseph Cuneo, General Manager of the Medico Drug Co., West Street that the Medico Fountain, which has been closed for a number of weeks will open again today. The fountain, newly painted and decorated, will be under the direct supervision of the Medico Drug Co., with Edith McDannald acting as manager.

Healdsburg Tribune, Enterprise and Scimitar
September 21, 1950

MONTE RIO

- **Tomasco's Pharmacy** (Ralph A. Tomasco)
- Expanded into R. H. Campbell's candy store, January 1926; opp. NWP depot
- June 1925 – 1929

Tomasco to Conduct Monte Rio Pharmacy

The Tomasco Drug Company of this city will open a branch drug store in Monte Rio for the summer season, it was announced yesterday by Ralph Tomasco, proprietor. Tomasco and Angelo Franchetti will be in charge of the river town store, while George Fagan, pharmacy student at the University of California, will manage the establishment here.

Press Democrat
May 15, 1925

Tomasco to Enlarge Monte Rio Branch

Plans for expansion of the branch business conducted by Tomasco's Pharmacy at Monte Rio were revealed here yesterday with filing in the county recorder's office of a notice of intended sale to the pharmacy owners of R. H. Campbell's candy store in the river resort town. Tomasco's now conducts a Monte Rio branch, which has been combined with the candy store, according to R. A. Tomasco. The sale will be completed January 10.

Press Democrat
December 29, 1925

Ralph A. Tomasco yesterday announced the purchase of the R. H. Campbell store at Monte Rio. He stated that he would install a modern pharmacy with soda fountain and ice cream service.
The drug store is located on the principal thoroughfare directly opposite the Northwestern Pacific Railroad Depot. The new pharmacy will be operated as a branch of the Santa Rosa pharmacy located in the new Elk's building at Fourth and A Streets, and will be open the entire year.

Santa Rosa Press Democrat
January 13, 1926

- **Torr's Drug Store** (Lee Otto Torr Jr. and his sister, Clare M. Torr)
- 1932 – 1943

MRIO-D-01
>Paper label:
>Net Contents ……………..Fld. Oz.
>CAMPHORATED OIL
>TORR'S DRUG STORE
>PRESCRIPTIONS
>…Depot   MONTE RIO
>Clear abm, metal screw cap
>3 3/4 inches tall
>Base: ILLINOIS 13-0-1
>Merle Avila collection

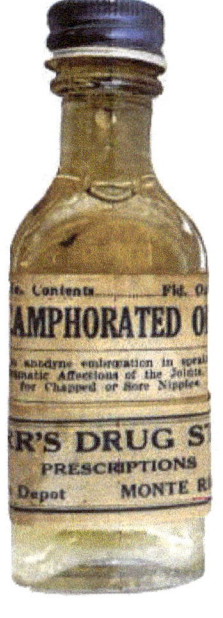

MRIO-D-02
>Paper label:
>Net Contents ……………..Fld. Oz.
>SPIRITS CAMPHOR
>ALCOHOL 86 PER CENT
>DOSE- From 5 drops to a teaspoon. First added to sugar and mixed with water.
>TORR'S DRUG STORE
>PRESCRIPTIONS
>Phone 37   MONTE RIO, CALIF.
>Clear abm, plastic screw cap
>3 inches tall
>Base: OWENS 17 <O> 4
>Merle Avila collection

Torr's Drug Store after a rare Monte Rio snow storm, circa 1940

PENNGROVE

- **Penngrove Drug Store**
- Schieck Bldg., Main Street, next to postoffice
- March 1910 – 1913: Dr. Arthur G. Lumsden
- 1916: Arthur Benson
- 1923-24: Mrs. Domenicini

DRUG STORE AT PENNGROVE

Penngrove is to have a drug store on the first of the month. Dr. Lumsden will occupy the vacant room in the Schieck building and will put in a full line of drugs.

Petaluma Argus-Courier
February 18, 1910

Penngrove Drug Store

Large Stock of Drugs and Novelties

All your drug wants promptly attended to. Prescription druggist. Prescriptions filled promptly with accuracy and skill.

ARTHUR BENSON, Prop.

Petaluma Courier
June 30, 1916

PENNGROVE DRUG STORE

Large Line of Chicken Remedies Coperas, Sulphuric Acid, Epsom Salt, Permaganate of Potash, Carbolic Acid and other remedies.

ARTHUR BENSON,
Prescription Druggist
Near Dr. Francis' Office

Press Democrat
July 30, 1916

Herman Schieck and family, 1917
This building was home to the Penngrove Drug Store
Courtesy, Sonoma County Library

PETALUMA

James E. Keyes, Ph.G. stands in front of Chicken Pharmacy
at 176 Main St. which he founded in 1923.

Courtesy, Sonoma County Library

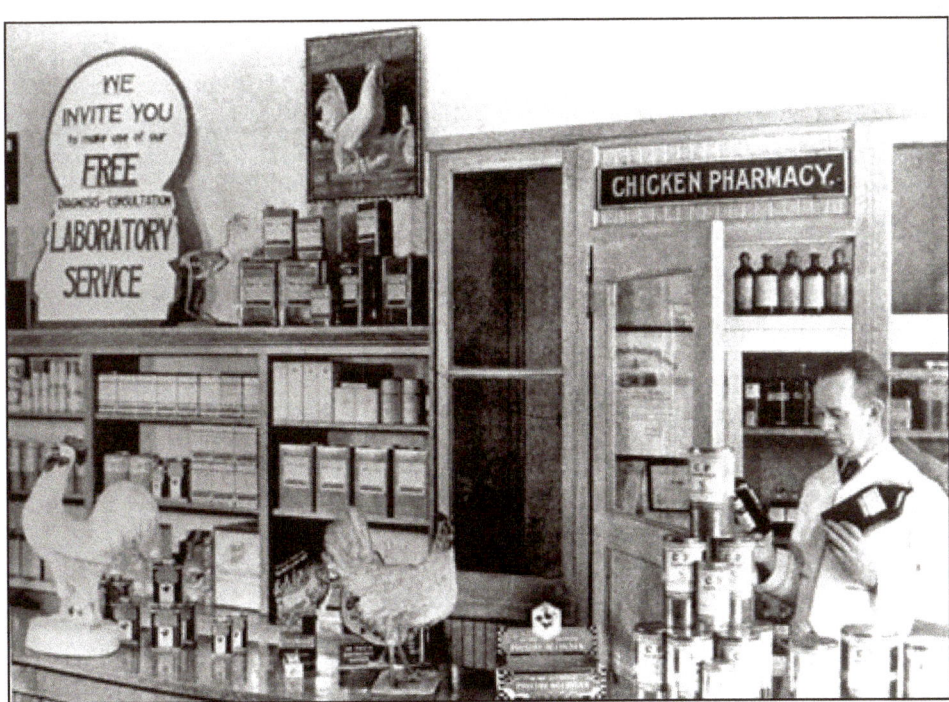

Pharmacist Watson McFadden on duty at the Chicken Pharmacy.

National Geographic Magazine
February 1939

- **Stephen Clayton Haydon** (lived 1826-1873)
- August 1855 – August 12, 1858
- North end of Phœnix Block in 1857, see page 141
- Sold to Smith D. Towne

S.C. Haydon's first store
circa 1856

FALL OF A HOUSE IN PETALUMA.—The Petaluma *Journal*, on Monday, Aug. 4, gives the following account of a somewhat unusual occurrence:

About fifteen minutes before 3 o'clock, this morning, our citizens were aroused from their slumbers by a crashing sound, and the cry of fire! A few moment's time was sufficient to summon together at the scene of destruction a large portion of our inhabitants.

The cause of the alarm proved to be the falling of the two story fire-proof building, on Main street, owned by Messrs. Gowen & McKay, and occupied on the first floor by L. Chapman, as a furniture store, and on the second by the Odd Fellows and Masons.

The front of the building fell into the street, the north side upon the adjoining building, (a wooden structure,) owned and occupied by Mr. S. C. Haydon as a drug store and Express Office of Wells, Fargo & Co., completely demolishing the building and destroying the stock of goods. The south side slid down an embankment into the cellars excavated on the two adjoining lots, preparatory to erecting a brick block over them. The rear wall is left standing, but badly cracked. The building is one mass of ruins.

Mr. Haydon's loss cannot be less than $2,000. Mr. Chapman's loss must of necessity be heavy, as the flooring of the second story has fallen upon his goods. Probably from $2,000 to $2,500. The loss sustained by the Odd Fellows and Masons is considerable, as they had but recently fitted up the Hall, at an expense of some $1,500. The building was erected about twelve months since, at an expense of $5,000, by Messrs. Gowen & McKay. Their loss cannot be much less than the original cost of the structure. The alarm of fire was occasioned by the igniting of some camphene and chemicals. The flames, however, were fortunately immediately extinguished. The accident was occasioned by the removal of the earth from the base of the south wall in order to excavate a basement story for the new block of Messrs. Wells and McKay—the embankment giving way beneath the pressure.

Mr. Haydon narrowly escaped immediate death from the falling building. At the occurrence of the accident he was asleep in a room adjoining his store. He was aroused by the crash, a falling brick striking him at the same moment. He sprang from his bed, and made an ineffectual attempt to escape by the door. At this instant the roof of his store fell, but fortunately the foot of the rafters on the side to which he had fled remained resting above his head. His cries for help brought immediate relief. The bed in which he was sleeping was found to be covered several feet with bricks.

The workmen are actively engaged removing the ruins.

Petaluma Journal
August 4, 1856

While the massive Phœnix Block was being built, Haydon came close to tragedy.

DEATH OF S. C. HAYDON

S. C. Haydon, a pioneer resident of this county, died recently in Hollister, Monterey County, where he has resided the past few years. Mr. Haydon came to California in 1849. He was first employed in the Custom-House in San Francisco under tax collector Collier. In 1852 he purchased a place on Petaluma Creek, which for a long time was known as Haydon's Landing.

He was a druggist by profession, and started the first drug store in the town of Petaluma. He sold the business to S. D. Towne and eventually moved to San Francisco, where he lived for some time. He was one of the original purchasers of the plot of land on which East Petaluma now stands. He was also owner in one of the first additions of Healdsburg.

Sonoma Democrat
November 29, 1873

- **Smith Darius Towne** (lived 1824-1891)
- Successor to Stephen C. Haydon
- North end of Phœnix Block: Aug. 12, 1858 – Nov. 1872 (then 1 door north to 42 Main)
- 42 Main St. (aka 821 and 155 Main): Nov. 1872 – January 1913; 171 Main St.: 1913 – 1919
- Store operated by son Walter Towne, Oct. 1891 – July 1919. See pages 121-123, 156.

Drugs and Medicines!
BOOKS AND STATIONERY!
Also---FLOWER & GARDEN SEEDS.
SMITH D. TOWNE,

HAVING purchased of Mr. *S. C. HAYDON*, **HIS ENTIRE STOCK,** would respectfully ask for a continuance of the patronage heretofore extended to this old established House.

A Full Assortment of Everything
In the
Drug & Medicine, Book & Stationery Line
Constantly on hand, and will be sold at prices much reduced for cash.

Physicians' prescriptions carefully compounded.

I have this day sold to Mr. Smith D. Towne my stock of Medicines, Books, &c., and would respectfully solicit for him a continuance of the liberal patronage formerly bestowed on myself.
S. C. HAYDON.
Petaluma, August 12th, 1858.–a19-3m

Sonoma Democrat
August 19, 1858

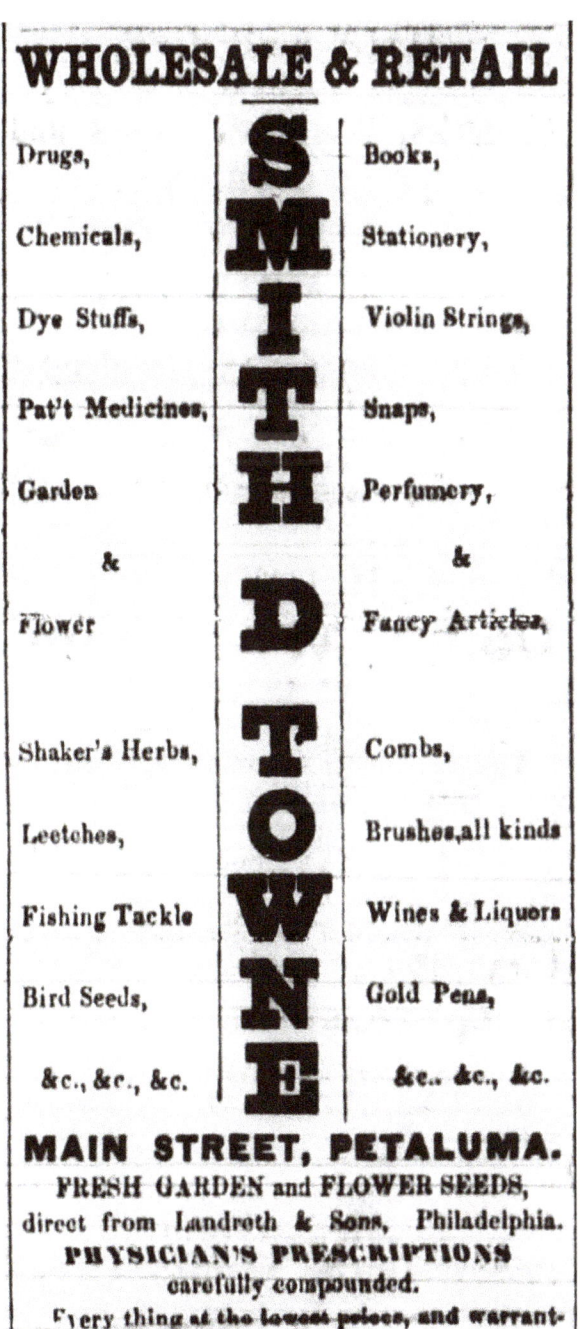

WHOLESALE & RETAIL

Drugs,	**SMITH D TOWNE**	Books,
Chemicals,		Stationery,
Dye Stuffs,		Violin Strings,
Pat't Medicines,		Soaps,
Garden & Flower		Perfumery, & Fancy Articles,
Shaker's Herbs,		Combs,
Leetches,		Brushes, all kinds
Fishing Tackle		Wines & Liquors
Bird Seeds,		Gold Pens,
&c., &c., &c.		&c., &c., &c.

MAIN STREET, PETALUMA.
FRESH GARDEN and FLOWER SEEDS, direct from Landreth & Sons, Philadelphia.
PHYSICIAN'S PRESCRIPTIONS carefully compounded.
Every thing at the lowest prices, and warranted to give satisfaction.   23-3m

Sonoma County Journal
June 17, 1859

DRUGS AND MEDICINES!

SMITH D. TOWNE,
DRUGGIST
AND
APOTHECARY,
Phenix Block, Petaluma,

HAS in store and is constantly receiving direct from New York, a supply of

Drugs,	Perfumery,
Medicines,	Hair Oils,
And Chemicals,	Lily White,
Fancy Articles,	Rouge,
Toilet Soaps,	Puff and Powder
Combs and Brushes,	Boxes, etc., etc.

Spirits Turpentine, Castor Oil, Castile Soap, Whiting, Lampblack, Canary and Hemp Seed, Hops, Potash, Sal Soda, Baking Soda, Cream Tartar, etc.

Jayne's, Ayres', Holloway's, Scovill's, and all other popular Patent Medicines, at New York Prices.

☞ Physicians' Prescriptions accurately prepared.

Orders from the country by stage or express, are solicited, and will be promptly attended to.

51 tf SMITH D. TOWNE.

Sonoma Democrat
November 1, 1860

FOR THE PAST TWENTY-FIVE YEARS Mr. TOWNE has been dealing in Seeds, and has won quite a reputation throughout Sonoma and Marin Counties for the great superiority of Seeds and the low prices. His Seeds are purchased direct by him from well-known and reliable Seed-growers in the East, and may be relied upon as being

FRESH AND GENUINE.

—o—

S. D. TOWNE,
Druggist and Chemist,

42 MAIN STREET,
PETALUMA.

Petaluma Argus
March 3, 1883

The Wholesale and Retail Drug Store of S. D. Towne, formerly in Phœnix Block, is now one door north of the old store, Hinshaw's building, Petaluma.

Sonoma Democrat
November 30, 1872

PET-D-01
> mortar & pestle
> S. D. TOWNE
> APOTHECARY
> SDT (monogram)
> PETALUMA 1855
> Clear rectangular
> Tooled top
> 4 1/8 inches tall
> Base: W T & CO A
> Helmut & DeAnna collection
> 5 1/4 inches tall
> 5 5/8 inches tall
> Base: W T & CO
> Dan Brown bottle shown

Note: "1855" on S.D. Towne bottles refers to start date of his predecessor, S.C. Haydon.

PET-D-02
> mortar & pestle
> S. D. TOWNE
> APOTHECARY
> SDT (monogram)
> PETALUMA
> 1855
> Clear square
> Tooled top
> 5 1/8 inches tall
> Base: W T & CO
> Dan Brown shown
> 5 1/4 inches tall
> Base: W T & CO A L
> Helmut & DeAnna collection

PET-D-03
    S. D. TOWNE
    DRUGGIST
    PETALUMA, CAL
    Aqua rectangular panel
    Tooled top
    7 1/4 inches tall
    Base: W T & CO
    Dan Brown collection

PET-D-04
    S. D. TOWNE
    DRUGGIST
    PETALUMA
    1855
    Aqua ball-neck panel
    Tooled top
    7 inches tall
    ex Frank Sternad collection

PET-D-05
> S. D. TOWNE
> DRUGGIST
> PETALUMA
> 1855
> Clear ball-neck panel
> Tooled top
> 7 1/4 inches tall
> Base: W T & CO.
> Dan Brown collection

PET-D-06
> S. D. TOWNE
> PHARMACY
> PETALUMA
> Clear rectangular
> Tooled top
> 3 5/8 inches tall
> Base: W T & Co
> Dan Brown collection

PET-D-07
S. D. TOWNE
DRUGGIST
PETALUMA
1855
Clear square
Tooled top
6 3/8 inches tall
Base: #1
Dan Brown collection

PET-D-09
S. D. TOWNE
scales/wreath
DRUG GIST
ESTABLISHED (conical graduate) 1855
PETALUMA
Clear square
Tooled top
7 ½ inches tall
Base: W T & CO.
Dan Brown collection

PET-D-10

S.D. TOWNE
PHARMACY
PETALUMA
Clear square
Tooled top
4 3/16 inches tall
Dan Brown collection

PET-D-11

S. D. TOWNE
PHARMACY
PETALUMA
Clear oval
Tooled top
4 ¼ inches tall
Base: W T & Co
Dan Brown collection

PET-D-12
    S. D. TOWNE
    PIONEER
    DRUGGIST
    1855
    PETALUMA
    Clear square
    Tooled top
    5 5/8 inches tall
    5 7/8 inches tall
    Base: W T & Co
    Dan Brown bottle collection

PET-D-13
    S. D. TOWNE
    PIONEER
    DRUGGIST
    1855
    PETALUMA
    Clear rectangular
    6 inches tall
    W T & CO B
    Helmut & DeAnna Jordt collection

S.D. Towne's sidewalk signs direct customers to his store in the 3-story Phœnix Block. People are spilling out windows to watch a parade on Main Street, circa 1870.
ex Frank Sternad collection

PET-D-14
    S. D. TOWNE
    PHARMACY
    PETALUMA
    Clear square
    5 inches tall
    Base: A
    Helmut & DeAnna Jordt collection

PET-D-16
    S. D. TOWNE
    DRUGGIST
    PETALUMA, CAL.
    Aqua panel
    5 ½ inches tall
    Base: W T & CO
    Helmut & DeAnna
      Jordt collection

PET-D-17
S. D. TOWNE
DRUGGIST
PETALUMA
1855
Clear square
4 1/8 inches tall
Base: E
Helmut & DeAnna Jordt collection

A Sudden Death

Smith D. Towne, one of our oldest and most respected citizens, passed quietly. He was found dead in bed when a messenger was sent to summon him to breakfast yesterday morning. He had been seemingly well and attended to business the day before, and his death is a definite shock.

Smith Darius Towne was born in St. Louis, Mo., sixty-eight years ago. He came to California in 1851, settling near Petaluma. In 1855 he established his home in this city and has lived here continuously since.

Mr. Towne was married in Petaluma in December 1859 to Amanda Munday. His wife died in November 1883, leaving seven children, all of whom survive their parents. They are: Charles of Tacoma, Florence, Clarice, Beverly M., and three additional sons, all druggists— Frank M. of San Bernardino, Lester B. and Walter Towne. The absent sons have been summoned by telegraph and are expected to arrive today.

Petaluma Daily Courier
October 7, 1891

Note: Following S. D. Towne's death, his son Walter J. Towne (lived 1868-1932) and other members of the family continued Towne's Drug Store until Walter was named sole owner in 1898. He moved the drug business from 155 to 171 Main St. in 1913, converting the old location to *The Candy Shop*, operated until September 1915.

PET-D-17A
FROM
TOWNE'S
DRUG STORE
PETALUMA, CAL
Clear rectangular
Tooled top
4 3/8 inches tall
Base: S B W
6 1/8 inches tall
Base: W T & CO A U. S. A. PAT. Jan 5, 1892
Merle Avila collection
6 inches tall
Base: S B W
Dan Brown bottle shown

Petaluma Argus Courier
June 14, 1900

Some New Drinks at Towne's.	
Champagne Cider....	5c
Celery Phosphate, nerve tonic......	5c
Coca-Kola Phosphate, invigorator...	5c
Orange Phosphate, Towne's........	5c
Pepsin and Malt Tonic, for weak stomachs........................	5c
Iced Bouillon, refreshing, strengthening and delicious.............	5c
Egg Chocolate, rich and delicious..	10c
Egg Phosphate, Towne's...........	10c

Walter Towne was an accomplished photographer and published his own postcards circa 1905-1910 signing them "Photo by Towne." This view looking south on Main Street was taken north of Washington Street in 1905. Also see page 156.

Walter Towne moved his drugstore to 171 Main Street in the Derby Block in 1913. A sign reading "Towne the Druggist" is visible above the nearest automobile. His "Candy Shop" at 155 Main is down the block with large rigid awning over the sidewalk.

Courtesy, Sonoma County Library

ANNOUNCEMENT

We desire to express our great appreciation to Petalumans, those formerly residing here as well as those now in our midst, who have favored us with their patronage at any time during these many years.

The Towne family has been identified with the drug business in this city since 1852 and there has been a Towne's Drug Store here since 1855 while our own connection with the business dates from 1886, making, we believe, the oldest established business house in this city today.

It is, with becoming pride we look back over the eexistence of this house reflecting most brightly on the scrupulously painstaking, careful, exacting, conscientious and ethical policy adopted and followed, always safe in hazardous work, always trustful in confidences imposed.

We have always felt the seriousness of our calling and gave our best. We are now retiring from business in favor of a gentleman we have long trusted, Mr. Louis James, able and well qualified to carry on our work and we hope for him a generous confidence and liberal patronage.

WALTER TOWNE.

Walter Towne sells store to Louis James
Petaluma Argus-Courier - July 31, 1919

- **James' Drug Store** (E. Louis James)
- Successor to Towne's Drug Store
- 171 Main Street: July 1919 – June 1924
- 117 Kentucky St. (Schoeningh Building, aka The Fair): June 1924 – September 1929
- Prescription files sold to Petaluma Drug Company.

NOTICE

Prescription file of James' Drug Store has been acquired by Petaluma Drug Co. Prescriptions formerly filled at James' Drug Store can now be filled at Petaluma Drug Co.

Petaluma Argus-Courier
September 26, 1929

NOTICE

Mr. E. Louis James is now located at O'Neill Drug Co., 9 Lower Main Street, where he will be pleased to meet and serve his old customers and friends.

Petaluma Argus-Courier
September 1929

James' Drug Store in *The Fair* building on Kentucky Street, circa 1925
Courtesy, Sonoma County Library

- **Petaluma Drug Co.**
- 130 Kentucky Street
- Otto H. Poehlmann, Clarence B. Maggetti, Arnold J. Piezzi: Oct 1, 1920 – Dec 30, 1924
- Lewellyn T.O. Rule, sole owner: December 31, 1924 – June 6, 1925
- Arnold "Nolda" J. Piezzi and Joseph H. Schoeningh: June 6, 1925 – February 1930
- Joseph H. Schoeningh: February 1930 – June 1, 1942
- Sold to Antlers Drug Store (Paul Elmore and William Naye), NE corner Western & Kentucky

Kodak as you go

Use the new fresh films we sell for best results

Let Us Develop Your Films

Our Photographer is a wonder
A trial will convince you.

We have a complete line of Eversharp Pencils and Tempoint Pens.

DON'T SAY CANDY—
SAY PIG'N WHISTLE

PETALUMA DRUG CO.

Prompt, Intelligent Druggists
We give S. & H. Green Trading Stamps
Phone 100   Directly Opposite Postoffice

Petaluma Daily Courier
June 4, 1921

Pharmacist Technician Joseph H. Schoeningh is at Camp Patrick Henry in Virginia en route home after spending the greater part of his service in China. Upon applying for discharge he was returned to this country and is expected to arrive here shortly. Schoeningh is the son of Mr. and Mrs. Joseph Schoeningh, of 210 English street, and brother of Herman (Ham) Schoening, a civilian prisoner of war of the Japs. His wife, Isabel, and daughter, Barbara, reside in San Francisco.

Petaluma Argus-Courier
August 10 1945

PETALUMA DRUG CO.

Prescriptions — Drugs — Seeds

January 1923

- **Petaluma Drug Store** (east side of Main St., opposite Phœnix Block)
- Unknown proprietor: May 1856 – September 1857
- Charles P. Lovegrove & Co. (E. Parker): September 1857 – December 5, 1857
- Charles P. Lovegrove: December 25, 1857 –June 25, 1858

NEW DRUG STORE.
On Sale at the 'Petaluma' Drug Store.
EAST SIDE OF MAIN STREET.

Cod Liver Oil, Castor Oil, Olive Oil, Sponges, Tartaric Acid, Carbonate of Soda, Hair Oil, Eau de Cologne, Carter's Spanish Mixt., P. Davis' Pain Killer; Wright's, Brandreth's, Moffat's, Lee's, Cook's, Radway's, Hollway's, and other family Pills; Townsend's, Shakers', Sand's, Bailey's and Guysott's Sarsaparilla; Quinine, Iodide of Potassium, Epsom Salts, Bay Rum & Bay Water, Radway's Ready Rel'f, Mustang Liniment, Tulington's Balsam, Wistar's Balsam of Wild Cherry, Enema Pipes, Seidlitz Powders, Camphor, Hair Tonics, Arrowroot, Syringes, Bed Pans, Calomel, Opium, Trusses, Brown's Es. of Ginger, Sassafras, Chloride of Lime, Tamarinds, Collodion, Chloroform, Tooth Powders, Tooth Brushes, Cream of Tartar, Gentian Root, Thermometers, Leeches—Hungarian, fresh imported;

Small Pox.

CHILDREN and Adults, Vaccinated daily at the Petaluma Drug Store, from fresh, healthy Matter.
If requested, families will be attended at their residence.

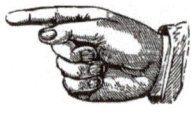

Sonoma County Journal
June 7, 1856

CHAS. P. LOVEGROVE & Co. Druggists & Practical Apothecary
Respectfully solicit public patronage Having opened a new Drug Store on
MAIN STREET, NEXT DOOR ABOVE McCUNE & CO.'s They offer for sale all the popular
FAMILY MEDICINES AS WELL AS DRUGS AND MEDICINES

Sonoma County Journal
September 18, 1857

NOTICE
The partnership heretofore existing between E. Parker & Charles P. Lovegrove, under the name and style of Lovegrove & Co., is this day dissolved by mutual consent for Self and Partner.
C. P. LOVEGROVE   December 5, 1857

Sonoma County Journal
December 25, 1857

Fresh Stock.

CHARLES P. LOVEGROVE having removed into the store so long and favorably known as the "Petaluma Drug Store," east side of Main street, and nearly opposite to the Phenix Block, has just now laid in a large stock of nearly

Every Requisite of the Drug Trade,

With the addition of a variety of articles in the

PERFUMERY LINE,

and trusts to be favored with a continuation of patronage hitherto afforded him.

To Physicians, he would state that having had *nine years experience* in one of the largest and most respectable establishments in the Eastern States, they may rely on the accuracy with which any prescription intrusted to his care, will be filled up.

Also, for their accommodation, as well as that of the public, the Store will be kept open night as well as day, himself in attendance.

No Drugs but those selected *as the best* by care and experience, will be found in his Store.

Among the immense variety, the following, just received, may be mentioned: Sulphate, Muriate and Acetate of Morphia, Sulphate of Quinine, P. & W. Syrup of Ferri Iodido, Iodine, Nitrate of Silver, in stick and in crystal, Liquor Potassa, Strychnine, Chloroform, "Baltey's Sedative Solution of Opium," Liquor Plumbi Subacetates, Holloway's Pills and Ointment, all sizes. All the favorite Sarsaparillas of the day; Essential Oils, Annotta, Blue Stone, &c. Also,

Leeches! Leeches!!

☞ Look out for the BIG RED MORTAR.
Petaluma, Dec. 25, 1857.   19-tf

Sonoma County Journal
March 19, 1858

J. ROBBINS, PRACTICAL DRUGGIST,

(LATE OF THE STEAMER J. L. STEPHENS,)

HAVING purchased the Petaluma Drug Store, formerly kept by Dr. Trevor, enlarged and improved it, and replenished it with an entire stock of

New Drugs, Medicines, Chemicals, PERFUMERIES, DRUG-GROCERIES,

And a variety of articles belonging to the Drug Business, would respectfully inform his numerous friends and acquaintances who have traveled with him on the steamers John L. Stephens, California, Panama and Tennessee,—as well as families generally, that he is prepared to furnish them with any article connected with the Drug business, and at as *low prices as any store in the State.*

By strict attention to business and a desire to please, he hopes to merit and receive a liberal portion of public patronage.

Personal care will be given to the compounding of Physician's Prescriptions and Family Recipes, as well as to the preparation of Horse and Cattle Medicines; and that too, without making the usual exorbitant charges.

Families will find it to their advantage to call and examine my assortment of articles of daily use.

Physicians supplied with Drugs, &c., at very reasonable prices. Orders from the country promptly attended to, carefully put up, and forwarded.

☞ Don't mistake the place:—Sign of the Red Mortar, East side Main street, Petaluma, a few doors below Washington street.

Petaluma, June 25, 1858.   45-3m

Sonoma County Journal
September 24, 1858

- **Petaluma Drug Store** (continued)
- J. Robbins: June 25, 1858 – July 1859
- Robbins & Vaslit: July 1859 – May 25, 1860;
- J. Robbins alone until May 1861
- Robbins was a private in the Petaluma Guard in January 1859

CARD TO THE PUBLIC

Having studied and practiced Medicine for six years with some of the eminent Physicians of Europe, I am prepared to give advice gratuitously in all diseases, particularly the diseases of Children, and perform all the minor operations of Surgery, at the

PETALUMA DRUG STORE

Main Street near Washington.   J. ROBBINS

Sonoma County Journal
February 25, 1859

PETALUMA DRUG STORE

Having associated Dr. Vaslit with me in the Drug Business, I take this opportunity of informing the public that we are prepared to give Medical Advice Free, at the Petaluma Drug Store, and perform all the minor operations of surgery.

Dr. Vaslit comes from Napa highly recommended, where he has been practicing for two years with Dr. Stillwagon. He has also studied at the Worchester Medical Institute, Mass.

I will also reiterate, that I served a regular apprenticeship of five years with the late Dr. H. G. Harbord of Liverpool, and that I feel competent to give advice in every branch of the Medical profession; and having studied two years to the Liverpool Opthalmic Institution, I am qualified to treat all Diseases of the Eyes, whether acute or chronic.

I will guarantee a permanent cure in all chronic diseases of the synovial membrane of the knee, commonly called white swelling, by local treatment.

Physician's Prescriptions carefully prepared, and Medicines dispensed at all hours of the night. There will be a light in the window, and a night bell attached to the store. Constantly on hand, a fresh supply of Homeopathic Medicines, Leeches, &c.

The largest and best assorted stock of Drugs and Medicines in the County, for sale at San Francisco prices, either in small or large quantities. Physician's supplied on reasonable terms, Foreign and Native Wines and Liquor of best quality, and English Ale and Porter in Pints, for Medicinal use, for sale.

ROBBINS & VASLIT, Pharmacists
Petaluma Drug Store, Main Street near Washington Street.

Sonoma County Journal
July 8, 1859

PETALUMA DRUG STORE
HAVING ENLARGED OUR STORE
AND INCREASED OUR STOCK
We now sell for cash,
PATENT MEDICINES & EVERY OTHER ARTICLE
Connected with the Drug Business,
CHEAPER THAN ANY OTHER STORE
IN THE COUNTY.
Prescriptions Dispensed Night or Day
ROBBINS & VASLIT
Prescribing Druggists and Agents for Patent Medicines.

Sonoma County Journal
October 21, 1859

DISSOLUTION OF PARTNERSHIP

The partnership heretofore between Robbins & Vaslit in the drug business, has been dissolved by mutual consent. The business will hereafter be conducted by J. ROBBINS, who will settle all outstanding debts.

All parties indebted to the old firm are requested to make immediate payment. I take this opportunity to thank the public for past favors, and solicit a share of their patronage in the future.
J. ROBBINS   Main St. near Washington St.

Sonoma County Journal
May 25, 1860

Mortar & pestle trade sign, late 19th century

- **Adolph Lessel**
- German Drug Store, SW corner Main & Washington Streets
- 1880 – March 1882
- Sold to E.M. Treuholtz

GERMAN DRUG STORE!

ADOLPH LESSEL,

Graduate of Breslan, Prussia, with 27 years' practice

Physicians' Prescriptions Carefully Compounded.

Cor. Main and Washington sts., Petaluma.
20t

Petaluma Courier
July 21, 1880

Adolph Lessel has sold his German Drug Store on the corner of Main and Washington Streets to Dr. E. Treuholtz, formerly of El Dorado County. Mr. Lessel will soon visit the old country and business.

Petaluma Courier
March 22, 1882

- **Ernest Magnus Treuholtz**
- German and American Drug Store, successor to Adolph Lessel
- After E.M. Treuholtz died in March 1892, his sons Anthony and Francis took over, moving the store to 867 Main St. by January 1893. The store was sold to D.T. Ruffin in Dec 1893.
- March 1882 – December 27, 1893

GERMAN & AMERICAN DRUG STORE!

E. M. TREUHOLTZ,

Apothecary & Chemist,

(Successor to A. Lessel)

Cor. of Main and Washington Sts., Petaluma.

Has on hand and is constantly receiving a full and fresh stock of Drugs, Medicines, Chemicals, Patent Medicines, Perfumery, Fancy Goods, Etc.

CIGARS, TOBACCOS, CIGARETTES,

Etc. A superior stock constantly on hand.

PRESCRIPTIONS and FAMILY RECEIPTS compounded with accuracy and of the PUREST DRUGS.

EILER'S EXTRACT OF TAR & WILD CHERRY for Coughs, Colds, Consumption and Bronchitis—a sure cure for the above complaints.

UNCLE SAM'S NERVE & BONE LINIMENT has no superior. TRY it and be CURED.

All Orders from the Country promptly filled. 31 tf

Petaluma Courier
July 26, 1882

When in Need
—OF—
DRUGS AND PATENT MEDICINES,
You Want the Best.

Our Stock is Fresh and Genuine

Prescriptions a Specialty.

TREUHOLTZ BROS.
DRUGGISTS-
Main Street, Petaluma, Opp. Hale Bros.

Petaluma Courier
January 25, 1893

A BUSINESS CHANGE

D. T. Ruffin of San Francisco has purchased the Treuholtz Drug Store, the deal having been consummated Wednesday morning, and has taken possession of the same. The newcomer is a young man of excellent repute who has been in the drug business for more than a dozen years, the last three years in Steele's Palace Hotel. He is a pharmacist of high ability and a very affable young man who evidently possesses the attributes calculated to make and hold patronage. The *Courier* welcomes him to the Petaluma business world.

Petaluma Courier
December 27, 1893

- **David Taylor Ruffin**
  - 867 Main Street
  - Successor to Treuholtz Bros.; sold to F.N. Hitchcock
  - December 27, 1893 – June 1899 (Ruffin moved to Marysville, CA)

Petaluma Daily Morning Courier
January 11, 1895

NO-TO-BAC GUARANTEED TOBACCO HABIT CURE

Over 1,000,000 boxes sold. 300,000 cures prove its power to destroy the desire for tobacco in any form. No-to-bac is the greatest nerve-food in the world. Many gain 10 pounds in 10 days and it never fails to make the weak impotent man strong, vigorous and magnetic. Just try a box. You will be delighted. We expect you to believe what we say, for a cure is absolutely guaranteed by druggists everywhere. Send for our booklet "Don't Tobacco Spit and Smoke Your Life Away," written guarantee and free sample. Address **THE STERLING REMEDY CO.**, Chicago or New York.

SOLD AND GUARANTEED BY D. T. RUFFIN.

Petaluma Daily Courier
November 12, 1896

PET- D-18

D. T. RUFFIN
DRUGGIST
PETALUMA, CAL.
Clear oval
Tooled top
5 1/8 inches tall
Dan Brown collection

- **Black's Fine Drugs** (Charles A. Black, born 1867)
- Kentucky Street
- August 29 – November 10, 1909   [An exercise in futility]

BLACK'S DRUG STORE OPENS

The opening of C. A. Black's new Drug Store on Kentucky Street on Saturday was a very successful affair. Mr. Black is very much pleased with the outlook.

On Saturday morning, the store was swamped with expectant customers and the clerks had more business than they could handle. Four hundred and fifty souvenirs were given out before ten o'clock. Mr. Black had expected that this number would be sufficient for the entire day's business and was somewhat chagrined that he had so underestimated the demand, but he considers the opening a great success.

Miss Ruth Carter of 749 Bremen Street was the winner of the $5 prize and Miss Kate Hanley of 35 Bassett Street won one of the $1 prizes. The balance of the winners has not yet reported.

Petaluma Daily Morning Courier
August 29, 1909

AN ADDRESS
TO THE PEOPLE OF PETALUMA

First, I will ask you, do you know that for years you have been paying out your good money in support of a system that is iniquitous, right here in Petaluma?

Whenever you hear the findings of the Grand Jury, exposing some public graft, you are horrified, and justly so.

Now, there is a system of graft, which for years has been thriving in Petaluma over which the Grand Jury has no justification. I refer to *PERCENTAGES PAID TO CERTAIN DOCTORS BY CERTAIN DRUGGISTS TO WHOM THESE DOCTORS SEND THEIR PRESCRIPTIONS*. I know of no other town in the state, which is so cursed with this evil, excepting San Francisco. And this percentage graft has obtained such a grasp in the metropolis that medical journals throughout the country have been urging steps so that this diabolical graft shall cease.

In San Francisco, there are certain stores which pay doctors sending their prescriptions to their stores as high as fifty-percent of the price of the prescription. That is, if the druggist charges $1 for the medicine the doctor prescribing it gets 50 cents on the dollar.

IS IT NOT PLAINLY APPARENT THAT THE PATIENT MUST PAY A HIGHER PRICE FOR THEIR MEDICINE IF THE DOCTOR DEMANDS OF THE DRUGGIST HALF THE PRICE OF THEIR MEDICINE THE DRUGGIST FURNISHES ON THE DOCTOR'S PRESCRIPTION.

The druggist must have his profit, and if the doctor gets half the money charged for the medicine, that is, 50 cents out of the dollar, the druggist's profit must come out of the remaining 50 cents. To avoid this *THE PATIENT MUST PAY DOUBLE PRICE FOR THE MEDICINE*, is this not plain?

The percentage paid to the doctors, (those doctors who will accept this percentage) *IS ONE THIRD OF THE PRICE CHARGED FOR THE MEDICINE*. If the medicine ought to cost 50 cents, a charge of 75 cents will be made, in order that the druggist may give the doctor his one-third, without loss to himself. Or if the right price of the medicine would be one dollar, a charge of $1.50 will be made.

THE DRUGGIST SURELY WILL NOT GIVE ONE-THIRD OF THE DOLLAR TO THE DOCTOR, IF THE RIGHT PRICE OF THE MEDICINE WOULD BE ONE DOLLAR, FOR THAT WOULD NOT LEAVE THE DRUGGIST ENOUGH PROFIT TO COVER HIS TIME COMPOUNDING THE PRESCRIPTION, OR A REASONABLE MERCHANDISE PROFIT.

I have been in the drug business twenty years, and never in all that time payed a percentage to any physician sending prescriptions to my store. Though I was told, when ready to open my drug store in Petaluma that it was generally the custom to pay doctors a percentage for sending their prescriptions to certain drug stores designated by them, and it was intimated that I would have to do this to get any prescription business. But I want to say this:

I have a family to support; have recently gone through a long period of business depression where I was located before coming to Petaluma; have put all my eggs in a Petaluma basket; --- but *I NEVER WILL, AS LONG AS I LIVE, STOOP TO PETTY GRAFT TO DO BUSINESS OR MAKE A LIVING!*

There are some doctors in Petaluma who do not --- *WHO WOULD NOT* --- accept percentages from the druggist. If your physician insists that you go to any certain drug store to have his prescription filled, his action is open to suspicion, to say the least.

YOU HAVE THE RIGHT TO TAKE YOUR PRESCRIPTION YOUR DOCTOR WRITES TO ANY DRUG STORE YOU CHOOSE.

And you have also the right to demand that your prescription be written so any qualified druggist may fill it --- *AND NOT WRITTEN IN SECRET CHARACTERS UNDERSTOOD ONLY BY THE DOCTOR AND THE DRUGGIST FROM WHOM HE TAKES A PERCENTAGE.*

This latter expedient is often resorted to. Another is to telephone the prescription to the druggist. By this latter means, the prescription never gets into the hands of the patient. I respectfully submit these statements to the people of Petaluma for your consideration.

Sincerely, C. A. BLACK
BLACK'S FINE DRUGS
OPPOSITE POST OFFICE – PETALUMA

Petaluma Argus Courier
September 28, 1909

BLACK DRUG STORE CLOSED

The Kirk, Geary Company of Sacramento, the assignees of the C. A. Black drug store of Kentucky street, have closed the store. Today the doors were closed. C. A. Black was in the city and his intentions are not known. The store has been in financial difficulty for some time.

Petaluma Daily Courier
November 10, 1909

- **Francis Newton Hitchcock**
- Yellow Front Drug Store, 867 Main St.
- June 1899 – December 1901 ; Hitchcock relocated to Napa
- Successor to D.T. Ruffin; sold to E.O. Webb

Francis N. Hitchcock, circa 1885

Petaluma Argus-Courier
April 17, 1901

PET-D-19

F. N. HITCHCOCK
DRUGGIST
PETALUMA, CAL
Aqua rectangular panel
Tooled top
7 7/8 inches tall
Base: W. T. & CO. USA
Dan Brown collection

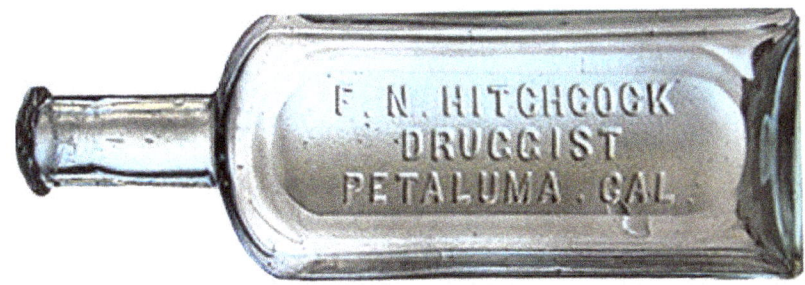

- **Edward O. Webb**
  - Webb's Yellow Front Drug Store, 867 Main Street (also see page 156)
  - Successor to F.N. Hitchcock; John L. Clark acquired 50% interest in October 1905 to form Webb-Clark Drug Co. Webb was located in Marysville, Cal. In 1901.
  - January 1902 – 1906

Save 15 Cents

Overstocked on Palmer's Perfumes, one ounce size.

This week we sell regular 50 cent bottles for.......... 35c

Call and see our display of perfumes and toilet articles.

Genuine, Old-time Horehound Drops

A sure stop for throat-tickle.

Delicious and not disturbing

Old fashioned, genuine horehound flavor

Large packages

5 AND 10 CENTS.

A good thing for children

Webb's Yellow Front Drug Store

Low Prices,   Telephone, Main One.

Petaluma Argus Courier
December 9, 1902

COUGH HANGS ON!

Don't let it hang on much longer.
It will become chronic if you do.

Webb's Cough Cure

Is a splendid remedy for hard coughs, old coughs, and a reliable relief for night coughing spells.

Price 50 cents a bottle.

Prepared only at

WEBB'S Yellow Front Drug Store

Petaluma Daily Morning Courier
April 28, 1903

- **Clark Drug Co.** (John L. Clark and Joseph W. Tuttle)
- Yellow Front Drug Store, 867 Main Street (aka 113 Main St. by May 1908)
- Successors to Webb-Clark Drug Co.; *The Rexall Store* after 1915
- Tuttle & R.L. Squires were proprietors. by September 1919
- 1906 – 1926   (name changed to Tuttle Drug Co. about April 1926)

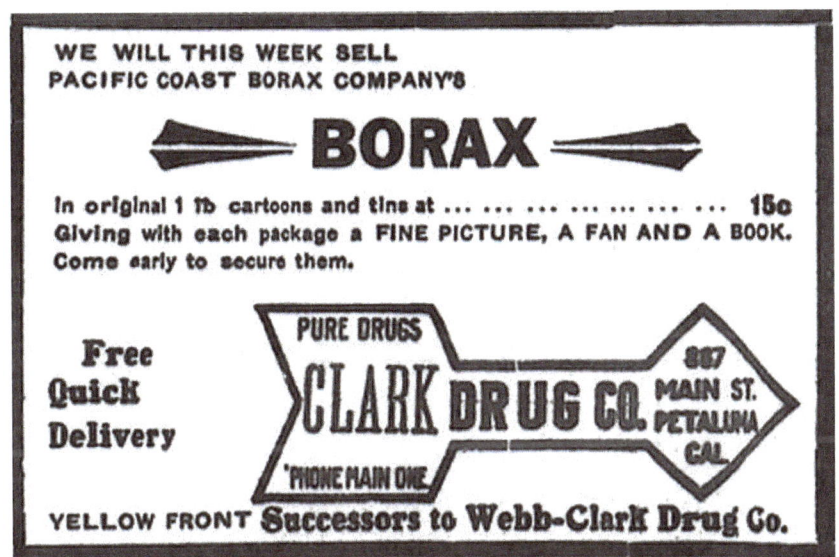

Petaluma Argus Courier
August 17, 1906

Petaluma Argus Courier
December 9, 1906

PET-D-20
    CLARK DRUG CO.
    PETALUMA, CAL.
    Clear square
    Tooled top
    2 inches tall
    Base: W T CO U.S.A.
    Helmut & DeAnna Jordt collection

PET-D-21
    CLARK DRUG CO.
    PETALUMA, CAL.
    Clear nurser, graduated back
    Tooled top
    6 3/8 inches tall
    Dan Brown collection

December 17, 1907
Petaluma Argus

- **Blackburn Drug Co.** (Charles Walter Blackburn & Tupper S. Malone)
- 171 Main Street (purchased Young Drug Co.); Blackburn formerly employed by McGuire's
- November 1909 – Dec. 2, 1912 (sold to Walter Towne who relocated from 155 Main)

WALTER TOWNE BUYS BLACKBURN DRUG CO

A deal was closed today when the Blackburn Drug company, who have been in business in the Maynard building for the last three years, sold the business to Walter Towne, the well known pioneer druggist, who took immediate possession.

Mr. Towne will continue to conduct the store in the same location and will remove his stock of drugs from his present store to the new place of business. He will convert the store, which he now occupies, into an ice cream and confectionary parlors and will engage in the business on a large scale.

Mr. Blackburn who established the Blackburn Drug store and who was associated with Tupper Malone in conducting the drug store, will after January 1st travel, selling his stomach remedies. He has long been anxious to get out of the business so that he could travel.

Petaluma Daily Courier
December 2, 1912

An Excellent and Reliable Remedy for Dyspepsia and Indigestion. Recommended for Bloating, Gas, Sourness, Fermentation, Belching, Heartburn, Smothering, Heart Palpitation, Nausea, Difficult Breathing, Vomiting, Nervous Indigestion, Cramps, Sleeplessness and all Stomach Distress.

PRICE 50c and $1.00.

Press Democrat
March 17, 1911

Announcement

We, C. Walter Blackburn and T. S. Malone have sold out our entire Interest in the Blackburn Drug Co. to Walter Towne who will continue to conduct the business at the same stand. We heartily appreciate the patronage of our friends in the past and sincerely wish every one of you to continue your patronage with the store as we believe Mr. Towne most capable and most anxious to give you the best possible drug store service.

Very Respectfully
C. WALTER BLACKBURN

Towne's Cut Rate Store
"THE QUICK AND CAREFUL DRUGGISTS"

Petaluma Argus-Courier
December 2, 1912

- **George L. Edelmann**, Ph.G.
- Red Front Drug Store
- 859 Main Street, opposite Hale Bros. & Co.
- February 1898 – May 1901

Edelmann's branch store at Tomales,
Marin County, circa 1900

Petaluma Argus-Courier
October 25, 1900

..... EDELMANN'S .....
Headquarters for Murdock Poultry Prescriptions
GOOD THINGS FOR SUNBURN
Edelmann's Complexion Cream 25 cents
Almond and Benzoia Cream 25 cents
Talcum Powder (Borated) in Sprinkle Top Cans
10 cents or three for 25 cents
Bring us your prescriptions.
We will price them cheerfully and guarantee accuracy and material.

Petaluma Argus-Courier
August 7, 1900

PET-D-22

Geo. L. Edelmann, Ph. G.
Pharmacist
859 Main St. Petaluma, Cal.
Clear rectangular
Tooled top
3 1/16 inches tall
4 3/4 inches tall
5 3/16 inches tall
Dan Brown collection
3 inches tall
5 5/8 inches tall
Helmut & DeAnna Jordt collection
7 3/16 inches tall
Dan Brown bottle shown

S.H. Wagener's Drug Store on left, S.C. Haydon's store on right, Phœnix Block, Main Street, circa August 1857 (note Wagener's sign being installed).

- **Samuel H. Wagener & Co.**
  - Phenix Drug Store, Main St., south end of Phœnix Block (see previous page)
  - Successor to C. Hopkins; sold to Frank T. Maynard
  - August 1857 – April 22, 1861

Phenix Drug Store,
Phenix Block, Main st., Petaluma

S. H. WAGENER, successor to C. Hopkins

Physicians Prescriptions carefully Compounded.

Patent Medicines,	Books & Stationery,
Guysott's Sarsaparilla,	Law Blanks,
Townsends Sarsaparilla,	Blank Books,
Jayne's Family Medic's,	School Books,
Cherry Pectoral,	Perfumery,
Life Balsam,	Lubins' & Edrehi's ex-
Morse's Cordial,	tracts,

Fever & Ague Pills, and Balm of 1000 Flowers, all the popular Patent Fancy Soaps, &c. Medicines of the day.

Petaluma, Aug. 21, 1857.   3-1-tf

Sonoma County Journal
September 25, 1857

S. H. WAGENER & CO.,
dealer in
DRUGS & MEDICINES,
Books and Stationery, &c.
Physicians Prescriptions carefully put up
Phenix Block, Main st.,
PETALUMA.   [8-tf

Sonoma County Journal
August 10, 1860

NOTICE
We have this day sold to Mr. F. T. Maynard our entire stock of Drugs, Medicines, Books, and Garden Seeds, and cordially recommend him to our customers.
           S. H. WAGENER & CO.   Petaluma, April 22, 1861
Referring to the above, the undersigned would respectfully solicit a continuance of the patronage of the late firm of S. H. Wagener & Co., and from his long experience as a Druggist and Dispensing Apothecary he hopes to give satisfaction to all.   F. T. MAYNARD   April 30, 1861

Petaluma Argus
July 16, 1861

- **F. T. Maynard & Co.** (Frank T. Maynard & Henry L. Hoyer, his brother-in-law)
- 36 Main Street, south end of Phœnix Block; successor to S. H. Wagener & Co.
- 79 Main Street 1876-78; 13 Main St. (aka 805 and 171 Main) by 1885.
- April 22, 1861 – 1898; store then run by F. T. Maynard's son, Harry Maynard—see pp.152-3

Petaluma's Emmett Rifles, an all-Irish company mustered into the California National Guard.
The unit stands in front of Frank T. Maynard's drug store in the Phœnix Block, 1862.
Courtesy, Sonoma County Library

F. T. MAYNARD & CO.,
DRUGGISTS & APOTHECARIES
Main Street, Petaluma.

IMPORTERS AND RETAILERS OF

DRUGS, MEDICINES,
SPONGES, CORKS, SPICES,
....PURE....
WINES and BRANDIES,
....PERFUMES....

Fine Toilet Goods, and Landreth's Garden Seeds.

We keep the very best of everything in our line, purchased from first hands in the Atlantic cities. All goods leaving our counter are neatly put up and properly labeled. Owning our business premises and doing our own work enables us to sell at the lowest possible rates. We have recently reduced the price of our Fluid Extract Sarsaparilla in quart bottles from $1 50 to $1, and Citrate Magnesia from 50 cents to 10 cents per bottle. 28-3m

F. T. MAYNARD.................H. L. HOYER.

Petaluma Courier
October 1, 1870

"In Medicine quality is of the first importance"

F. T. MAYNARD,
DRUGGIST AND APOTHECARY,
79 MAIN STREET, - - - PETALUMA

IMPORTER AND RETAILER OF

SELECT DRUGS, MEDICINES,
CHOICE PERFUMERY,
TOILET GOODS,
SPONGES,
SHOULDER BRACES,
TRUSSES,
COMBS,
PATENT MEDICINES,
BRUSHES,
GARDEN SEEDS,
WINES,
BRANDIES,
WHISKIES,
ETC., ETC., ETC.,

ALL OF WHICH ARE BOUGHT FROM FIRST hands and sold at the lowest price. 4 tf

Petaluma Argus
October 26, 1876

Frank Turner Maynard (1823-98)
Photo taken circa 1870
ex Frank Sternad collection

PET-D-23
F. T. MAYNARD
DRUGGIST
eagle/mortar & pestle/wreath
PETALUMA, CAL.
Aqua square
7 3/8 inches tall
Base: W T & CO
Helmut & DeAnna Jordt collection

PET-D-24
F. T. MAYNARD
PETALUMA, CAL
Clear square
3 ½ inches tall
Base: W T & CO 1
Helmut & DeAnna Jordt collection

PET-D-25
F.T. MAYNARD
PETALUMA
Teal green oval
Tooled top
6 5/8 inches Tall
Base: W T & CO   A C USA
Helm & DeAnna Jordt collection

PET-D-26

F. T. MAYNARD
PETALUMA
Clear rectangular
Tooled top
3 1/2 inches tall
4 1/4 inches tall
4 5/16 inches tall
Base: W. T. & CO.
Dan Brown collection

PET-D-27

F. T. MAYNARD
PETALUMA
Clear rectangular
Tooled top
4 1/8 inches tall
Base: U.S.A. PAT. DEC. 11, 1894
Dan Brown collection

PET-D-28

F. T. MAYNARD
PETALUMA, CAL.
Clear oval
Tooled top
3 ½ inches tall
4 1/4 inches tall
4 5/16 inches tall
Base: W. T. & CO.
Dan Brown collection

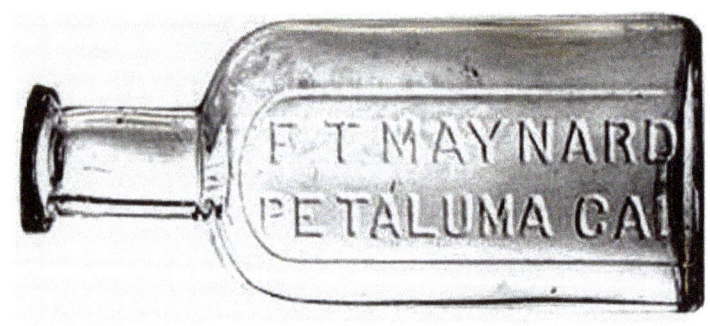

PET-D-28A

F. T. MAYNARD
PETALUMA, CAL.
Aqua oval
Applied top
4 1/4 inches tall
Base: W. T. & CO.
ex Frank Sternad collection

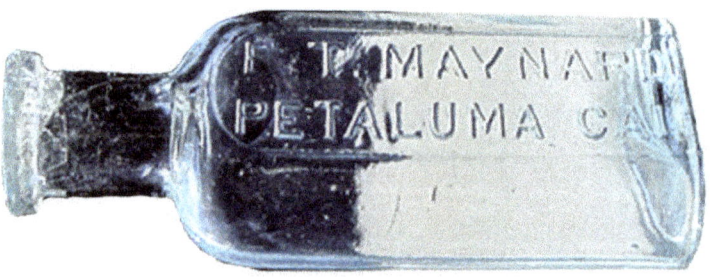

PET-D- 29
F. T. MAYNARD
PETALUMA, CAL.
Aqua square
Tooled top
4 3/4 inches tall
Base: W T & CO T
6 5/8 inches tall
Base: A
Helm & DeAnna Jordt collection
5 3/4 inches tall
Base: 2
Dan Brown bottle shown

PET – D- 30
F. T. MAYNARD
mortar & pestle
DRUGGIST
FTM (monogram)
PETALUMA, CAL.
Clear rectangular
Tooled top
5 1/4 inches tall
Base: *** A U.S.A. PAT Dec. 11, 1894
Dan Brown collection

PET-D-30A
F. T. MAYNARD
DRUGGIST
PETALUMA, CAL.
Clear medicine glass
1 7/8 inches tall
Base: N
Dan Brown collection

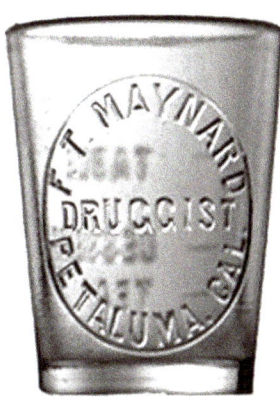

PET-D-31
    mortar & pestle
    F. T. MAYNARD/
    DRUGGIST/
    PETALUMA/
    CAL (in double lined garter)
    FTM (monogram in center)
    Aqua or clear square
    Tooled top
    5 inches tall
    Base: 8
    Dan Brown collection
    5 1/4 inches tall
    Base: W T & CO C
    Helmut & DeAnna Jordt collection

PET- D-32
    mortar & pestle
    F. T. MAYNARD/
    DRUGGIST/
    PETALUMA/
    CAL (on double lined garter)
    FTM (monogram in center)
    Clear oval
    Tooled top
    5 inches tall
    ex Frank Sternad collection

PET-D-33
F. T. MAYNARD
DRUGGIST
eagle/mortar & pestle/wreath/shield
PETALUMA, CAL.
Aqua or clear oval
Tooled top
5 inches tall
Base: W T & CO V
6 5/8 inches tall
Base: 4
Helmut & DeAnna Jordt collection

6 3/4 inches tall
Base: 4
Dan Brown bottle shown

PET – D-34
MAYNARD'S
PHARMACY
PETALUMA (in circle)
Clear seal square
Tooled top
5 inches tall
5 ½ inches tall
Dan Brown collection

5 5/8 inches tall
Base: S B W
Merle Avila collection

PET-D-35
    F. T. MAYNARD
    DRUGGIST
    PETALUMA, CAL.
    Aqua citrate of magnesia
    Tooled top
    7 1/8 inches tall
    Base: W T & CO 5 U.S.A.
    Rick Siri collection

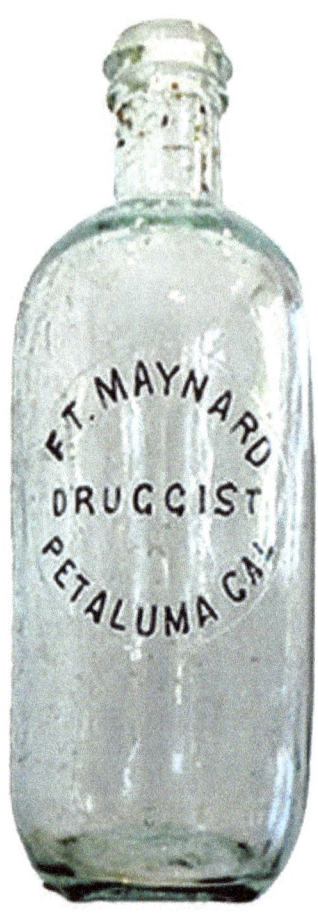

PET-D-36
    F.T. MAYNARD
    mortar & pestle
    PETALUMA
    Clear round
    Tooled top
    3 7/8 inches tall
    Helmut & DeAnna Jordt collection

    7 Inches tall
    Merle Avila collection

    See page *ix*

PET-D-38
F. T. MAYNARD
mortar & pestle
DRUGGIST
FTM (monogram)
PETALUMA, CAL.
Clear square
Tooled top
5 inches tall
Helmut & DeAnna Jordt collection

Notice.

WE have this day sold to Mr. F. T. MAYNARD our entire stock of Drugs, Medicines, Books and Garden Seeds, and cordially recommend him to our customers.

S. H. WAGENER, & CO.
Petaluma, April 22, 1861.

REFERRING to the above, the undersigned would respectfully solicit a continuance of the patronage of the late firm of S. H. WAGENER & Co., and from his long experience as a Druggist and Dispensing Apothecary, he hopes to give satisfaction to all.

F. T. MAYNARD.
Petaluma, April 30, 1861.   12-tf

Petaluma Argus
July 16, 1861

DIED.

MAYNARD—In Petaluma, Cal., August 20, 1898, Frank Turner Maynard, husband of Mary A. and father of Harry H. Maynard, Mrs. Eva E. Fairbanks and Mrs. Grace R. Nelson, a native of Lyme, Connecticut, aged 75 years.

The funeral will take place from the late residence on Liberty street Tuesday at 10 A. M. Interment Cypress Hill cemetery.

Petaluma Daily Courier
August 20, 1898

- **Harry Hoyer Maynard** (lived 1861-1933)
- 805 Main Street, Maynard's Drug Store
- 1898 – August 31, 1904; business sold to Dilberger & Lynn
- Maynard sold building and lot March 1905 to Mrs. Eva Fairbanks

DO YOU WANT $500.00

Or any part thereof. If so buy your drugs where every 10-cent purchase gives you an opportunity to get part of this sum which is to be

Given Away February 22d at

H. H. MAYNARD'S

Petaluma Argus-Courier
January 13, 1902

ONLY 1 DAYS TO WAIT

The date of the distribution of the $500.00 in eight big gifts at this store, February 22, is drawing near. Got any tickets yet? Every 10c purchase gets one. The more you have the more chance you have to secure one or more of the big gifts.

H. H. MAYNARD'S

Petaluma Argus-Courier
February 21, 1902

THE LAKEVILLE TRAGEDY.

Harry Maynard Arraigned for the Shooting of Winnie Gossage.

The Story of a Remarkable Hatred Told by the Prosecuting Attorney.

SANTA ROSA, CAL. March 10.—The trial of Harry Maynard for the shooting of Winnie Gossage is occupying the attention of Judge Dougherty and a jury in the Superior Court. From the opening statement of Prosecuting Attorney T. J. Butts and the evidence of the witnesses for the prosecution a remarkable story of deep hatred and attempted vengeance is adduced.

Ed Phelps, who was foreman of Senator Fair's big ranch near Lakeville at the time of the shooting in December last, became involved in a quarrel with an ex-employe of the ranch named Collins. The latter, since leaving the ranch, had been keeping a saloon at Lakeville and being a big, husky fellow had nothing to fear from a fair fight with either Phelps or Maynard. Maynard was a warm friend of Phelps and conceived the idea of going down to the ranch to assist Phelps either in making peace or whipping Collins. Not having proven a shining success as a fighter in the numerous rows he had engaged in about Petaluma, he induced Winnie Gossage to go along on the pretext of taking medicine to a sick friend. Gossage is a well-built, active young man who, though very good-natured when sober, is easily induced to fight after imbibing a few drinks, and the theory of the prosecution is that Maynard expected to get Collins into a row and, with the assistance of Gossage, administer a severe beating to him.

They arrived at the Collins saloon about midnight armed with a Winchester rifle, a revolver and a pair of brass knuckles. Collins was aroused and after some bluster on the part of Maynard consented to go with his visitors to see Phelps. The three men entered the buggy and Collins and Gossage soon began to quarrel. According to the testimony Maynard tried to steal Collins' revolver from his pocket during the row and Collins, becoming alarmed, jumped from the rig and disappeared in the darkness.

Maynard, so the prosecution declares, seeing that his prey had escaped was filled with rage at both Gossage and Collins, and in his drunken madness conceived the idea of killing Gossage and throwing the blame on Collins. Gossage testifies that he had alighted from the buggy to open a gate and was standing near the fore wheel when he saw a blinding flash come from the buggy and fell to the ground unconscious from a rifle ball through the chest.

It is said that Maynard then turned the horse loose, and leaving his victim to his fate, struck across the fields for home. The wounded man, after lying for three hours where he had fallen, managed to reach a barn near by, where he was discovered the next morning.

Dr. Gossage of Petaluma, a brother of the wounded man, says that Maynard told him that the buggy was surrounded by a band of armed men, who did the shooting, conveying the impression that Collins was responsible, and the District Attorney declared in the courtroom to-day that had Gossage been killed that night it would be Collins and not Maynard who would now be on trial.

San Francisco Call
March 11, 1896

PET-D-39

HARRY H. MAYNARD
DRUGGIST
805 MAIN ST. PETALUMA, CAL.
Clear rectangular
Tooled top
5 inches tall
Dan Brown collection

Harry H. Maynard parked in front of his store at 805 Main St., circa 1900
ex Frank Sternad collection

- **Dilberger & Lynn** (Frederick C. Dilberger & C. Walter Lynn)
- The Maynard Pharmacy, Deutsche Apotheke, 805 Main Street
- Purchased from Harry H. Maynard; sold to Cyrus Young (see page 165)
- August 31, 1904 – January 3, 1905

SALE OF MAYNARD'S DRUG STORE PENDING

On Wednesday, negotiations were pending for the sale of H. H. Maynard's pioneer drug store to Fred C. Dilberger, a prominent young druggist of Oakland, and C. W. Lynn, a prominent capitalist of that city and the future father-in-law of Mr. Dilberger. The sale was practically closed on Wednesday, save for formal transfer, and will be consummated on Wednesday evening.

Petaluma Argus-Courier
August 31, 1904

Petaluma Argus-Courier
September 21, 1904

COMPANY INCORPORATES

Articles of incorporation of the Dilberger & Lynn Drug Company of Petaluma were filed with the county clerk today. The company is formed with a ten-thousand-dollar capital stock of a par value of one dollar, and five dollars have been subscribed of that amount. A general mercantile, manufacturing and commission business will be conducted, real estate purchased and stock of corporations secured. The directors are C. Walter Lynn, Linnie A. Linn and Boyden Linn of Oakland, and Ethel B. Dilberger and Frederick C. Dilberger of Petaluma.

Santa Rosa Republican
November 18, 1904

TO THE PUBLIC

We desire to announce that we purchased the drug store formerly owned by Harry H Maynard and will continue the business at the same location. The store will be known as

"The Maynard Pharmacy."

After remodeling we will have one of the Finest Appointed and Best Stocked Drug Store north of San Francisco. We will conduct the business in an up-to-date manner. Our PRICES will be right. The utmost courtesy and kindness will be extended to all.

We pay PARTICULAR attention to the WANTS and COMFORTS of our LADY PATRONS. Our aim will always be to please. If we haven't what you want we will get it for you.

Free delivery. Phone Red 322. Telephone orders promptly attended to. Prescriptions and domestic receipts carefully compounded.

Inviting your patronage, we are yours for quality in drugs.

DILBERGER & LYNN.

Petaluma Courier
September 7, 1904

WHO FILLS YOUR PRESCRIPTIONS?

In soliciting your trade for our Prescription Department we will state that this branch of the business is at all times in charge of a First Class Registered Pharmacist. Mr. C. H. Young, our prescription man has always given special attention to the art of dispensing. This gives our patrons confidence and the assurance that all prescriptions and domestic receipts will always be correctly and scientifically compounded. Bring in your Prescriptions, we use only the purest drugs, also the utmost caution in putting them up, and our prices will always be the lowest.

Dilberger & Lynn, Props.

Phone Red 322.   THE MAYNARD PHARMACY.   Free Prompt Delivery.

N. B.--Mr. Fred C. Dilberger, junior member of our firm and manager will at all times be in our store to personally look after the wants and comforts of our patrons

Petaluma Argus-Courier
September 19, 1904

F. DILBERGER SELLS OUT

An important deal was consummated on Tuesday when Dilberger & Lynn sold The Maynard Pharmacy to Cyrus Young, who has had charge of the prescription department.

The firm was doing a splendid business and Mr. Dilberger was loathe to sell, but his father-in-law, Mr. Lynn, desired very earnestly to have Mr. Dilberger assume a half interest in his extensive mining business, which will occupy all of his time.

And besides, Mr. & Mrs. Lynn desired to have their only daughter, Mrs. Dilberger, near them and they could not move to Petaluma for business reasons. So, they have purchased a beautiful home adjoining their own which they are furnishing as a gift to Mr. & Mrs. Dilberger.

Mr. Young begins business under the brightest auspices and will no doubt receive a liberal share of trade.

Santa Rosa Republican
January 3, 1905

PETALUMA – JUNE 1905

Looking south on Main Street from Washington. Derby Block at right.

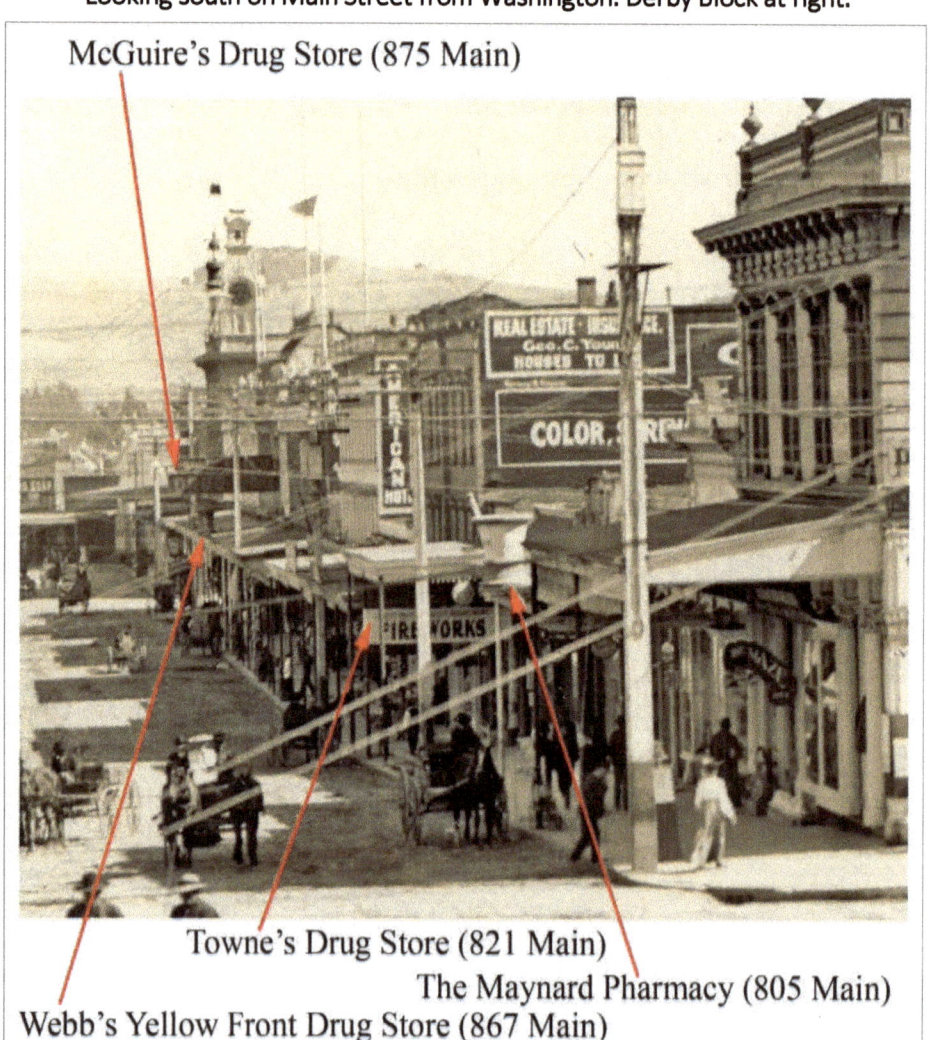

Photo by Walter Towne

- **Dean & Young** (Louis Dean & Cyrus H. Young)
- The Maynard Pharmacy, 805 Main St.
- January 3 – June 15, 1905 (see page 165)

TAKE A TONIC!

A good sensible Tonic that will sharpen your appetite and put new go in your nerves and muscles.

PORT WINE AND IRON

A nerve tonic, blood builder and delightful appetizer. Put up in pints, 50c; quarts, 75c.

The Maynard Pharmacy

Deutsche Apotheke.
Free Prompt Delivery.
Tel. Red 322.
Dean & Young, Props.

Petaluma Daily Courier
February 17, 1905

Of having your prescriptions filled here. No matter how simple it may be, it is filled by an experienced registered pharmacist with accuracy. Only the purest drugs are used by us in compounding prescriptions—that means quality. Our prices are the lowest that can be charged for pure, fresh drugs—that means full value for every cent you spend.

Dean & Young
Props.
Free Prompt Delivery.
Phone Red 322

The Maynard Pharmacy

Petaluma Argus-Courier
May 5, 1905

- **Thomas McGuire** (lived 1840-1902)
- First store was on east of side Main, opp. American Hotel, then to Hinshaw's Bldg. above Washington in 1873. McGuire moved to 44 (aka 819) Main by 1882; 875 Main by 1896.
- April 1872 – 1902 (Thomas McGuire died Aug. 26, 1902, succeeded by his son Thomas T.)
- McGuire's Drug Store (Thomas Talbott McGuire, U.C. Graduate in Pharmacy--Ph.G.): 875 Main (aka 105 Main). 1902 – April 1914. Also see page 156; sold to Warren Geary.

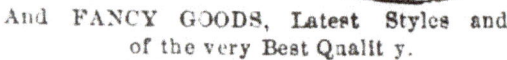

Petaluma Weekly Argus
September 6, 1872

Petaluma Weekly Argus
September 18, 1874

Petaluma Argus-Courier
December 12, 1882

ELEGANT.—Our popular druggist, Thomas McGuire, has added to the many attractions of his store a large and elegant glass show case which was made in Cleveland, Ohio, whence it was shipped by steamer to Chicago, and thence by rail to San Francisco. It is eight feet long, two feet three inches wide and four feet high, with an oval cover, and is much the finest piece of furniture of the kind that can be found in this part of the State. It is filled with a good many dollars worth of toilet articles.

Petaluma Weekly Argus
August 6, 1875

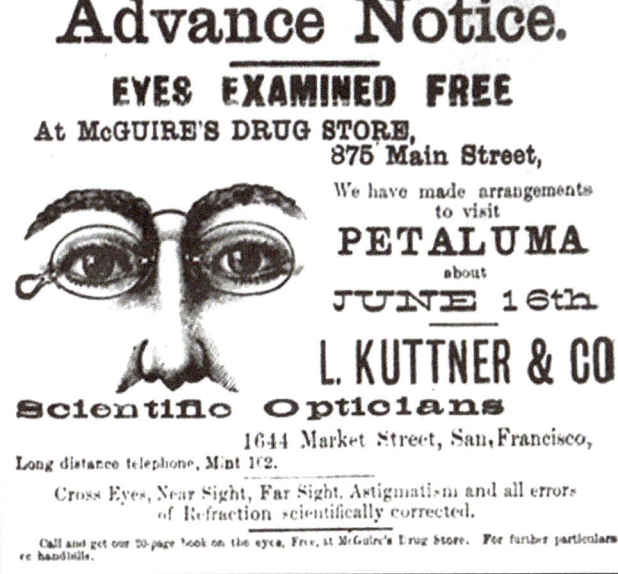

Petaluma Argus-Courier
April 15, 1896

They Are Going Fast!

You had better come around as soon as possible and look over our

CHRISTMAS GOODS

We may have just the thing you want. No trouble to show goods.

McGuire's Pharmacy.
ONLY REGISTERED CLERKS EMPLOYED.

Petaluma Argus-Courier
December 15, 1902

Jot it Down.

McGuire's Tooth Ache Drops Stop the Ache

Jot That Down

And the next time you have the Toothache, Try

McGuire's Toothache Drops

Guaranteed and sold only at

McGuire's Pharmacy

875 Main Street.

Petaluma Argus
October 19, 1903

Perfumes Free this Week—

at McGUIRE'S

All this week we will sell our 50 cent extracts for 35c — we have all the leading odors and invite your attention.

——— SPECIAL NOTICE ———

To the first forty ladies bringing this ad to our store we will give absolutely free a 25c bottle of Society Le Grand the new perfume for which we are exclusive agents for Petaluma.

THIS OFFER IS FOR LADIES ONLY— and there are only forty bottles to be given away.

McGuire's Drug Store

Petaluma's Independent Drug Store under the personal supervision of Thos. McGuire, P. H. G.

THE STORE THAT SAVES YOU MONEY

Petaluma Argus Courier
February 23, 1912

For Your Chickens Sake...

— WE QUOTE —

Epsom Salts, lb............4c
Feenegreuk Powder, lb.....15c
Mustard Powder, lb........13c
Capsicum Powder, lb.......14c
Flax Seed Powder, lb......10c
Sulphur Powder, lb........10c

McGuire's Drug Store
Whosesale and Retail
THE STORE THAT SAVES YOU MONEY

Petaluma Argus Courier
March 16, 1912

PET – D- 40
THOS. Mc GUIRE
DRUGGIST
PETALUMA, CAL.
Reverse: TABLE
 DESSERT
 TEA
Clear medicine glass
2 inches tall
Base: C
Helmut & DeAnna Jordt collection

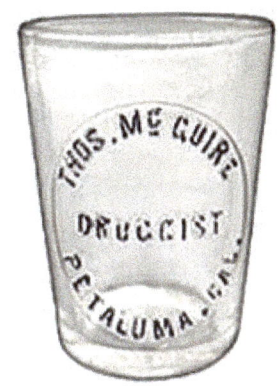

PET-D-41
McGUIRE
DRUGGIST
PETALUMA CAL.
Clear rectangular
Tooled top
4 1/4 inches tall
Merle Avila collection
4 3/16 inches tall
4 13/16 inches tall
5 3/8 inches tall
6 1/16 inches tall
6 13/16 inches tall
Base: *** A USA PAT. DEC. 11, 1894
Dan Brown collection

PET-D-42
Mc GUIRE
DRUGGIST
PETALUMA, CAL.
Clear rectangular
Tooled top
5 inches tall
Base: W T & CO F USA/
 PAT JAN 5, 1892
Helmut & DeAnna Jordt collection

PET-D-43
>   Mc GUIRE
>   DRUGGIST
>   PETALUMA. CAL.
>   Clear rectangular
>   5 3/8 inches tall
>   Base: W .T. & CO.
>   Merle Avila collection

PET-D -44
>   PURITY ACCURACY (in double circle)
>   OUR SUCCESS (inside double circle)
>   T. McGuire
>   Ph.G.
>   Petaluma, Cal.
>   Clear rectangular
>   Tooled top
>   4 13/16 inches tall
>   6 inches tall
>   Base: W T CO
>   Dan Brown collection

PET-D-45
>   T. McGuire
>   Ph.G.
>   Petaluma, Cal.
>   3 inches tall
>   Helmut & Deanna Jordt collection
>   3 1/4 inches tall
>   3 ½ inches tall
>   Base: *** B U.S.A.
>   Merle Avila collection

PET-D-46

Mc GUIRE
DRUGGIST
PETALUMA CAL.
Clear oval
Tooled top
4 ½ inches tall
5 1/8 inches tall
Base: W T CO CC
6 1/4 inches tall
Base: H
Helmut & DeAnna Jordt collection

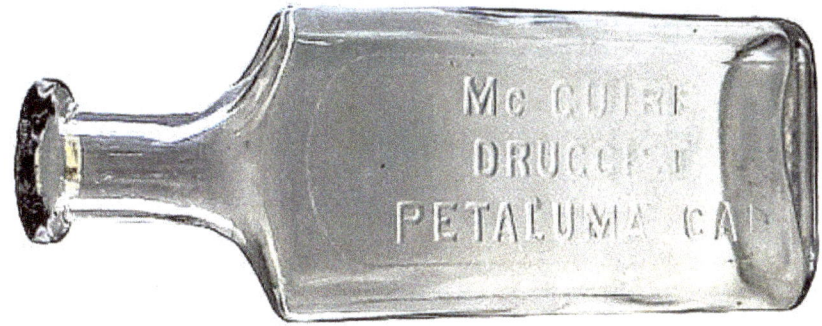

PET-D-47

T. Mc. GUIRE
DRUGGIST
PETALUMA, CAL.
Cobalt citrate of magnesia
Tooled top
7 inches tall
Base: W. T. & Co.
Eric McGuire collection

PET-D-48

T. Mc. GUIRE
DRUGGIST
PETALUMA, CAL.
Aqua citrate of magnesia
Tooled top
7 1/4 inches tall
Base: W T & CO 6 U.S.A.
Rick Siri collection

PET-D-49

Labeled clear oval
TEL. MAIN 8
McGuire's Pharmacy
875 MAIN ST.
PETALUMA, CAL.
ONLY LICENSED CLERKS EMPLOYED
4 ½ inches tall
Base: A
Merle Avila collection

Petaluma Daily Courier
August 27, 1902

THOMAS McGUIRE.

Thomas McGuire, the pioneer druggist of Petaluma, passed away at his residence, corner of Fifth and D streets, at 10:15 o'clock last evening.

Thomas McGuire was a native of Cincinnati, Ohio, and was sixty-two years old. When he was a boy his father was appointed consul to Edinborough, Scotland, and later to Rio Janeiro, Brazil. In the latter city Thomas and his brother, now deceased, attended a Portuguese school, and Thomas soon learned to talk Portuguese, Spanish and Italian, better than the natives. After his father's term as consul had expired he returned to the United States.

When he came to Petaluma he embarked in the drug business, and at the time of his death he was the oldest druggist in Petaluma. He had established himself here so long that his probity and business ability had built up one of the solid institutions of the city. He had no brothers nor sisters living, and his father and mother were both dead, the latter dying about a year ago.

- **Young Drug Co.** (Cyrus H. Young and Harry Herold)
- Acquired Dean & Young's *The Maynard Pharmacy*, 805 Main Street
- June 15, 1905 – August 15, 1909; sold to Charles W. Blackburn

Looking south on Main Street from Washington Street in 1908. An overhead sidewalk sign for Young Drug Company can be seen behind the power pole at right. The store's street address was changed by the City of Petaluma from 805 to 171 Main in early 1908.

Courtesy, Sonoma County Library

Petaluma Daily Courier
July 7, 1909

- **Young- Herold Drug Co.** (Cyrus H. Young and Harry Herold)
- Store #1 in Canepa Building, 163 Kentucky St., SW corner Washington St.
    August 15, 1909 – May 1, 1915
- Store #2 in new Gossage Building, No. 9 Lower Main St.
    October 30, 1909 – May 1, 1915

ANNOUNCEMENT

Harry Herold announces the purchase of C. H. Young's interest in the Young-Herold Drug Company. The firm in the future will be known as the HEROLD DRUG CO. Same dependable goods and prompt service from our two handy stores; Kentucky and Washington streets and No. 9 Lower Main street. Our quick delivery service which we have in the past featured is even going to be improved on for beginning today we are going to make it LIGHTNING DELIVERY—so when you want drugs in a hurry just Phone 10 or 36.

Petaluma Argus-Courier
May 1, 1915

PET-D-51

YOUNG-HEROLD DRUG CO.
PETALUMA, CAL.
Reverse: TABLE
　　　　 DESSERT
　　　　 TEA
Clear medicine glass
2 inches tall
Base: W. T. CO. A N U.S.A.
Helmut & DeAnna Jordt collection

- **Herold Drug Co.** (Harry Herold, his wife Ida C., and other partners, e.g. Raymond Momboisse 1929-38, Albert L. Battaglia 1942-55)
  - Store #1 in Canepa Building, SW corner Kentucky & Washington (renamed Herold Building when Harry Herold became owner in 1923): May 1, 1915 – 1964
  - Store #2 in Gossage Building, No. 9 Lower Main St.: May 1, 1915 – 1918
  - Harry Herold died suddenly in his store November 15, 1932 at age 50
  - Inventory sold to Tuttle Drug Co. in 1965.

Herold Drug Co. in Canepa Building, SW cor Kentucky and Washington Streets, circa 1918

Courtesy, Sonoma County Library

Labeled carton
BORACIC ACID
HEROLD DRUG CO.
DEPENDABLE DRUGGISTS
KENTUCKY & WASHINGTON STS. PETALUMA, CAL.
3 ½ inches tall
John Louder collection

- **Warren F. Geary**
  - Geary Pharmacy, 105 Main Street
  - Purchased McGuire's Drug Store; sold to Weck & Wood Drug Co.
  - April 1914 – March 1921

PET-D-52

GEARY PHARMACY
PETALUMA, CAL.
Reverse: TABLE
　　　　　DESSERT
　　　　　　TEA
Clear medicine glass
2 inches tall
Base: W. T. CO. A L U.S.A.

Helm & DeAnna Jordt collection

WARREN GEARY OFF FOR THE SOUTH

Warren Geary of this city left Sunday by auto for Los Angeles where he will remain a month acting as relief druggist for a friend, and on his return will have charge of the drug store of Cyrus Young at Redwood City during the absence of Mr. Young. Then he will leave for Arizona with a friend to prospect for precious stones.

Petaluma Argus-Courier
May 5, 1914

Petaluma Argus-Courier
June 6, 1921

- **Weck & Wood Drug Co.** (Charles E. Weck and Farley Eugene Wood)
- 105 Main Street
- Agents for Owl Drug Company products
- March 1921 – August 8, 1923
- Sold to Morris Drug Co. of Napa

LIFE AND DEATH

Often Times Depends Upon Your

Doctor and Druggist

WECK & WOOD Drug Co. Successors to Geary Pharmacy

The patient deserves the best results and so does your doctor, for prescriptions represent his skilled diagnosis. Prescriptions brought to us are filled with care and accuracy from the purest Drugs and Chemicals by Graduates in Pharmacy.

WECK & WOOD Drug Co. Successors to Geary Pharmacy

Phone, giving us the privilege of calling for your prescriptions and we will deliver them as soon as careful compounding will permit.

Free Delivery — Our prices are Right.

WE GIVE THE S. & H. GREEN TRADING STAMPS

 **Weck & Wood Drug Co.**
SUCCESSORS TO GEARY PHARMACY
Phone 8　　　105 Main St.　　　Petaluma

Petaluma Argus-Courier
April 6, 1921

- **Morris Drug Co.** (Harry H. Morris and Albert B. Scanlon)
- SW corner Main Street and Western Avenue (Masonic Hall, under the clock)
- Morris Drug Co. of Napa bought out Weck & Wood; Scanlon was put in charge and store was moved to Masonic Hall in January 1924.
- August 8, 1923 – February 5, 1931

To The Public—

We are now in "Our New Home" (under the Town Clock), corner Main and Western Ave., and although we are not entirely settled, are ready to serve you. We wish to announce that on and after Jan. 15th, all rebate tickets bearing the name "Weck & Wood" will be null and void, at our store; only those with the "Morris Drug Co." name appearing thereon, will be honored.

—

The Morris Drug Co.
A. B. SCANLON, RES. PROP.

S. W. corner Main and Western Ave., Phone 8   Petaluma

We give S. & H. Green Trading Stamps

Petaluma Argus Courier
January 3, 1924

- **O'Neill Drug Co.** (Fred Arthur O'Neill, lived 1882-1949)
- 9 Lower Main Street, Gossage Building (former Herold Drug Co.)
- 1918 – June 1, 1946
- Sold to William A. Perry Jr. who created a rear entrance to the store at 21 Fourth Street in 1951. Franchised agency for Rexall Drug Co. products

O'Neill Drug Co., 9 Lower Main St., circa 1940
Courtesy, Sonoma County Library

O'Neill Drug Co., enlarged to occupy entire ground floor of Gossage Building.
Main entrance at 9 Lower Main Street, *Rexall* signage, circa 1975.

SANTA ROSA

Druggist bottles in the downtown area became instantly rare on April 18, 1906

Looking north on Mendocino Ave. about 1900.
F.H. Newman's drugstore is visible under the witch's hat.

The same intersection, Fourth and Mendocino, after the "San Francisco" earthquake.
Duplex postcards published by Winslow S. Hosmer, Santa Rosa stationer

Santa Rosa sits on an alluvial plain above the Rodgers Creek-Hayward Fault system, and dangerously close to the San Andreas, two of Northern California's most seismically active. In the early morning of April 18, 1906 this combination proved fatal when the area was severely shaken by an estimated magnitude 7.8 earthquake. Eight blocks of the downtown area were reduced to rubble, and some 85 people died from trauma and the ensuing fire.

Fronting the devastated blocks were most of Santa Rosa's drugstores —sitting along Fourth Street from Wilson to D Street, and around Courthouse Square. Harry Newman's building on the NW corner of 4th and Mendocino collapsed, and Newman, who was sleeping in an apartment above, was killed. When it came to rebuilding, some businesses like Newman's and Michael Dignan's at 4th and B would not return. Others, like Wm. McK. Stewart's St. Rose Drug Store, still standing at at the corner of 4th and A, and those of Nels Juell, C.F. Keller, and Hahman Drug Company were entirely restored and operations resumed.

Fragile glass bottles, of course, failed to survive—their shards were among the tons of debris loaded onto flat cars and transported to dump sites. The custom lettered molds used to produce embossed bottles, however, were kept at glassworks like Whitall Tatum Co. in Millville, New Jersey; and new stocks of bottles could be ordered from existing plates and molds. In such cases, pre- and post-quake bottles are practically identical; but all Sonoma County druggist bottles from that period, for one reason or another, are now very scarce to rare in collectors' hands.

- **William Green Alban** (physician and druggist)
- Previously in Nevada City, Virginia City, NV and Sacramento
- January 25, 1860 – November 1861 (east side of plaza)

W. G. ALBAN, D. M'LAREN, T. A. THOMAS.
ALBAN, THOMAS & CO.,
[Successors to THOMPSON & BORRADAILE,]
Importers and Wholesale Dealers,
IN
DRUGS, MEDICINES, PAINTS,
Glass, Herbs, Extracts, Hops, Bird Seed, Chemicals, Quicksilver, Camphene, Burning Fluid, Polar, Sperm, Lard, Olive and Neatsfoot Oils, Turpentine, White Lead, Varnishes, Alcohol, Brushes, Combs, Perfumery, Soaps, Toilet Articles, &c., &c..
—Also—
Agents for JAYNE'S MEDICINES, and all the Extracts of Sarsaparilla and Genuine Medicines of the day. New Goods constantly arriving per Express and Clippers.
Prescriptions accurately prepared by experienced Apothecaries, as all engaged in the store have served severally from twelve to seventeen years in the business. Everything retailed at the lowest rates.
No. 161 J Street, corner of Sixth,
SACRAMENTO.   17f-1m

Sacramento Bee
February 22, 1857

Dr. W. G. ALBAN,
Druggist,
Apothecary and Chemist,
Having purchased the stock of Drugs and Medicines belonging to Dr. Hendley, is
NOW RECEIVING
One of the Best Selected Stocks of
DRUGS
Ever brought to Sonoma Co.,
Consisting of
English, French and American Drugs, Medicines and Chemicals,
Paints, Oils and Dye Stuffs;
BRUSHES OF ALL KINDS;
Extracts, Perfumery;
Shaving and Toilet SOAPS;
FANCY ARTICLES,
&C.,
Trusses, Supporters, and Instruments;
Bronzes, Gold Leaf and Artists' Paints;
GARDEN SEEDS
Of ALL KINDS, FRESH;
SHAKERS' HERBS & ROOTS;
Together with every article comprising the stock of a Druggist and Physician.
Santa Rosa, Sonoma Co., January 25, '60.

Sonoma Democrat
January 26, 1860

FORMER NEVADA RESIDENT DEAD

Mrs. Alice G. Cunningham, who spent her girlhood at Virginia City, died February 27 in Sacramento, according to reports received here. She was born in Nevada City, Calif., in 1854.

Mrs. Cunningham's father, Dr. William G. Alban, and his wife moved to Virginia City from Nevada City shortly after Mrs. Cunningham was born. There, he was a friend and physician to Mark Twain during the Comstock Lode boom.

Dr. Alban, finding Virginia City too rough a place to raise a family, moved later to Santa Rosa, then to Ukiah, Calif., eventually ending in Seattle, Wash.

Mrs. Cunningham was married in Ukiah to the late Thomas W. Cunningham.

Reno Gazette Journal
March 1, 1941

- **Bacci Drug Store**, John J. Bacci. Prop.
- 401 Mendocino Ave., NW cor. 5th Street (Upton Bldg.)
- August 5, 1935 – May 1943 (sold to Mario Corsiglia in March 1943)

BACCI PHARMACY TO CARRY FULL LINE OF DRUGS
City's Newest Drug Store to Feature Nyal Line of Products

Bacci's Drug Store, newest pharmacy of the North Bay district, already well known to scores of Santa Rosans who visited it last week which time it has been open for business, will hold its formal opening today in conjunction with the opening of the 405-Market next door.

The drug store, housed in the corner location, 401 Mendocino Avenue, in the Upton Building, is one of the most up- to- date pharmacies in the area. It has been completely remodeled, finished in an interior trim of cream and two pastel shades of green, with the new type of display cases, combination display and service units, to house the varied stock of the establishment.

The store is featuring the famous Nyal line of drugs and drug sundries, as well as other nationally advertised lines of merchandise.

John Bacci, son of A. Bacci, is owner of the business, and is well known in Santa Rosa, where he was educated and where he has worked since a boy in pharmacies. He is assisted in the store by Claude O. Howard, formerly of Oakland, registered pharmacist of 31 years' experience.

Press Democrat
August 9, 1935

Trade Token
Merle Avila
Collection

AN INVITATION

OUR NEW, MODERN DRUG STORE IS READY TO SERVE YOUR EVERY NEED . . . and WE CORDIALLY INVITE YOU TO VISIT US and SEE WHAT WE BELIEVE TO BE THE FINEST DRUG STORE IN SANTA ROSA

For The Ladies!
A corsage will be presented to every lady visiting our store today

A Drug Store of Friendly Service Carrying a Complete Line of Drugs - Sundries - and Nationally Known Drug and Toilet Preparations . . .

We specialize in prescription work—accurately compounded by registered Pharmacists!

Bacci Drug Store
Mendocino Avenue at Fifth Street
TELEPHONE 433

"We Will Never Knowingly Be Undersold"

Press Democrat
August 9, 1935

BACCI DRUG STORE TO OPEN FOUNTAIN

In keeping with progressive times, the Bacci Drug Store has recently installed a modern fountain at the corner of Mendocino and Fifth Street, which will be formally opened tomorrow. Sandwiches and fountain items will be served at all hours, and Golden State ice cream will be used exclusively.

Announcement is also made that on opening day between the hours of 12 and 3 p. m., free ice cream cones will be given to the children if accompanied by an adult.

Press Democrat
October 25, 1940

Press Democrat
October 25, 1940

MARIO'S PHARMACY IS THE NEW NAME OF DRUG STORE HERE

Announcement has just been made that the Bacci Drug Company store on Fifth Street and Mendocino Avenue will become known as Mario's Pharmacy.

The name is being changed by Mario Corsiglia, who purchased the store from the former owner approximately two months ago. During the short period that Corsiglia has owned the store, many new lines of drugs, sundries, wines and liquors have been added.

The prescription department has also been restocked with new preparations from leading pharmaceutical houses. Refrigeration equipment for the preservation of insulin, serums and other perishables has also been installed. The fountain will continue to serve breakfast and lunch dishes as well as short orders and all of the popular fountain food and confections.

Corsiglia has owned and operated drug stores in San Francisco for the past 22 years and is well known in the field.

Press Democrat
May 16, 1943

- **Baldwin Drug Company** (Warren Earle Baldwin and Frank C. Baldwin)
- 621 Fourth Street until December 1916, then moved to 507 Fourth St.; *The Rexall Store*
- April 1915 – April 22, 1926 ; purchased from Nels Juell, sold to Standard Drug Co.

NEW DRUG FIRM FOR SANTA ROSA

The Juell Drug Store at 621 Fourth Street was sold Saturday to W. E. Baldwin of Modesto, who takes over the active management of the business this week. The new firm name will be the Baldwin Drug Company. Dr. N. Juell, the retiring proprietor, will devote his time to his medical practice. His son, Rolfe Juell, will remain in the employ of the new firm.

The new firm has perfected arrangements whereby it will have the exclusive agency of the Rexall products in Santa Rosa. The new proprietor, although a young man, has been directly interested in the drug business for twenty-three years. For the last three years he has been at Modesto. He has secured apartments for himself and mother at the Upton.

Press Democrat - April 4, 1915

BALDWIN DRUG COMPANY

The *Rexall* Store

Has Moved to Its New Location

507 FOURTH ST.

Special for the Christmas Holidays

STATIONERY, PERFUMES, FRENCH IVORY

Call at once and make selections for the Holidays

BALDWIN DRUG COMPANY

The Rexall Store

Press Democrat - December 13, 1916

Walter Pancoast has arrived and will take charge of the Baldwin Drug Store, Mr. Baldwin having entered the service of the country.

Press Democrat - September 26, 1918

W. E. BALDWIN
F. C. BALDWIN

PHONE 237
621 FOURTH STREET

BALDWIN DRUG CO.

The *Rexall* Store

Letterhead, circa 1916

- **Standard Drug Company** (Harry D. Norton and Oliver R. Tuttle)
- 507 4th Street, *The Rexall Store*
- Successors to Baldwin Drug Co.; sold to Tomasco Drug Co.
- April 22, 1926 – July 28, 1941

SANTA ROSA MEN BUY PHARMACY HERE

The purchase of the Baldwin Drug Store, in a deal consummated within a few hours after it was first broached, was announced last night by H. D. Norton and O. R. Tuttle, well known Santa Rosa pharmacists. The new owners will take over the Baldwin Drug store this morning, and will rename it the Standard Drug Company.

Norton and Tuttle are both Santa Rosa boys and both learned rudiments of pharmacy work in the Hahman Drug Store here, later graduating from the University of California. Norton has experience in managerial capacity at Tacoma, Washington and Westwood, California, and operated his own business in Livingston, California, and spent time as a travelling salesman for a wholesale drug house.

Tuttle is the proprietor of the Exclusive Pharmacy whose business is to be merged with the new store. He worked two years in San Francisco in addition to his experience in Santa Rosa.

Press Democrat
April 22, 1926

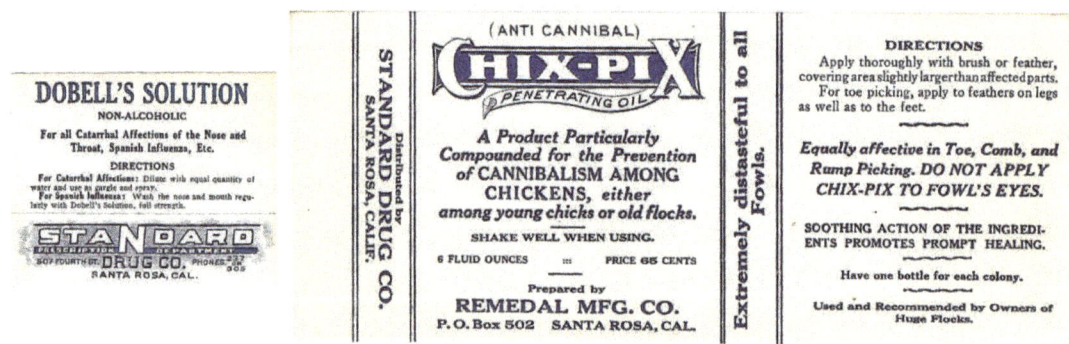

John Burton collection

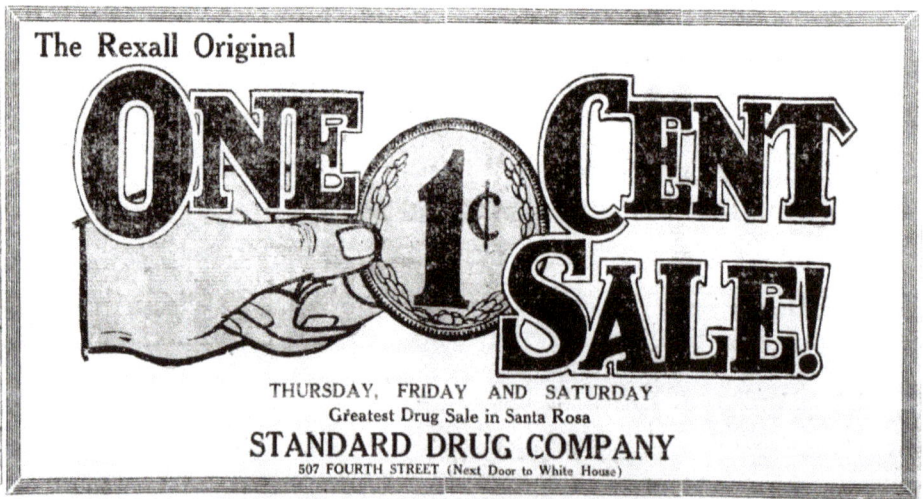

Press Democrat
April 14, 1927

- **Belden & Upp** (Benjamin C. Belden & Arthur Frank Upp)
- 443 4th Street in Occidental Hotel Building by 1908
- February 1907 – November 1919; sold to J. Walter Claypool (see page 188)
- Branch store in Guerneville: August 1910 – November 1915 (see page 34)

BELDEN & UPP, Prescription Druggists, Occidental Hotel Bldg., 443 Fourth St., Phone Main 24, Santa Rosa, Cal.

Portfolio of Santa Rosa and Vicinity. H.A. Darms, 1909, p.100

Occidental Hotel circa 1908. Belden & Upp's drugstore is left of Keegan Bros. at 443 4th St.

E-RU-SA CURES PILES or $50.00 PAID
No Mercury, Narcotics, or other poisons. United States
Dispensatory recommends every ingredient of E-RU-SA
False statements are criminal. Price $1.00 per box
FOR SALE by BELDEN & UPP
Occidental Hotel Building   Santa Rosa, Cal.

Press Democrat
October 11, 1908

Branch Store at Guerneville
CERTIFICATE OF PARTNERSHIP

We hereby state that we are partners transacting business at Guerneville, Sonoma County, in the State of California, under a designation not showing the names of the persons interested in such business, to wit; BELDEN & UPP DRUG COMPANY.

The names of the partners are: Arthur Frank Upp, residing at Santa Rosa; Benjamin C. Belden, residing at Santa Rosa; and Newton Allen Lark, residing at Guerneville.

Press Democrat
October 25, 1912

Benjamin C. Belden, retired Santa Rosa pharmacist, died early yesterday afternoon at his home in Cherry street following an extended illness. He had been in ill health for several years, and because of poor health was forced to retire from professional life five years ago.

Belden, a native of Cloverdale, was the son of the late C. C. Belden, pioneer Sonoma county business man, who died here two months ago. The younger Belden came to Santa Rosa with his parents at an early age and received his elementary education in Santa Rosa schools. After completing his college course in pharmacy he entered business here with Frank Newman. Following the earthquake in 1906, Belden became associated with Arthur T. Upp in the drug business, their first store being where the Crown Machine works now stands. Later they moved to Fourth street. After being in business here 15 years, Belden sold his equity in the drug store and went to San Francisco where he engaged in business.

Press Democrat
March 18, 1927

- **Elizabeth McG. Bennett** (nee Lizzie J. McGaughey)
- 547 Fourth Street, NW corner Mendocino (Doyle & Overton Bldg.)
- Purchased William C. Reed's drugstore; sold to W.B. Snodgrass
- May 5, 1887 – July 30, 1892 (also opened branch store in Sebastopol, see page 289)
- Proprietor of the Oroville Drug Store by February 1893.

San Francisco Call
March 10, 1895

Santa Rosa Pharmacy,
L. J. MCGAUGHEY.
A Complete Stock of Drugs.
AND PATENT MEDICINES.
TOILET ARTICLES, PERFUMES, SPONGES, ETC., ETC., ETC.
Physicians Prescriptions carefully compounded day or night.
Cor. Fourth and Mendocino Streets,
SANTA ROSA, CALIFORNIA.

Sonoma County and Russian River Illustrated, 1888

Among the little band of women pharmacists — practical, self-reliant, self-educated, skilled and enthusiastic—which we have within the borders of our State, one of the most prominent is Mrs. Elizabeth McGaughey Bennett, formerly of Santa Rosa, now of Oroville. Indeed so successful has this lady been in her chosen profession that her example cannot fail to be a help and encouragement to all women whose tastes and inclinations lead them to take up this branch of work and study.

Mrs. Bennett, who is one of a decidedly medical family, three members of which, a sister and two brothers, are successful physicians, began her business life on the foundation of an excellent education, as a teacher in the city schools of Winona, Minnesota, afterward teaching four years in Sonoma County, in this State. An enthusiastic student of chemistry even in her schoolgirl days, she early determined to become a practical pharmacist, and to that end entered the College of Pharmacy in this city, afterward working at the business for several years under the direct supervision of one of the best druggists on the coast.

At the expiration of this self-imposed season of probation Mrs. Bennett, with a fine courage which augured success, purchased a drugstore in Santa Rosa, burdening herself with a debt of $5500 borrowed money, and started in business for herself. "I was obliged to succeed," she says simply, "for I had to pay back that money with interest, and," with a sigh of satisfaction, "I did."

Mrs. Bennett has been particularly fortunate in her chosen calling, for the community in which she established herself was exceptionally free from anything like trade jealousy and narrow-mindedness and gave her the heartiest support, both moral and financial. She found few, if any, prejudices to combat, and the popularity of her store, and its owner, were unquestioned from the first.

A branch store in Sebastopol was soon started by this enterprising lady, and conducted by her for two years, at the expiration of which it was sold at a handsome profit. Later on Mrs. Bennett sold her large drugstore in Santa Rosa, and removed to Oroville, where she has built up a flourishing business, and identified herself with the best interests of the town.

Mrs. Elizabeth McG. Bennett.
[From a photograph.]

It is needless to say that this lady is a strong advocate of pharmacy as a profession for women, provided that they are equal to its requirements. "The business demands long hours, close confinement, much drudgery and constant study," she says, "and carries with it heavy responsibilities. Sex cuts little figure in the matter, but individuality makes all the difference in the world, and she who wishes to be successful must love the profession and devote to it her whole time and energy. I never argue the matter, but I think I am proving by my work that a drugstore is just the place for me, as it is for any woman whose tastes and education fit her for such a position; and I hope to see the time when every first-class pharmacy will employ at least one woman prescription clerk."

Mrs. McG. BENNETT IS IN CHARGE OF THE DRUG STORE

Mrs. Lizzie McG. Bennett, sister of attorney Francis McG. Martin of this city, is commuting to Sebastopol these days and taking charge of the T. R. Worth Drug Store during Mr. Worth's vacation. Mrs. Bennett is an experienced pharmacist of many years. She was the owner of a drugstore here for years and also in other cities, and at the time of the big fire she owned one in San Francisco. It is very convenient these days to be able to be a "sub" in any profession.

Press Democrat
July 9, 1918

- **James Alexander Bogle** (b. 1825 North Carolina)
- Bogle's Drug Store, Main Street (aka C St.) opposite Grand Hotel
- November 1874 – February 1875

Dr. Bogle, formerly of Chinese Camp in Tuolumne County and Visalia, called at his office on Tuesday. He has determined to settle in Santa Rosa. Dr. Bogle has a number of friends in Sonoma County. He is highly pleased with the place and surroundings.

October 17, 1874
Sonoma Democrat

NEW DRUG STORE

Dr. J. A. Bogle is fitting up a drugstore in Hood's Building on Main Street, adjoining Wise & Goldfish, and will keep on hand a full assortment of drugs, medicines and fancy articles.

November 21, 1874
Sonoma Democrat

DR. J. A. BOGLE,

PHYSICIAN AND SURGEON,

Having permanently located in Santa Rosa, Respectfully offers his professional services to the citizens of Santa Rosa and surrounding country, in the practice of Physic and Surgery

OFFICE IN

BOGLE'S DRUG STORE,

Main Street,

opposite the Grand Hotel, Santa Rosa.   no21 tf

Sonoma Democrat
November 28, 1874

MOVING BACK TO VISALIA

Dr. Bogle, who occupied a portion of George Hood's building on C street as a drug store, has moved to Visalia, Tulare County, and will open a drug store in that place.

Sonoma Democrat
February 27, 1875

- **W. E. Bryant**
- Plaza Drug Store, 6 Ridgway Block, next to Savings Bank, west side of plaza
- Successor to T.F. Hudson; sold to Oscar Morrison (page 238)
- March 3, 1880 – January 7, 1882

TO THE PUBLIC

I would respectably announce that my stock of drugs, chemicals, stationary, and all articles pertaining to the drug trade, is now complete. The drugs, chemicals, and liquors have been selected with care as to their medical strength and purity.

Also, the services of Mr. J. B. Westgate, who was formerly with Mr. T. F. Hudson, have been secured, who will have charge of dispensing physicians' prescriptions at all hours, day and night. His qualifications in that capacity are considered unquestionable. I would assure Mr. Hudson's patrons and others that it is my intention to carry on the drug and prescription business on a purely fair and square basis.

Respectfully, W. E. Bryant, late of Denver, successor to T. F. Hudson.
Note--The establishment hereafter will be known as the Plaza Drug Store.

Sonoma Democrat
March 20, 1880

Labeled inverted show globe
ALUMIN. & POTASS. SULFATE MERCK
John Burton collection

- **Butler-Winans Drug Co.** (Clarence Raymond Butler and Ray J. Winans)
- 443 Fourth Street - Occidental Hotel Bldg.
- Purchased Claypool's Pharmacy; merged with Mario's to form Medico Drug Co., Aug. 1944
- March 1, 1923 – July 1944 (Butler sold his share to Winans in September 1935; see p. 203)

Butler-Winans Drug Co. at 443 Fourth St., 1931
photo by Frank Patterson

BUTLER-WINANS BRANCHING OUT TO CLOVERDALE

Branching out in the drug business, Butler-Winans Drug Company has entered into partnership with William Oldham, licensed pharmacist here, in the purchase of Beaulieu Candy store in Cloverdale. Oldham is a partner in the Cloverdale drugstore, but the Santa Rosa store will remain under the control of Butler-Winans.

For the Cloverdale store, the complete agency for the United Cigar Stores Company has been taken and the work of installing their fixtures is under way. The candy store, soda fountain, newspaper and magazine agencies will also be run in connection with the drug store.

Oldham Drug Company will be the name of the store and Mr. and Mrs. William Oldham will move their residence to Cloverdale where Oldham will take charge.

Press Democrat
September 27, 1925

BUTLER TO CLOSE OUT INTEREST IN DRUG STORE HERE

The Butler-Winans Drug Company partnership, organized in March of 1923 will be dissolved next week, a notice of sale filed with the county clerk yesterday indicates.

This notice announces sale of all title and interest in the business by Clarence Ray Butler to Ray J. Winans, his partner. Butler has not decided as to his future course, he announced yesterday, but at least for the present he will remain in Santa Rosa.

Press Democrat
September 20, 1935

- **Medico Drug Company** (merger of Butler-Winans and Mario's Pharmacy)
- 401 Mendocino Avenue, NW corner 5th Street (former Mario's Pharmacy)
- August 1944 – 1983 (Incorporated December 10, 1948; 10 stores in 4 counties by 1951)

MEDICO DRUG SLATES GRAND OPENING HERE

Ray Winans to Manage Remodeled Store at Corner of Fifth and Mendocino for Firm

Santa Rosa's newest pharmacy—the Medico Drug Company—at Fifth street and Mendocino avenue, will observe its grand opening Monday under the management of Ray Winans, popular local pharmacist.

Owned and operated by a group of well-known druggists from Santa Rosa and other nearby communities, the new store is a combination of the Butler-Winans Fourth street store and the Mario pharmacy, the former Bacci pharmacy, at Fifth and Mendocino.

Owners of the store are Graham B. Mann and A. J. Franchetti of Santa Rosa; Arch R. Hill of Vallejo, Irvin J. Hill, Sebastopol; Joseph T. Cuneo of Healdsburg and Arch Reid of Vallejo.

The location of the former Mario pharmacy has been completely remodeled and doubled in size to accommodate the new Medico Drug Company's store. The prescription department especially has been greatly increased in size, with the prescription records and facilities of both the former stores incorporated in it.

On the staff, with Winans, will be P. Merrill, pharmacist who has been in Santa Rosa for years; Mrs. M. Franchetti, cosmetician; Charles Gould, who was associated with Winans in the Butler-Winans pharmacy, as salesman.

A fountain and lunch counter in the store is under lease to Jess Reynolds and under the management of Mrs. A. Anderson.

Winans, manager of the new store, has been in the business for years, operating his own store at 443 Fourth street.

Franchetti, one of the owners of the new business, too, is a veteran in the drug business here, having been the managing owner of the Tomasco pharmacy at Fourth and A streets for years.

MEDICO DRUG MANAGER—Ray Winans, popular Santa Rosa pharmacist, who will manage the enlarged drug store at the corner of Mendocino avenue and Fifth street for the Medico Drug Company. Winans was formerly a partner in the Butler-Winans pharmacy, recently purchased by the Medico Drug Company.

Press Democrat
August 20, 1944

DRUIDS ENLARGE BUILDING FOR MEDICO DRUG CO.

A building permit was issued this week to the Druid's Temple in an estimated amount of $1500 for a 20-by-47-foot addition on the west side of the existing building, according to C. J. Herbold, building and electrical inspector for the city. The owners will handle their own contracting.

The addition is to provide additional space for the Medico Drug Co., which will open at the location of the post office in a few weeks, when it moves to its new location on Broad street. The drug company now operates stores in several other communities and is opening in Cloverdale because of its recent growth in population.

Cloverdale Reveille
January 20, 1951

The Butler-Winans Drug Co. has combined with Mario's Pharmacy to form the MEDICO DRUG COMPANY, located at MENDOCINO AVE. and FIFTH ST. This event is to acquaint you with Santa Rosa's new, modern drug store ● The two managements express their appreciation for your patronage in the past and invite you to visit our new location where we will endeavor to serve as efficiently and courteously as in the past.

MEDICO DRUG CO.,
Ray J. Winans, Manager

Special!
FILMS FILMS
V127--V120
V620--V116
V616
SHOP EARLY to avoid disappointment. We have a limited quantity.

Special!
KLEENEX
200 Sheets 13¢
To celebrate our opening we offer this hard-to-get item.

Interior and exterior views of Santa Rosa's new and modern drug store at Mendocino Ave. and Fifth.

Press Democrat
August 20, 1944

FREE DELIVERY!

Let Our "Medicine Dropper" drop off your prescriptions 7 days a week until 9 p.m.

FREE   FREE

THREE LOCATIONS TO SERVE YOU

- **TOMASCO DRUG CO.** 4th & A Streets, Santa Rosa 545-0236
- **MEDICO DRUG CO.** 5th & Mendocino Ave. Santa Rosa 545-2190
- **MEDICO PRESCRIPTION CENTER** 1132 Montgomery Drive, Santa Rosa, Opposite Memorial Hospital 545-0290

Rx —PROMPT —ACCURATE —REASONABLE Prescription Service
We Gladly fill State Welfare Prescriptions

Press Democrat - January 30, 1966

Tomasco and Medico merged in 1975

Labeled pasteboard box:
PUMICE, N. F.
AN ABRASIVE
DISTRIBUTED BY
MEDICO DRUG CO. Inc.
425 SEBASTOPOL ROAD
SANTA ROSA, CALIF.
3 ½ inches tall
John Burton collection

Note: 425 Sebastopol Rd. was location of Medico Drug's warehouse facility, 1949-74.

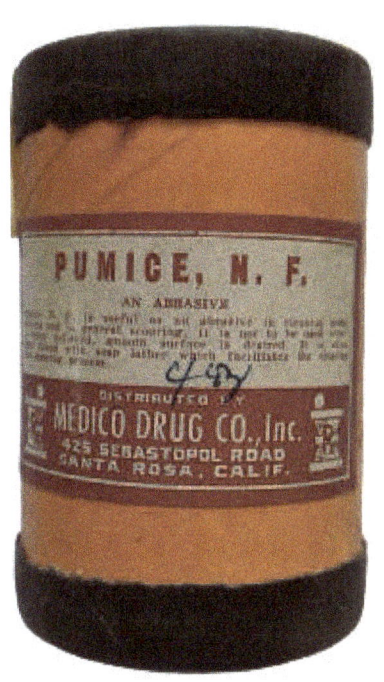

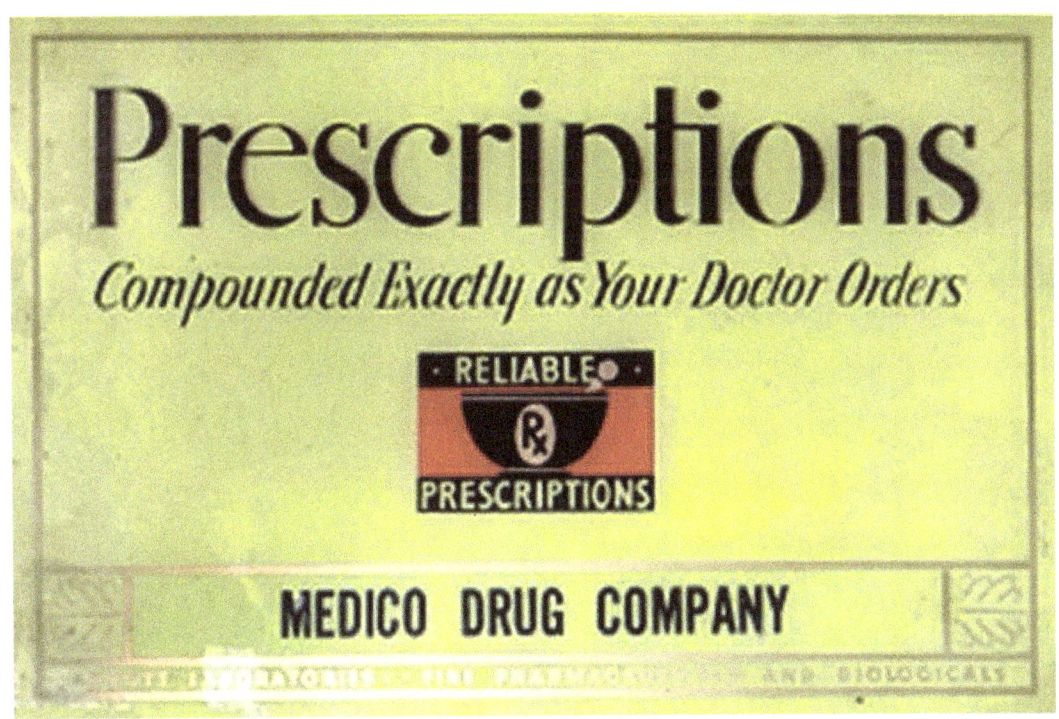

Glass sign provided druggists by Abbott Laboratories of Chicago
Courtesy Richard Siri

- **Claypool's Pharmacy** (Jeremiah Walter Claypool; pharmacy operated by Mrs. Mollie Claypool following her husband's death on February 15, 1921 at age 47)
- J.W. Claypool had previously been a partner in Hahman Drug Co., see page 210
- Purchased Belden & Upp's Drug Store at 443 4th Street; sold to Butler-Winans Drug Co.
- November 1919 – March 1, 1923

DONALD PERCY GOES TO CLAYPOOL DRUG STORE

Donald Percy who has been with G. M. Luttrell for a year or more, will take a position with J. W. Claypool in his drug store in the Occidental Hotel. Mr. Percy has a large circle of friends here and it will be good news to them to know he and family will remain here.

Press Democrat
February 1, 1920

Captain J. Walter Claypool, one of the best known residents of the county and who had many friends here, died Tuesday morning at the family home in Santa Rosa, after having made a brave fight for life.

He was a son of Mrs. Ellen Claypool and brother of Mrs. Jesse F. Thorsen of Lakeville; S. B. Claypool; Mrs. Ralph Welden, Misses Mildred, Alice, Lily and Carrie Claypool. His aged mother, who makes her home with Mrs. Thorsen at Lakeville is in a precarious condition having recently suffered two strokes of paralysis.

The deceased was born at Healdsburg, Aug. 13, 1873, his parents being the late Jeremiah Claypool, who died some years ago, and Mrs. Ellen Claypool, who resides with her daughter at Lakeville.

He is survived by his widow, who was formerly Miss Mollie Dearborn.

Petaluma Courier
February 17, 1921

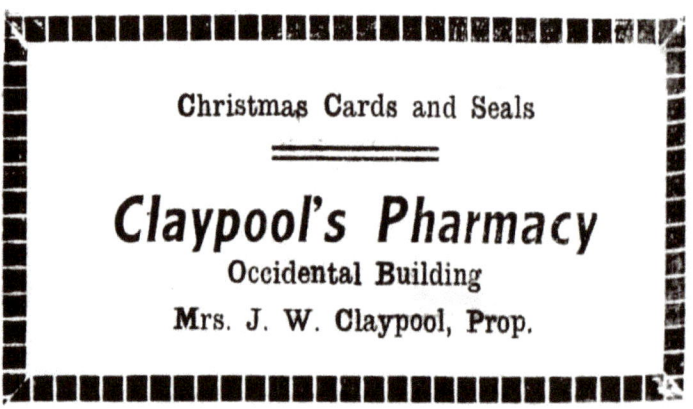

Santa Rosa Republican
December 17, 1921

PETALUMANS PURCHASE CLAYPOOL DRUG STORE

Mrs. Mollie T. Claypool, proprietor of the drug store on Fourth Street, has disposed of her interests to C.R. Butler and Ray Winans of Petaluma, who will take possession on March first.

Butler has been employed in the Tuttle and Squires Drug Store at Petaluma, and Winans has been employed by the Harry Herold Pharmacy of the same city. The business is to be conducted under the name of the Butler-Winans Drug Company.

Some years ago, the drugstore was purchased by Jerry W. Claypool from Belden and Upp. Since the death of Claypool, the store has been conducted by his widow.

Press Democrat
February 28, 1923

- **Harry S. Davis**
  - Model Drug Store, 401 4th St., NE corner A St.; purchased from Martin Muller (see p.237)
  - January 1902 – May 1904; sold to William McK. Stewart (see page 257)
  - Opened store at 518 5th St. after quake; sold to G. M. Luttrell in Oct. 1906 (see page 233)

THE MODEL DRUG STORE BOUGHT BY H. S. DAVIS

On Wednesday morning H. S. Davis, a well-known druggist who came here from Sacramento, entered into possession of the Model Drug Store on the corner of Fourth and A Streets which he purchased from Martin Muller. Mr. Davis is an experienced druggist and chemist and hopes to extend the business and get a good share of patronage.

Press Democrat
January 16, 1902

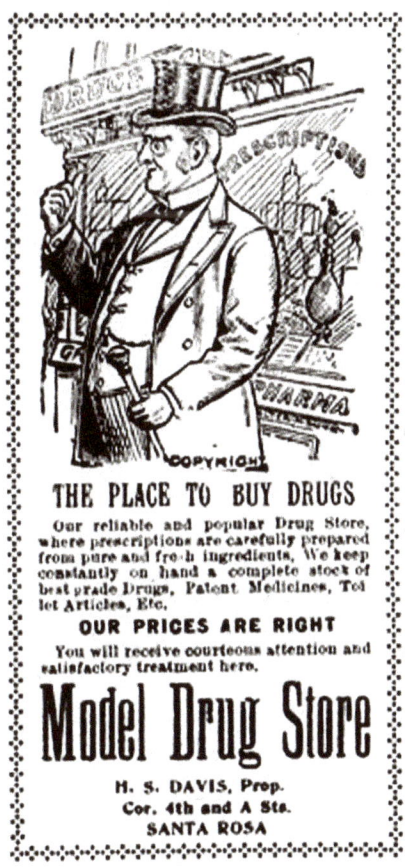

Press Democrat - May 3, 1902

STILL WORKING

We fill prescriptions written by ANY PHYSICIAN, correctly or NOT AT ALL
and we tell you honestly, we do NOT SUBSTITUTE. It's hard to buy
Drugs but we've done our best to get everything essential in prescription work.
H. S. DAVIS
PRESCRIPTION DRUGGIST – The place to buy drugs.
518 Fifth Street near Fire Department

Press Democrat - June 5, 1906

- **James B. Dean**
  - 503 Fifth Street: July 1908 – November 1910; successor to Charles F. Keller (see page 229)
  - 229 Fourth Street, Donovan Block, NW corner Washington: November 1910 – 1912

FILES PHARMACIST'S CERTIFICATE

In the office of the County Clerk Fred L. Wright on Thursday, J. B. Dean filed his pharmacist certificate for registration in Sonoma County.

Press Democrat
July 10, 1908

Press Democrat
July 30, 1908

J. B. DEAN MOVES HIS STORE TO 4th

J. B. Dean, who has conducted a drug store on Fifth Street for several years since he bought out C. F. Keller's business, has moved into a new location. He is now installed in the C. Donovan Building at Fourth and Washington Street. He will have a very attractive store, and will have it well equipped and stocked. Mr. Dean will undoubtedly be pleased with the new location.

Press Democrat
November 24, 1910

190

- **Michael Henry Dignan**
- Successor to Hill & Eberhard
- City Drug Store, 500 Fourth Street, SE corner B St.
- July 1887 – April 18, 1906

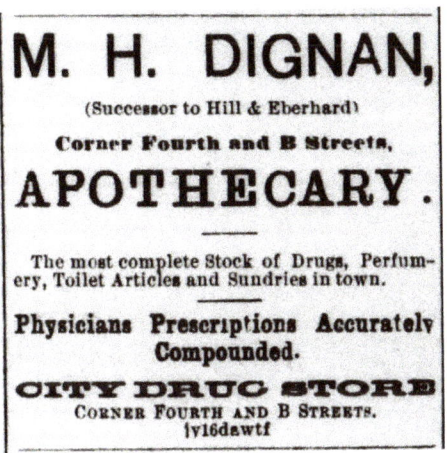

Sonoma Democrat
July 16, 1887

Press Democrat
March 9, 1898

Press Democrat
September 3, 1898

A WORD TO THE WISE

Pure and well compounded medicines prevent and cure illness and for that reason their preparation is the most important function of the druggist. Accordingly, we give to our prescription department the most careful attention.

Every prescription is compounded by an expert pharmacist, and we make it a special object to secure drugs of undoubted purity and efficacy. We also carry a full line of standard and reliable medicines; which experience has shown to be good things to have in the house.

M. H. DIGNAN   PRESCRIPTION DRUGGIST

Sonoma Democrat
June 21, 1895

SR-D-01

M. H. DIGNAN
PRESCRIPTION DRUGGIST
SANTA ROSA, CAL.
Clear rectangular
Tooled top
6 inches tall
2 3/4 inches tall
Base: *** F U. S. A. PAT JAN 5, 1892
Dan Brown collection

SR-D-02

M. H. DIGNAN
PRESCRIPTION
DRUGGIST
SANTA ROSA, CALIF.
Clear oval
Tooled top
3 inches tall
4 1/8 inches tall
Base: W. T. & CO. PAT. JAN. 1881 U. S. A.
5 inches tall
6 inches tall
Helmut & DeAnna Jordt collection

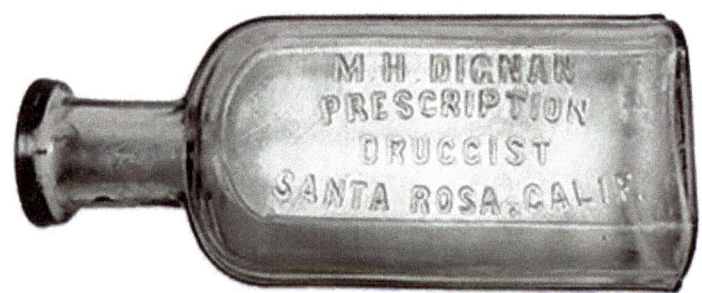

SR-D-03

M. H. DIGNAN
CHEMIST
SANTA ROSA, CAL.
Aqua rectangular panel
Tooled top
5 1/4 inches tall
Base: W. T. & CO. 1 USA
Dan Brown collection

Note: One of Dignan's clerks, Chester Allen Trudgen, age 21, was killed in the April 18, 1906 earthquake and fire. Newton A. Lark, also a drug clerk at the time, cut his hand to the bone trying to rescue Trudgen who was trapped under burning timbers, to no avail.

- **Dozier & Hall** (Linwood Dozier & Walter R. Hall)
- Successor to R.P. Smith – 449 Fourth Street, under Occidental Hotel
- December 1879 – July 1880
- Walter Hall, as surviving partner, sold to John W. Warboys in Sept. 1881 – see page 283

ANOTHER CHANGE

Linwood Dozier purchased the drug store lately owned by Dr. R. Press Smith Jr. on Monday last and will continue the business at the old stand. Mr. Dozier is an active, enterprising young man, and will doubtless meet with success.

Sonoma Democrat
December 20, 1879

STANDS THE TEST

Messrs. Dozier & Hall's imported Old Kentucky Bourbon has been tested by the best judges and pronounced superfine. They order it especially for medicinal purposes.

Sonoma Democrat
January 31, 1880

Dozier & Hall have erected a tasteful sign in front of their drug store and have put up a new awning.

Sonoma Democrat
January 31, 1880

CAMPHORATED or SAPONACEOUS TOOTH POWDER

Those teeth will continue to grow more and more tender and gradually decay and will in a few brief months subject you to the rack and torture of that dreadful instrument, the dentist's forceps. People who do not seem to realize the fact that there is a substance in nature within the reach of all which if applied to the teeth once a day will strengthen the gums, beautify and preserve the teeth, and if they are not too badly decayed will delay the evil day for years. Ask for Camphorated or Saponaceous Tooth Powder, prepared at Dozier & Hall's Pharmacy, Fourth Street, Santa Rosa.

Sonoma Democrat
January 24, 1880

ANOTHER CHANGE

Walter R. Hall has purchased the interest of his partner, Linwood Dozier, in their Drug Store, and will continue in the business on his own responsibility. In common with Walter's numerous friends we wish him unlimited and unbounded success.

Sonoma Democrat
July 3, 1880

DOZIER AND HINCKSON BODIES FOUND

The bodies of Linwood Dozier and his companion, Add. C. Hinckson, drowned by the upsetting of their boat, were found in the overflow above Sacramento City on May 6. Dozier's remains were taken to Rio Vista for interment.

Sonoma Democrat
May 15, 1886

- **James E. Ewing**
  - The Peoples Drug Store, 223 Exchange Avenue, next to Savings Bank of Santa Rosa
  - Purchased Carl G. Fischer's interest in R.B. Reedy & Co. in December 1897
  - Purchased Ray B. Reedy's interest in March 1898; sold to Nels Juell
  - December 24, 1897 – February 1902 (see pages 237, 247)

NEW DRUGGIST

Mr. J. E. Ewing of Healdsburg has purchased an interest in the Peoples Drug Store on Exchange Avenue and will hereafter be identified with that establishment. Mr. Ewing is a pharmacist of experience, having been for the past eight years engaged in that business in Healdsburg and prior to that time in San Francisco for seven years. With R. B. Reedy, the former manager of the store, the people may have assurances of good service and faithful attention.

Press Democrat
December 25, 1897

A WORD TO THE PUBLIC

The practice of Pharmacy is dangerous. We understand our calling. The accurate dispensing of Prescriptions with the best materials is a specialty of which we excel.

THE PEOPLES DRUG STORE

Press Democrat
January 26, 1898

PURCHASED DRUG STORE

The lights were out at the Peoples Drug Store on Exchange Avenue Monday evening and the door was locked. On the door was a notice to the effect that M. Prince had purchased the drug store [building].

Press Democrat
March 8, 1898

PEOPLES DRUG STORE

James E. Ewing of the firm of R. B. Reedy & Co., the Peoples Drug Store on Exchange Avenue, has purchased Reedy's interest in the business and is now sole proprietor of the store.

Press Democrat
March 9, 1898

James E. Ewing of the drug firm of R. B. Reedy & Co., Santa Rosa, has purchased Reedy's interest in the business and is now sole proprietor of the People's Drug Store. Mr. Ewing, who lately left Healdsburg to engage in business in Santa Rosa, has had many years' experience in his vocation as a druggist, and he has a first-class location in the County Seat. He will undoubtedly do a lucrative business. We wish him well.

Healdsburg Tribune, Enterprise, and Scimitar
March 17, 1898

The Peoples Drug Store

HAS A FULL LINE OF

Holiday Goods .

GLOVE BOXES,
HANDKERCHIEF BOXES,
COMBS, BRUSHES,
MIRRORS,
PERFUMES

223 Exchange Avenue, next to Savings Bank

Press Democrat
January 1, 1898

A Word

TO THE PUBLIC.

The practice of Pharmacy is dangerous. We understand our calling. The accurate dispensing of Prescriptions with the best materials is a specialty at which we excel.

The People's Drug Store
223 Exchange Avenue

Sonoma Democrat
January 12, 1898

- **Eugene Columbus Farmer** (lived 1878-1943)
  - Farmer's Drug Store; see page 224 for pre-quake partnership
  - 738 4th Street: Jan 1907–1908; 701 4th St. NE corner D St.: 1908–September 1911
  - 647 4th Street NW corner D St.: September 1911–1958
  - Eugene Farmer died in 1943; his wife operated store until sold to David T. Smith in 1958
  - Smith merged with Empire Drug in October 1971 to form Farmers-Empire Drug (see p. 203)

EUGENE FARMER
Prescription Druggist

738 Fourth Street
Next to Public Library

Free Delivery   Phone Red 2291

Press Democrat
May 7, 1907

EUGENE FARMER WILL HAVE ELEGANT STORE

Eugene C. Farmer, the druggist at the corner of Fourth and D streets, will have an elegant new store in the future. He has taken a lease on the corner store of the handsome new Manville Doyle building on the opposite corner to where he is now located. Mr. Farmer will arrange the interior in the most up-to-date and modern manner, and will add materially to his already large lines of toilet articles, drugs and the various things carried by persons in his line of business.

Santa Rosa Republican
August 28, 1911

When Minutes Count --- Call 50
FARMER'S DRUG STORE
PRESCRIPTION DRUGGISTS
On the Corner of 4th and D Sts.

We carry a complete stock of fresh, clean, up-to-date Pharmaceuticals, chemicals and biologics, ready for any emergency.

We Recommend That You CONSULT your PHYSICIAN and DENTIST More Frequently

May We Fill Your Next Prescription?
Free Delivery

Press Democrat
October 1937

SR-D-05

Labeled clear abm corker:
NET CONTENTS…FLD. OZS.
GLYCERIN
EUGENE C. FARMER
DRUGGIST
Fourth St. Cor. D   SANTA ROSA, CAL.
4 ½ Inches tall

Rick Siri collection

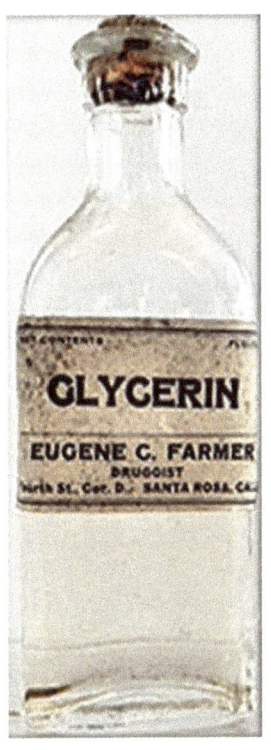

SR-D-06

Labeled green abm screw cap:
SPT. OF TURPENTINE, U.S.P.
Not for Medicinal Use
Net Contents…Fld. Ozs.
DISTRIBUTED BY
FARMER'S DRUG STORE
PRESCRIPTION DRUGGISTS
647 4th STREET   SANTA ROSA, CALIF.
Phone 50
5 Inches tall
Base: Illinois

John Louder collection

Labeled pasteboard carton:
Net Contents ...*4*... Avoir. Oz.
POWDERED ALUM
EUGENE C. FARMER
—DRUGGIST—
FOURTH STREET, Cor. D.   SANTA ROSA, CALIF.
PHONE 50

Labeled pasteboard carton:
CASSIA BUDS
Net Contents ...... Ozs.
EUGENE C. FARMER
DRUGGIST
Fourth Street, Cor. D.   SANTA ROSA, CALIF.
Phone 50

Richard Siri collection

Labeled pasteboard carton:
Flax Seed
Net Contents...Fld. Ozs.
EUGENE C. FARMER
—DRUGGIST—
FOURTH STREET Cor. D.   SANTA ROSA, CALIF.

James Arietta collection

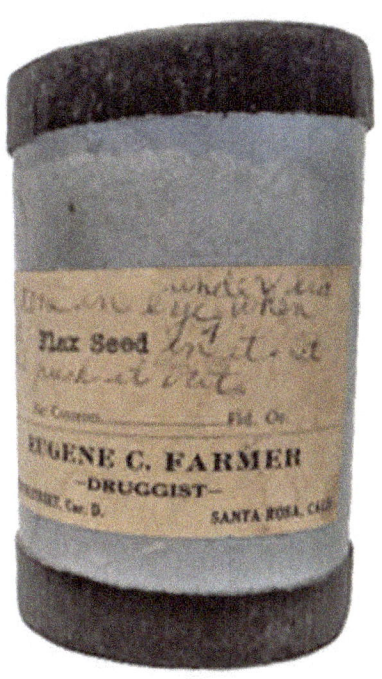

Farmer's Drug Store, NW corner Fourth & D Streets, 1941
Courtesy, Sonoma County Library

"PROGRESS" from 1870 to the present – a window display of vintage and modern pharmacy equipment and drugs, featuring photos of Farmer's Drug Store over the years.

Photo by Don Meacham, 1960
Courtesy, Sonoma County Library

- **Charles DeWitt Frazee**
- Pioneer Drug Store
- June 1869 – August 1887
- Main Street, two doors south of plaza: December 1872–1879
- 223 4th Street: January 1880 – September 1883
- 611 4th Street: 1884 – August 1887
- Sold to Richard J. Pye (see page 242)

C.D. Frazee was born in Rensselaer County, NY, October 20, 1828. He worked as a druggist in New York City and in St. Louis until 1851, New Orleans until 1854, then traveled west to Oregon and Siskiyou County, California where he engaged in mining. He returned to San Francisco in 1858, found employment in Petaluma 1865-68, and opened his Pioneer Drug Store in Santa Rosa in 1869. Charles D. Frazee died August 13, 1893 and is buried in the Santa Rosa Rural Cemetery.

C. D. FRAZEE,
Chemist & Apothecary,
MAIN STREET,

Two Doors south of the Plaza, Santa Rosa,

KEEPS CONSTANTLY ON HAND A FULL and carefully selected stock of Drugs, Medicines, Chemicals, Perfumery, Toilet Articles, Stationery, Pocket Cutlery, and Garden, Field and Flower Seeds.   de16se13 w

Sonoma Democrat
December 16, 1872

Signage for C.D. Frazee's 611 4th St. store is seen behind this 1884 fire company

SR-D-07

CDF (monogram)
C. D. FRAZEE
CHEMIST
SANTA ROSA
Clear oval
Tooled top
4 3/4 inches tall
5 3/4 inches tall
6 inches tall
Base: W. T. & CO. H
6 3/4 inches tall
John Burton collection

C.D. Frazee's embossed druggist bottles represent some of the earliest in Santa Rosa

C. D. FRAZEE
Heads the list as one of the early pioneer merchants of this city. He became established in the drug business on Main street in 1869 with a stock not worth to exceed $1800. As business began to make its way to Fourth street, Mr. Frazee also moved in the same direction, and in 1884 became established at 611 Fourth street, where with the aid of two clerks he still continues to dispense drugs to one of the largest prescription trades in the city. Most of his pharmaceutical goods, fluid extracts, tinctures, etc. are manufactured. Nothing but drugs of the purest quality are dealt in, and prescriptions receive the most careful attention.

Sonoma Democrat
January 8, 1887

- **Empire Drug Company** (Alvin J. Gambini, prop.)
- C. Raymond Butler was a non-invested partner; franchised Rexall Store starting in 1952
- 623 Fourth Street; sold to Healdsburg druggist Merle Bartel in February 1964.
- November 20, 1936 – October 1971
- Bartel merged with Farmer's Drug to form Farmers-Empire Drug at new location, 640 4th St.

ALVIN GAMBINI WILL OPEN NEW S.R. DRUG STORE

Further expansion in the downtown shopping district of Santa Rosa, was revealed today when Alvin Gambini, widely known local pharmacist, announced that he would open the Empire Drug Company here on or about November 1.

Gambini has taken a long term lease on the store at 623 Fourth street, vacated last week by the Redwood Market. The building is being revamped and modernized to house a modern up-to-date drug store, specializing in prescription service.

For the past ten years Gambini has been a member of the staff at the Rutherford Drug store here and is widely known throughout the Santa Rosa shopping area.

Under the proposed plan the Empire Drug Company will feature the entire line of the United Cigar Stores, which include cigars, cigarettes, specialities and liquors of all kinds. An exclusive franchise for the service has already been signed, it was said. No particular line of drugs will be featured, but the store will be stocked with all nationally-advertised drugs and household remedies.

Specially designed fixtures are now being constructed for the new store, and all the latest types of merchandising counters and stands are to be used.

Announcement of the personnel of the new store was not made.

Santa Rosa Republican
October 13, 1936

C. Raymond Butler

Services have been held for C. Raymond Butler, 89, who died Sunday at his Santa Rosa home.

A native of San Francisco, he lived in Sonoma County 60 years. He was a pharmacist and a partner in Tuttle's Drugs in Petaluma.

He was a veteran of World War I, and a member of American Legion's Theodore Roosevelt Post No. 21 and Barracks No. 21 of Veterans of World War I. He was an honorary life member of Knights of Columbus (Third Degree) and a member of St. Rose Roman Catholic Church.

He attended the Physicians and Surgeons College in San Francisco and received his pharmacist's license in 1920. In 1923 he bought the Claypool Drugstore on Fourth Street in Santa Rosa with a partner, Ray Wymans. He later sold his interest to Wymans and in 1936 he and Alvin Gambini opened the Empire Drug Co.

During World War II, Butler and his nephew, Lester Pometta, bought the Tuttle Drugstore in Petaluma. He retired from the drug business in 1946.

He is survived by his wife, Emily Butler, Santa Rosa, and sister, Bernice Mehl, San Francisco.

Eggen and Lance Mortuary was in charge of arrangements. Burial was at Calvary Catholic Cemetery.

Press Democrat
January 4, 1984

NEW DRUG STORE TO OPEN TODAY AT 623 FOURTH ST.

Another new business establishment will open its doors to the public in downtown Santa Rosa this morning. The latest addition to the communities growing business area is the Empire Drug Company, located at 623 Fourth Street, an up-to-date firm with an extensive and varied stock that will enter a strong bid for drugstore patronage.

Al Gambini, popular young Santa Rosa pharmacist for ten years was connected with Rutherford's Drug Store as the proprietor.

Completely remodeled, modernly decorated, and equipped with the latest drug store display fixtures, the interior of the Empire Drug companies presents both an attractive appearance and an exceptionally convenient arrangement for shoppers. Among the many innovations is a glass enclosed prescription department in the rear center of the store where prescriptions are filled within sight of the patrons rather than in some hidden rear room.

A well-stocked liquor department is included in the store with popularly priced brands being featured. Sundries of all kinds are included in the stock, with an exceptionally large supply of novelties and gifts for the Christmas season.

Cosmetics and beauty preparations of all kinds, standard brand drugs, candy, and every other type of merchandise that can be found in completely stocked drug stores will be handled by the Empire Drug firm according to Gambini.

The complete Whelan line of low-priced drugs distributed only through the United States Cigar Company will be featured.

"We believe that we can offer Santa Rosa and the surrounding area as complete and as varied a stock to choose from as any drug store in the North Bay area, and also as fine a prescription department," Gambini declared last night. "No expense has been spared in making our store a worthwhile addition to the business district and community."

Press Democrat
November 20, 1936

SR-D-08

Labeled amber abm screw cap:
SPIRITS CAMPHOR
ALCOHOL 86%
DISTRIBUTED BY
EMPIRE
DRUG CO.
623 4th ST. PHONE 12 SANTA ROSA, CALIF.
3 ½ inches tall
Base: 2 oz. A U S A S2
James Arietta collection

SR-D-09
    Labeled amber abm screw cap:
    PHONE 12
    EMPIRE DRUG CO.
    The Rexall Store
    623 4th St. Santa Rosa, Calif.
    Dr. *Norman*
    12.22.53
    4 ¼ inches tall
    Face: *Duraglas*
    Base: 7 I 57-3 oz. 20
    James Arietta collection

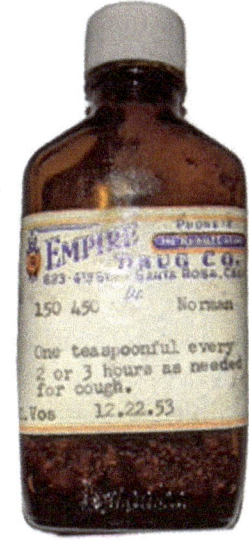

SR-D-10
    Labeled amber abm screw cap:
    PHONE 12
    EMPIRE DRUG CO.
    The Rexall Store
    623 4th St. Santa Rosa, Calif.
    Dr. *Norman*
    9/12/60
    KEEP OUT OF THE REACH OF CHILDREN
    5 1/4 inches tall
    Base: 23 I 9 – 6oz. 3506-P-4A
    James Arietta collection

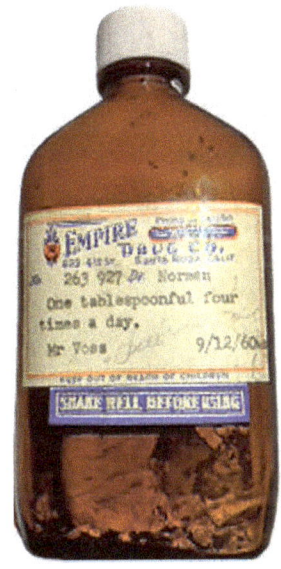

Press Democrat
August 23, 1964

- **The New Service Drug Store**
- 518 Fourth Street; purchased from Herman Lauchere (see page 231)
- June 1930 – May 1932: Carl H. Garloff, prop.
- May 1932 – 1933: George C. Butler and George R. Butler, props.

SALE ADVERTISED

Herman Lauchere will sell to C. H. Garloff next Friday morning at 10 o'clock the stock in trade and fixtures of the Service Drug Store in this city for $1,292 according to notice of sale filed with the county recorder.

Press Democrat
June 25, 1930

CARL GARLOFF BUYS SERVICE DRUG STORE

Carl Garloff of Cunningham District has purchased the Service Drug Company at 518 Fourth Street from Herman Lauchere. The store was recently moved to 518 Fourth Street from 521 Fourth Street. New business policies have been inaugurated, with Ben Carbinas manager.

New furniture and a completely new stock of drugs and sundries have been put in Garloff stated. A new prescription department has been installed and will be under the direction of a registered pharmacist. The concern had adopted a slogan "We never substitute."

Press Democrat
July 11, 1930

The New Service Drug Store

518 FOURTH STREET

Agents for
HELENA RUBINSTEIN COSMETICS
THE OWL DRUG CO. PRODUCTS
PAGE AND SHAW CANDIES

Prescriptions carefully and accurately compounded by Registered Licentiate Pharmacists.

**PHONE 3 FOR YOUR DRUG STORE WANTS
FREE DELIVERY**

Santa Rosa Republican
August 2, 1930

NOTICE

Carl Garloff

Has Purchased

The Service Drug Store

518 Fourth Street

And is now its sole owner. The (NEW) Service Drug Store is now in its NEW location with NEW stock, NEW furniture and fixtures, WITH A NEW BUSINESS POLICY.

New management—A new prescription department stocked with new and high grade drugs and pharmceuticals, under management of a registered licentiate pharmicist, with a new special delivery service.

ALSO

THE (NEW) SERVICE DRUG STORE CARRIES THE HIGHEST GRADE OF DRUG SUNDRIES, COSMETICS AND PERFUMES AND SUCH OTHER MERCHANDISE AS IS CARRIED BY FIRST-CLASS DRUG STORES.

When you want the best—remember

The NEW Service Drug Store

nothing but the best and
"NEVER SUBSTITUTE"

Press Democrat
July 11, 1930

New Service Drug Store

518 Fourth Street

FRIDAY AND SATURDAY SPECIALS

LEADING THE TREND TO LOWER PRICES

Owl Milk of Magnesia Tooth Paste. Regular 50c	39c
Fancy Box Writing Paper, Regular 75c	39c
Watches Guaranteed	98c
Alcohol Rubbing	37c
3 for	99c
Owl Sanitary Napkins 1 dozen	29c

Rubber Goods 20% Reductions

PHONE 3   FREE DELIVERY

We Never Substitute

Santa Rosa Republican
August 22, 1930

FORMER RESIDENT REOPENS SERVICE DRUG STORE

After an absence of nearly 30 years, George C. Butler has returned to Santa Rosa and again is in the drug store business. Butler recently took over the stocks, prescription lists, and fixtures of the Service Drug Stores and will combine both into one down-town store, 518 Fourth Street.

Prior to the earthquake and fire, Butler was associated with the old Dignan drugstore, at that time located on the corner of Fourth and B Streets, the present location of Rosenberg's. For a number of years, he operated stores in Los Angeles and San Francisco and just recently retired from his store in the Flood Building in San Francisco which he operated for the past seven years.

Associated with Butler in the Service Drug Company will be his son, George R. Butler, who is also a registered pharmacist. The store will continue to stock all high-quality drugs and home remedies and will specialize on prescription work.

As an opening event, the store will conduct a "Two for One" sale starting this morning and continuing until Saturday night. This sales event affords the purchaser an additional advertised item of the same value or two similar items for and additional one cent. Practically all items in the store, with the exception of some nationally advertised and controlled merchandise will be included in this two for one sale.

"I have always looked forward to returning to Santa Rosa," Butler stated, "and I welcomed the opportunity to re-open the Service Drug Store. We shall continue to maintain only the highest quality merchandise and household remedies."

Santa Rosa Republican
May 27, 1932

- **Louis Goldberg**
- 521 Fourth Street; Owl Drug Company agent
- Successor to George M. Luttrell; sold to Herman Lauchere (see page 231)
- March 1924 – October 1927

DRUG STORE SPECIALS AT GOLDBERG'S TODAY

Goldberg's Drug Store which is a bargain spot weekly for store patrons, will give away toilet sets with every dollar purchase at his store today. The sets are regularly on sale for $2.50, according to Goldberg. An unusual list of specials is on sale today.

Press Democrat
August 29. 1925

BUYER OF GOLDBERG DRUG COMPANY STORE

Louis Goldberg, owner of Goldberg Drug Company, has sold his store to Herman Lauchere of San Jose and plans to take a partnership in a string of six stores in the southern part of the state. Rumors of an impending deal have been heard around Santa Rosa for several days, but confirmation came with the announcement that a notice of intended sale had been filed with the county recorder, and a letter of introduction of Lauchere from the San Jose Merchants Association was received by the Chamber of Commerce here.

Just what company he will be affiliated with in the south, Goldberg declined to state yesterday. It is understood that the Goldberg home, one of the most attractive in the city on Denton Way will be placed on the market.

Press Democrat
October 23, 1927

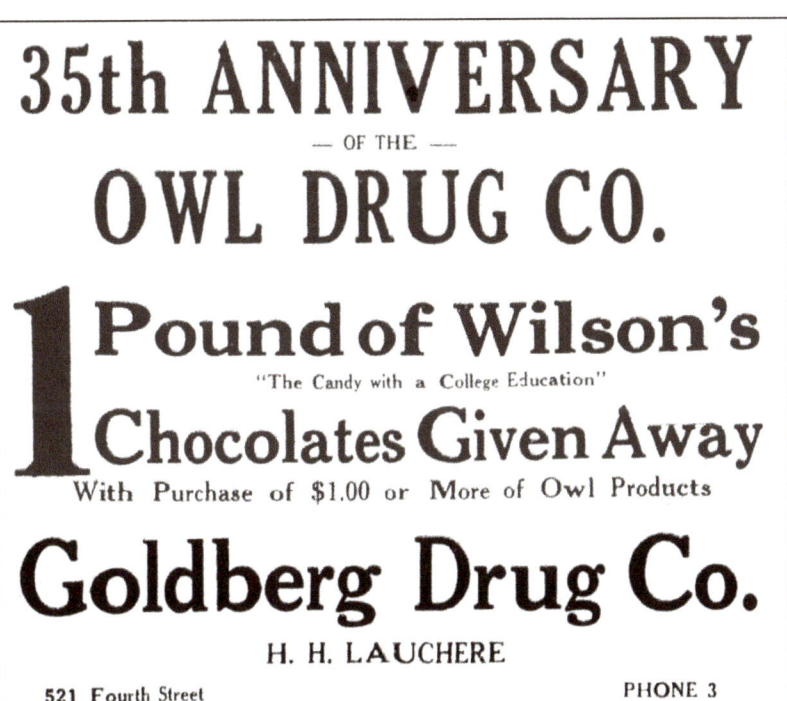

Santa Rosa Republican
October 31, 1927

- **Paul Theodore Hahman** (lived 1864-1942)
- Hahman & West (Paul T. Hahman & Edward F. West) Exchange Ave.: April 1891–1893
- Paul T. Hahman (Family Drug Store) 215 Exchange Ave.: 1893–December 1903
- Hahman Drug Company (P.T. Hahman & J. W. Claypool):
    215 Exchange Ave.: January 1, 1904– April 18, 1906
    504 Mendocino Ave. (temporary post-quake location): May 20, 1906–December 1907
    213 Exchange Ave. (new building): December 19, 1907–September 1966
- J.W. Claypool left the partnership in October 1919; Paul T. Hahman retired January 1932.

Santa Rosa Daily Democrat
April 10, 1891

To the Public.
Having purchased the drug business and stock of the late W. C. Reed, we wish to inform our friends and the public in general that we will continue at the old stand on Exchange avenue, between the banks, where we will carry a full line of Pure Drugs, Chemicals, Etc., and give special attention to compounding physicians' prescriptions and family recipes.
PAUL T. HAHMAN,
Formerly with R. J. Pye & Co.
ED F. WEST,
*d   Formerly with J. W. Warboys.

Labeled pasteboard carton, 3.75 inch dia., circa 1900
John Louder collection

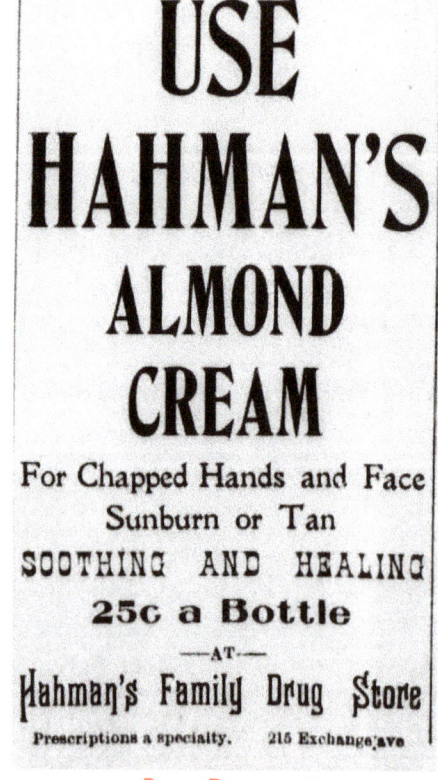

Press Democrat
September 3, 1898

Paul T. Hahman, The Family Drug Store
215 Exchange Ave., circa 1895
Courtesy, Sonoma County Library

The Family Drug Store, circa 1900. Paul T. Hahman at left
Courtesy, Sonoma County Library

A NEW FIRM

J. W. Claypool to Be Associated in Business with P. T. Hahman

On and after January 1, the old established drug business conducted by P. T. Hahman on Exchange Avenue will be merged into Hahman Drug Company on account of the fact that J. Walter Claypool has gone into co-partnership with Mr. Hahman. This will be very interesting news for Mr. Claypool's friend, who will be greatly pleased to learn of the move. For ten years, Mr. Claypool has been with Mr. Hahman as his clerk and assistant and has made himself deservedly popular with everyone.

Mr. Hahman and Mr. Claypool are both Native Sons of California and Santa Rosa. The former has been in business here for nearly fourteen years and has been met with marked success. The many friends of the co-partnership formed wish the principles continued success and prosperity in the new year and years that are to come.

Press Democrat
December 31, 1903

WILL HAVE A FINE NEW STORE

Paul T. Hahman of the Hahman Drug Company recently purchased the Old Savings Bank building, for years the telephone "central" on Exchange Avenue, adjoining his present place of business, and has awarded the contract to Simpson & Roberts for transforming the building into a splendidly equipped modern drug store into which the company will move within sixty days. The work of remodeling the building will begin this week, and will be carried out as soon as possible.

The remodeling will include the lowering of the floor, the putting in of a modern and attractive front, a gallery running clear around the interior, and completely new fixtures will be installed. The prescription department, a feature of the business, will occupy a separate room in the rear and other facilities will be added. The new building will afford considerable room.

Fifteen years ago, Mr. Hahman went into the drug business at the present location, being a member of the firm of Hahman & West. Two years later he purchased the interest of Mr. West and conducted the business alone with J. Walter Claypool as assistant until 1904 when Mr. Claypool became a partner and the firm name was changed to the Hahman Drug Company. In addition to their large retail business the company also has an extensive jobbing business with the druggists throughout the county. The property Hahman purchased was owned by the Savings Bank.

Press Democrat
April 8, 1906

Ten days later the entire Exchange Avenue block was destroyed

---

To the Public
OF SANTA ROSA AND VICINITY

We saved our Prescription Books from the **FIRE** and can refill any prescription ever put up at our store. Our stock is now almost as complete as ever, and new goods are being received daily. Try us before going elsewhere. Have your doctor phone your prescription day or night.

'PHONE THIRTY-TWO.

HAHMAN DRUG CO.
Prescription Druggists

504 Mendocino Street - Santa Rosa
Above Johnson
See the Street Banner

Press Democrat
May 26, 1906

OPENING DAYS OF THE HAHMAN DRUG CO.

Opening days, Dec. 19, 20, 21

Opening Day No. 1, Thursday, Dec. 19
On this day we will give Cash Purchasers a discount of 20 per cent from any article in Leather Goods or Box of Stationery in our stock. This day only.

Opening day No. 2, Friday, Dec. 20
On this day we will give Cash Purchasers a discount of 20 per cent from any Mirror, Dressing Case, Manicure Set or Holiday Goods in our stock. This day only.

Opening day No. 3, Saturday, Dec. 21
On this day we will give Cash Purchasers a discount of 20 per cent from any package of Perfumery in stock, except Hudnut's which we are under contract not to sell below list prices. This day only.

These goods are all our regular stock and are Not Marked Up for the occasion but even now are Marked Lower than Usual. Call and be convinced. Call and see the Most Complete and Handsomest Drug Store in northern California and at the same time save money on your holiday purchases.

213 Exchange Ave — Next to big Santa Rosa Bank Building

Santa Rosa Republican
December 18, 1907

PAUL T. HAHMAN TO BUILD

Paul T. Hahman is preparing to rebuild his structure on Exchange avenue purchased a short time before the April fire. He has plans and specifications prepared for a splendid structure, which will be the future home of the Hahman Drug Company, one of the oldest and best known firms of this city. Mr. Hahman hopes to have the building completed without delay that he may resume the location formerly occupied by the firm before the devastating fire.

Santa Rosa Republican
November 12, 1906

The first plate glass window installed during the rebuilding of Santa Rosa was for Hahman Drug Company's new storefront.

Hahman Drug Company's post-quake building at 213 Exchange Ave., circa February 1909. It sits next to the new Santa Rosa Bank, presently called the Empire Building.
Frank Sternad collection

EXPLOSION STARTS FIRE

The auto chemical [fire engine] was called to Hahman's Drug Store on Exchange Avenue yesterday morning just before 10 o'clock. A small explosion of chemicals having started a blaze. Only slight damage was done and the fire was extinguished before the fire department arrived owing to the prompt work of J. Walter Claypool, Clyde Hudson, and Roy Tuttle. Mr. Claypool was badly singed about the hands, wrists and eyebrows.

Press Democrat
May 24, 1913

Hahman Drug Company, circa 1910. J.W. Claypool center, P.T. Hahman at right
Courtesy, Sonoma County Library

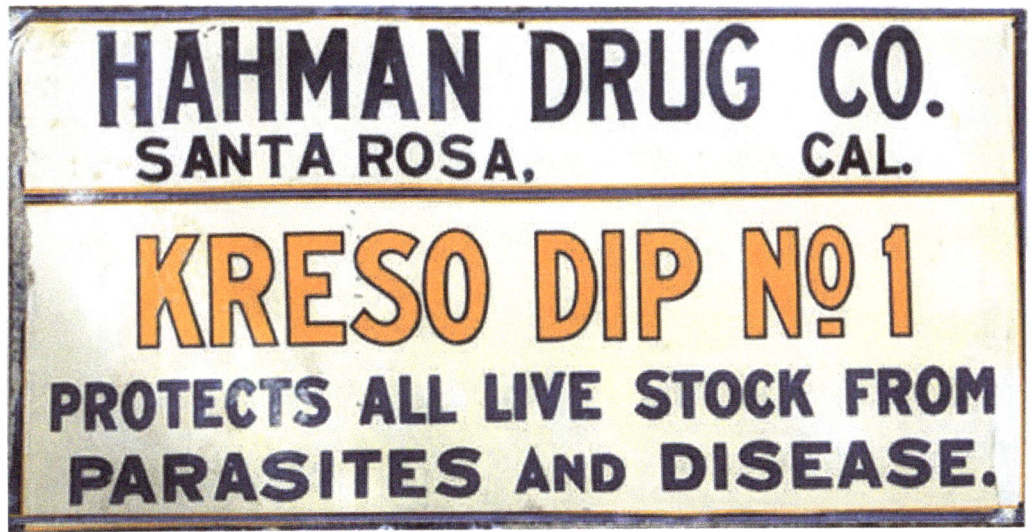

Tin advertising sign
Richard Siri collection

Hahman Drug Company's storeroom. P.T. Hahman and J.W. Claypool at rear, circa 1915.
Courtesy, Sonoma County Library

Jerry Claypool and P.T. Hahman at work in the prescription department of Hahman Drug Co., 213 Exchange Ave., circa 1915.
Courtesy, Sonoma County Library

SR-D-11
    Labeled clear abm screw cap:
    GLYCERIN, U.S.P.
    1 FL. OZS.
    HAHMAN DRUG COMPANY
    PRESCRIPTION DRUGGISTS
    EXCHANGE AVE.   SANTA ROSA, CAL.

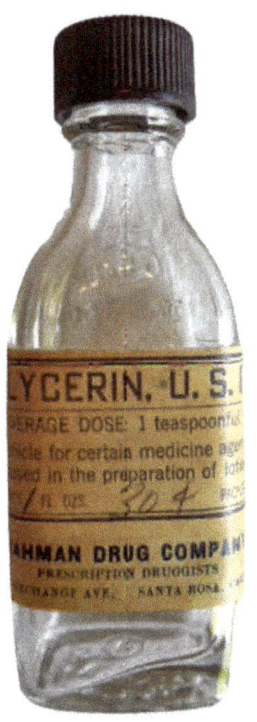

SR-D-11A
    HAHMAN DRUG CO.
    SANTA ROSA, CALA.
    Clear square, stone ground lip
    3 inches tall
    Not shown

SR-D-12
    HAHMAN DRUG CO.
    PRESCRIPTION DRUGGISTS
    SANTA ROSA, CAL.
    Clear citrate of magnesia, porcelain stopper
    8 Inches tall
    Base: 100 - H
    Frank Sternad collection

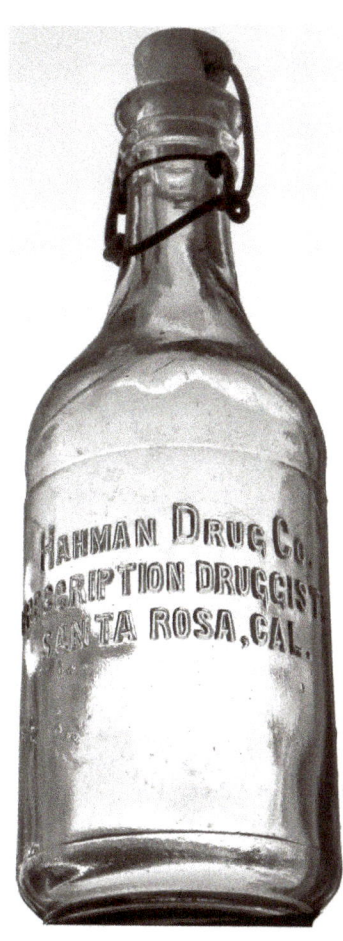

- **Hall Brothers Drug Co.** (Theron E. Hall and Lowell Harry Hall)
- Purchased Rutherford Drug Co. in 1936; changed name to Hall Brothers in 1941
- 529 Fourth Street
- May 6, 1936 – May 8, 1970 (sold to Tomasco Drug Co.)

Halls to Operate Drug Store Here Under Own Name

One of Santa Rosa's oldest established firms, the Rutherford's Drug Store, will henceforth continue in business under the name of Hall Brothers' Drug Company.

Conveniently located in the central business section of the city, the store was purchased five years ago by Theron and Lowell Hall, brothers who are now conducting the business under their name.

Both brothers are Santa Rosa men and both are graduate pharmacists of the University of California.

Prior to purchasing the Rutherford store, they were associated with leading drug firms in the bay area for eight years.

In the past five years, they have added many new lines to the store and now feature quality products at competitive prices.

The Hall brothers operate a modern and well-stocked prescription department with one of them on duty at all times.

Also operated is a large fountain where lunches, milkshakes, ice cream and other confections are served. The store is open daily from 8:00 a. m. to midnight.

Included in the store is a large perfume and cosmetic department completely stocked with latest nationally known products. Miss Alice Blois, beauty consultant, is on duty daily to assist with the selections of creams, powders and other beauty aids.

In addition, the store maintains free delivery service from 8:00 a. m. to midnight. The two partner-brothers employ a staff of seven others in operation of the various departments of the store.

SANTA ROSA DRUG FIRM ASSUMES NEW NAME

One of the longest-established drug stores in the city continues business under a new name with the rechristening of Rutherford's Drug Store at 529 Fourth street as Hall Brothers' Drug Company. Theron Hall, upper, and Lowell Hall are brothers who five years ago purchased the store and are now conducting the firm under their name. The store front is shown.

Press Democrat
March 28, 1941

SR-D- 13
    Labeled clear abm screw cap:
    GLYCERIN, U. S. P.
    FLD. OZS.
    HALL BROTHERS
    PRESCRIPTION PHARMACY
    529-4th ST. PHONE 100
    SANTA ROSA, CALIFORNIA
    3 3/8 inches tall
    Base: 23 I 49 AA
    James Arietta collection

SR-D-17
    Labeled clear abm screw cap:
    Milk of Bismuith (S. & D.)
    HALL BROTHERS
    PRESCRIPTION PHARMACY
    529 – 4th St. PHONE 100
    SANTA ROSA, CALIFORNIA

    Richard Siri collection

- **John Hendley**
- Santa Rosa Drug Store
- East side of plaza; a general merchant who advertised as druggist for 14 months
- November 1858 – January 25, 1860 ; served as Sonoma County Treasurer in 1860
- Sold to William G. Alban

```
JOHN HENDLEY,
General Merchant.
East Side of Public Square,
Santa Rosa.

KEEPS constantly on hand, a large and full
  supply of
    Dry Goods,        Groceries,
    Clothing,         Queensware,
    Shoes & Boots,    Woodware,
    Hats & Caps,      Hardware,
    Bonnets,          Rope & Nails.
            ....ALSO....
A large stock of
   Drugs, Medicines and Chemicals.
all of which will be sold at the lowest market
price either for
        CASH or the PRODUCE
of the country.
    The highest prices paid for Butter Eggs,
Wheat, Barley and Oats.
```

Sonoma Democrat
October 22, 1857

```
NEW DRUG STORE:
JOHN     HENDLEY,
```

```
DRUGGIST.
EAST SIDE OF PUBLIC SQUARE,
       —SANTA ROSA—
HAS now on hand, and is constantly receiving
   a full assortment of
PURE AND FRESH DRUGS,
  MEDICINES, CHEMICALS,
Patent and Family Medicines,
       PERFUMERY,
            AND
    FANCY ARTICLES.
The attention of Physicians and the public are
respectfully invited to the same.    nov10-1m
```

Sonoma Democrat
November 10, 1858

NEW DRUGS, MEDICINES, &c.,
AT THE
SANTA ROSA DRUG STORE.

I HAVE just received and offer for sale, a large stock of—

DRUGS, MEDICINES, PAINTS, OILS, AND FANCY GOODS,

as low as can or will be sold this side of the Bay. The trade of Physicians is respectfully solicited to my stock of regular

Drugs, Medicines, Chemicals and Drug-Groceries, in their line.

JOHN HENDLEY,
East side of Plaza.

je30-1m

Sonoma Democrat
October 20, 1859

Funding the Debt of Sonoma County.

NOTICE is hereby given, that in accordance with the provisions of an Act of the Legislature, entitled "An Act to fund the debt of Sonoma county, and to provide for the payment of the same," "Approved March 20th, 1860," that from, on and after this date, the funding of the now outstanding indebtedness of Sonoma county will commence, and the time for funding the said debt will remain open for the term of ninety days from this date.

JOHN HENDLEY,
Treasurer of Sonoma County.
Santa Rosa, October 1st, 1860.   8-4w

Sonoma County Journal
October 26, 1860

NEW FIRM
—AND—
NEW GOODS.
HENDLEY & FARMER,

ARE now in receipt of, and just opening, a Large and Well Selected Stock of

DRY GOODS, CLOTHING, SHOES, BOOTS, HATS, CAPS, GROCERIES, Hardware, Queensware, &c., &c.,

Which they will sell LOW For Cash, or Country Produce.

We would invite the attention of the Ladies to our LARGE STOCK of

DE LAINES, BEREGES, SILKS, GINGHAMS, CALICOS, & WHITE DRESS GOODS, BONNETS, TRIMMINGS, GOODS OF ALL KINDS, LADIES' VEILS, GLOVES, RIBBONS, ETC.,

Which we are now selling LOWER than has ever been offered in this market.

The attention of the public is especially called to our

Large and Well Assorted Stock of **Gentlemen's and Boys' COATS, PANTS, SHIRTS, BOOTS and SHOES,**

And Furnishing Goods generally

HENDLEY & FARMER,
East Side Public Plaza.

Santa Rosa, April 17, 1860.   3m-27

Sonoma Democrat
May 24, 1860

- **Hill & Eberhard** (Harvard W. Hill & Charles E. Eberhard)
- Successors to Hill & Wheeler (November 1884 – May 1885)
- 516 Fourth Street, south side between B and Exchange: May 1885 – April 1886
- 500 Fourth Street, corner of B St. (Overton's new block): April 1886 – June 4, 1887
- Sold to M.H. Dignan (see page 191)

HILL & WHEELER, DRUGGISTS.

Invite you to call at their elegant Drug store, 516 Fourth street, where you will find a large and complete stock of Pure Drugs, Chemicals, Perfumery, Patent Medicines, Combs, Brushes, Sponges and the largest stock of Druggists' Sundries in town. Also a full line of Paints, Oils, Varnishes and Artists' materials at lowest prices.

PRESCRIPTIONS ACCURATELY PREPARED. NIGHT BELL PROMPTLY ANSWERED.

HILL & WHEELER
dec20dawtf

Sonoma Democrat
December 20, 1884

HILL & EBERHARD DRUGGISTS.

Invite you to call at their elegant Drug store, 516 Fourth street, where you will find a large and complete stock of Pure Drugs, Chemicals, Perfumery, Patent Medicines, Combs, Brushes, Sponges and the largest stock of Druggists' Sundries in town. Also a full line of Paints, Oils, Varnishes and Artists' materials at lowest prices.

PRESCRIPTIONS ACCURATELY PREPARED. NIGHT BELL PROMPTLY ANSWERED.

HILL & EBERHARD.
dec20dawtf

Sonoma Democrat
May 9, 1885

HILL & EBERHARD

Successors to Hill & Wheeler; established in the spring of 1885 in Overton's Building, with a stock valued at $500. Within the past year and a half, they have increased their stock to $7,000 and occupy one of the finest corners in the city. Their trade is wholesale as well as retail, and they fill large orders from Guerneville, Sebastopol, Windsor and Sonoma. Most of their pharmaceutical goods are manufactured in the store. Their stock of fancy goods and toilet articles is second to none in the city. The central office of the Sunset Telephone Company is located in their store.

Sonoma Democrat
Jan 8, 1887

DISSOLUTION OF CO-PARTNERSHIP

Notice is hereby given that the co-partnership existing under the firm name of Hill & Eberhard was on the 4th day of June, 1887 dissolved by mutual consent. H. W. Hill will continue the business and settle all accounts.   —Chas. E. Eberhard

Sonoma Democrat
June 4, 1887

- **Joab N. Hooper**
- Hooper's Drug Store
- 611 Fourth Street; successor to John H. Lunn
- February 1903 – April 1904

PURCHASED DRUG BUSINESS

J. H. Lunn, the druggist of upper Fourth Street, has sold out his pharmacy to J. N. Hooper of Friend, Nebraska. The new proprietor has taken possession. W. McK. Stewart will remain with Mr. Hooper and will retain his position as assistant, in which he is popular and efficient. Mr. and Mrs. Hooper and their son are located here.

Press Democrat
February 20, 1903

J. N. HOOPER Successor J. H. LUNN
DRUGGIST

Having purchased this old established business I propose renovating the premises and bringing it up-to-date in every respect. All orders br telephone promptly filled and delivered to any part of the city. Prescriptions a specialty.

W. McK. Stewart, will still have charge of the Prescription Department. When you need medicine at night, ring phone Red 624. All night calls answered promptly

Telephone Red 43   611 FOURTH STREET

Press Democrat
March 12, 1903

EYE TESTING —AND— GLASS FITTING

Has advanced to a science. In our testing and glass fitting we use separate and distinct methods by means of the best instruments known to optical science and guarantee our glasses to be right in every minute detail. The accurately fitting of glasses is our business exclusively.

If you are particular about your glasses call on us. Examination free.

Lawson Optical Co.
With Hooper's Drug Store.   611 Fourth St. Santa Rosa

Press Democrat
April 1, 1903

611 FOURTH ST. DRUGS AND TOILET ARTICLES

Call for what you want and get what you call for is our motto. We allow no substitution and keep only the Purest Drugs. We deliver goods promptly to any part of the city. Careful attention given to Prescriptions.

Hooper's Drug Store
611 FOURTH ST.   PHONE RED 43

Press Democrat
March 16, 1904

- **Hooper & Farmer** (Joab N. Hooper & Eugene C. Farmer)
- 611 Fourth Street
- April 1904 – June 4, 1906

HOOPER & FARMER

Eugene Farmer came up from San Francisco on Thursday night and will enter into business at once in the new firm of Hooper & Farmer, Druggists.

Press Democrat
April 4, 1904

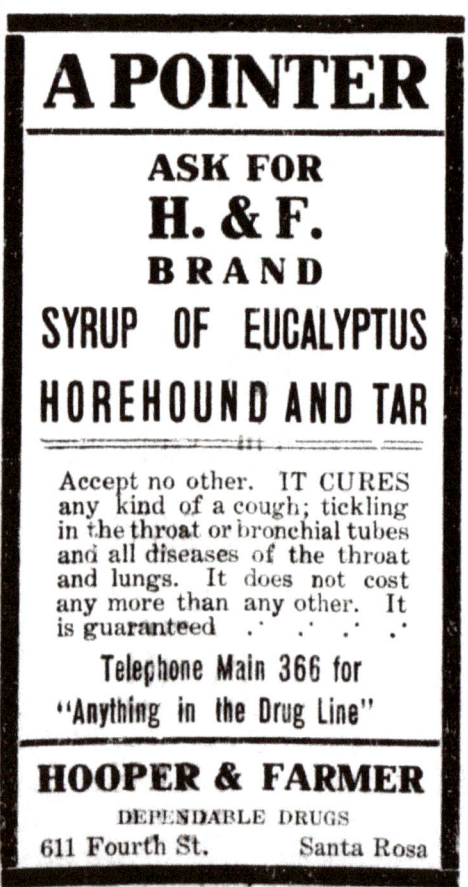

Press Democrat
January 19, 1906

Press Democrat
January 27, 1906

NOTICE TO THE PUBLIC

The public will hereby take notice that the firm of Hooper & Farmer has dissolved partnership by mutual consent, Eugene C. Farmer continuing the business. All bills owing to Hooper & Farmer previous to this date will be paid to J. N. Hooper at 738 Fourth St.

J. N. Hooper   Eugene C. Farmer

Santa Rosa June 4, 1906

Press Democrat
June 8, 1906

- **T. F. Hudson** (lived 1846-1932)
  - July 1874 – March 3, 1880 ; previously in Ukiah and Cloverdale
  - 6 W. Plaza (Ridgway Block); Paul T. Hahman was an apprentice under Hudson
  - Sold to Dr. W. E Bryant

DRUGGIST T.F. HUDSON TO LEASE SHOP

Mr. T.F. Hudson, who had a drug store in Cloverdale for the past two years, has leased one-half of the store occupied by Mr. Nilson the jeweler, Ridgway Block, and will open it with a large assortment of drugs, medicines, perfumery, etc. next week. Mr. Hudson is an experienced and reliable chemist, a good businessman, and having a large circle of friends we predict for him success in business.

Sonoma Democrat - July 1874

T. F. HUDSON, Druggist, Santa Rosa, is manufacturing a Poison for Squirrels, Gophers, Rats, Mice, &c., which is sure death to those pests. Numerous testimonials from those who have used it, point to the fact that it is all that it is represented to be. Persons who are troubled with these pests should give Mr. Hudson a call and secure a box of Hudson Poison. It is only 75 cents per pound can. may27-wtf

Sonoma Democrat – May 27, 1876

Paulson's Handbook of Sonoma County, 1874

SR-D-14

T.F. HUDSON
APOTHECARY
SANTA ROSA
Clear oval
Tooled top
6 1/8 inches tall
Merle Avila collection

SR-D-15

TFH (monogram in mortar & pestle)
T. F. HUDSON
APOTHECARY
SANTA ROSA
Clear oval
Tooled top
5 1/8 inches tall
Base: 6
ex Frank Sternad collection

Note: After selling out to W.E. Bryant, Taliaferro Fleurnoy Hudson (his full name) traveled to Tombstone, Arizona Territory and opened another drugstore. One of Hudson's first civic duties in that boomtown was to serve on a grand jury impaneled to investigate the famous October 26, 1881 shootout at the O.K. Corral.

- **Guy A. Johnson Drug Store**
- 637 Fourth St., F.G. Hahman Block
- Sold to J.W. Cummings, formerly of Oroville, who in turn sold to A.F. McLain in December 1891, see page 236
- January 1889 – September 1891

IS COURTSHIP A FAILURE?

Once a charming, charming, charming
  Nice young man, (considered so).
Learned, alas, that streams of true love
  Never, never smoothly flow.

He'd been loving, loving, loving
  A fair maiden long and well:
And at last had mustered courage
  All his treasured hopes to tell.

He'd not whispered, whispered, whispered
  Then into his maiden's ear,
But had penned them and had sent them
  To the one he loved so dear.

He grew thinner, thinner, thinner
  Like his shadow every day
Till we all were apprehensive
  That he soon would blow away.

He was lucky, lucky, lucky
  For it saved him sure as fate.
Some one told him he had better
  Try the famous "Golden Gate."

He has used it, used it, used it,
  And is portly now, and tall;
And his clothes already fit him
  "Like the paper on the wall."

Making money, money, money,
  Till he out of debt has got.
He has made the Chinese happy,
  And has bought a house and lot.

And he told me, told me, told me
  That his lady-love of late
Wrote for him to call and see her.
  SHE HAD TAKEN "GOLDEN GATE!"

We were present, present, present,
  And the wedding feast was fine;
But we noticed on the table,
  "GOLDEN GATE" INSTEAD OF WINE.

This wonderful medicine is to be found at the following drug stores in Santa Rosa:

M. H. DIGNAN,
  GUY A. JOHNSON.
    MRS. L. BENNETT,
      J. W. WARBOYS,
        R. J. PYE AND CO.
          T. J. RILEY

my3wtf

Santa Rosa Democrat – May 3, 1889

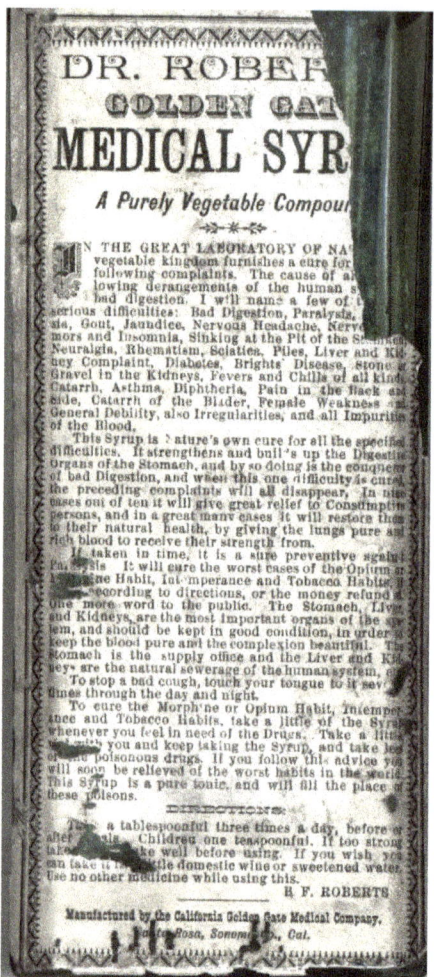

Paper label courtesy Lou Lambert

SANTA ROSA, January 5, 1889. Why don't men die? Because they have found they can buy a bottle of Roberts' Golden Gate Medical Syrup at Guy A. Johnson's, druggist and pharmacist, 637 Fourth street, Santa Rosa. Every bottle guaranteed if taken according to directions.

Sonoma Democrat – Jan. 5, 1889

Note: Guy Anderson Johnson (b. 1861), a Santa Rosa druggist since 1884, had become a gardener at the California State Capitol in Sacramento by 1896.

- **Juell's Drug Store** (Dr. Nels Juell, lived 1850-1928)
- 223 Exchange Avenue: Feb. 1902 – April 1904 (bought People's Drug from James Ewing)
- 545 Fourth Street: 1905 – April 18, 1906
- 215 B Street: August 1906 – September 1909
- 621 Fourth Street: March 10, 1910 – April 1915
- Sold to Warren E. Baldwin (see page 177)

DRUG STORE CHANGES HANDS
THE PEOPLES DRUG STORE

Dr. N. Juell, recently from Redwing, Minnesota, has purchased the Peoples Drug Store at 223 Exchange Avenue. The recent proprietor, J. E. Ewing, intends to go to Carchecan, Alaska and engage in mining. Dr. Juell is a physician as well as a druggist, and has had thirty-five years' experience in the two kindred professions.

Press Democrat
February 9, 1902

Note: Nels Juell's son, Rolfe Juell, was granted a State of California registration as Asst. Pharmacist in October 1912. He took over the drug business in October 1914 when his father resumed his medical practice in the Santa Rosa Bank building.

SR-D-16

Juell's
SANTA ROSA, CALIF.
Clear oval
Tooled top
4 ½ inches tall
5 1/4 inches tall
Base: MARVEL
John Burton collection

SR-D-17

Juell's DRUG
STORE
SANTA ROSA, CAL
Clear rectangular
Tooled top
5 ½ inches tall
Base: MARVEL
John Burton collection

SR-D-18

PURITY ACCURACY (in double circle)
OUR SUCCESS (inside double circle)
Juell's
SANTA ROSA
Clear rectangular
Tooled top
4 ½ inches tall
8 ½ inches tall
John Burton collection

SR-D-19

ʒvi
Juell's DRUG
         STORE
SANTA ROSA, CAL.
Clear rectangular
Tooled top
6 ½ inches tall
Base: W. T. CO. USA
John Burton collection

SR-D-20

ʒviii
Juell's DRUG
         STORE
SANTA ROSA, CAL.
Clear rectangular
Tooled top
6 ½ inches tall
Merle Avila collection
6 3/4 inches tall
Base: W. T. CO. USA
John Burton collection

Go to	**JUELL'S PHARMACY**	for Perfumery, Soaps and Toilet Articles
223 Exchange Avenue, Santa Rosa, Cal.		Tel. Red 123

1903 Santa Rosa city directory

- **Charles F. Keller, Jr.**
  - Keller occupied J.W. Warboys' store at 505 Fourth St.: Jan. 16–March 1, 1905
  - 535 Fourth Street: March 1, 1905 – April 18, 1906
  - 707 Fourth Street: May-June 1906
  - 503 Fifth Street: July 1906 – July 1908
  - Successor to John W. Warboys; sold to J.B. Dean (see p. 190) and returned to Eureka, CA

Press Democrat
January 29, 1905

Keller at 535 Fourth St., circa 1905
Courtesy, Sonoma County Library

C. F. KELLER MOVES TO NEW DRUG STORE
C. F. Keller who recently purchased the J. W. Warboys Drug Store, moved into his new location at 535 Fourth St., formerly the J. M. Dickson Dry Goods Store. The new store is well located and gives plenty of room for the proper display of the large stock Mr. Keller offers. The show windows will be neatly arranged and very soon everything will be in good shape for the transaction of business.

Press Democrat
March 3, 1905

BUSINESS RESUMED
Temporary location 707 Fourth Street.
Good stock of drugs; more arriving. Kodaks and supplies. Everything new.
C. F. KELLER Jr.

Press Democrat - May 19, 1906

William Keller, a brother of C. F. Keller the local druggist, was among successful applicants passing the recent examination for pharmacists in San Francisco. He passed with high honors and will be associated with his brother in business in Santa Rosa.

Press Democrat - February 21, 1908

- **Hiram Delaney Kellogg**
  - Attended Rush Medical College 1867; registered as physician in E. Oakland, CA, Nov. 1891
  - 442 Fourth Street; July 1889 – February 1890
  - Formerly ran drugstores in Arkansas City, Kansas and San Jose, CA

> DR. H. D. KELLOGG.   L. V. COOMBS
>
> ## Kellogg & Coombs
> ——AT THE——
> ## "NO. 33"
> Drug Store on the corner opposite the Cowley County, Bank, have fitted up one the finest and best
> ## DRUG STORES
> In the State. Everything Neat, New and convenient, where you will find a large stock of New Drugs, Paints, Oils, Toilet Articles, Perfumery, Patent Medicienes and everything pertaining to the drug business.
> **** We are sole agents for Sal-Muscatelle English Grape Cure for Sick Headache, Dyspepsia, &c.

Arkansas Valley Democrat
January 22, 1886

Note: Kellogg arrived in San Jose, CA from Arkansas City, Kansas in May 1887

T. J. Riley, of this city, and H. D. Kellogg of San Jose have traded drug stores. Mr. Kellogg has already arrived and taken possession. Mr. Riley expects to depart for San Jose on Monday. We welcome Mr. Kellogg into our midst and express regret at the departure of Mr. Riley. [see page 248]

Press Democrat
July 6, 1889

> ## Histogenetic System of Medicines
> —OF—
> ### Dr. J. E. Jordan of Seattle, W. T.
>
> Prepared from animal glands and tissues—tasteless. Remedies for every variety of diseases, and all absolute cures.
>
> ### Sold by H. D. KELLOGG, Druggist,
> SANTA ROSA, CAL.
>
> Local Agent, MRS. E. BURNEY,
> 213 THIRD STREET
> Books explaining given free.   se7-dwtf

Sonoma Democrat
September 7, 1889

- **Herman Henry Lauchere** (lived 1900-1987)
- Purchased Goldberg Drug Co., 521 4th St. in October 1927 (see page 209)
- Changed name to Service Drug Store, March 1928; moved to 518 4th St. in March 1930
- Sold to Carl Garloff in April 1930 (see page 206)

> Have you seen any of the gay Colleen Moore gift sets of toilet articles. **THE SERVICE DRUG STORE** has them and loads of others. Red Feather, Darnee, Yardley's and a full line of the famous new Rubenstein toilet preparations. Every woman loves exquisite toilet preparations for Christmas gifts—such necessary vanities.

Press Democrat
December 9, 1928

Herman Lauchere, Santa Rosa druggist, will go before Federal Justice Frank H. Kerrigan in Sacramento Friday for sentence on three counts involving prohibition law violations, to which he pleaded guilty before the court yesterday. Lauchere was under indictment by the Federal Grand Jury on the counts, which charged conspiracy in the handling of whiskey prescriptions.

Press Democrat
April 16, 1930

LAUCHERE SURRENDERS AT JAIL, STARTS TERM
Herman Lauchere, local druggist surrendered himself at the county jail yesterday to begin service of a 90-day sentence imposed in federal court at Sacramento yesterday following his plea of guilty to three counts of violation of liquor laws.

Press Democrat
April 20, 1930

Herman Henry Lauchere, Ph.G. (UC) paid for his poor judgement in 1930, and went on to lead a full and prosperous life, dedicated to pharmacy and to public service. During WWII he played a part in formation of the US Army Pharmacy Corps at Scott Field, Illinois.

HERMAN LAUCHERE

U. S. INDICTS FOUR DOCTORS IN LIQUOR NET

Federal Grand Jury Acts in Cases of Santa Rosa Physicians

SACRAMENTO, Feb. 24 (P)—Establishing a record in the United States District Court today, ninety-five indictments and forty-three informations were filed, making the largest number to be presented at a single term of court.

The majority of the defendants named in the indictments and informations are charged with violating sections of the national prohibition act. The Federal Grand Jury presented the indictments to United States District Judge Harold Louderback, who is here to preside over the February term of court, while the United States District Attorney's office filed the informations.

Four Santa Rosa doctors and a druggist of that city stand charged with violating the national prohibition act as the result of indictments returned by the inquisitorial body.

The doctors are Leighton Ray, Cuthbert Fleissner, A. M. Bowles and A. M. Thomson, while the druggist is Herman Lauchere of the Service Drug Company, 521 Fourth street, Santa Rosa.

The indictments charge the doctors knowingly issued wholly false and fictitious whisky prescriptions and that the persons designated as patients were not under treatment for any ailment or disease.

Lauchere, the druggist, is indicted on counts of possession and sale of illicit liquor.

San Francisco Chronicle
February 25, 1930

- **James Henry Lunn** (lived 1841–1915)
- Pioneer Drug Store, J.H. Lunn Drug Co.
- Successor to R. J. Pye; sold to J.N. Hooper; member of Stewart Manuf. Co. (see page 257)
- 611 Fourth Street
- July 1, 1901 – February 1903

Pioneer Drug Store
A CARD!

To Our Former Patrons and the Public Generally:

Having disposed of our business to MR. J. H. LUNN, we wish to express our thanks for your former patronage.

Mr. Lunn will be able to give more personal attention to the business than has been possible for me lately. I ask a continuance of your friendship to the store. Mr. Lunn proposes to keep everything in his line of business.

A graduate in pharmacy will have charge of the prescription department and only the best drugs will be used. Call and make the acquaintance of the new proprietor. Yours respectfully,

R. J. PYE.

7c11tf   611 Fourth St., Santa Rosa, Cal.

Press Democrat
July 11, 1901

A Pharmacy

We conduct one, with an up-to-date supply of

TOILET ARTICLES
DRUGS AND CHEMICALS

Special attention given to PRESCRIPTION WORK
Call and interview our Soda Water Artist.

The J. H. Lunn Drug Co.

611 FOURTH ST.   TELEPHONE RED 43

Press Democrat
August 14, 1901

LUNN DRUG CO.
611 Fourth Street - Santa Rosa
Always have on hand a full and complete line of Drugs, Medicines, Chemicals, Fancy and Toilet Articles, Sponges, Combs, Brushes and Perfumery. Physicians' Prescriptions Carefully compounded. Our stock of medicines is warranted genuine and best of quality.

Press Democrat
March 5, 1902

- **George McClure Luttrell**
- 518 Fifth Street: October 1906 (purchased Harry S. Davis' post-quake store)
- 527 Fourth Street: March 11, 1907 – February 1922, Luttrell Drug Company
- 521 Fourth Street: February 1922 – March 15, 1924 (branch store at 5th & B Streets)
- Sold to Louis Goldberg (see page 209)

LUTTRELL'S NEW STORE

G. M. Luttrell, the druggist, who purchased the late Harry Davis' drug store, has moved into his handsome new store on Fourth Street. He has a fine place and it is attractively furnished. Mr. Luttrell is doing a big business, and since coming here has made many friends.

Press Democrat – March 12, 1907

Decorative plates

"Complements of G.M. Luttrell, Druggist"

Dan Brown collection

Press Democrat
January 13, 1907

Press Democrat
April 26, 1907

233

Labeled pasteboard carton:
SULPHUR
LUTTRELL DRUG Co.
PHONE 3
527 Fourth St. SANTA ROSA, CAL.

Richard Siri collection

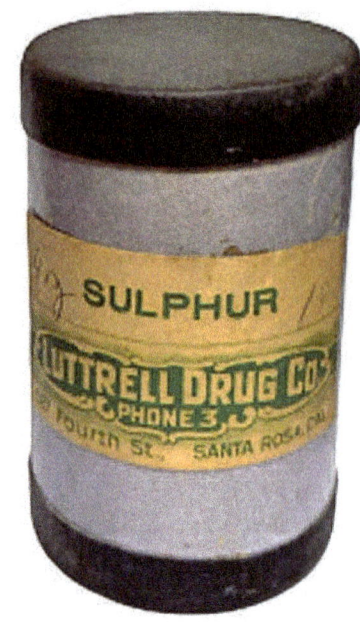

LUTTRELL'S
White Pine Comp.
with Tar, Menthol and Eucalyptus.
The best remedy we know of for Coughs and Colds
25 cents and 50 cents
Luttrell Drug Co., Prescription Druggist
Phone 3 - 527 Fourth Street
Press Democrat
December 28, 1915

LUTTRELL SELLS PHARMACY HERE

G. M. Luttrell, for seventeen years proprietor of the Luttrell drug store here, yesterday announced the sale of his business to Louis Goldberg of Larkspur, Marin county.

Luttrell has no plans for the future. For the present he will remain at the store assisting the new proprietor. Goldberg, who came to Marin county from Los Angeles, is a graduate pharmacist. He will make his residence here.

Press Democrat
March 16, 1924

LUTTRELL DRUG CO.

We are now settled in our new store at 521 Fourth street—two doors west of our old location. We are now in a position to serve you better than ever before.

Dependable Drugs and Reasonable Prices

Let us fill your prescriptions.

LUTTRELL DRUG CO.

BRANCH STORE COR. FIFTH AND B

Press Democrat
February 25, 1922

GEORGE LUTTRELL IS REGISTERED AS STATE PHARMACIST

George M. Luttrell, Jr., son of George M. Luttrell, former Santa Rosa pharmacist, has just passed his state pharmacy board examination and has been awarded his licentiate papers.

Young Luttrell, who is spending a vacation in Santa Rosa, received word today from the state board that he had passed the test with a high rating. He plans joining his father in Southern California soon.

Santa Rosa Republican
August 6, 1930

- **Luttrell & Rutherford Drug Company** (an interim partnership)
- 527 Fourth Street
- December 1914 – June 25, 1915

RUTHERFORD TO BE PARTNER WITH LUTTRELL

W. E. Rutherford, who with his family has been a resident of this city for several years past, has purchased an interest in the drug store conducted by Geo. M. Luttrell on Fourth Street, and henceforth will devote his time to his new work. Mr. Rutherford has long waited for the time when he could resign his position as a traveling salesman with the Coffin-Redington Company in order to settle down with his family. The opportunity to gratify this desire offered itself when he contemplated the purchase of a partnership in Mr. Luttrell's business.

Both gentlemen are well known in this vicinity. The Luttrell drug store has established and maintained a good patronage for a number of years and with two widely experienced men in the business it will be raised to a higher point of efficiency in attendance to the wants of its patrons.

Press Democrat
December 23, 1914

WHAT AWAITS YOU HERE
A comfortable chair
A telephone
A writing desk & material for writing your letters
General information about Carnival
A comfy restroom and you are very welcome
LUTTRELL & RUTHERFORD
PRESCRIPTION DRUGGIST
527 Fourth St. - Santa Rosa
Phone 3   Free Delivery

Press Democrat
May 12, 1915

SPECIAL AGENCY

Goods that we carry a complete stock of: Adlerika, Vinol, Eastman Kodaks and Supplies, A.D.S. Remedies, Dr. David Roberts' Veterinary Remedies and

REXALL REMEDIES

LUTTRELL & RUTHERFORD
PRESCRIPTION DRUGGISTS
527 Fourth St., Santa Rosa
Phone 3   Free Delivery

Press Democrat
June 23, 1915

DISSOLUTION OF PARTNERSHIP

Notice is hereby given, that G. M. Luttrell has acquired all the interest of W. E. Rutherford in the partnership known as Luttrell & Rutherford Drug Company, and in the business conducted by said former firm at 527 Fourth St., Santa Rosa, Cal., and that said partnership is dissolved.

From and after this date, viz: June 25th, 1915 all accounts owing said firm are payable to G. M. Luttrell, and all indebtedness of said firm will be settled by him.

G. M. LUTTRELL
W. E. RUTHERFORD

Press Democrat
June 27, 1915

- **A. F. Mc Lain**
- 637 Fourth Street, F.G. Hahman Block
- Sold to R.B. Reedy & Co.; business moved to 401 4th St. (see page 237)
- December 22, 1891 – September 27, 1895

NOTICE.

I take pleasure in informing the public generally that having purchased of Mr. J. W. Cummings, the store formerly known as the

Guy A. Johnson Drug Store

SITUATED IN THE

Habman Block, Adjoining the Athenæum

WHERE I PROPOSE TO CONDUCT A

First Class Pharmacy in every Respect

The public can rely upon being served with Fresh Drugs and Medicines, all of the best quality. The PRESCRIPTION DEPARTMENT will be a specialty, my assistant being a competent, qualified and experienced Pharmacist.

In conjunction with the store I will open a

DENTAL OFFICE

Where I will be pleased to receive my old friends and patrons as well as all others who may need dental services.

A. F. McLAIN, M. D., D. D.

de22dwtf

Sonoma Democrat
December 22, 1891

Having disposed my Drug Store to Mr. R. B. Reedy & Co., a worthy, competent pharmacist, I take method of returning thanks to my friends and patrons for the liberal support they have heretofore given me; and would at the same time earnestly bespeak the continuance of the same to my successor. I can be found in my office for professional or other business matters.

A. F. McLain

Sonoma Democrat
October 5, 1895

TO THE CRESCENT CITY

Dr. A. F. McLain leaves Santa Rosa today for Louisiana where he will practice dentistry. His health has not been good for some time past and he makes the change in hopes of being benefited. He has been in Santa Rosa eleven years. He sold out his drug store a short time ago. He has been an active officer and member of the Congregational Church. His wife will remain here for the present.

Sonoma Democrat
December 21, 1895

- **R. B. Reedy & Co.**
  - The Model Drug Store, 401 Fourth Street, NE corner A Street
    - Ray B. Reedy (purchased A.F. McLain's stock): October 1895 – January 1897
    - Ray B. Reedy & Martin Muller: Jan-June 1897 (then Muller alone until Jan. 1902)
  - The Peoples Drug Store, 223 Exchange Ave. (see pages 194, 247)
    - Ray B. Reedy & Carl G. Fischer: June 24–December 1897
    - Ray B. Reedy & Jas. Ewing: Dec. 1897–March 1898 (then Ewing alone to Feb 1902)

R. B. Reedy, a San Francisco pharmacist, has bought the drug store of A. F. McLain and will restock with a full and complete line of drugs, druggist's sundries, and other stock usually carried by a first-class drug store. Mr. Reedy has enjoyed a previous successful business career in San Francisco.
Sonoma Democrat - September 28, 1895

Martin Muller, who until recently was steward and superintendent at the county hospital, has purchased half-interest in the Model Drug Store and is now to be found there.
Sonoma Democrat - January 30, 1897

THE PEOPLES DRUG STORE
C. G. Fischer, Proprietor — R. B. Reedy, Manager
223 Exchange Avenue, next to Savings Bank
Opens Today with a full line of Drugs, Chemicals and Fancy Goods.
Press Democrat - June 24, 1897

SR-D-21

THE MODEL
DRUG STORE
R. B. REEDY & CO.
SANTA ROSA, CAL.
Dose glass
2 inches tall
Reverse: TABLE
DESSERT
TEA
Base: W. T. & CO. AT USA

Helmut & DeAnna Jordt collection

Press Democrat
December 1, 1898

A BRANCH POSTAL STATION
Is now located in Martin Muller's drugstore on the corner of
Fourth and A Streets.
Money orders and stamps can be obtained and letters can be registered there.
Press Democrat - March 4, 1899

Note: Raymond Berthold Reedy (1847-1923) had been a druggist in San Jose and San Francisco before opening a store in Santa Rosa in 1895. He moved to Honolulu, Hawaii in 1898.

- **Oscar Morrison** (lived 1847-1910)
- 6 Ridgway Block (west side of plaza)
- January 7, 1882 – October 1883; formed short-lived partnership with H.W. Hill (page 240)
- Purchased W.E. Bryant's Plaza Drug Store (page 183)
- Sold to John W. Zimmerman – see page 287

OSCAR MORRISON PURCHASES BRYANT DRUG STORE

Oscar Morrison has purchased the Bryant Drug Store on Exchange Avenue and has placed it under the management of M. F. Patterson, an experienced chemist from the east.

Sonoma Democrat
January 7, 1882

OSCAR MORRISON,
— DEALER IN —
DRUGS, MEDICINES
And Chemicals!
PERFUMERY, SOAPS!
COMBS AND BRUSHES,
TRUSSES, SHOULDER BRACES, FANCY AND TOILET ARTICLES, BOOKS, STATIONERY, JEWELRY AND NOTIONS, OILS, LAMPS AND CHIMNEYS, GARDEN SEEDS, ETC., ETC., ETC.

PURE WINES AND LIQUORS!
For Medicinal Purposes.
Patent Medicines, Etc.
— AGENT FOR THE —
NEW FAMILY SINGER SEWING MACHINE.
Sewing Needles for All Machines.

The Drug Department is under the management of MR. M. F. PATTERSON, an experienced Druggist and Chemist. Physicians' Prescriptions accurately compounded AT ALL HOURS.

NO. 6 RIDGWAY BLOCK, SANTA ROSA.
(Next door to Savings Bank.)

Sonoma Democrat
April 8, 1882

MORRISON'S DRUG STORE

No. 6 Ridgway Block, Santa Rosa,

Next door to Santa Rosa Savings Bank, has just been re-opened with a new, fresh and complete stock of

DRUGS, MEDICINES

PERFUMERY, TOILET ARTICLES, ETC.,

Under the management of H. W. HILL, a Practical Druggist.

☞ Prescriptions carefully compounded, day and night.　　　　　　　　　my8-daw-1m

Sonoma Democrat
May 8, 1883

Physician's prescriptions carefully compounded
At Morrison's Plaza Drug Store

A line of beautiful toilet preparations
And fine perfumery just received
At Morrison's Drug Store

Morrison's Plaza Drug Store
is now open for business with fresh stock of
drugs, under the management of H. W. Hill.

Sonoma Democrat
August 24, 1883

DEATH CALLS FOR OSCAR MORRISON

Mr. Morrison was a resident of the county and State for about half a century and was engaged in business in Santa Rosa and Guerneville. In Santa Rosa he conducted a drug store and dry goods store and in Guerneville he was proprietor of similar stores and a lumber yard. He was widely known and to many of his friends, who were not aware of his illness, his death came as a surprise on Thursday.

The deceased was a native of Iowa and was a son of the venerable Samuel Morrison, one of Santa Rosa's highly esteemed and aged residents.

Press Democrat
January 28, 1910

- **Morrison & Hill** (Oscar Morrison and Harvard W. Hill)
- 516 Fourth Street (between B and Exchange - Overton Bldg.)
- May-November 1884 (see Hill & Wheeler, page 222)

Morrison & Hill,

Have just opened with a new and complete stock of

DRUGS, MEDICINES, PERFUMERY, ARTISTS MATERIALS, PAINTS, OILS, WINDOW GLASS, ETC.

At 516 Fourth Street, Santa Rosa.

Tuttle & Chamberlin's old stand.

EVERYTHING IN OUR NEW STORE WILL BE FOUND FIRST CLASS AND PRICES WAY down. We extend a cordial invitation to all, especially our old patrons and friends, to come and see us.

Prescriptions prepared at all hours from pure drugs by OSCAR MORRISON.

H. W. HILL, Druggist.

my5-dawtf

Sonoma Democrat
May 5, 1884

Note: Harvard W. Hill, a trained chemist, moved to Los Angeles and by 1903 was the president of a proprietary medicine firm, the Hill Yerba Lip-Tus Company.

CALIFORNIA YERBA LIP-TUS

THE DESTROYER OF CATARRH, either nasal or catarrh of the stomach, indigestion or dyspepsia.

YOU WON'T BELIEVE it will cure you; this proves you have never used Yerba Lip-Tus or even heard of it or the grateful testimony of others.

I had catarrh for 30 years, but Yerba Lip-Tus cured me.
JAMES D. TODD,
774 San Julian Street.

I suffered 15 years with catarrh of the stomach and nervous dyspepsia. The Yerba Lip-Tus remedies cured me.
MRS. W. SUESS,
550 South Grand Avenue.

Either remedy 50c at druggists or by mail.

Hill Yerba Lip-Tus Co.
786 San Pedro Street

Los Angeles Herald
December 16, 1903

- **Felix Harry Newman** (lived 1870-1906)
  - The Santa Rosa Pharmacy, 547 Fourth Street, NW corner Mendocino Avenue
  - March 1896 – April 18, 1906

F. H. NEWMAN

The drug store owned by Mr. Newman occupies as good a location as there is in the city. It is neatly kept and finely appearing store and well stocked. The soda fountain that graces that part of the store nearest the door is one of the finest in the city.

Mr. Newman is a graduate of the California College of Pharmacy, class of '91. He was connected with drug houses in San Francisco and the southern part of the state until March of this year when he purchased the present store.

He is the manufacturer of the California Compound Cough Syrup, and Traill's Cream Balm, two specialties that are of considerable merit and have met with a good sale. The Cream Balm is very effective in treating sunburn, tan, etc. He is agent for Warren's London Corn Cure, a sure cure for corns, bunions, warts, etc.

He makes a specialty of prompt and careful service in the prescription department. Someone is in attendance at all hours of the day and night.

Sonoma Democrat
November 21, 1896

F. H. Newman has secured the appointment as U. S. postal agent, and will hereafter keep stamps and stamped envelopes for sale at his drug store.

Sonoma Democrat
June 5, 1897

Felix Harry Newman was killed during the April 18, 1906 earthquake (see page 173)

Press Democrat
March 9, 1898

The Pleasure of Cleanliness

Looking after the little things. The little articles which make the toilet pleasant and perfect are the things you are interested in. You may not know the difference there is in soaps, brushes, or soft appliances but they are the important things you should consider. Let us give you some pointers.

The Santa Rosa Pharmacy
F. H. NEWMAN, Prop.
Cor. 4th and Mendocino Street, Santa Rosa

- **Richard John Pye** (lived 1859-1913; "Major" was his title as IOOF drillmaster)
- Pioneer Drug Store, 611 Fourth Street
- Successor to C.D. Frazee; sold to James H. Lunn (page 232)
- December 1887 – July 1, 1901

The Frazee
PIONEER DRUG STORE !

Carries the best of Everything in its Line.

DRUGS, CHEMICALS AND SURGICAL APPLIANCES,
TOILET ARTICLES, STATIONERY, CIGARS AND SEEDS.

Manufacturing Pharmacy. Prescriptions carefully compounded night and day. NIGHT BELL. A fine line of Holiday Goods at lowest rates.

R. J. PYE & CO.
de8dawtf   Successors to C. D. Frazee

Press Democrat
December 8, 1887

SR-D-22

Chemists
R. J. PYE & CO.
Druggists
Santa Rosa
Clear rectangular
Tooled top
4 3/8 inches tall
Base: S B W
Rick Siri collection

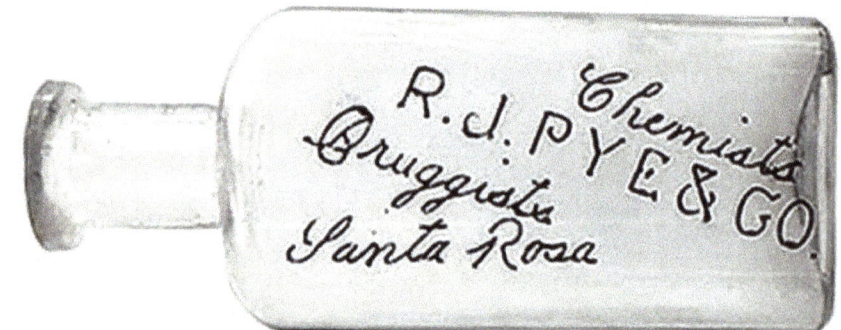

Major Pye Disposes of the Pioneer Drugstore

The many friends of Major R. J. Pye will be surprised to learn that he is no longer owner of the well-known Pioneer Drug Store on Fourth Street. On Monday he sold the business to J. H. Lunn of Salem, Oregon, who arrived here yesterday morning and is in possession of the store.

For some time, past, Mr. Pye has been contemplating the disposal of his business because of ill health, acting on the advice of his physician. His plans for the future he has not outlined definitely, but it is understood that he will engage in business that will not confine him to so much indoors. He has been proprietor of the Pioneer Drug Store since 1887 and during his fourteen years of business life here he has been prominently identified with many leading projects in Santa Rosa. The friends of Mr. and Mrs. Pye hope that they will decide to remain in Santa Rosa.

Mr. Lunn is an experienced man in the drug business and is a very genial gentleman. He has been in business in Oregon, and while here for a short time he took a great fancy to Santa Rosa. Mrs. Lunn and family will arrive here in a few days.

Press Democrat
July 3, 1901

- **Joseph Henry Richardson** (lived 1828-1911)
- East side of plaza: October 1861 – May 1866 ; sold to Thomas Spencer
- SW corner plaza, Miller's Bldg., *Santa Rosa Drug Store*: June 1866 – April 1870. This location was formerly occupied by Dr. Joshua L. Downing and by W.D. Dixon.

DRUGS AND MEDICINES.

J. H. RICHARDSON & CO.,
SANTA ROSA,
Keep constantly on hand a
COMPLETE ASSORTMENT OF
Daugs, Medicines,
Chemicals,
Paints and Oils,
Camphene,
Perfumery,
Patent Medicines.

Also, the Largest and Best Assortment of
BOOKS, Stationery, Legal and Other BLANKS,
FANCY GOODS
Of Every Description,
MUSICAL INSTRUMENTS,
Paper Hangings, etc.,
Ever offered in this market. Remember the place.
☞ EAST SIDE OF PLAZA. ☜
October 16th, 1861.   1 tf

Sonoma Democrat
October 16, 1861

J. H. RICHARDSON
Druggist and Apothecary
East Side of Plaza
Keeps consistently on hand
A LARGE ASSORTMENT OF
Pure Drugs, Medicines, Chemicals, Paints, Varnishes, Oils,
Genuine Patent Medicines, Fancy Goods, Toilet Articles, etc.
Prescriptions Compounded
BOOKS & LEGAL STATIONARY
October 28, 1862
Sonoma Democrat

DRUG STORE FOR SALE.

I OFFER FOR SALE the well established Drug Store, now kept by me, on the most reasonable terms.

THERE IS BUT ONE DRUG STORE IN THE TOWN,

and an excellent opportunity is offered

FOR A PRACTICAL DRUGGIST

to make money.

For further particulars apply in person or by letter to

J. H. RICHARDSON,

27tf   Santa Rosa, Cal.

May 27, 1863
Sonoma Democrat

DRUGS, DRUGS! DRUGS!!

J. H. RICHARDSON,

DRUGGIST,

South-West Corner Plaza, Santa Rosa, Cal.,

WOULD RESPECTFULLY ANNOUNCE TO his many patrons and friends that he has now on hand, and is constantly receiving, the largest and best selected stock of Drugs ever brought to Sonoma county, consisting of

English, French and American Drugs, Medicines and Chemicals,

Paints, Oils and Dye Stuffs;

BRUSHES OF ALL KINDS,

Extracts, Perfumery,

SHAVING AND TOILET SOAPS,

FANCY ARTICLES, ETC.:

Trusses, Supporters, and Instruments

Bronzes, Gold Leaf and Artists' Paints.

— ALSO —

School Books, Stationary,

CIGARS AND TOBACCO.

Remember the Place,

SANTA ROSA DRUG STORE,

South west Corner, Plaza, Santa Rosa, where the undersigned will be found at all hours, DAY AND NIGHT.

J. H. Richardson, Druggist.

May 16, '68-tf.

Sonoma Democrat
May 16, 1868

- **William Carson Reed** (lived 1829-1891)
- 225 Fourth Street: June 1875 – June 1876; Occidental Block, 4th and B Sts.: 1876 – 1877
- 613 Fourth Street (Taylor Building): 1877 – 1885
- 547 Fourth Street (Doyle & Overton Bldg., NW corner Mendocino Avenue):
  August 1, 1885 – May 5, 1887 (sold to Elizabeth J. McGaughey)
- Reed's estate sold a store on Exchange Ave to Hahman & West in April 1891 (see page 210)

W. C. REED

Elegant establishment at the corner of Fourth and Mendocino Street.

W. C. Reed established in this city near the depot in 1875 (225 4th St.), being unable to procure a better location farther up town. At the expiration of one year, in June 1876, he moved to the Occidental block at Fourth and B Sts.; and one year later moved into the Taylor Building where he remained for nine years (613 4th St.) until moving into the handsome store where he is now located. His store is as finely located as any in the city, and he continues to cater to a first-class trade which he has held since his establishment here.

Sonoma Democrat
January 8, 1887

CASH DRUG STORE.—Drugs sold and prescriptions filled at Eastern prices by W. C. Reed, in the office of Wells, Fargo & Co., Occidental Building.   je19-6t

Press Democrat
June 19, 1877

Ed West, clerk in W. C. Reed's drug store, while engaged in mixing and pulverizing some corrosive sublimate Wednesday narrowly escaped being blinded. Some of the powder flew up in his left eye and burned the interior of it badly.

Press Democrat
June 3, 1886

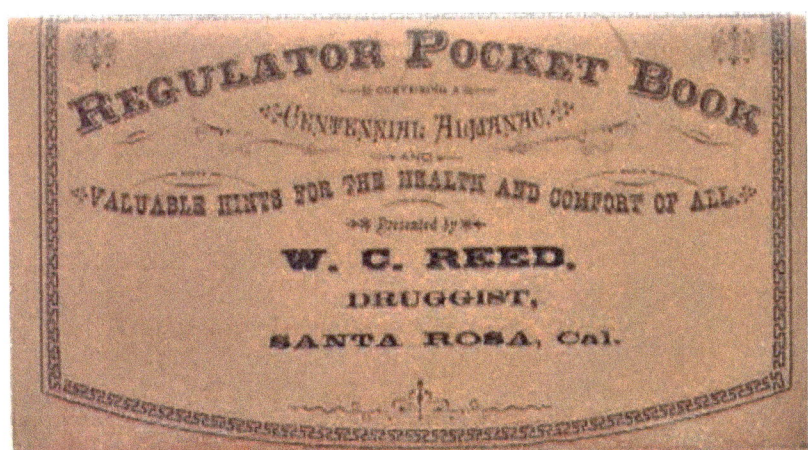

REGULATOR POCKET BOOK and CENTENNIAL ALMANAC
Pocket calendar and health advisor, 1886-1887
ex Frank Sternad collection

Important Notice.

Santa Rosa, Cal., Sept. 25, 1890. We the undersigned druggists, of Santa Rosa, do agree and promise, to enter into and abide by the following agreement, and publish the same that the public may know that he who violates it has broken his word of honor, and should this be broken public notice shall be given with the firm's name violating the same.

We agree that all but one drug store shall be closed on Sundays after the hour of 10:30 A.M. The store being open shall be furnished in rotation, due notice being given by all others, provided, that any store may be opened, at any time, on personal application in case of necessity and for that purpose only.

We understand the "store closed" to mean no business shall be done and ask the public to make arrangements accordingly. This to take effect the first Sunday in October, 1890.

R. J. PYE & CO.
L. McG. BENNETT,
W. C. REED,
GUY A. JOHNSON,
J. W. WARBOYS,
M. H. DIGNAN.

Press Democrat
October 3, 1890

A New Firm.

Ed West, formerly with J. W. Warboys, and Paul Hahman, with R. J. Pye & Co., Saturday, concluded the purchase of the drug store on Exchange avenue from the W. C. Reed estate. Ed and Paul have spent their lives in Santa Rosa and have the confidence of our people. They are are practical pharmaceutists and their knowledge of the business is such as to insure them a prosperous future in their undertaking.

Sonoma Democrat
April 11, 1891

- **The Peoples Drug Store**
  - 223 Exchange Ave. (west side of plaza); see pages 194, 237
  - Ray B. Reedy and Carl G. Fischer: June 24–December 1897
  - Ray B. Reedy and James Ewing: Dec. 1897 – Mar. 1898 (then Ewing alone until Feb. 1902)
  - Sold to Nels Juell (see page 227)

The Peoples Drug Store on Exchange Ave., circa 1897; Hahman's drugstore at left
Courtesy, Sonoma County Library

Vindicated.

After two trials, the case against Druggist R. B. Reedy, has been dismissed. It was developed at the trial by the testimony of Mr. John Calvert, secretary of the State Board of Pharmacy, that the prosecution was inspired by the complaint of several druggists of Santa Rosa, who probably, prefer not to compete with Mr. Reedy, with his 36 years experience as a druggist. But notwithstanding these complaints on the part of these rival druggists, after a careful and patient investigation the case has been dismissed and Mr. Reedy fully exonerated.

Mr. Reedy will be found, as heretofore at the Peoples' Drug Store, next to the Savings Bank on Exchange avenue, and his 36 years' experience as a druggist, and the reputation he has made during his two years' business as a druggist in Santa Rosa, must convince the people that they will make no mistake in giving that drug store their patronage. Physician's prescriptions compounded from absolutely pure drugs and chemicals, will be made a specialty in the future as in the past, at the Peoples' Drug Store. *

Sonoma Democrat
September 18, 1897

- **Thomas J. Riley & Son**
- Golden Eagle Drug Store
- 442 Fourth Street, opposite Occidental Hotel
- August 27, 1887 – July 1889 (exchanged stores with H.D. Kellogg of San Jose)

Sonoma Democrat
October 29, 1887

GOLDEN EAGLE DRUG STORE
Onward Bound.
Ahoy There! Look Out for Breakers!

Look out for our new goods; Look out for our Low Prices; Look out for our Big Bargains.
The attention of Everyone is invited to our

NEW STOCK OF DRUGS, CHEMICALS, ETC.
T. J. RILEY & SON,
THE ONWARD BOUND DRUGGISTS.

Progressive Methods, Quick Time, and no waste of Money; Best accomodation for all; Low Prices on all lines; The rapid sale system. Down breaks. Stop at the GOLDEN EAGLE PHARAMACY. That's our Store. Receiving new goods every day! Receiving a Booming Trade!

Hear that Whistle. See Old High Prices Get Off the Track

THE ECONOMY RAIL ROAD.

TO SUCCESS.	TO EXCELENCE.	TO QUALITY.	TO SAVINGVILLE.
TO PLENTY.	TO SATISFACTION.	TO RAPID SALES.	TO RELIABILITY.
TO LOW PRICES.			

RUNS DIRECT TO 442 FOURTH STREET.
That's Our Store.
FREE PASSES To Economy, Prosperity and any and all the above points issued every patron of

T. J. RILEY & SON,
Golden Eagle Drug Store, 442 Fourth St., Santa Rosa, Cal.
NIGHT BELL.

SR-D-22A
GOLDEN EAGLE
DRUG STORE
SANTA ROSA
Clear dose glass

T. J. Riley of this city and H. D. Kellogg of San Jose have traded drug stores. Mr. Kellogg has already arrived and taken possession. Mr. Riley expects to depart for San Jose on Monday. We welcome Mr. Kellogg into our midst and express regret at the departure of Mr. Riley. [see page 230]

Press Democrat
July 6, 1889

- **William Edward Rutherford** (lived 1876-1962)
- 401 Mendocino Ave., NW cor. Fifth St., The Quality Drug Store: July 1915 – October 1922
- 601 Fourth St., NE corner Mendocino Ave. (Rosenberg Bldg.): October 7, 1922 – June 1932
- 529 Fourth Street (Rutherford Drug Co.): June 1932 – May 6, 1936
- Sold to Theron and Lowell Hall (see page 218)

> **MOVED**
> and ready for business
> **Rutherford's Drug Store**
> **PHONE 100**
> **Rosenberg Building**
> **COR. 4th AND MENDOCINO**

Santa Rosa Republican
October 7, 1922

SPRAY TO PREVENT "FLU"
Germs enter the system through the nose and throat. Nose and throat treated with a strong germicidal anti-septic solution clears and purifies the passages and destroys the germs at point of attack.
CACTUS ANTI-SEPTIC SOLUTION
is the best for the purpose. Also fine as a mouth wash, for all ulcers, sores and anti-septic uses.
RUTHERFORD'S DRUG STORE
FOURTH AND MENDOCINO
OPEN SUNDAYS

Press Democrat
January 17, 1923

Mrs. Mollie Claypool to Join W. E. Rutherford
Mrs. Mollie Claypool, who conducted the drug store in the Occidental Hotel building for a number of years after the death of her husband, has accepted a position with W. E. Rutherford in his drug store, where she will be glad to see her many friends.

Press Democrat
October 18, 1925

C.R. BUTLER NOW WITH RUTHERFORD
Clarence Raymond Butler, well known Santa Rosa pharmacist, is now associated with the Rutherford Drug Company. Butler has been a leader in pharmacy in Santa Rosa the past 13 years and is well known throughout Sonoma County.

Press Democrat
December 28, 1935

SR-D-23

Labeled clear abm plastic screw cap:
Net Contents...*2*...Ozs. *SAT. SOL.*
BORACIC ACID
(BORIC ACID)
RUTHERFORD'S DRUG STORE
PRESCRIPTION DRUGGISTS
COR. FOURTH ST. & MENDOCINO AVE. SANTA ROSA

Richard Siri collection

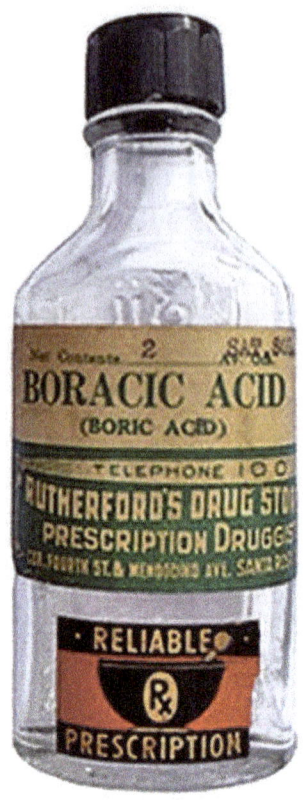

Rutherford's Drug Store, NE corner Fourth and Mendocino, circa 1925

RUTHERFORD'S IS SOLD

The sale of Rutherford Drug Co. at 529 Fourth Street to Theron E. and Lowell H. Hall, former Santa Rosa youths who for the past seven years have been district managers for a coast-wide drug concern, was announced yesterday. The Hall brothers are sons of C.T. Hall, partner in Hall Brothers Hardware Store on Roberts Avenue.

With the sale, William E. Rutherford, former mayor of Santa Rosa, will retire from the retail drug business in this city, with which he has been connected for 20 years. His plans for the future are indefinite, he said. Notice of intention of sale was filed by Rutherford yesterday in the county recorder's office.

The Hall brothers will arrive here today from Berkeley to complete arrangements for the taking over of the Fourth Street store, constructed four years ago by Rutherford after he had moved from the corner of Mendocino and Fourth, where he operated a drug store for 10 years. Prior to that time, Rutherford was in business at Fifth and Mendocino.

Both graduate pharmacists, the Hall brothers have been connected with the Owl Drug Company, Theron managing one of the company's stores in Berkeley, while Lowell has been in charge of the concern's branch in Spokane, Washington.

Rutherford who is president of the California Pharmaceutical Association, came to Santa Rosa in 1914 from San Francisco, where he had been in the wholesale drug business. He opened his first store here in January of the following year [Luttrell & Rutherford]. He served as mayor of Santa Rosa in 1918, '19, and '20 and at the present is a member of the Sonoma County Probation Committee. He has been connected with the National Retail Druggists association for 18 years.

"Other than that, I will retire from the retail drug business. My plans are indefinite, although, as far as know now, I will continue to maintain my home here," he said. "I have about two months more work with the state pharmaceutical association and after that I'm not sure what I will do."

Both Hall brothers attended local schools, but have not lived here since they left to attend college.

Press Democrat
May 7, 1936

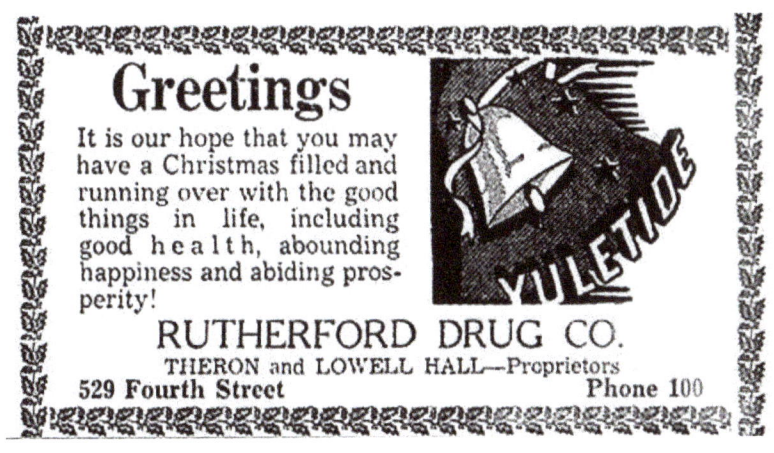

Press Democrat - December 25, 1938

- **Thomas Spencer**
  - Successor to Joseph H. Richardson, east side of plaza
  - May 1866 – October 14, 1871
  - August 1870 moved to new brick "Post Office Building" on NW corner of Main and 2nd Sts.
  - Sold stock to Rufus A. Temple who in turn moved business to his own "Postoffice Building" on Fourth Street (see page 267).

Dr. Spencer of this place is having his new brick building on Main Street fitted up in excellent style. It will be used as a drug store and post office, and the Doctor informs us that he doesn't intend any similar establishment this side of the Bay City to surpass it in appearance.

Sonoma Democrat
May 28, 1870

Dr. SPENCER RELOCATING

Dr. Spencer is now preparing to move his Drug Store from the old stand which he has occupied for many years to his fine new building on Main Street, opposite the Kessing Hotel. He has fitted this building up in fine style, and it will now compare favorably with any similar establishment this side of the Bay City.

Sonoma Democrat
July 2, 1870

THOS. SPENCER,

Druggist and Apothecary,

POST OFFICE BUILDING, SANTA ROSA,

KEEPS CONSTANTLY ON HAND a large and well-selected stock of pure, fresh

Drugs, Patent Medicines, Perfumery,

WINES AND BRANDIES,

And everything usually kept in a First-class Drug Store.

Also, School Books, Pens, Ink, Envelops, Legal Blanks, Writing Paper, Etc.

Physicians' prescriptions carefully prepared at all hours.

Agent for Phœnix and Home Fire Insurance Company.   au27 ly

Sonoma Democrat
August 27, 1870

- **Robert Press Smith, Jr.** (lived 1839-1899)
  - One of Sonoma County's early physicians (office at J.H. Richardson's drugstore 1868-69)
  - Purchased Rufus A. Temple's stock and moved to NW corner Fourth and B Streets
  - August 1876 – December 1879; sold to Dozier & Hall (see page 193)

NEW TO-DAY.

R. PRESS SMITH, M. D.,
PHYSICIAN & SURGEON,

HAS removed his office from the Drug Store of J. H. Richardson, and may be found for the present in Roney's Brick building, up-stairs, second door.
Santa Rosa, April 2d, 1870.tf

Sonoma Democrat
April 2, 1870

CHANGE OF FIRM.

R. P. Smith having bought R. A. Temple's

DRUG STORE

Solicits the patronage of the public in Santa Rosa and vicinity.

WILL KEEP A FULL SUPPLY OF FRESH Drugs, Chemicals, Perfumery and other articles usually found in a well-kept Drug Store. Also an assortment of

STATIONERY AND SCHOOL BOOKS.

Prescriptions carefully and promptly filled by a competent Druggist and Apothecary. The store has been removed to the

Corner of Fourth and B streets,
Under Occidental Hotel, Postoffice Building.
au2-dwtf

Press Democrat
August 2, 1876

DR. SMITH'S WILL

Petition Filed In the Probate Court Yesterday

The Deceased Physician Left All His Property to His Wife Who Is Executrix

The will of the late Dr. Robert Press Smith was filed yesterday for probate in the Superior Court by the sole executrix named therein, Mrs. Nellie M. Smith, through her attorney, W. E. McConnell.

In his olographic will made in 1896, the deceased bequeaths all his property to his wife with the exception of a bequest of some notes and fifty dollars to his son, Edwin DuBose Smith. He states that in leaving all his property to his wife he knows she will look after the interests of the minor children. Mrs. Smith is named as sole executrix without bonds. The testator provides that when the estate is settled his wife may make another bequest of an amount she deems fit, to E. D. Smith.

The property in the main consists of 72 acres of land in Sonoma county valued at about $7500, a half interest in 131 acres of land on Mark West Creek valued at about $1500, building lots in Ludwig's addition valued at about $1000, the family residence and lot on A street, Santa Rosa, valued at about $5000. The total value of the property does not exceed $15,000.

Press Democrat
October 25, 1899

Robert Press Smith, Jr., MD
circa 1870

SR-D-24
    RPS (monogram)
    DRUG STORE
    SANTA ROSA, CAL.
    Clear oval
    Tooled top
    2 3/4 inches tall
    3 3/4 inches tall
    4 1/4 inches tall
    Base: W. T. & CO. B
    John Burton collection

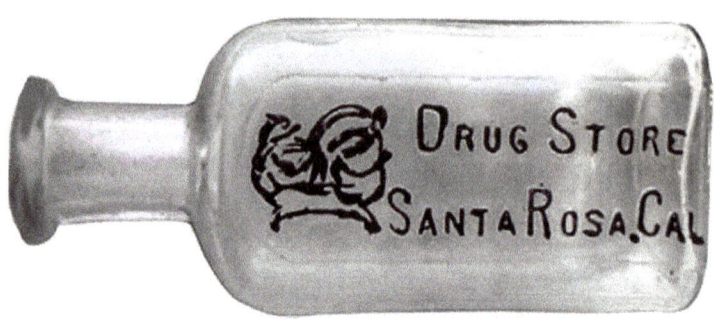

SR-D-25
    RPS (monogram)
    DRUG STORE
    SANTA ROSA, CAL.
    Clear oval
    Tooled top
    5 1/8 inches tall
    Base: W. T. & CO. 9
    Dan Brown collection

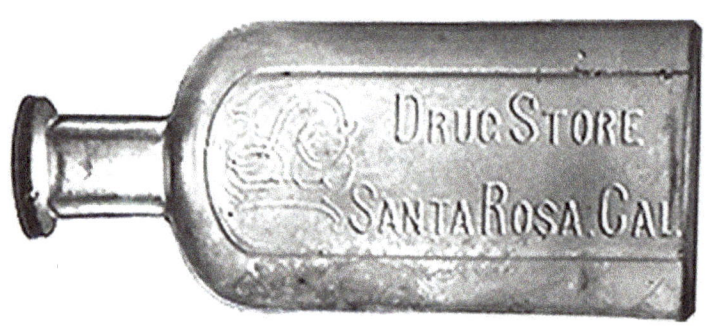

DR. SMITH DEAD.

Old and Highly Respected Resident of Santa Rosa.

SANTA ROSA, Oct. 19.—Dr. R. Press Smith, one of the best known and oldest physicians of Sonoma County, died at his residence in this city to-night after a critical illness. He was universally respected and at the time of his death was Health Officer of Santa Rosa. He was a prominent Mason and belonged to a number of other fraternal societies. Dr. Smith was a native of Charleston, S. C. He came to California in 1868 and since then has resided in Santa Rosa. During the civil war he was a captain in the First South Carolina Regiment and served with distinction. He was a member of the Episcopal Church vestry and one of the best known churchmen in this State, having served a number of years as a member of the standing committee. He leaves a widow and eight children.

San Francisco Call
October 20, 1899

- **William Benjamin Snodgrass**
- Druggist in Portland, Oregon in 1890
- July 30 – December 24, 1892; sold to Charles C. Van Valkenburg
- 547 Fourth Street, NW corner Mendocino (Doyle & Overton Bldg.)

SNODGRASS PURCHASES MRS. BENNETTS DRUG STORE

Mr. Snodgrass, late of Sisson, purchased the drug store on the corner of Fourth and Mendocino Streets from Mrs. Bennett. Mr. Snodgrass is an experienced pharmacist and will be welcomed as a valuable acquisition to our city.

Sonoma Democrat
July 30, 1892

C. C. Van Valkenburg has purchased the drug store at the corner of Fourth and Mendocino Streets from W. B. Snodgrass.

Sonoma Democrat
December 24, 1892

BULLET KILLS BOY BY ACCIDENT.

SPECIAL DISPATCH TO THE CALL.

IONE, Or., Sept. 15.—While playing around the hardware store of W. B. Snodgrass, Arthur Cochran, eight years old, was shot in the head and almost instantly killed by a revolver in the hands of the proprietor of the store. The shooting was purely accidental, and no blame attaches to Snodgrass, but the storekeeper is overcome with grief. Snodgrass was examining a 32-caliber revolver. He knew it was loaded, but in some manner the weapon was discharged the bullet entering the boy's right eye and lodging in his brain. Snodgrass came here recently from San Francisco, where he was burned out and nearly lost his life in the recent disaster. The parents of the dead boy are old residents of this place. They are very much distressed by the sad occurrence.

San Francisco Call
September 16, 1906

- **Sontag Drug Store**
  - 627 Fourth Street
  - An early discount chain drugstore
  - August 22, 1937 – June 1942

WORK BEGUN ON NEW DRUG FIRM

Alterations of the former Mitchell building in Fourth Street to house the Sontag Drug Store was started yesterday by workmen from the Unit Built Fixture company of San Francisco, the firm manufacturing and installation of all fixtures and store fronts for the drug chain.

Under plans announced yesterday the entire portion of the building, formerly occupied by the Economy Market, will be rebuilt to permit thirteen-foot show windows and a fifty-foot display floor. All the latest type fixtures are being installed, workmen said. The completed installation will cost in excess of $7,000. The store is expected to open about August 1.

Press Democrat
July 22, 1937

SONTAG OPENS BRANCH STORE

Santa Rosa shoppers added another modern new store to their list Friday with the formal opening of the Sontag Drug Store on Fourth Street.

View of the front of the new Sontag Drug Store, 627 Fourth street, which opened yesterday

The new firm, latest branch of a chain of 47 throughout California, specializes in the sale of all nationally advertised merchandise at the lowest possible prices. A complete stock is carried in drugs, sundries, liquors and tobaccos.

The store, completely modern throughout, is one of the first air-conditioned shopping havens in the city. It is the first of the Sontag chain in the North Bay, which started from a single store in Los Angeles.

A staff of five, headed by A. Rustigan, manager, offers ready and efficient service. Rustigan is assisted by Brinley Williams of Santa Rosa. Others on the staff are Lois Puffer, Carolou Western and Mabel Rider. D. A, Hart, district supervisor, is temporarily here to aid in launching the store successfully.

Santa Rosa Republican
August 23, 1937

- **William McKenzie Stewart** (lived 1859-1928)
- Stewart Manufacturing Co. incorporated March 31, 1902
- Stewart's Drug Store, 401 Fourth St., NE corner A Street (former Model Drug Store run by H.S. Davis): May 1904, renamed St. Rose Drug Store March 20, 1905.
- This brick building survived the April 18, 1906 earthquake and fire. Stewart was open for business at same location within a month.
- William's son Even McK. Stewart had interest in store since 1921; William died July 3, 1928
- Proprietorship styled Stewart & Stewart 1929-1934 ; also St. Rose Drug Co. 1931-1943
- May 1904 – May 1943 (business sold to Tomasco Drug Co. at 331 Fourth St., see page 266)

NEW COMPANY INCORPORATED

Articles of Incorporation of the Stewart Manufacturing Company were filed in the County Clerk's office on Monday. The incorporators are: Wm. McKenzie Stewart, Prince Albert Meneray, M. D., J. H. Lunn, L. B. Lawson, all of this city, and R. M. Brown of Oakland. These five men also compose the board of directors.

The capital stock of the concern is $75,000, divided into shares of the par value of $100 per share. The amount of capital stock subscribed is $55,000, of which Stewart has $15,000, Meneray $10,000, Lunn $10,000, Brown $5,000, Mrs. Mary Stewart $2,500, and Belle Tannahill $2,500. The principle place of business is Santa Rosa.

The purpose of incorporation is to manufacture and sell drugs, etc. Some time ago, William McKenzie Stewart, who is with the Lunn Drug Company, perfected a tasteless castor oil, and the oil will now be manufactured and placed upon the market.

Press Democrat – April 1, 1902

Note: *Stewart's Odorless and Tasteless Castor Oil* was registered with the U.S. Patent Office on July 8, 1902 (Label No. 9293). Purification of castor oil is achieved by a vacuum steam distillation process which removes volatile substances responsible for undesirable flavors, colors, and odors.

STEWART'S DRUG STORE

I am pleased to announce to the residents of Santa Rosa and vicinity that about May 23rd I will open a new Drug Store with a new and select stock of Fresh Drugs and Druggist's Sundries, in the building formerly known as the "Model Drug Store," corner Fourth and A Streets, Santa Rosa.

An experience of years as a prescription druggist qualifies me to compound the prescription of any physician correctly to ensure beneficial effect intended by the doctor. None but the best quality of drugs will be used in my prescription department and scrupulous exactness may be relied on in the filling of all prescriptions.

Respectfully, Wm. McK. Stewart, Apothecary
401 Fourth St., corner of A

Santa Rosa Republican
May 20, 1904

ST. ROSE DRUG STORE

Wm. McK. Stewart, who conducts a drugs store at 401 Fourth Street, corner of A Street, has given his establishment the name of St. Rose Drug Store by which it will be known as hereafter.

Press Democrat
March 21, 1905

Stewart's Drug Store.
401 Fourth Street, Corner A   **Santa Rosa, Cal.**

When there is illness in your home, and the critical period approaches, you find yourself wondering if the medicine is really the best to be had. So much **depends upon the medicine.** Bring your prescriptions to us, and you can be sure that NONE but the highest standard drugs and chemicals will be used, and that every prescription will be filled with as much carefulness and accuracy as if the medicine were for one in our own family. We would like an opportunity to DEMONSTRATE THESE FACTS TO YOU.

Phone Red 341   **WM. McK. STEWART**

Press Democrat
June 23, 1904

FOR ALL MEDICAL PURPOSES USE STEWART'S ODORLESS AND TASTELESS CASTOR OIL

Santa Rosa Republican
September 12, 1904

IMPORTANT SCIENTIFIC DISCOVERY

For years it has been the ambition of chemists to remove from castor oil its obnoxious taste and odor. Heretofore the nearest approach was by sweetening and flavoring but the desired effects by this means disguise is brief for the patient is soon conscious that it is the same old Castor oil that he has taken with all its disagreeable features in evidence.

It remained for a Santa Rosa Druggist, Mr. Wm. McK. Stewart, proprietor of the St. Rose Drug Store, to effectually solve the problem and render Castor oil not only pleasant to the taste but palatable, while the medicinal properties are unimpaired.

Mr. Stewart's discovery has before been rendered by the Press Democrat and we are now pleased to note the Stewart's Odorless and Tasteless Castor Oil is being given the preference by physicians and is attaining popular favor wherever introduced, and in fact may now be obtained from up-to-date druggist's throughout California.

Press Democrat
July 7, 1905

St. Rose Drug Store
WM. McK. STEWART, Proprietor
Fourth and A Sts., Santa Rosa

**Best Prescription Work,
The Best Drugs,
The Best Perfumes,
The Best Toilet Articles.**

I keep in stock all the standard Patent Medicines and Druggists' Sundries. I have a well selected stock of Trusses, Abdominal Supporters, Elastic Stockings, Knee Caps, Anklets, Shoulder Braces, Hot Water Bottles. Fountain Syringes, Etc.

Press Democrat
July 6, 1907

St. Rose Drug Store, NE corner 4th and A Sts., survived the 1906 earthquake and fire
Views of Santa Rosa and Vicinity, Before and After the Disaster. Temple Smith, 1906, p.16

St. Rose Drug Store, Wm. McK. Stewart, Proprietor
NE corner 4th & A Streets

Portfolio of Santa Rosa and Vicinity. H.A. Darms, 1909, p.87

1912 St. Rose Drug Store advertising calendar
Richard Siri collection

SR-D-26

℥viii
ST. ROSE DRUG STORE
SANTA ROSA, CAL.
Clear rectangular
Tooled top
6 3/4 inches tall

John Burton collection

SR-D-27

℥ii
ST. ROSE DRUG STORE
SANTA ROSA, CAL.
Clear rectangular
Tooled top
4 ½ inches tall

Dale Chase collection

SR-D-28

Labeled clear tincture bottle:
BROWN MIXTURE
ST. ROSE DRUG STORE
WM. McK. STEWART, Prop.
4th & A STREETS SANTA ROSA, CAL.

Richard Siri collection

Labeled pasteboard carton:
TUMERIC (misspelling of Turmeric)
ST. ROSE DRUG STORE
WM. McK. STEWART, Prop.
4th & A STREETS   SANTA ROSA, CAL.

Richard Siri collection

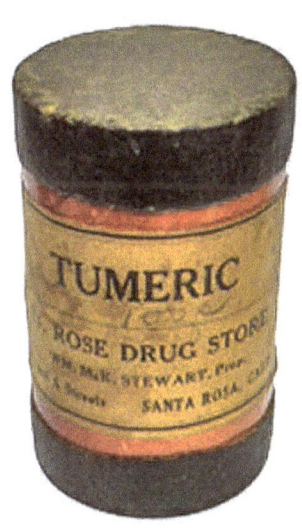

Press Democrat - June 26, 1927

Labeled pasteboard carton:
Net Contents....6....Av. Ozs.
FLAX SEED
ST. ROSE DRUG STORE
STEWART & STEWART, PROPS.
4th & A STREETS   SANTA ROSA, CAL.

Richard Siri collection

Labeled pasteboard carton:
EPSOM SALT
ST. ROSE DRUG STORE
STEWART & STEWART, Props.
4th & A STREETS   SANTA ROSA, CAL.

Richard Siri collection

NUE-OVO A Pure Herbal Remedy — It Removes the Cause for Rheumatism, Neuritis, Lumbago, Articular, Muscular and Inflammatory.

We Give S. & H. Green Stamps

Phone 76 St. Rose Drug Store N.E. Cor. 4th and A

STEWART & STEWART, Props., Santa Rosa
"THE PLACE WHERE YOU GET A SQUARE DEAL"

Santa Rosa Republican
October 30, 1931

FOR COLDS
California Eucalyptus Cough Remedy
Eureka Cold Capsules

—Si Parla Italiano—

Phone 76 St. Rose Drug Store N.E. Cor. 4th and A

STEWART & STEWART, Props., Santa Rosa
"THE PLACE WHERE YOU GET A SQUARE DEAL"

Santa Rosa Republican
March 30, 1934

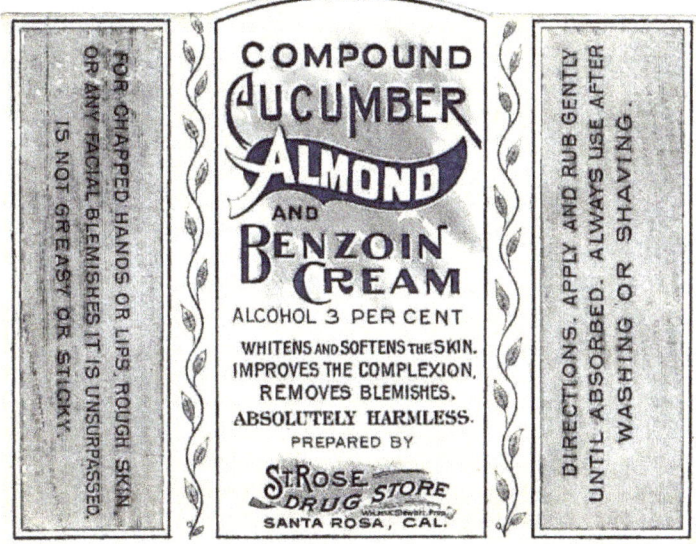

Proprietary remedy labels, circa 1907-1928
John Burton collection

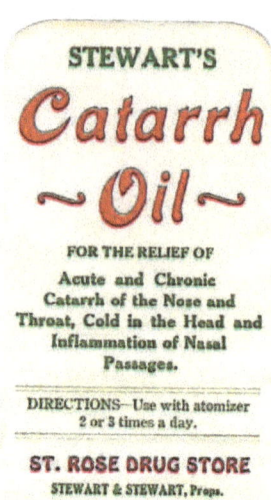

St. Rose Drug Store, 4th & A, circa 1930, looking north to Post Office on 5th St.

Proprietary remedy labels, circa 1929-1943
John Burton collection

Labeled pasteboard carton
(label is for bottled product):
STEWART'S
CELERY
BRAND
NERVINE
ST. ROSE DRUG STORE
EVEN McK. STEWART, Prop.
401 Fourth St.   Santa Rosa, Calif.
7 ½ inches tall
Metal cap
John Burton collection

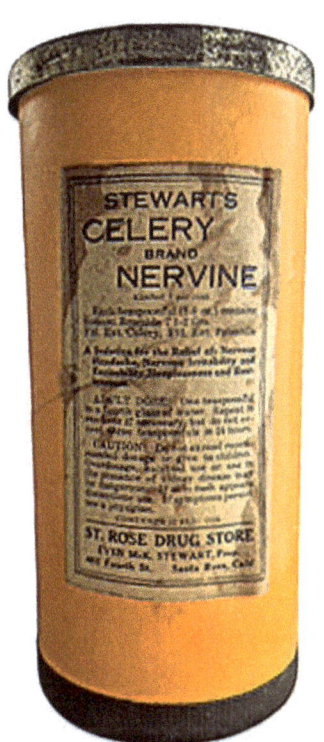

Members of Northwestern Bottle Collectors Assn. digging the former site of St. Rose Drug Store on April 22, 1972 (looking west to A Street and the Elk's Building).

Photo by Frank Sternad

St. Rose's Drug Company Is Purchased by Tomasco Firm

The St. Rose Drug Store, pioneer Santa Rosa business establishment, has been purchased by the Tomasco Drug Co., it was announced yesterday.

Stock, store records, and prescription files have been moved across A street to the Tomasco store, where charge accounts of the St. Rose store will now be available to its customers.

Even McK. Stewart, former proprietor of the St. Rose store, will be associated with the Tomasco firm.

At present on a two-week vacation, he will join the Tomasco firm as one of the three registered pharmacists there. Others include the owner, "Ang" Franchetti, and Oliver Roy Tuttle.

The St. Rose Drug Store, located at Fourth and A streets, was established in May 1, 1905, by the late William McK. Stewart, who was active in the store until his death in July of 1928. His wife took over his interest in 1928 and was active in the business until her death in 1930. Even McK. Stewart entered the business as a partner in 1921. Since the death of his mother he has operated the establishment.

To Our Friends and Patrons:

WE HAVE CLOSED!

Our Entire Stock Including Our Prescription Files and Other Records Have Been Moved to the

TOMASCO DRUG CO.

Elks' Building, Santa Rosa

Where They Will Be Available To Our Former Patrons

"I take this opportunity to thank my friends and customers for their kind patronage during the years we have been in business. On and after May 15th I will be at the Tomasco Drug Company. I will be glad of the opportunity to continue serving you there." EVEN McK. STEWART.

ST. ROSE DRUG STORE

Press Democrat
May 2, 1943

- **Rufus A. Temple**
- Fourth Street, NW corner Mendocino Avenue, *Postoffice Building*
- November 1871 – August 1876
- February 10, 1872 Temple appointed Postmaster of Santa Rosa, replacing Thomas Spencer.
- Sold to Dr. Robert Press Smith (see page 253)

RUFUS A. TEMPLE,
Druggist and Apothecary,
Postoffice Building.
FOURTH STREET, : : : SANTA ROSA,

KEEPS CONSTANTLY ON HAND A large and well selected stock of pure, fresh

Drugs, Patent Medicines, Perfumery,
WINES AND BRANDIES,

And everything usually kept in a first-class drug store. Also, school books, pens, ink, envelops, legal blanks, writing paper, etc.

Physicians' prescriptions carefully prepared at all hours

Agent for Knowlton & Co.s' Inks, Liquid Blueing, &c.

de2 1y

December 2, 1871
Sonoma Democrat

RUFUS A. TEMPLE,
Druggist and Apothecary,
POSTOFFICE BUILDING,

Fourth street......................................Santa Rosa,

KEEPS CONSTANTLY ON HAND A FULL and well selected stock of Drugs, Patent Medicines, Perfumery, Wines and Brandies, and everything usually kept in a first-class Drug Store.

Also, School Books, Pens, Ink, Envelopes, Legal Blanks, Writing Paper, Etc.

Physic'ans' Prescriptions carefully prepared at all hours.

Agent for Knowlton & Co's Inks, Liquid Blueing, Etc.   de2 1y

Press Democrat
December 14, 1872

- **I. S. Titus & Co.** (Isaac Spicer Titus, lived 1863-1934)
- 11 Exchange Avenue; Plaza Drug Store
- Successor to J.M. Zimmerman; sold to R.J. Humphreys
- July 1885 – October 1887 (insolvent debtor January 1888; druggist in San Francisco by October 1888, Arizona by February 1889)

I. S. TITUS & CO.

Established in their present stand on Exchange Avenue in the spring of 1885, the successor to John M. Zimmerman. The stock was considerably run down when Titus & Co. took possession, and would not invoice more than $1200, but by their skill and experience as druggists, and dealing directly in accordance with business principles, and handling nothing but first-class goods, they have increased it to $4000. The stock is the freshest in town and embraces nothing but strictly pure goods. They also make a specialty of fancy toilet articles, perfumes, colognes, etc.

Sonoma Democrat
January 8, 1887

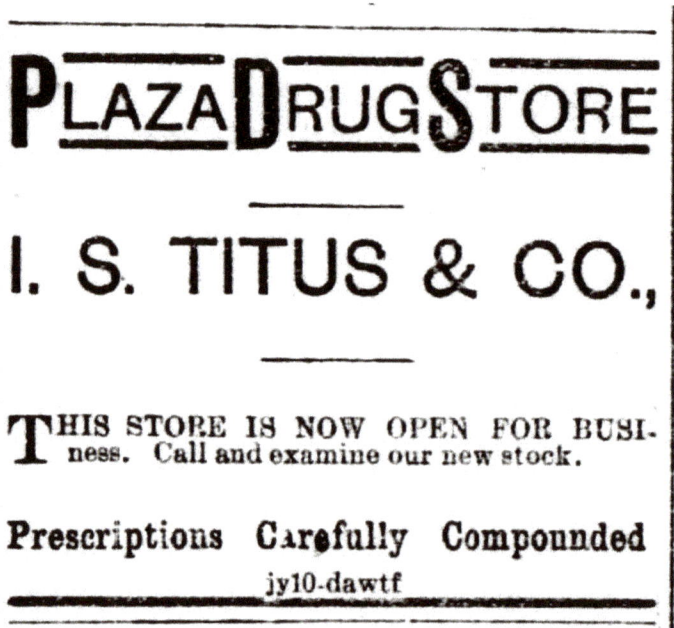

Sonoma Democrat
July 10, 1885

I. S. Titus, Jr., formerly of Santa Rosa, has secured a position of apothecary in the Territorial Insane Asylum at Phoenix, Arizona.

Sonoma Democrat
February 8, 1889

Note: Isaac S. Titus, Sr. (1828-1892) was medical superintendent at the Asylum.

- **Tomasco's Pharmacy** (July 1913 – 1935)
- Tomasco Drug Company (1935 – May 1975)
- Ralph A. Tomasco (1888-1954), Angelo J. Franchetti (1902-1968), Michael A. Franchetti (1937-2018).
- 305 Fourth Street, 3 doors east of Washington St.: July 1913 – December 1919
- 301 Fourth Street, NE corner Washington St.: January-July 1920
- 231 Fourth Street, NW corner Washington St.: May 1923 – December 1925
- 331 Fourth Street, NW corner A St. (Elk's Bldg.): December 3, 1925 – December 3, 1944
- 401 Fourth St., NE corner A St. (former St. Rose Drug Co.): December 3, 1944 – May 1970
- A.J. Franchetti became a full partner September 30, 1925; purchased the company in 1928.
- Following the October 1969 earthquake in Santa Rosa, Tomasco Drug Co. purchased Hall Bros. Drug Co. at 529 4th St. and moved their flagship Fourth and A store to that location in May 1970. Tomasco Drug Co. and Medico Drug Co. merged to form the Medico-Tomasco Drug Co. in May 1975.

Tomasco's Pharmacy, 305 Fourth St., circa 1915
Richard Siri collection

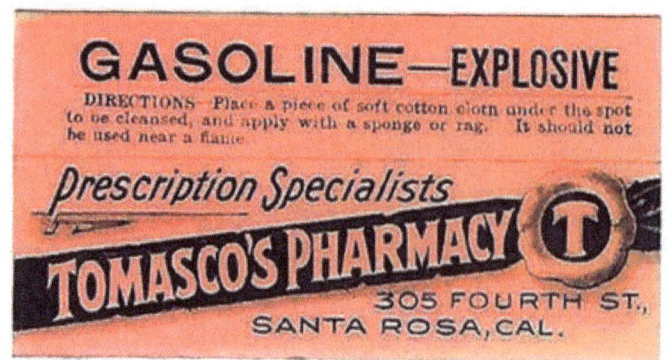

Paper labels
Tomasco's Pharmacy
305 Fourth Street
John Burton collection

The Mutual Girl Visits Tomasco's Pharmacy

Tomasco's Pharmacy at 305 Fourth street, was a place that I had been wanting to go to for a long time, but I failed to get around to it until last week. I told Mr. Tomasco that I didn't think that I wanted to purchase any thing in particular, although I knew better, but he never-the-less greeted me with fine courtesy and told me to make myself at home and he would assist me in the selection of anything I desired, or would be pleased to make suggestions.

When I had my teeth fixed by Dr. Crawford in The Elks building, he recommended a certain preparation for preserving my teeth, and I found that I was able to get it from Mr. Tomasco.

As I was completely out of a lot of toilet requisites, and the stock carried here was so large and of so many varieties, I was easily able to get what I wanted without fail.

Java Rice Powder, was one thing, then I got a can of Squibbs' Talcum, and a box of Colgate's Cashmere Bouquet Toilet Soap, a bottle of Peroxide and some toilet water.

I had lost my nail buffer and broken my file, so I looked at some manicuring outfits. Mr. Tomasco showed me a very neat little set that just caught my eye. It was the Parisian Ivory, and it was so very pretty that I just had to treat myself and buy it, or else yearn for it forever after. I think now that I have it I am cheating some of these manicuring girls out of a job, as I use it regularly.

I was feeling tip top and had no use for prescriptions of any kind, however, I find that this is the most important part of Mr. Tomasco's establishment. He feels that when a doctor hands his patient a prescription that the prescription should be filled in the most painstaking manner, with clean, fresh and pure drugs in order to get the desired results. Therefore, Mr. Tomasco fills them exactly as they should be filled.

As a result of this careful and skillful service, combined with only the best drugs and articles obtainable, Mr. Tomasco has won a fine reputation as a pharmacist, and has drawn a splendid and ever-growing patronage to his establishment.

As I had been informed that Mr. Tomasco had such an exceptionally good reputation for skill and reliability in these lines I was glad to purchase a number of little home remedies on his recommendation, and I have since found those I have used to be all that is claimed for them.

THE MUTUAL GIRL

Press Democrat
March 21, 1915

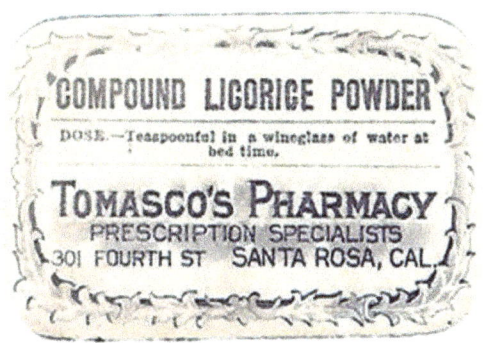
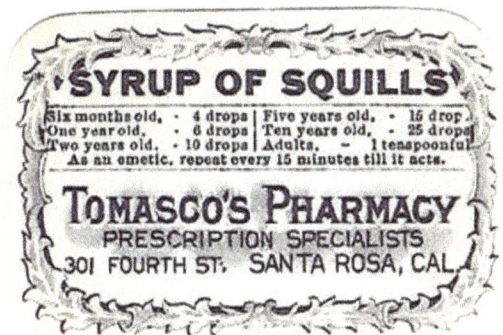

Paper labels – Tomasco's Pharmacy – 301 Fourth Street
John Burton collection

Newspaper coupon – Tomasco's Pharmacy – 231 Fourth Street
Santa Rosa Republican
July 5, 1924

Paper label – Tomasco's Pharmacy – 231 Fourth Street
John Burton collection

OPENING THURSDAY, DECEMBER 3
Tomasco's Pharmacy

TOMASCO'S PHARMACY IS THE MOST PERFECTLY LIGHTED STORE IN SANTA ROSA

Fixtures and Electrical Work
FURNISHED BY
Mundell Electric Co.
416 Fourth Street — Phone 321

Santa Rosa's Newest and Finest
DRUG STORE
IN THE
New Elks' Building
Fourth and A Streets
3 Big Days
Thursday-Friday-Saturday—December 3-4-5
To welcome you in our new location
FREE BALLOONS FOR THE KIDDIES

The New Tomasco's Pharmacy

Painted and **Decorated**
— BY —
Gambini & Co.
521 Fifth Street
PHONE 49

Elk's Building, 331 Fourth Street, NW corner A St., Grand Opening December 3, 1925

Press Democrat
December 2, 1925

SR-D-29

2 OZ (embossed)
SHAKE WELL BEFORE USING
TOMASCO'S
CHILLBLAIN REMEDY
APPLY FREQUENTLY
TOMASCO'S PHARMACY
PRESCRIPTION SPECIALISTS
ELKS. BLDG. SANTA ROSA
Clear square
4 inches tall
Base: FERG. CO. 882

James Arietta collection

(PARKE-DAVIS)
PURE EXTRACT OF VANILLA
ALCOHOL 30%
NET CONTENTS   OZ.
TOMASCO'S PHARMACY
DEPENDABLE DRUGGISTS.
ELK'S BLDG.   SANTA ROSA, CALIF.
PHONE 17

Tomasco Plans Open House at New Quarters

Expressing gratification for the support given his business in the opening days in his new location in the Elks building, Ralph Tomasco, proprietor of Tomasco's drug store, yesterday announced that in appreciation of the public interest in his new venture he will hold open house all of this week, offering many special bargains to his customers.

"We expected a big crowd for the opening Thursday," said Tomasco, "but the attendance was even greater than we anticipated. Every department was busy from opening until closing time. The beauty shop was constantly busy, and the soda fountain did a big business and six clerks were kept on the jump behind the prescription counter all day long. Opening day was a splendid surprise to us, but in the two days following even bigger crowds visited the store."

Tomasco says he believes his new pharmacy, at the Fourth and A street corner of the new Elks building, is the most modern and best-equipped drug store in northern California. It represents a cash outlay of more than $20,000, according to the proprietor.

Press Democrat
December 6, 1925

Tomasco Drug Co., Elk's Building, NW cor 4th & A Sts., 1936 – Courtesy Sonoma County Library

Remodeled soda fountain, April 1936

TOMASCO DRUG STORE TO HOLD 'OPEN HOUSE'

New Displays Planned To Celebrate Completion Of Alterations

The new, bigger and busier Tomasco Drug company will hold "open house" today and all next week, commemorating the completion of extensive alterations of the exterior and interior of their store, located at the Elks' building, Fourth and A streets, which have been under way for several weeks.

With all work completed and displays of merchandise and new departments installed, the Tomasco Drug company, established here in 1913, presents one of the finest and most modern type of stores of its kind in northern California.

The firm, owned and operated by A. F. (Ang) Franchetti and George J. Fagan, announces a great sale in honor of the remodeled store. The firm also operates a store at Sebastopol.

In speaking of the "open house" celebration, Franchetti said: "We are pleased to present our new store to the people of Sonoma county and feel that it is one of the most modern in northern California."

The personnel of the Tomasco Drug company includes A. J. Franchetti and George J. Fagan, proprietors, and registered pharmacists: Graham Mann, registered pharmacist; Miss Elsie Novelli, saleslady; Jack Cooper, soda fountain manager; Mark Body, soda fountain clerk; Donald Spittler, apprentice in pharmacy; Joseph Colabella, apprentice in pharmacy; Virginia Hesseltine, soda fountain clerk; Joseph Basso and Leland Gleason, deliveries.

Typically a modern drug store, the Tomasco Drug company has many important departments. On the main floor will be found drug and prescription departments, as well as the toiletries department, soda fountain, health food, toasted nuts, cigars, candy, liquor and stationery departments. On the mezzanine floor of the store may be found a modern beauty shop with a hair cutting department in conjunction as well as a surgical appliance department and a telephone and rest rooms for convenience of patrons.

The department, which has always been a feature of the Tomasco Drug company and which has attracted statewide attention since its installation in 1925, is the open glass front prescription department. Since its installation it has been viewed by interested druggists from all parts of the state and has been duplicated in many large stores in larger cities. This department has a refrigeration system for storage of biological and other perishable pharmaceuticals, thus assuring freshness and safety in the use of serums, antitoxins and other biological products and drugs. Besides a complete stock of prescription pharmaceuticals, this department is also operated as a supply depot for biological products, oxygen and other hospital supplies.

The toilet goods department is one of the most complete in this section, featuring nationally popular lines such as Richard Hudnut, Rubenstein, Primrose House, Tussy, Max Factor, Leon Loraine, Yardley, Coty, Houbigant, Lesquendieu, Bourjois and Guerlain. At the perfume counter milady can fill her every desire. The mirrored sampling counter featuring all popular fragrances is an outstanding feature.

Miss Novelli, who is in charge of this department, is an expertly trained beautician and is prepared to advise patrons on problems in the care of the skin.

The surgical department, located on the mezzanine floor, is considered the only complete surgical appliance stock north of San Francisco. Here we find individual fitting rooms for men and women and both men and lady fitters in charge. This department features nationally known lines of surgical supports and appliances such as Camp belts and supports, Honest John trusses, Little Doctor trusses, Jung's Foot appliances and other surgical appliances including hearing devices, elastic hosiery, foot appliances, shoulder braces, back and abdominal supports and trusses.

The Battle Creek Health Food department maintained in the Tomasco Drug company is under the management of Miss Elysie Novelli, who is also a graduate Battle Creek health food dietitian. Problems of diabetic, reducing and other health diets are outlined by her to those interested in health diet.

The new Tomasco soda fountain is one of the finest and largest in this section of the state, having accommodations for 21 persons. The fountain is modernly equipped with 100 feet of electrical refrigeration, a broilator, a Stovex Silex coffee unit, a Russ salad and sandwich refrigerated table as well as a complete equipment for refrigeration and serving of ice cream and fountain soft drinks and dishes. At the candy counter of the soda fountain are featured the nationally famous Whitman, Alegrettiss and Walgreen lines of candies as well as the famout Double Kay freshly toasted line of nuts.

In the cigar, wine and liquor departments the open type feature of display has been employed to its greatest advantage. Here the customer may shop in a leisurely, self-serve manner allowing the patron the advantage of the inspection of the entire stock in these departments before purchasing.

The floor in the new store is of the Masonite-Pressdwood type, now employed in larger drug and department stores throughout the country.

The exterior of the building, with its new corner entrance and larger display windows facing both Fourth and A streets are additional features which make the Tomasco Drug company another outstanding shopping center in our community.

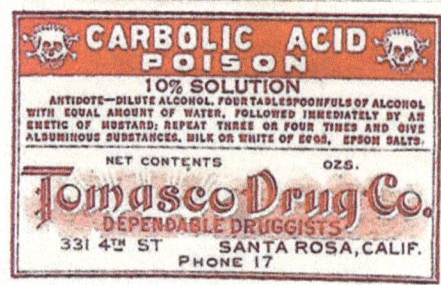

Press Democrat, April 11, 1936 — Remodel of Tomasco Drug Co. in Elk's Building

TOMASCO MOVES ACROSS THE STREET

After many months of planning, constructing and remodelling, the management of TOMASCO DRUG COMPANY announce the opening of their new store at 401-403 Fourth street, Santa Rosa, Calif. The new store is located directly across A street from the location in the former Elks' building occupied by this firm for almost twenty years. The management takes this opportunity to extend thanks to the many firms and workmen who have made the store possible. They also send an invitation to the people of this area to visit this new store, one of the largest and most highly departmentized drug stores in California.

ANG J. FRANCHETTI
GRAHAM B. MANN, Partners
TOMASCO DRUG COMPANY

View of the new TOMASCO DRUG CO. store at 401-403 Fourth street, Santa Rosa. The three street entrances in the new store are an added customer convenience. The many feet of display windows are to accommodate the items of the many departments of the store.

Press Democrat
December 3, 1944

Angelo John Franchetti

The prescription department of the new store is one of the largest in this area and includes all the facilities of modern prescription filling. This department is equipped with dual telephone service for doctor and patient convenience and has refrigeration facilities for perishable drugs and biologicals. The pharmacists in picture are, left to right: Ang J. Franchetti, Graham B. Mann, Leonard P. Bertoli and Ewen McK Stewart.

Press Democrat
December 3, 1944

Press Democrat – May 1, 1975

- **Eugene Joseph Toschi** (lived 1899-1979)
- Economy Drug Store
- 205 Exchange Avenue: October 1935 – August 1940
- 646 Fourth Street, SW corner D St. (Masonic Bldg.): August 1940 – July 1, 1962
- Sold business to Hahman Drug Co. when building was scheduled for demolition.

ECONOMY DRUG STORE TO OPEN HERE SATURDAY
Cut Rate Prices Will Be Featured on All Merchandise

The Economy Drug Store, newest Santa Rosa business establishment, will open its doors to the public tomorrow morning with a sale of nationally advertised drug products. The new store, located in the Leppo-Churchman building at 205 Exchange Avenue, is owned and operated by Eugene J. Toschi, who recently came here from San Francisco.

In opening the new store, which will feature cut-rate prices on all merchandise, Toschi points out that his store is not a part of any chain. For eight years he has successfully operated a drug store in the Marina district of San Francisco. After disposing of that business, he made a survey of northern California cities and chose Santa Rosa because of the possibilities he saw here for future development, he said.

The policy of the new store will be to offer nationally advertised merchandise at the lowest possible prices. "We will never knowingly be undersold in Santa Rosa," Toschi declared. "In our prescription department we will use merchandise such as Squibb, Upjohn, Parke-Davis, and Lilly prescription products."

Toshi announced that only registered pharmacists will be employed and that a strictly cash and carry business will be operated. By eliminating charge accounts and deliveries, the store will be able to maintain the lowest prices.

All fixtures installed in the store were purchased here and local labor was employed in redecorating the store and installing lighting fixtures.

Toshi has established a home here with his wife and baby daughter and plans to take an active part in the community.

Press Democrat
October 4, 1935

ECONOMY DRUG MOVES TO NEW LOCATION HERE
Special Two-Day Sale Will Start Today to Celebrate Change, Modernization

Completely modernized and in a new location, the Economy Drug Store offers its wide variety of select stock at minimum prices to Santa Rosa patrons at Fourth and D Streets [Masonic Building].

Located for the past five years at 205 Exchange Avenue, the new store is one of the most attractively appointed north of San Francisco and will provide its large clientele with the same high quality of merchandise and superb service in a handsome new setting. Completely renovated, the new store is decorated in white and ivory, with a marble linoleum floor.

The modern-type shelving and display counters are specially designed to attract the eye and to make the selection of merchandise easy. All items are price-marked, leaving no confusion in the customers mind as to the bargains offered by the firm.

The shop is the only fluorescent-lighted drugstore in Northern California, the lights having been custom built and specially installed to fit the decorative scheme of the interior.

Eugene Toschi, proprietor and prominent Santa Rosa Pharmacist, assured his large patronage faithful to the store for the past five years that he would continue to conduct his business on the policy of selling nationally known merchandise at lowest prices possible.

In celebration of moving into the new location, Toschi has announced a special for today and tomorrow, offering drug items at astonishingly low prices.

Toschi makes a specialty of prescription work and compounds his prescriptions in a modern department, fully stocked with nationally known products.

In addition, the store is the local agent for Agfa films, cameras and all supplies for both amateur and professional photographers. Himself a photography hobbyist, Toschi is always eager and ready with advice and assistance.

Santa Rosa Republican
August 16, 1940

Eugene Toschi's Economy Drug Store in new location at SW corner of Fourth and D Streets, 1941
Courtesy, Sonoma County Library

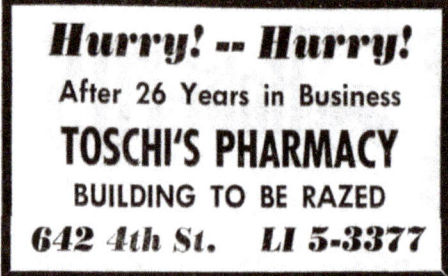

Press Democrat - May 24, 1962

- **George Ernest Traill** (lived 1865-1896)
- Successor to Charles C. Van Valkenburg; formerly at Del Monte Drug Store, Monterey, Cal.
- City Pharmacy, aka Santa Rosa Pharmacy, 547 Fourth St., NW corner Mendocino Ave.
- April 1894 – November 1895

G. E. Traill, the successor to Dr. Van Valkenburg in the City Pharmacy on the corner of Fourth and Mendocino Streets, finds a warm welcome at the hands of the enterprising businessmen like himself. We are as glad to receive him as Monterey was sorry to lose him.

The *New Era* says: "G. E. Traill, who for nearly three years past has occupied the position of dispensing druggist for J. F. Moore of the Del Monte Drug Store, left on Thursday for Santa Rosa to go into business for himself. Mr. Traill, by his skill and care in his professionalism and the uniform courtesy and affability of his disposition, has contributed to the success of the Del Monte Drug Store, and his genial presence will be greatly missed by the patrons of the establishment.

Sonoma Democrat
April 21, 1894

A letter has been received from G. E. Traill the druggist by a friend in this city. He reports an improvement in his health and says the weather is delightful and bracing in the mountains near Auburn.

During druggist Traill's absence, Julian Oliver Kelton will have charge of the store. Mr. Kelton is a graduate in pharmacy of the University of California and comes highly recommended. He graduated with high honors and has since had experience in the drug business in San Francisco.

Sonoma Democrat
March 16, 1895

Julian O. Kelton, who has been clerking at G. E. Traill & Co.'s drug store for some months, leaves in a few days for Ukiah where he has accepted the position of pharmacist at the State Insane Asylum.

Sonoma Democrat
July 13, 1895

Albert G. Rankin of San Francisco, a graduate pharmacist, has taken charge of G. E. Traill & Co. pharmacy.

Sonoma Democrat
July 20, 1895

Death of George Traill.

George Traill, who formerly owned the Santa Rosa Pharmacy on Fourth and Mendocino, has recently died at his old home, Austin, Ill. He was a victim of consumption. His health has not been good for some time and from here he went to Arizona and finally to Illinois where he died.

Sonoma Democrat
March 7, 1896

- **Oliver Roy Tuttle** (lived 1894-1976)
- Exclusive Prescription Pharmacy
- 621 Fourth Street
- July 1925 – April 1926 (merged with Baldwin Drug Store to form Standard Drug Co. at 507 Fourth Street, see page 178)
- Tuttle graduated from Santa Rosa Business College in 1914, and UC College of Pharmacy in 1918. During 1918-19 he was a Pharmacist's Mate in the U.S. Navy.

TUTTLE OPENS EXCLUSIVE PHARMACY STORE HERE

O. R. Tuttle, who began his career twenty years ago in a local drug store, has gone into business for himself and has opened the Exclusive Pharmacy at 621 Fourth Street, where he will conduct a strictly drug business and cater exclusively to prescription buyers.

Press Democrat
July 23, 1925

ANNOUNCING THE OPENING OF AN

EXCLUSIVE PRESCRIPTION PHARMACY

At 621 Fourth Street

A considerable demand for a Prescription Specialist has made itself felt in Santa Rosa, and my New Pharmacy will seek to meet this condition.

This means that you will not find a Drug-Department Store here, but a Pharmacy supplied with the Purest and Freshest Prescription Ingredients and devoting its entire knowledge and energy to providing the very highest character of professional service.

You may come here fully assured of Utmost Accuracy, Prompt Service and Reasonable Charges.

Exclusive Prescription Pharmacy

OLIVER ROY TUTTLE

DRUGS—PHARMACEUTICALS—BIOLOGICS

621 FOURTH STREET

Press Democrat
July 22, 1925

- # R. J. Humphreys
- October 1887 – May 1888
- Plaza Drug Store, 11 Exchange Ave.

STORY OF A LOTTERY TICKET WHICH CAUSED R. J. HUMPHREYS' DEATH

While Coroner John Tivnen was in town Saturday, he related to a *Democrat* reporter the interesting history of the cause of R. J. Humphreys' accidental death in this city two years ago. R. J. Humphreys, most of our people will remember, bought the Plaza Drug Store from Titus & Co. on Exchange Avenue, and conducted business about eight months prior to his death. He was very much a gentleman and made many friends who sincerely mourned his sad and untimely death which occurred on May 26, 1888.

It seems that he had long been in the habit of sending money to New Orleans for lottery tickets every month. About three days after the May drawing, he received an envelope containing a ticket, the number of which called for no prize. Before opening the envelope, he had noticed marks upon it that made him suspect it had been tampered with, and when he found that his ticket was not among the lucky numbers, his suspicions were confirmed and he telegraphed to the lottery company to learn what number had been sent to him. The answer left no further room to doubt that he had been robbed of his ticket, which drew $5,000, on its way from New Orleans.

He immediately corresponded with Wells Fargo & Co., in San Francisco, and the detectives of the company traced the robbery to an agent on one of the divisions between New Orleans and this coast by the name of Filmore. He confessed to opening the envelope and taking out the ticket. He subsequently collected the $5,000 through Wells Fargo & Co., and loaned $2,500 to a friend to pay off a mortgage on the latter's house and $900 of the amount he spent. Filmore paid over to the company $1,600 in cash and gave a note for $2,500. After securing this settlement from its dishonest clerk, the company wrote to Humphreys, offering to compromise with him in the same manner, but he refused to accede to the proposition unless the company would endorse the note, which the latter refused to do.

At this stage in the proceedings Humphreys, who feared that he would be swindled out of his winnings, went on a spree which lasted over a week and terminated in his untimely death from an overdose of morphine, taken while suffering from nervous prostration. After the inquest had been held, John Tivnen, Coroner and Public Administrator, took charge of the dead man's store and personal effects. While searching among the papers of the deceased, a holographic will was found bequeathing everything to James L. Patterson, a mining superintendent of Calico, San Bernardino County. Mr. Patterson, it seems had been an intimate friend of Humphreys and loaned him the money with which to purchase the drug store in this city.

Proof of the strong affection existing between the two men was had when Mr. Patterson visited this city a few days after Humphreys had been buried and before the will was found. W. H. Grissom took Mr. Patterson out to the cemetery and showed him where the unfortunate man lay beneath the sod. Mr. Patterson was very much affected and before leaving the precincts of the dead, instructed that a coping be placed around the lot and a marble slab erected, even though it cost the full amount of the debt owed him by the deceased.

Messrs. Ed West, John Shearer and W. C. Reed were appointed appraisers of the drug stock and fixed a valuation on it of $1,600. It was afterwards sold for $1,200 and all claims were paid off. Mr. Tivnen then instituted proceedings against the Pacific Bank in San Francisco for the full amount of the ticket which was cashed through Wells Fargo & Co. It seemed to be a hopeless case but our faithful Administrator stuck to it and would have spent his own funds in order to get the dead man's dues if necessary. But it was not necessary. The express company, finding that there was an honest determination back of the proceedings, made overtures which were finally accepted Friday by Mr. Patterson, the sole legatee under the will, and Mr. Tivnen. Through the former's lawyers, Messrs. Messick, Maxwell and Phelan, Wells Fargo & Co., offered to settle the claims for $4,527 and acting on the advice of attorneys the offer was accepted and the money paid over.

Press Democrat
October 12, 1890

A CARD.

$50,000.

NEW ORLEANS, April 19, 1888.

The undersigned certifies that he held for collection, for account of R. J. Humphreys, Santa Rosa, Cal., through Pacific Bank of San Francisco, Cal., one-tenth of ticket No. 19,862, Single Number, Class D, in the Louisiana State Lottery, which drew the Second Capital Prize of FIFTY THOUSAND DOLLARS, on Tuesday, April 10, 1888, and that the amount was promptly paid, by a check on the New Orleans National Bank, on presentation of the ticket at the office of the company.

R. JOS. DURHAN,
Runner State National Bank, New Orleans, La.

New Orleans Times Picayune
April 29, 1888

R. J. Humphreys, a druggist of Santa Rosa, died at that place on the 26th. It appears that deceased had sent direct to New Orleans for a ticket in April drawing of the Louisiana Lottery. The day after the ticket was mailed to him the drawing took place. On reading the prize list, he found Santa Rosa was down for $5,000. Believing his ticket had been intercepted, Humphreys wrote to New Orleans asking the number of the ticket that was sent him. The answer was that the ticket was 19,863, which did not correspond with the number on the ticket he had received. The matter was at once put in the hands of the detectives, who succeeded in recovering the greater portion of the money. Humphreys had been drinking hard for two weeks, which resulted in his sudden death.

Mendocino Beacon
June 2, 1888

- **John Walter Warboys** (lived 1851-1923)
- 449 4th St., NW corner B St. under Occidental Hotel: Sept.-Dec. 1881 (purchased W. R. Hall's store, see p. 193; subsequently occupied storefronts on 4th St. just east of B St.)—
- 179 aka 511 Fourth Street: December 1881 – 1887
- 509 Fourth Street: 1888 – 1893
- 515 Fourth Street: 1893 – 1897
- 505 Fourth Street: 1898 – January 15, 1905 (sold to Charles F. Keller, Jr. – see page 229)

J. W. Warboys carries as complete and handsome stock in this line as any of his competitors. He purchased the store of Walter R. Hall in 1881, and has been increasing it ever since. From a $2,000 stock he has increased it to $7,000, and at his present stand, 511 Fourth Street, may be seen as a complete stock of drugs and pharmaceutical goods as there is in the city. He supplies a large prescription trade and has never yet failed to give satisfaction.

Sonoma Democrat
January 8, 1887

SADLER LEAVING J. W. WARBOYS

A. Sadler, who has been in charge of J. W. Warboys Drug Store since the owner's departure for the East, leaves this city today to assume the management of a large drug store in Oakland.

Sonoma Democrat
July 1, 1890

W. R. CARITHERS BUYS THE BUILDING OCCUPIED BY WARBOYS DRUGS

On Tuesday, W. R. Carithers of the firm of Carithers and Forsyth of the White House, purchased from the Byrne estate the brick two-story building adjoining the White House on Fourth street which is occupied by J. W. Warboys Drug Store. [505 Fourth St.] The new owner has made up his mind as to what future plans, if any that he may have in connection with the property. The Carithers block now extends clear through to B Street in an unbroken line.

Sonoma Democrat
June 26, 1902

SR-D-30

J. W. WARBOYS
DRUGGIST
SANTA ROSA
Clear dose glass
2 ½ inches tall
Reverse: Table 2 – 8 TEA
                         4
                         2
                         1

Base: W. T. & CO.
Helmut & DeAnna Jordt collection

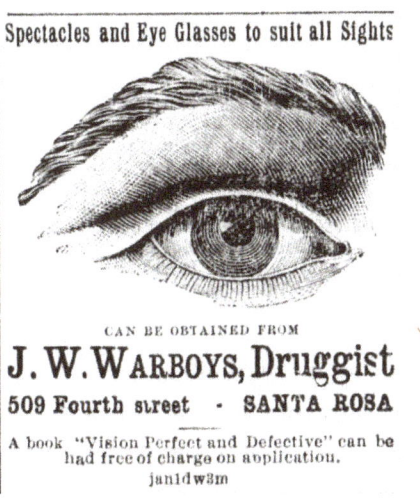

Sonoma Democrat
January 1, 1892

SR-D-31
J. W. WARBOYS
DRUGGIST
SANTA ROSA, CAL.
Amber rectangular
Tooled top
4 ½ inches tall
Base: W. T. & Co. U. S. A.
John Burton collection
3 ½ inches tall
Base: W T & Co/1/USA PAT. JAN 5, 1892
Helmut & DeAnna Jordt bottle shown

SR-D-32
J. W. WARBOYS
DRUGGIST
SANTA ROSA, CAL.
Aqua oval
Tooled top
4 3/8 inches tall
5 1/4 inches tall
6 3/4 inches tall
Base: W T & Co/1/USA
John Burton Collection

SR-D-33
J. W. WARBOYS
DRUGGIST
SANTA ROSA, CAL.
Clear rectangular
Tooled top
3 ½ inches tall
5 inches tall
John Burton collection
6 inches tall
Dan Brown collection

SR-D-34   J. W. WARBOYS
DRUGGIST
SANTA ROSA, CAL.
Clear oval
Tooled top
5 Inches tall
6 ½ inches tall
6 3/4 inches tall
Base: W T & Co/1/USA, or S B W
Dan Brown and Jordt collections

SR-D-35   J. W. WARBOYS
DRUGGIST
SANTA ROSA, CAL.
Clear rectangular
Tooled top
3 ½ inches tall
4 Inches tall
4 3/4 Inches tall
5 Inches tall
5 1/4 inches tall
6 inches tall
7 inches tall
Base: W.T. & CO., or S B W
Dan Brown and John Burton collections

SR-D-36   J. W. WARBOYS
DRUGGIST
SANTA ROSA, CAL.
Clear oval
Tooled top
4 1/4 inches tall
Base: W T & Co. Q
Helmut & DeAnna Jordt
   collection
4 7/8 inches tall
Base: W T & Co L
Dan Brown collection

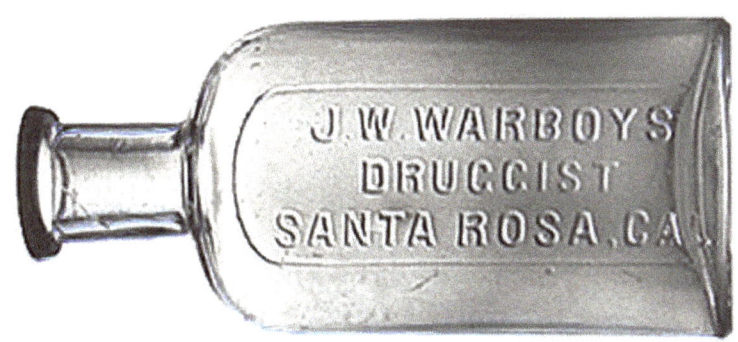

J. W. Warboys' Drug Store, Santa Rosa, Cal.

515 Fourth Street; John W. Warboys standing behind counter at right
Illustrated Atlas of Sonoma County, California. Reynolds & Proctor, 1898, page 12

Graduated set of J.W. Warboys bottles - John Burton collection

- **John M. Zimmermann**
- Plaza Drug Store, 6 Ridgway Block (west side of plaza); 11 Exchange Ave. by 1884
- October 1883 – July 1885
- Purchased Oscar Morrison's Plaza Drug Store; sold to I. S. Titus

PLAZA GERMAN DRUG STORE!

JOHN M. ZIMMERMANN, Ph. D.

(German Graduate Pharmacy.)

—DEALER IN—

PURE DRUGS, CHEMICALS,

—AND—

PHARMACEUTICAL PREPARATIONS.

Having recently purchased of Oscar Morrison, his

PLAZA DRUG STORE

NO. 6 RIDGWAY BLOCK

Offers special inducements to the trade. My preparations will always be found up to the standard, and my

Prices Reasonable.

GERMAN AND FRENCH PREPARATIONS

A Specialty.

Prescriptions Accurately Compounded at all hours.

oct31dawtf

Sonoma Democrat
October 31, 1883

SEBASTOPOL

- **Model Drug Store,** Norman C. Finley, prop.
  - 1896 – June 1897 (sold stock to R.B. Reedy, see page 247)
  - 15 N. Main St., west side, opposite Janssen Hotel

The MODEL DRUG STORE
Opposite Janssen's Hotel, Sebastopol.

MEDICINES---Patent, Proprietary, Official.

Stationery and the Highest Grade Perfumes, Soaps and Toilet Articles.

Prescriptions Correctly and Carefully Filled

At Lowest Prices.

N. C. FINLEY, Proprietor.

Sonoma West Times
December 23, 1896

RECENT BUSINESS CHANGES

Lee Bros. moved the Model Drug Store stock from this place (Sebastopol) to Santa Rosa last Monday. A new pharmacy will be established there by R. B. Reedy.

Sonoma West Times
June 10, 1897

Janssen Hotel, circa 1885
Courtesy, Sonoma County Library

Not Unfounded Rumors.

This is not an advertising scheme, but the plain truth. My goods are the best to be procured and I again repeat that I pay no percentage for prescriptions, consequently I can save you money.

Model Drug Store.   NORMAN FINLEY.

Sonoma West Times
March 10, 1897

- **L. McG. Bennett**
- "L" for Lizzie, short for Elizabeth; "McG." is abbreviation of her family name, McGaughey.
- 19 N. Main Street
- May 24, 1889 – July 19, 1890; sold to William W. Parr
- Mrs. Bennett also owned a drug store in Santa Rosa from 1887 to 1892 (see page 181)

The branch drug store of Mrs. L. McG. Bennett in Sebastopol was opened Friday.
Press Democrat - May 25, 1889

Well Known Minnesota Physician Visiting Relatives Here

Dr. J. B. McGaughey, one of the best-known physicians of Winona, Minnesota, is in Santa Rosa for a visit with his sisters, Mrs. A. McG. Stuart, Mrs. Francis McG. Martin and Mrs. Lizzie McG. Bennett.

Dr. McGaughey is always a welcome visitor when he comes to Santa Rosa. For years he has been paying Santa Rosa a call, and this is his first in a couple of years. He has many old friends here. He is one of the leading citizens of the state of Minnesota and is prominent man of affairs there.
Santa Rosa Press Democrat - November 12, 1907

L. McG. Bennett's Drug Store and U.S. Post Office,
Independent Order of Good Templars upstairs.
19 North Main Street
Courtesy, Sonoma County Library

- **William W. Parr** (b. 1867)
- Sebastopol Drug Store: 19 N. Main St. for 4-5 years, then 25 N. Main Street, west side.
- July 1890 – March 6, 1899
- Sold to Thomas R. Worth

W. W. Parr has purchased Mrs. Bennett's Drug Store in Sebastopol.
Sonoma Democrat - July 19, 1890

SEB-D-01

W.W. PARR
APOTHECARY
SEBASTOPOL, CAL.
Clear rectangular
Tooled top
3 3/4 inches tall
Base: *** D U.S.A. PAT. JAN 5 1892
Merle Avila collection

SEB-D-02

W.W. PARR
APOTHECARY
SEBASTOPOL, CAL.
Clear rectangular
Tooled top
4 ½ inches tall
Base W.T. & CO. C- U.S.A./
         PAT. JAN 5 1892
Merle Avila collection

SEB-D-04

W.W. PARR
APOTHECARY (on horseshoe)
P (center of horseshoe)
SEBASTOPOL
CAL.
Clear rectangular
Tooled top
5 inches tall
5 ½ inches tall
6 inches tall
Base *** U.S.A. PAT. JAN 5 1892
Merle Avila collection

W. W. Parr, Mrs. Lozer and Miss Lillian Strobel went to San Francisco Thursday morning to attend the commencement exercises of the graduating class of the California College of Pharmacy. Mrs. Parr, wife of our popular druggist has the honor of being a member of the graduating class. She has spent the past two years in the study of pharmacy and on Saturday will return to Sebastopol to assist Mr. Parr in vending drugs and medicines.

Sonoma Democrat
November 21, 1896

W. W. PARR.

Proprietor of Sebastopol's "Up-to-Date" Pharmacy.

Among the attractive and finely-arranged business institutions of Sebastopol is none better, if as well equipped, both in stock and fixtures, as the modern drug store owned by Mr. W. W. Parr.

Mr. Parr has had a long experience in the drug business, having been connected with it for fifteen years. He has been ere for six years and a half. Mrs. Parr also a registered pharmacist, having recently graduated from the California College of Pharmacy.

In addition to a fine stock of drugs, toilet articles, patent medicines, etc., a good supply of stationery of all kinds is always on hand, and an elaborate soda fountain is run during the summer months.

Mr. Parr is also local agent for the Sunset Telephone Co.

This store is one of which Sebastopol may well be proud.

Sonoma Democrat
December 19, 1896

William W. Parr's Sebastopol Drug Store
25 N. Main Street, Forsyth Building, circa 1896

SALE OF PARR'S DRUG STORE

W. W. Parr, who for the past eight or ten years has been one of the most energetic and wide-awake business men of Sebastopol, sold his drug store last Monday to T.R. Worth & Co., and he will now retire to private life for a time at least. No one had knowledge of the pending negotiations and therefore the sale caused a little astonishment.

Mr. Parr is well known in western Sonoma County and if he decides to relocate in some other part of the State, both himself and his wife will leave many warm friends in Sebastopol.

Mr. Worth, who will now manage the business, comes from San Francisco highly recommended, and as he is a pleasant gentleman, the store will retain its reputation as being the finest pharmacy in Sonoma County.

Sonoma West Times
March 8, 1899

PURCHASED A DRUG STORE

W. W. Parr has purchased one of the most prominent drug stores in Spokane, Washington, and will hereafter reside there. The many Sebastopol friends of Mr. and Mrs. Parr will wish them every success in their new field. The latest edition of the Spokesman-Review contains the following notice:

"To my many friends, patrons and the general public I wish to state that I have disposed my entire interest in the drug store, including the sole right to manufacture Anger's celebrated Compound Cough Syrup, Liver Nervine, and all of my other private specialties to the Parr Drug Company, a firm recently from California. Mr. Parr is a competent druggist of 16 years' experience and my earnest request is that they may patronize the new firm as liberally as they have me in the past."   —O. H. Anger

Sonoma West Times
October 4, 1899

- **Worth's Drug Store**, Thomas Renfro Worth (lived 1862-1938)
- 25 N. Main St., west side, formerly W. W. Parr's drugstore: March 6, 1899 –July 18, 1905
- 108 N. Main Street, east side, in Kingsbury Block: September 1905 –1931
- 109 N. Main Street, west side, former 25 N. Main: 1932 – March 20, 1936
- Sold to Fred and Burtis Hite who retained the Worth name, see page 300

Thomas R. Worth (left) and colleague in 25 Main Street store, 1903
Courtesy, Sonoma County Library

Worth's Drug Store interior, circa 1905
Courtesy, Sonoma County Library

Worth's Drug Store in the Kingsbury Block, NE corner Main and Santa Rosa Ave., circa 1912.
Petaluma & Santa Rosa Railway interurban car 59 is returning from Forestville.
Albert Walter photo
Courtesy, Sonoma County Library

Main Street looking south, Worth's Drug Store at left, circa 1925
Courtesy, Sonoma County Library

Note: All Worth's prescription bottles are embossed "KINGSBURY BLOCK"—the two-story stone building constructed in 1905 on the NE corner of Main and Santa Rosa Ave. (now Sebastopol Ave.). Worth had been burned out of his store in the Forsyth Bldg. (25 N. Main) on July 18, 1905, then relocated in the new Kingsbury Block (108 N. Main) by September. The April 18, 1906 earthquake leveled several buildings in Sebastopol, and the Kingsbury building, less than a year old, was badly damaged. It was repaired, however, and the resilient T.R. Worth resumed business.

SEB-D-06
1 oz.
mortar & pestle
Worth's Drug Store
KINGSBURY BLOCK
Sebastopol Cal.
Clear rectangular
3 3/4 inches tall
Dan Brown collection

SEB-D-07
6 OZ.
mortar & pestle
Worth's Drug Store
KINGSBURY BLOCK
Sebastopol, Cal.
Clear rectangular
5 7/8 inches tall
Base: 207
Merle Avila collection

SEB-D-08
8 oz.
mortar & pestle
Worth's Drug Store
KINGSBURY BLOCK
Sebastopol, Cal.
Clear rectangular
6 1/4 inches tall
Base: W. T. CO. USA
Helmut & DeAnna Jordt collection

SEB-D-09

℥ ii
mortar & pestle
Worth's Drug Store
KINGSBURY BLOCK
Sebastopol, Cal.
Clear oval
3 1/4 inches tall
Helmut & DeAnna Jordt
    collection
3 3/4 inches tall
Base: W.T. CO.
Dan Brown collection

SEB-D-10

℥ iii
mortar & pestle
Worth's Drug Store
KINGSBURY BLOCK
Sebastopol, Cal.
5 inches tall
Base blank
John Burton collection

SEB-D-11

℥ iv
mortar and pestle
Worth's Drug Store
KINGSBURY BLOCK
Sebastopol, Cal.
Clear oval
5 ½ inches tall
Base: W. T. CO. USA
John Burton collection

SEB-D-12

    ℥ xvi
    mortar & pestle
    Worth's Drug Store
    KINGSBURY BLOCK
    Sebastopol, Cal.
    Clear oval
    8 7/8 inches tall
    Base: W. T. CO. -C-U.S.A.
    Merle Avila collection

SEB-D-13

    ℥ i
    mortar & pestle
    WORTH'S DRUG STORE
    KINGSBURY BLOCK
    SEBASTOPOL, CAL.
    3 ½ inches tall
    Base: W.T. CO.
    Dan Brown collection

Labeled glass tube:

    Worth's Drug Store
    Kingsbury Block
    Sebastopol, Cal.
    7 1/4 inches long
    Merle Avila collection

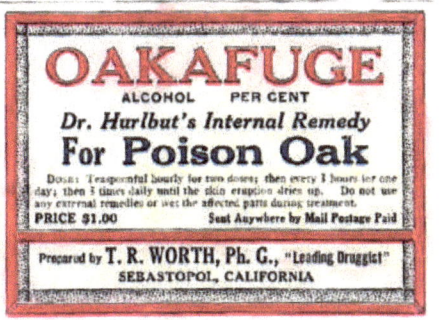 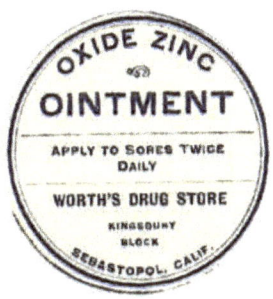 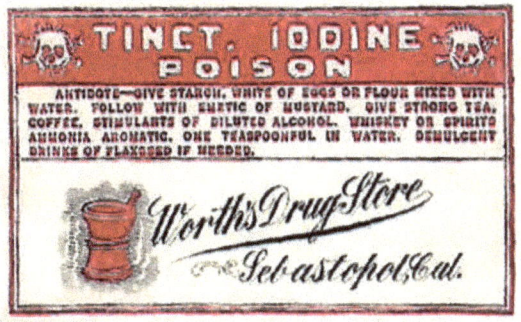

Product labels - John Burton collection

SEB-D-14

Labeled clear glass stoppered jar:
PRECIPITATED SULFUR
Worth's Drug Store
109 MAIN ST.
Sebastopol, Cal.
4 ½ inches tall

Merle Avila collection

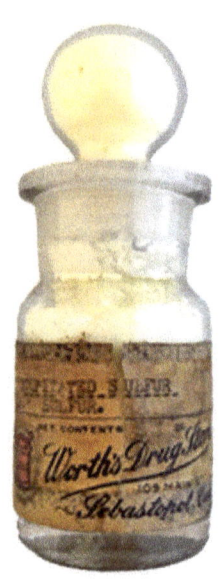

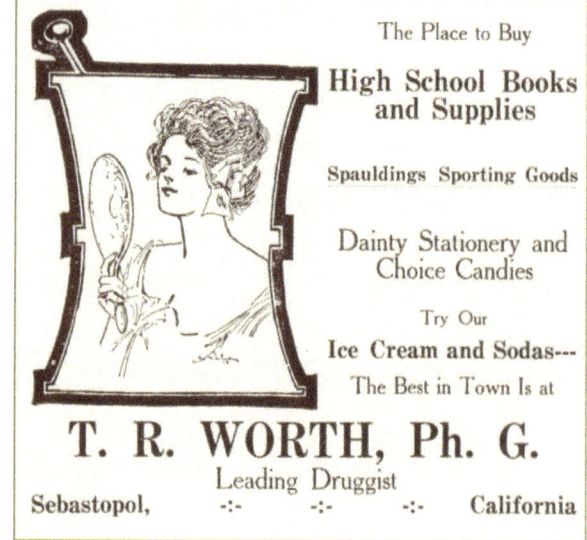

1911   Analy High School yearbooks   1913
Courtesy, Sonoma County Library

Spring Medicine.

Signs of Spring convey a warning that certain ailments—general debility, impure blood, dyspepsia, skin diseases, rheumatism, liver complaints, etc need attention. There is'nt anything to purify the blood that equals WORTH'S SPRING MEDICINE. It is pleasant to take and makes rich, red blood. It insures a fair skin and brilliant complexion. It cures constipation. By acting also on the kidneys and liver it aids the process of nutrition and restores the normal functions of the system. Only 75c. for a pint bottle.

T. R. WORTH & CO., Druggists

Sonoma West Times
March 6, 1901

Note: T. R. Worth's father, Thomas James Worth (1823-1871), sailed to California from New York and settled in the Eureka area as a rancher and farmer in the late 1850's. T.R. Worth's Native American mother, Annie, was about 18 when he was born in 1862. His uncle, David P. Worth, became his guardian when his father died. After working in an Arcata drugstore a few years, Thomas attended the California College of Pharmacy in San Francisco, earning a Ph.G. degree in 1891. He came to Sebastopol in 1899 and acquired W.W. Parr's drugstore in partnership with Col. James A. Hardin, uncle of his fiancé, Ella I. Hardin. His son, Thomas Andrew Worth (b. 1901) attended UC School of Pharmacy and started working with his father as a registered pharmacist in 1925.

Sources: *History of Sonoma County*. Honoria Tuomey, 1926, vol. ii, page 555;
U.S. censuses and Humboldt County probate records.

REXALL STORES

Rexall Drug Stores everywhere are adopting a very liberal plan by which customers may receive a choice from many valuable premiums at about half the market price. The system is operated as follows: For any purchase of Rexall branded goods from the Rexall Store in your locality, a coupon will be given. When the coupons amount to half the price of a selected premium, you pay the balance in cash, and the premium is yours at half the regular price—a saving worthy of your attention.

See the choice premiums at the Rexall Drug Store, T. R. WORTH, proprietor.

Sonoma West Times
November 25, 1916

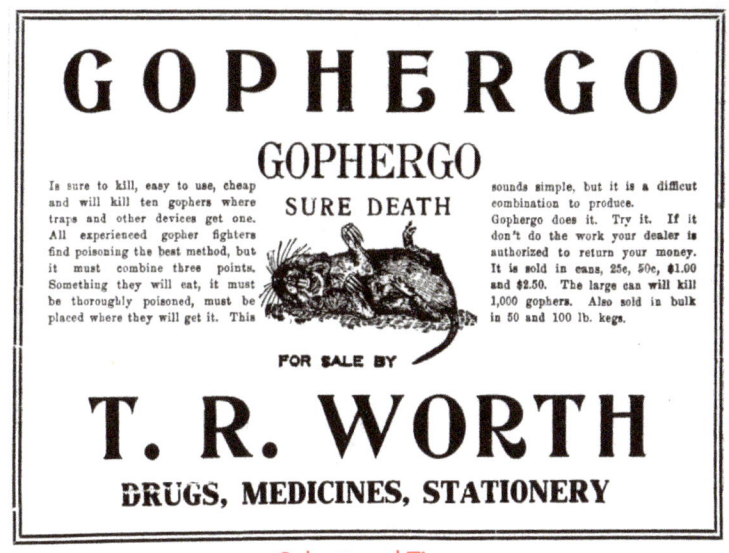

Sebastopol Times
December 2, 1911

EARDLEY HARDIN BUYS DRUG STORE IN SAN DIEGO

Eardley Hardin has passed the State Board of Pharmacy according to word received here by relatives. Hardin, who is nephew of Mrs. T. R. Worth, was employed for two years at Worth's Drug Store. He has many friends in the community who will wish him success in his chosen work.

Mr. Hardin has purchased the drug store owned by his father before his death, in San Diego, and will conduct it in the future. The store is located at First and Juniper streets in the Fair City.

Sonoma West Times & News
August 2, 1935

- **Worth's Drug Store**, Fred Arthur Hite and Burtis Allison Hite, props.
- 109 North Main Street
- Fred Hite and his son Burtis were pharmacists working in San Francisco in 1930
- March 20, 1936 – July 22, 1938
- Sold to Raymond Momboisse

Announcement

Having purchased the **Worth Drug Store** we respectfully solicit a continuance of your business and pledge ourselves to give you

SERVICE

Worth Drug Store

Burtis Hite, Proprietor

Sebastopol Times
March 20, 1936

WORTH'S DRUG STORE
THE REXALL STORE

Fred A. Hite and Burtis A. Hite, Prop.

Prescriptions a Specialty

Drugs   Stationery   Tobacco

Fountain   Kodak Supplies

109 Main Street
SEBASTOPOL, CALIF.

Sonoma West Times
March 27, 1936

New Owners in Charge of Worth Drug Store Here

Druggist Retires After 38 Years of Business in This City

Even though the personnel of the Worth Drug Store has changed, the business will continue under the name it has had for the last 38 years, being one of the oldest business concerns in the city of Sebastopol operating under the same name.

The new owners, Burtis Hite and Fred Hite of Crockett, took over the business formally Monday morning when the deal was completed.

Thomas R. Worth, who has faithfully filled the prescription needs here for many years, retires from active business to enjoy a well deserved rest. Mrs. Worth, who has made many friends by her friendly manner, has been at the drug store ever since the earthquake in April, 1906.

Mrs. A. R. Kirkpatrick, who has served in the drug store for four years as clerk, will continue with the new owners.

After taking a rest, Mr. and Mrs. Worth plan a tour of Europe and other sight-seeing trips.

Sebastopol Times
March 20, 1936

- **Worth's Drug Store**, Raymond Momboisse, prop.
- 109 North Main Street
- July 22, 1938 – February 1945
- Merged with Tomasco Drug Company

RAY MOMBOISSE BUY'S WORTHS DRUG STORE HERE

Raymond Momboisse of Petaluma recently disposed of his interest in the Herold Drug Co. to Mrs. Ida Carr-Herold, and on July 22nd purchased the former Worth's Drug Store from Fred A. and Burtis A. Hite. He took immediate possession of the established business which was operated for almost forty years by the late Thomas R. Worth. In addition to buying the business Mr. Momboisse also leased the building located at 109 North Main Street from the Sebastopol National Bank.

Since he disposed of his interest in the Herold Drug Store, Mr. Momboisse decided to locate in Sebastopol, and is enthused over the closing of the deal for the drug store. The present employees will be retained by the new owner. He graduated from the University of California College of Pharmacy and for 18 years was connected with the Herold Drug Co., first as an employee and later an owner.

He is popular in business, fraternal and social life being affiliated with the Petaluma Post No. 20 American Legion; Knights of Columbus; Petaluma Camp, Woodmen of the World; Harmony Grove of the Druids; Petaluma Parlor, N. S. G. W.; Petaluma Aerie, F. O. E.; and deputy state president of the Eagles Petaluma Rotary Club, Sonoma County Lafayette Club and Y. M. I. He has filled the chairs of several of the above-named organizations.

Sonoma West Times
July 29, 1938

Sebastopol Times
July 7, 1939

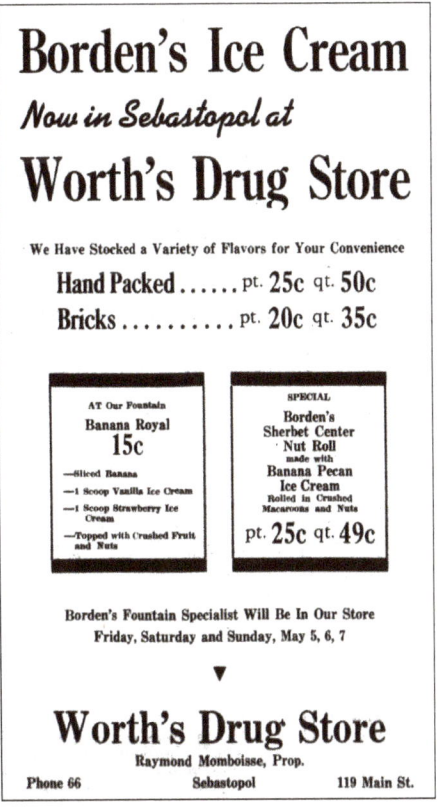

Sebastopol Times
May 5, 1939

- **Tomasco Drug Co.**
  - A.J. Franchetti, Irwin J. "Pete" Hill
  - 125 North Main Street; renamed Medico Drug Co. in 1950
  - February 9, 1934 – May 1975

Tomasco to Open Sebastopol Drug Store Tomorrow

Arrangements have been completed for the opening of the Tomasco Drug company's new store in Sebastopol tomorrow. Located in the Barnes building, 125 Main street, the new establishment has a modern front and windows, with the latest type fixtures of dark walnut, with natural gray ash trim.

Archie R. Hill, a registered pharmacist and connected with the company's Santa Rosa store, for several years, will be the manager of the Sebastopol establishment.

Departments will include drugs, sundries, prescription, and toilet goods, featuring complete lines of well known cosmetics. Among the cosmetic lines will be the Du-Barry, Primrose, Coty's, Elmo, Max Factor, and Colonial Dames.

Pharmacist Archie Hill (left) and clerk Ben Weeks stand behind counter of Tomasco Drug Co.
Photo by Bill Borba.

Press Democrat
February 8, 1934

RENOVATED TOMASCO BRANCH OPEN TODAY

Three months work of extensive improvements completed, the Tomasco Pharmacy branch at 125 North Main street in Sebastopol will have its formal opening in modern dress today. In operation since 1934 when Arch Hill, since located in Vallejo, opened as manager, the store will welcome clients to twice its former space. On display will be many new improvements including an entirely remodeled, modern storefront. Irwin J. Hill, brother of Arch Hill, continues in the position as manager which he has held for two years, assisted by Nick Collabella, pharmacist, and Norma Ciavarelli, cosmetician.

Press Democrat
November 15, 1940

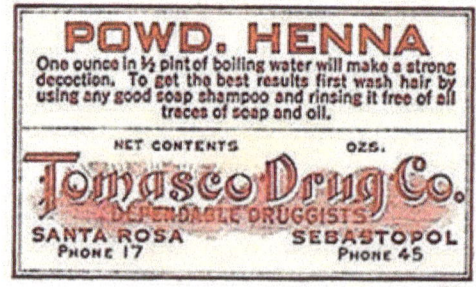

SEB-D-20
- Labeled clear abm metal screw cap
- OLIVE OIL U.S.P.
- Tomasco Drug Co.
- SANTA ROSA   SEBASTOPOL
- 5 ½ inches tall
- Base: 45-A-48- U. S. A.
- Merle Avila collection

Irwin J. "Pete" Hill

SEB-D-21
- Labeled clear abm metal screw cap
- AMERICAN
- MINERAL
- OIL
- Tomasco Drug Co.
- SANTA ROSA   SEBASTOPOL
- 8 inches tall
- Base: 18-A-47-U.S.A.
- Merle Avila collection

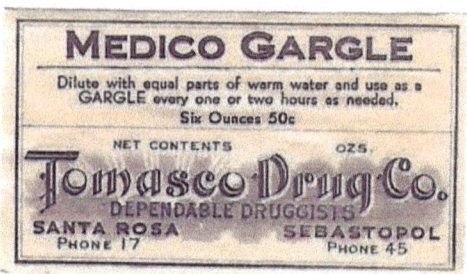

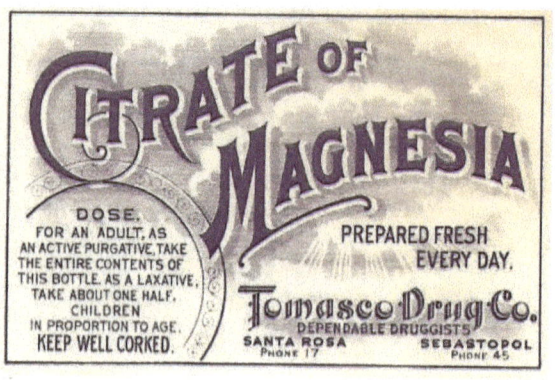

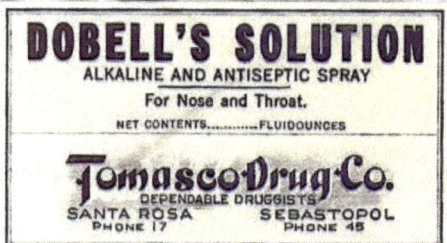

SEB-D-22
    Labeled clear abm plastic screw cap
    CASTOR OIL U.S.P.
    Tomasco Drug Co.
    125 N. Main St.   Sebastopol
    Phone 45
    3 ½ inches tall
    Base: 8-A-47- U.S.A.
    Merle Avila collection

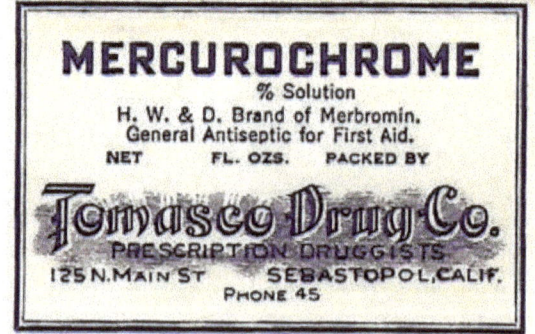

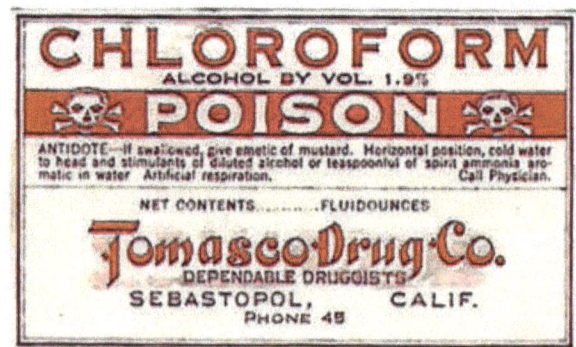

Paper labels: John Burton collection

TOMASCO DRUG COMPANY TAKES OVER WORTH'S DRUG

Because of wartime conditions and shortage of pharmacists, Worth's Drug Store combined with the Tomasco Drug Company this week. Ray Momboisse, who formerly managed Worth's, will be employed by Tomasco's in San Rafael.

Tomasco's will carry the same line of products which Worth's have carried in the past in addition to their own regular line. They will also carry the newspapers. Mr. and Mrs. Momboisse will continue to make their home in Sebastopol for the present, and Momboisse will commute to his new position.

Sonoma West Times
February 2, 1945

PRESCRIPTIONS and REXALL MERCHANDISE of WORTH'S DRUG STORE Will Be Obtainable at TOMASCO DRUG CO.

FAMOUS FILMO HOME MOVIE EQUIPMENT NOW OFFERED BY TOMASCO DRUG COMPANY

Movies of your family and friends, your vacations and travels, your sports and hobbies, are now available to you through the famous Bell & Howell line of Filmo personal motion picture equipment added recently by Tomasco Drug Company.

Tomasco Drug Co., invites all Sebastopol picture-making fans to come in and see the new line of Filmo personal movie cameras, projectors and accessory equipment now on display. Demonstrations are gladly given, they say,—and no obligation to buy.

TOMASCO DRUG CO.
-PRESCRIPTION DRUGGISTS-
Phone 45   We Deliver

Sebastopol Times
July 7, 1940

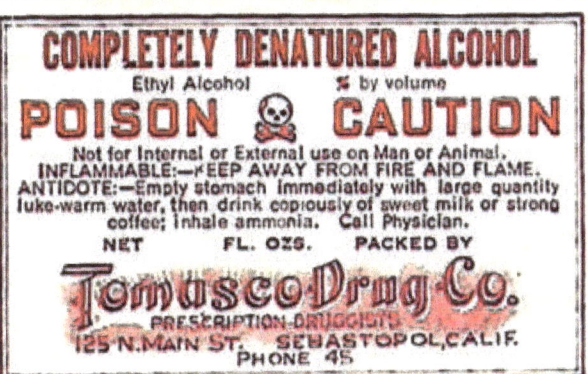

HEY!
What's your great hurry?

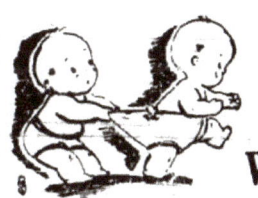

When it's a matter of winning a lovely pair of satin-covered hangers from us, no wonder he's in a rush.

And Mother, if your baby wins or not, it still means greater savings for you and better health for him if you purchase his vitamins, castor oil, and other nceessities from us!

TOMASCO DRUG CO.

Sebastopol Times
December 31, 1943

- **Towne's Drug Store**, Walter Towne and Lester B. Towne, props.
- 19 N. Main Street, west side, opposite P.O.
- January 1901 – March 1, 1906 ; sold to Fred Sellgren

WILL OPEN A DRUG STORE

A new drug store is to be opened in Sebastopol by the Towne Bros. of Petaluma. The room adjoining Burroughs's dry goods store in the new Baxter-Bennett brick block on Main street is being nicely fitted up for the accommodation of the stock. The new store will be opened about January 1st and Lester Towne will be in charge.

Sonoma West Times
December 12, 1900

TOWNE'S DRUG STORE

It is very generally conceded that there is no better conducted business in Sebastopol than Towne's Drug Store. It is a branch of Towne's Drug Store in Petaluma, originated by the late Smith D. Towne, father of Walter Towne, proprietor, and Lester B. Towne, manager of the Sebastopol branch.

Smith D. Towne, the founder of this astonishing business, came to California in the fall of 1850, and during the two years following he farmed in Green Valley, a few miles west of Sebastopol. In 1853 he went to Petaluma and took employment in the drug store which he purchased later. It was a pioneer drug store of Sonoma County. Of a family of seven children, four sons were raised in the drug business, and two of them, Frank M. Towne of San Bernardino and Lester B. Towne of Sebastopol, are acknowledged to have had more years of experience in the business than any other men of their ages in the state.

This store is one of the best in the county, and its reputation for pure fresh goods and excellent treatment of patrons in all respects is second to none. The manager is a businessman of the high-grade order, affable and courteous at all times and possessing in remarkable degree the qualities that commend the respect of the public.

Sonoma West Times - March 5, 1902

Do you Ever Have....

Spring Fever?

Do you Know what Spring Fever is?

It is that stuffy, lazy feeling that comes over you as soon as spring opens bright and warm; that good-for-nothing, no-account feeling that is so often described as THAT TIRED FEELING. It comes from the slow, labored coursing of your heavy winter blood through your veins. To cure it you must take TOWNE'S BLOOD BUILDER to freshen up your blood by encouraging your stomach, liver and bowels to work off the pressure on the veins. There are lots of sarsaparillas, but the best one is

TOWNE'S BLOOD BUILDER,
The Six Bit Sarsaparilla,
MADE AT ....
TOWNE'S DRUG STORE.

Sonoma West Times
March 12, 1902

TOWNE'S DRUG STORE

Towne's drug store, of which Lester B. Towne is proprietor, is one of the most up-to-date business houses in Sebastopol. A better drug store than this cannot be found in any town of Sebastopol's size north of the bay.

About three years ago Towne's drug store was established, and during that time a splendid patronage has been built up. There is probably not another druggist in Sonoma county who has been in the business as long as Mr. Towne. He is a son of the late Smith D. Towne, the pioneer druggist of Petaluma, and has been associated with the drug business ever since he was old enough to stand alone behind a counter. For years Mr. Towne was in the employ of leading wholesale and retail drug houses in the metropolis and other large cities, and no one is better qualified than he to successfully carry on the drug business. His store on Main street is a model of neatness. All of the best patent medicines and shelf goods are kept and prescriptions are compounded with exactness and promptness. As a side line Mr. Towne carries the finest of stationery, etc. A special feature of Towne's drug store is the delivery of country orders free of charge to all persons residing along the rural mail routes.

Lester Towne in his drugstore

LOOK AROUND
before you buy
CHISTMAS PRESENTS
You will find the best selection and the
LOWEST PRICES
in the county at
TOWNE'S DRUG STORE.
SEBASTOPOL.

Sonoma West Times - January 2, 1904

DEATH'S CALL WAS SUDDEN
Lester B. Towne of Sebastopol is Summoned Monday Morning by Apoplectic Stroke

Lester B. Towne, one of Sebastopol's most prominent citizens, passed to rest suddenly Monday morning. He breathed his last at 8:15 a.m. after a period of unconsciousness lasting five hours.

The deceased was born in Petaluma forty-three years ago. For nearly four years he has been engaged in the drug business in Sebastopol and there was no better known or highly and respected man in the community. He was almost as well-known and respected in Santa Rosa, and his death comes as a sudden shock to his friends there.

Santa Rosa Republican
September 24, 1904

- **Analy Drug Store**, Fredrick N. Sellgren, prop.
- 19 N. Main Street (formerly Towne's Drug Store)
- March 1, 1906 – June 1908 (Sellgren had run store since Lester Towne's death in Sept. 1904)
- Sold to Curtis M. Weeks

Dr. L. B. Lawson of the Lawson-Rinner Optical Co. of Santa Rosa will be at Sellgren's Analy Drug Store from 2 to 4 p.m. on the first and third Tuesdays of every month.

Sonoma West Times and News
February 15, 1908

PURE DRUGS.

And all the leading patent medicines at

THE ANALY DRUG STORE

We fill you Perscription exactly as ordered by your physician and with the greatest of care.

Stationery and Toilet articles.

Sonoma West Times and News
February 15, 1908

- **Analy Drug Store**, Curtis M. Weeks, prop.
- June 1908 – June 30, 1909
- Purchased from Fred Sellgren
- Estate sold store to Jesse Forsyth

CURTIS M. WEEKS SUCCUMBED TO HEART FAILURE ON ANNIVERSARY OF BIRTH

Curtis M. Weeks, a prominent resident of Sebastopol, dropped dead at his home on Bodega Avenue early Monday morning. A singular coincidence of the death is that it occurred on his 39th birthday.

Mr. Weeks was engaged in the drug business for some month's past, and had come down to his store Monday morning, opened the place of business, swept the sidewalk in front of the store and then returned home. After arriving at his residence, he collapsed.

Some months ago, Mr. Weeks sold his interest in the Crawford & Weeks grocery business and purchased the drug store formerly conducted by Mr. Sellgren.

Santa Rosa Republican
October 12, 1908

SEB-D-23
Labeled aqua oval
OLIVE OIL
ANALY
DRUG STORE
SEBASTOPOL, CAL.
6 inches tall
Tooled top
Base: 27F
Merle Avila collection

Horace Weeks, Jr., brother of the late Curtis Weeks, who has been with the Coulson Co., in Petaluma for the past three years, returned Monday with his wife to Sebastopol and has taken charge of the Analy Drug Store.

Petaluma Courier
November 7, 1908

- **Analy Drug Store**, Jesse T. Forsyth, prop.
- July 1, 1909 – December 2, 1911
- Purchased from estate of Curtis M. Weeks
- Sold to Mrs. F. E. Morse

Jesse Forsyth is studying in the College of Pharmacy in San Francisco.
Santa Rosa Press Democrat
August 27, 1901

JESSE FORSYTH BUYS ANALY DRUG STORE

Jesse Forsyth has purchased the Analy Drug Store at Sebastopol and on July 1st will take possession of the business. The Analy Drug Store was formerly conducted by Mr. Curtis M. Weeks and is a well-equipped establishment.

Mr. Forsyth has a large circle of friends who wish him every success. He will be sure to do well in his new location. For several years he has been assistant with Eugene Farmer, the local druggist, and prior to that ran a pharmacy of his own in Geyserville. He intends to make a number of improvements in his Sebastopol store and will carry a full line of everything.

Santa Rosa Press Democrat
June 27, 1909

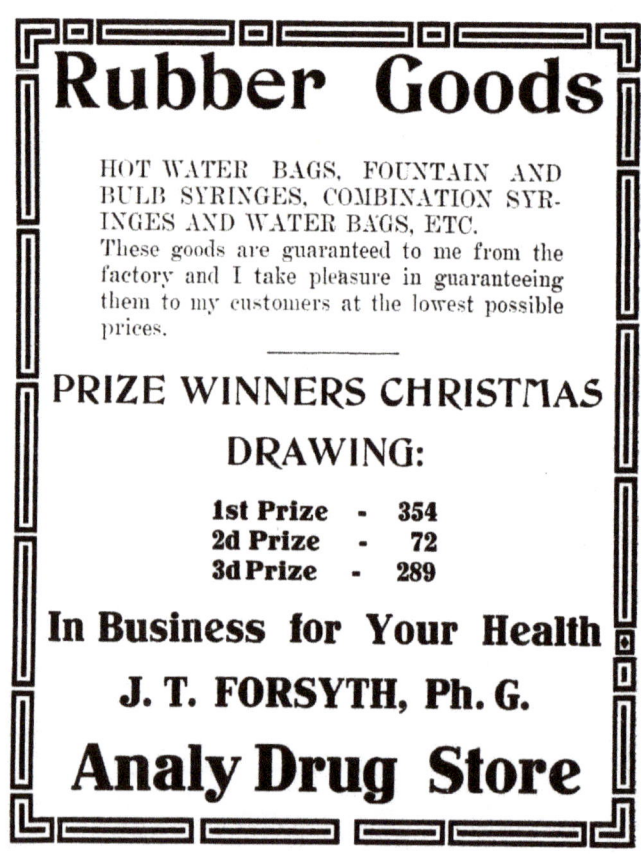

Sebastopol Times
January 22, 1910

- **Analy Drug Store**, Mrs. Frances E. Morse, prop.
- Erastus E. Rawlings, Manager
- 135 (aka 19) N. Main Street
- December 1911 – March 1912; sold to George Pease
- Mrs. F. E. Morse, widow of Stephen C. Morse, was Curtis M. Weeks' sister.

BRIEF LOCAL NOTES

Erastus E. Rawlings filed his pharmaceutical certificate with the county clerk on Tuesday.

June 11, 1907

Santa Rosa Republican

Analy Drug Store
NEW MANAGEMENT

MRS. F. E. MORSE
Proprietor

E. E. RAWLINGS
Manager

Sonoma West Times and News
December 2, 1911

SEB-D-24

Labeled clear oval
CASTOR OIL
ANALY
DRUG STORE
SEBASTOPOL, CAL.
6 inches tall
Base: 2325
Merle Avila collection

- **George Pease** (lived 1883-1974)
- Purchased Analy Drug Store from Mrs. F.E. Morse
- 133 N. Main St.: March 1912 – May 1919
- 109 N. Main St.: May 1919 – June 1932
- 104 N. Main St., NW corner Bodega Ave.: July 1, 1932 – January 25, 1963
- Sold to William R. and Patricia Collins of Santa Rosa
- Pease purchased the 2-story Crawford Building at 104 N. Main St. in January 1946

George Quincy Pease, circa 1908
Courtesy, Sonoma County Library

George Pease was born in Kansas and came to California as a young man in 1903, first locating in Geyserville. He went through high school in Kansas and completed a pharmacy course at the University of California.

One of the oldest establishments in Sebastopol, his drug store was first opened in 1912 at the present location of the five and ten-cent store. The store remained at that location for about 15 years, then moving to the present location of the Metcalf store. Then, following construction of the new building on the corner of Main and Bodega, he and Metcalf traded places and the store was moved to its present location about 11 years ago.

He was married in San Francisco, working for the Owl Drug Store there at the time. Later he moved to Healdsburg where he was a clerk in a drug store prior to buying the Sebastopol store.

He has two children, Marian, of Sebastopol, and George Leo, now owner of a store in Calistoga and father of three children.

Sonoma West Times
May 16, 1943

ANOTHER TO SEBASTOPOL

Sebastopol has won another of Healdsburg's good citizens – George Pease. Mr. Pease came to Healdsburg five years ago as a clerk for C. D. Evans, and he has held the same trusted position with druggist H. L. Huntington since the latter purchased Evans' store.

Mr. Pease has purchased the Analy Drug Store in Sebastopol, and left Healdsburg this week to enter business in that town. Many friends of Mr. Pease and family in Healdsburg will wish them abundant success in their new home.

Mr. Huntington has obtained the services of W. B. Whitney temporally until he engages a successor.

Healdsburg Tribune, Enterprise and Scimitar
March 28, 1912

Dr. Ruddock is employed at the Analy Drug Store during the absence of Mr. Pease, caused by his auto accident six days ago which almost proved fatal to himself and family.

Sonoma West Times
June 19, 1915

PEASE WILL INSTALL UNITED CIGAR LINE

George Pease, well-known local druggist, will open a fully equipped cigar stand, selling the United Cigar Stores line. Modern fixtures of the very latest design have been installed and smokers will be able to select from a very large stock.

Sonoma West Times
August 15, 1919

George Pease will move his drugstore into the building formerly occupied by the *Sebastopol Times* office.

Sonoma West Times
May 9, 1919

Sebastopol Times
April 26, 1918

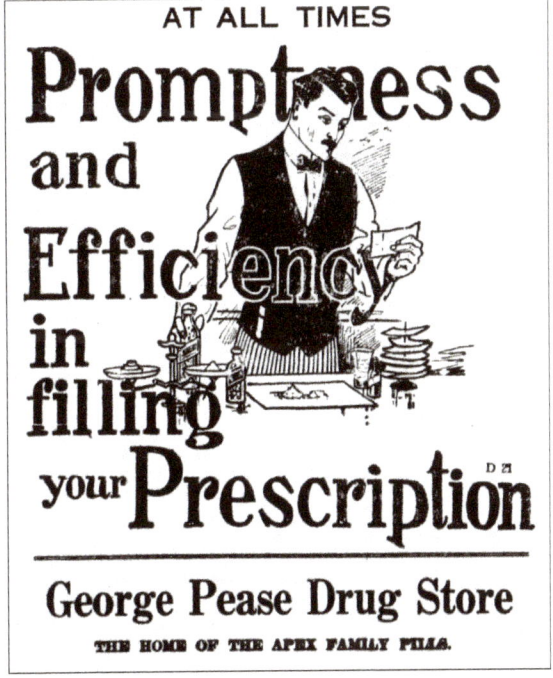

Sebastopol Times
June 7, 1918

SEB-D-25
> 2
> *Geo. Pease*
> *The Prescription Store*
> SEBASTOPOL, CALIF.
> Clear oval
> Fl. oz. and cc side markings
> 4 ½ inches tall
> Merle Avila collection

SEB-D-26
> 8
> *Geo. Pease*
> *The Prescription Store*
> SEBASTOPOL, CALIF.
> Clear oval
> Fl. oz. and cc side markings
> 7 inches tall
> Base: Half moon
> Helmut & DeAnna Jordt collection

SEB-D- 27
> Paper labeled amber rectangular abm, plastic screw cap
> *Dr. Ray*
> GEORGE PEASE
> Prescription Store
> 2 5/8 inches tall
> Base: 1558-7 -0 1
> Merle Avila collection

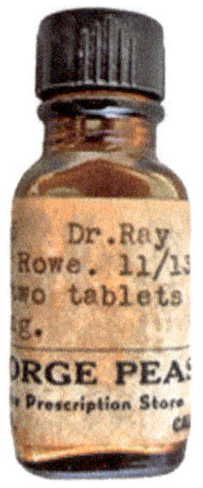

SEB-D-28
> Labeled clear rectangular, tooled
> TINCT. GREEN SOAP, U.S.P.
> Alcohol 28 to 32%
> GP GEORGE PEASE
> THE PRESCRIPTION STORE
> U.S. REG. NO. 1647   SEBASTOPOL, CALIF.
> 6 3/4 inches tall
> Merle Avila collection

SEB-D-29
Labeled clear abm oval,
    plastic screw cap
CAMPHORATED [OIL]
GEORGE PEASE
SEBASTOPOL, CALIF.
3 3/4 inches tall
Base: 10-0-7 ILLINOIS
Merle Avila collection

SEB-D-30
Labeled clear rectangular, tooled top
FLD. EXT. CASCARA AROM.
ALCOHOL 2 PER CENT
GEORGE PEASE
The Prescription Store
SEBASTOPOL   CALIFORNIA
5 1/4 inches tall
Merle Avila collection

SEB-D-31
Labeled clear oval, tooled top
OIL EUCALYPTUS U. S. P.
GEORGE PEASE
SEBASTOPOL   CALIFORNIA
5 5/8 inches tall
Base: 0 inside box
Merle Avila collection

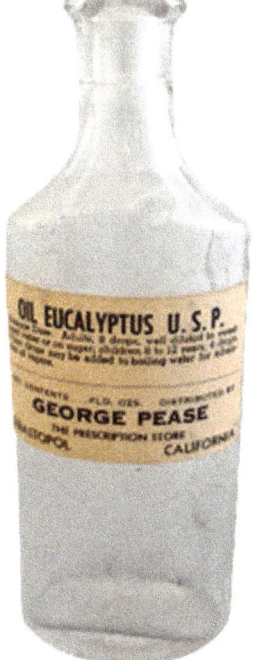

SEB-D-32
    Labeled clear square abm,
        metal screw cap
    Tincture Squills
    GEORGE PEASE
    SEBASTOPOL CALIFORNIA
    4 inches tall
    Base: 10-0-9
    Merle Avila collection

SEB-D-33
    Labeled amber rectangular abm,
        plastic screw cap
    ESSENCE OF PEPPERMINT
    GEORGE PEASE
    SEBASTOPOL CALIFORNIA
    8 inches tall
    Merle Avila collection

SEB-D-34
    Labeled amber oval abm,
        plastic screw cap
    SPIRIT CAMPHOR N. F.
    GEORGE PEASE
    SEBASTOPOL CALIFORNIA
    3 1/4 inches tall
    Base: A.H.M. 11M76
    Merle Avila collection

SEB-D-35
> Labeled clear oval, Rx
> GEORGE PEASE
> THE PRESCRIPTION STORE
> SEBASTOPOL   CALIFORNIA
> 3 ½ inches tall
> Base: 14-0-9
> Merle Avila collection

SEB-D-36
> Labeled clear oval abm,
>   plastic screw cap
> *Compound Tr. Benzoin*
> GEORGE PEASE
> The Prescription Store
> SEBASTOPOL   CALIFORNIA
> 4 ½ inches tall
> Base: OWENS 20-0-7
> Merle Avila collection

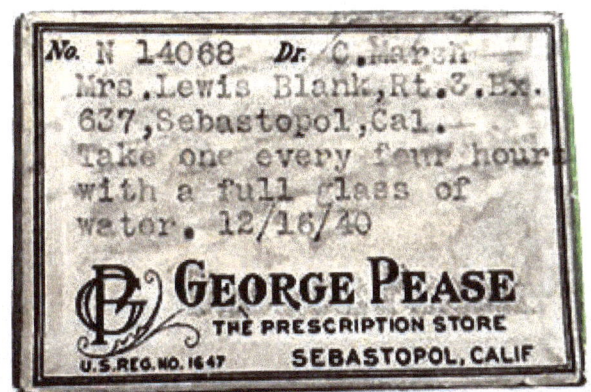

Labeled prescription box, filled December 16, 1940
Merle Avila collection

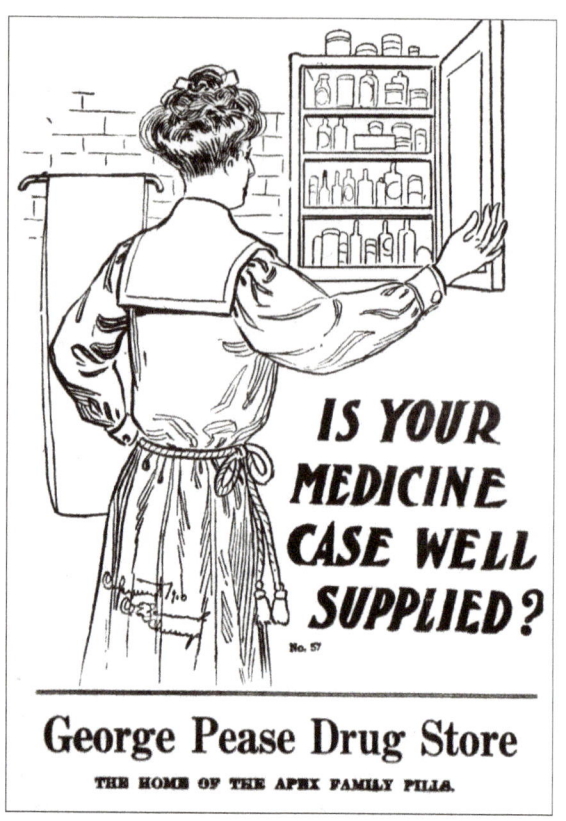

Sebastopol Times
June 28, 1918

Sebastopol Times
August 2, 1918

Geo. Pease Store In New Business Location Today

Today sees Sebastopol's newest and finest store building open for public inspection. Erected by Roy Crawford to replace the historic structure at Main street and Bodega avenue, this marvelous addition to Sebastopol's commercial section gives a tone of distinction to the surrounding area. George Pease has leased the entire main floor for his drug store business which has increased in size so much as to make his former location in the Forsyth building inadequate.

Downstairs has several features which fit in with the modern trend of the construction. The front part of the drug store has been arranged with the latest in cabinets, cases and shelfing.

Two stairways, one at the front on the Main street side and the other on Bodega next to Spooner's grocery, lead to the upstairs where rooms and suites for professional men have been arranged. Eleven rooms laid out and connected by a long corridor running the entire length of the floor makes available fine office spaces.

Metcalf Hardware company installed the plumbing, and Larry E. Naumann, resident of Sebastopol since 1907, had the painting and decorating contract.

Dr. Chester Marsh and Dr. A. P. Sweetnam have leased offices upstairs.

George Pease, proprietor of the drug store, came to Sebastopol in 1910 and has operated his business here continuously since. That period of time has seen him in two locations, this new place making the third.

Each move has found him in a bigger and nicer building and Mr. Pease in the hectic part of the moving this week vowed that it was the last.

Sebastopol Times
July 1, 1932

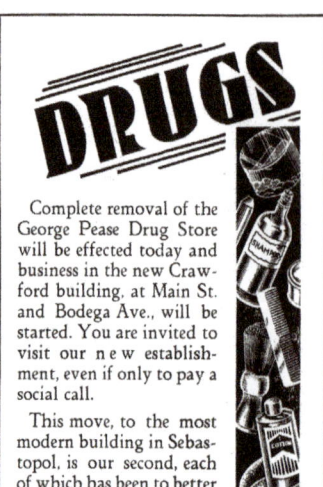

Complete removal of the George Pease Drug Store will be effected today and business in the new Crawford building, at Main St. and Bodega Ave., will be started. You are invited to visit our new establishment, even if only to pay a social call.

This move, to the most modern building in Sebastopol, is our second, each of which has been to better stores in the 22 years of business life in Sebastopol.

Larger stocks will be added to care for increasing demands and everything will be done to efficiently and satisfactorily care for our customers. To friends and customers we extend thanks for their patronage in the past and want them to view our new store.

GEORGE PEASE.

George Pease moved from 109 N. Main (Forsyth Bldg.) to 104 N. Main (Crawford Bldg.)

Leo Pease to Be Ass't. Pharmacist

Leo Pease, son of George Pease of Sebastopol, former local business man, has successfully passed his examinations as assistant pharmacist, and will be associated in the drug business with his father.

Healdsburg Tribune
Feb 4, 1933

George Pease and senior clerk, Mildred Meeker, circa 1950
Courtesy, Sonoma County Library

BILL COLLINS TAKES OVER AS OWNER OF PEASE DRUG STORE

William R. Collins, Jr., new owner of Pease Pharmacy, will not change the name of the store that has served Sebastopol so long, he said yesterday. And George Pease isn't getting out all of a sudden either. He will continue to help Collins in the pharmacy, at least for a while.

Collins was born in Oakland, attended Oakland High, San Francisco Junior College, Notre Dame, and graduated from the University of California, School of Pharmacy in June 1950.

He served as a U.S. Navy lieutenant in World War II, and for eight years has worked as a medical service representative for Eli Lilly Company, calling on doctors and pharmacies in Marin and Sonoma Counties.

The Collins family includes his wife Pat and their three children, Craig 12, Bront 9, and Kirk 7. They live in Santa Rosa now but plan on moving here later.

There is work cut out for him—he is also vice-president and coach of a Little League team in Santa Rosa.

Sonoma West Times
January 31, 1963

SONOMA

- **Edward Wegner** (lived 1837-1900)
- Westside of Plaza, corner of Napa and First
- 1870 – September 1900

ED. WEGNER DEAD.

Sonoma's Pioneer Druggist Succumbs to Lingering Illness of Several Months

Druggist Edward Wegner died at his home here early Monday morning from the dreaded ravages of consumption. After going out of business early in the fall he went up to his mountain ranch above town to see if the air of the higher altitude would not keep back the progress of the dreaded disease but to no avail. He gradually grew weaker and was brought home Thursday afternoon in a most critical condition. Everything possible was done to improve his condition but he only rallied long enough to have his will written out Saturday and passed away at a little before four o'clock Monday morning. His family was at his bedside when the final summons came.

With the death of Mr. Wegner Sonoma looses a good citizen who has ever been closely identified with the growth of the town since his arrival in 1868.

He was born in Berlin, Germany on November 3rd, 1837 and given a good education by his parents. At the age of seventeen he was apprenticed to the trades mason, carpenter and architect. He possessed a natural bent for chemical science and at the age of twenty he entered the scientific schools to perfect himself in chemistry.

In 1860 Mr. Wegner left Germany going to Valparaiso, Chili, where he engaged in the drug business. Later he was offered a position as builder by Godefroy & Co. to go to Siberia and assist in the building of one of the company's towns near Nikolaevsk. The offer was accepted and Mr. Wegner went to Siberia. Later the town was abandoned and he went to work for the company in their commission house at Hong Kong.

In 1867 he came to San Francisco and from there to Sonoma in 1868. He began work here as a carpenter and later went into the drug business and gradually enlarged his store until it contained a full line of general merchandise. By enterprise and good business ability he was able to leave his family in comfortable circumstances.

In 1883 when Sonoma was incorporated Mr. Wegner was elected a member of the first board of city trustees and was chosen as its president. His name is associated with several of the improvements that have been made in the town.

Deceased leaves besides a host of friends a wife and three daughters, Lydia, Freida and Isabelle, a brother in Texas.

Sonoma Valley Expositor
December 28, 1900

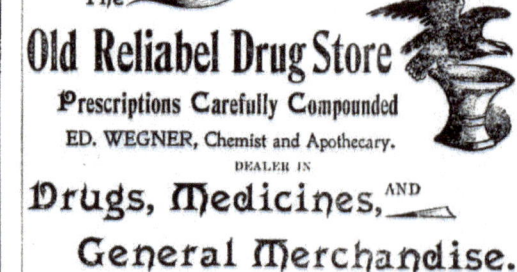

Sonoma Valley Expositor
June 1, 1900

- **Lloyd Scott Simmons** (lived 1871-1955)
- 29 East Napa Street, south side between Broadway and First Street East
- Son-in-law, Neal E. Dodge joined business in 1923; Simmons retired in 1945
- 1903 – 1954 (sold to Willis Helms)

Note: Lloyd S. Simmons was born in Independence, Kansas. His parents, Samuel B. Simmons and Lucetta Moon Simmons, brought their seven children overland to California in 1883, settling in the Los Angeles area. Lloyd attended the Woodbury Business College, studied pharmacy, and worked as a druggist in Pomona and Chino. By 1903 Lloyd had moved his wife and daughter to Sonoma where he set up the town's first professional pharmacy. Much of his stock was destroyed when the 1906 earthquake shook bottles off the shelves. Lloyd spent his entire career as a druggist. He died in 1955, aged 83, but his pharmacy at 29 East Napa Street remained in operation until 1986.

Trade token
Merle Avila collection

Simmons Drug Store, circa 1915, Lloyd S. Simmons at left
Courtesy, Sonoma State University Library

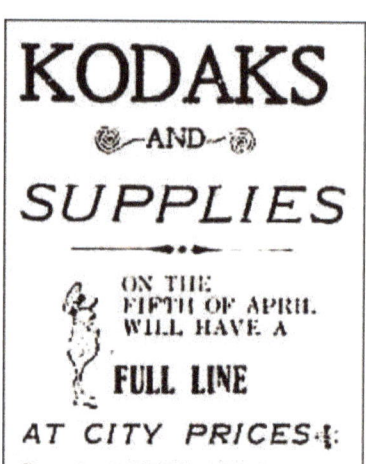

Sonoma Valley Expositor
April 4, 1905

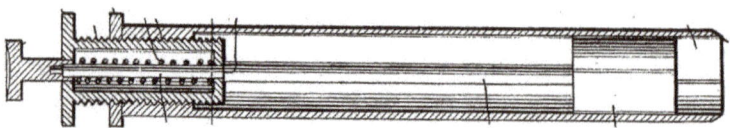

DRUGGIST INVENTS POWDER DIVIDER

Lloyd S. Simmons, a pharmacist of Sonoma, Cal., is the inventor of a powder divider on which he has received letters patent. The device consists of "a barrel, an adjuster having screw thread connection therewith, a plunger within the barrel and having sliding connection with the adjuster, and a spring disposed within the adjuster and normally acting to yield the plunger retracted in the barrel." It is claimed that the device will save much of the pharmacist's time, as only the original volume of the powder is weighed the device accurately dividing the powder into the required subdivisions. It is said that Mr. Simmons has already received an excellent offer for his invention.

Medicinal powder dispensing device patented by L.S. Simmons in 1922

Simmons Pharmacy, July 1941

- **Orin Eastland** (lived 1857-1939)
- E. Napa Street, 2 doors east of Simmons Drug Store (purchased from R.G. Shoults)
- 1906 – 1910

Note: Orin Eastland grew up on a farm in Palestine, Texas. In 1880, at age 23, he was listed as a medical student. He was working as a druggist in San Francisco in 1898, and the following year was granted California licensure as a pharmacist. Two years later he officially graduated from the California College of Pharmacy with a Ph.G. degree. Eastland worked primarily in San Francisco except for a few years following the 1906 earthquake when he and his wife Virginia ran a drugstore in Sonoma. He spent many years aboard oceanic vessels as a ship's doctor. His first voyage was to Balboa, Canal Zone in April 1919 on *S.S. City of Para*. Orin Eastman died in 1939 at age 81 while visiting relatives in Texas.

PHYSICIAN FILES DIPLOMA
Orin Eastland, who comes here from Monterey, has filed his certificate as pharmacist, and a diploma from the Missouri Medical College, with the county clerk.

Santa Rosa Republican
September 7, 1906

Orin Eastland
Photo taken Feb. 1919, age 61

Eastland's Model Pharmacy
THE LEADING DRUGGIST
SONOMA
Bring us your PRESCRIPTIONS

PURE DRUGS and Standard Medicines at reasonable prices. The people believe in us and have been our firm friends ever since we started in business.

Our rubber goods and sick room supplies are of the best quality made. Toilet articles, sponges, brushes, combs and perfumes sold here are brands of brands of known value.

Agents for celebrated Edison's Phonographs and Gold moulded Records with sweetest tones.

Sonoma Valley Expositor
May 17, 1907

SON-D-01

℥ vi
EASTLAND
THE LEADING DRUGGIST
SONOMA, CAL.
Clear oval
Tooled top
5 Inches tall
6 Inches tall
Mike Burgess collection

- **Louis Frank Lambert** (lived 1892-1945; registered as pharmacist May 1, 1918)
- SE corner of West Napa St. and First St. West, next to Union Hotel
- August 1921 – November 4, 1938

LAMBERT TO BUY SONOMA DRUG STORE

Notice of intention to sell his drug store at Sonoma to Louis F. Lambert of this city has been filed with the county recorder by J. McElney of Sonoma. [James McElney, who became a registered pharmacist in Sonoma County in 1910, owned The Corner Drug Store in Sonoma at least since 1913]

Santa Rosa Republican
July 29, 1921

VALUE OF FINGER SET AT $20,000

The right index finger of an expert masseur is worth $20,000 to him in his business according to a suit filed in the Superior court yesterday by Attorney G. F. Owens for J. J. Kaufman, who plies his art at Agua Caliente, against L. F. Lambert, a Sonoma druggist. Kaufman alleges that on Jan. 21 he treated the finger according to Lambert's advice and has since suffered serious disability through infection.

Mr. Lambert is a well known former Petaluman. He now has several drug stores in Sonoma valley.

Petaluma Argus
August 22, 1924

West Napa Street circa 1930 – L. F. Lambert drugstore at right

Peck Photo

SONOMA DRUGGIST GIVES BAIL HERE ON ALKY CHARGE

Louis F. Lambert, Sonoma druggist, was at liberty on $1,000 bail today, following arrest by federal agents last night on charge of illegal possession of alcohol.

The arrest was made when Prohibition agents and an inspector from the Bureau of Industrial Alcohol visited the Lambert Drug Store and inventoried his alcohol stock.

According to reports, the officers found a gallon and a half of alleged "bootleg" alcohol, not issued under government permit.

Lambert was brought to Santa Rosa for arrangement before U. S. Commissioner J. Harold McAlpine and was later freed on a bail bond.   [note: National Prohibition was repealed December 5, 1933]

Santa Rosa Republican
July 14, 1932

Complaint—Separate Maintenance

Mary M. Lambert vs. Louis F. Lambert. Wife seeks separate maintenance and support without divorce. Grounds, cruelty. Couple married June 15, 1918 and ceased living together March 15, 1936. L. G. Hitchcock, attorney for plaintiff.

Press Democrat
September 15, 1936

TO SELL DRUG STORE

Louis F. Lambert will sell his drugstore on Napa Street in Sonoma to Mary M. Lambert according to papers filed yesterday with the county recorder here. The sale will be completed November 4, at which time purchase price will be set.

Santa Rosa Republican
October 28, 1938

Louis Lambert, former Sonoma druggist, died suddenly in his store in Daly City on May 19. He had planned to open a branch store down the Peninsula, the next day, when stricken. He was a native of New York, aged 53 years, and located in Sonoma many years ago. He leaves a widow and five children.

Petaluma Argus
May 31, 1945

A busy, well-stocked California pharmacy, circa 1900

www.ingramcontent.com/pod-product-compliance
Lightning Source LLC
Chambersburg PA
CBHW061117070526
44583CB00028B/3327